Palestinian Commemoration in Israel

Stanford Studies in Middle Eastern and Islamic Societies and Cultures

Palestinian Commemoration in Israel

CALENDARS, MONUMENTS, AND MARTYRS

Tamir Sorek

Stanford University Press
Stanford, California

Stanford University Press
Stanford, California

Printed in the United States of America on acid-free, archival-quality paper

Library of Congress Cataloging-in-Publication Data

Sorek, Tamir, author.
   Palestinian commemoration in Israel : calendars, monuments, and martyrs / Tamir Sorek.
      pages cm--(Stanford studies in Middle Eastern and Islamic societies and cultures)
   Includes bibliographical references and index.
   ISBN 978-0-8047-9392-6 (cloth : alk. paper)--ISBN 978-0-8047-9518-0 (pbk. : alk. paper)
   1. Arab-Israeli conflict--Anniversaries, etc. 2. Muslim martyrs--Israel--Anniversaries, etc.
   3. Palestinian Arabs--Israel--Anniversaries, etc. 4. Collective memory--Israel.
   5. Memorialization--Israel. 6. Memorials--Israel. I. Title. II. Series: Stanford studies in
   Middle Eastern and Islamic societies and cultures.
   DS119.7.S635 2015
   394'.40899274--dc23
                              2015004813

ISBN 978-0-8047-9520-3 (electronic)

Typeset by Bruce Lundquist in 10/14 Minion

For Michelle, Tal, and Noah

CONTENTS

LIST OF FIGURES

ACKNOWLEDGMENTS

THIS BOOK IS THE FRUIT OF A STUDY that lasted almost fifteen years, through which I have been fortunate to benefit from the support, ideas, and inspiration of many individuals and institutions. Various parts of the study were supported by the Fulbright-Hays Faculty Research Abroad Fellowship, the Humanities Scholarship Enhancement Fund at the University of Florida, the Lucius N. Littauer Foundation, and a Post-Doctoral Grant by the Ginsberg Fellowship at the Hebrew University of Jerusalem. Since 2006 the Center for Jewish Studies at the University of Florida has been my academic home, and I am grateful for the continuous support I receive from the center and for the congenial environment created by the chair Jack Kugelmass. The last, and crucial, stage of writing was enabled by the Humboldt Fellowship for Experienced Researchers, which allowed me to dedicate undivided attention to the project throughout my stay in Berlin in 2013–2014. I would like to thank Klaus Eder from the Humboldt University of Berlin for the warm hospitality and the stimulating intellectual environment.

Some of the materials published in this book appeared earlier in the form of journal articles or chapters in edited volumes although the updates, additions, and changes created texts that are very different from the original. Chapter 1 is based on the article "Calendars, Martyrs, and Palestinian Particularism under British Rule," which appeared in *Journal of Palestine Studies* 43, no. 1, 2013. Chapters 4 and 5 constitute an extension and update of an article I published in *Comparative Studies in Society and History* 50, no. 2, 2008, titled "Cautious Commemoration: Localism, Communalism, and Nationalism in Palestinian Memorial Monuments in Israel." Chapter 7 is based on my article "The Changing Patterns of Disciplining Palestinian National Memory in Israel," in *States of Exception, Surveillance and Population Management: The Case of Israel/Palestine*, edited by Elia Zuriek, David Lyon, and Yasmeen Abu-Laban, published by Routledge in 2010. The argument in Chapter 10, appeared previously in "The Quest for Victory: Collective Memory and National Identification among the Arab-Palestinian Citizens of Israel," in *Sociology* 45, no. 3, 2011. Chapter 11 is based on my article "Public Silence and Latent Memories: Yitzhak Rabin and the Arab-Palestinian Citizens of Israel," in *Israel Studies Review* 28, no. 1, 2013.

Many of the insights I present in this book were developed with the significant help of friends, colleagues, and acquaintances who shared their knowledge or life experience with me, assisted in establishing relevant contacts, helped to refine my arguments, contributed their time and talent to read the text at various stages of its development, and provided useful criticism and valuable comments. I am grateful to Issam Aburaya, Gadi Algazi, Wadi' 'Awawde, Iyad Barghuthi, Linda Butler, Nabih Bashir, Irit Dekel, Hillel Cohen, Honaida Ghanim, Yousef Jabareen, Amal Jamal, Laleh Khalili, 'Emad Khamaysi, Nabil Khattab, 'Atef Mu'adi, Maqbula Nassar, Nasim Jarus, Tamar Rapoport, Keren Or-Schlezinger, Uri Ram, Shira Robinson, Wakim Wakim, Efrat Ben Ze'ev, Elia Zureik, and Tal Ben-Zvi. I am grateful also to the late author 'Ala 'Isa who shared with me rare video footage of past commemoration ceremonies in Kafr Qasim. My friend Youssef Haddad skillfully assisted me with the translation from Arabic to English of some especially challenging texts. I would like to thank as well Sammy Smooha who provided unpublished findings from his surveys. I also am grateful to Kate Wahl, my editor at Stanford University Press, and to the copy editor Leslie Rubin, whose editorial suggestions made an important contribution to the clarity of the text.

Above all, I would like to thank my wife, Michelle, whom I met when I first began to develop my ideas of investigating collective memory and commemoration among Palestinians in Israel. Throughout the years Michelle has been my most critical reader, commenting on innumerable texts related to this project, and making an important contribution to its quality. I am grateful for both her thoughtful reading and continuous loving support.

Palestinian Commemoration in Israel

INTRODUCTION

THE MONODRAMA *Herzl Said* tells the story of Khaled Majdalawi, a Palestinian history teacher in the Israeli school system. Khaled was a single and lonely man, cautious and obedient. He preferred to cite from textbooks rather than express his own views and feelings. He always carefully followed the official curriculum of the Israeli Ministry of Education and even rejected requests of his students to discuss the painful history of the Palestinian people. One day following a confrontation with a student who accused him of being a "Zionist," he was suspended and lost his dream of becoming a school principal.

Performed in Arabic with Hebrew subtitles, *Herzl Said* was first publicly presented in summer 2009 at the Eighth Masrahid Festival where it won first prize. The play presents the fear of the authorities, caution, and silence of the Palestinian citizens of Israel (approximately 17 percent of its 8.1 million citizens in 2013) and the difficult conditions under which they construct their historical remembrance. Khaled's character represents a common type of Arab teacher in the Israeli school system, one shaped by years of strict surveillance under the military government (which lasted until 1966), and then only partly liberalized after its removal. In the play, Khaled engages in a series of dialogues with key figures from his life, including his dead parents and an agent of the General Security Service (Shabak). Beyond telling his personal story, the play considers the impact of the first days of the al-Aqsa uprising in October 2000 when twelve Palestinian citizens of Israel were shot dead by the Israeli police.

A year before the play's public debut, the playwright Iyad Barghuthi invited me to attend a rehearsal in the old city of Acre. After the rehearsal I joined an informal conversation between Iyad, the actor Ghassan 'Abbas, and the director Munir Bakri. This was literally a conversation behind the scenes of the production of commemoration and collective memory. Ghassan voiced concern about the scene in which Khaled lists the names of the victims of October 2000 while the Israeli flag displays on a screen behind him, as if he blames the flag for their deaths. Ghassan wondered whether they were "going too far" in commemorating the event, whether this scene might provoke angry reactions. Iyad and Munir were unsure—and then all eyes turned toward me. As the only Jew in the room, I was asked to assess the extent to which the scene would hurt the sensitivities of Jewish Israelis. I found the situation ironic since I had considered the play itself to be a protest against this self-censorship exercised by so many Palestinian citizens of Israel. And yet, at the point that the play's protagonist breaks through the barrier of fear, his creators had become hesitant and wondered whether the barrier should be pushed in a less aggressive way.

In the end the scene was left unchanged, but even four years later in an interview in 2012, Iyad remained unsure if this was the right decision. He finds the scene too direct and therefore artistically unrefined, and he is ambivalent about the extent to which he is interested in antagonizing a Jewish audience:

> I think that the content might annoy people so I said, "Let's not annoy them so they won't disqualify the play from the very beginning only because it is critical against the establishment or the Zionist narrative." But at the same time, when I think about it—let them be annoyed, why not? My buddies and I are annoyed every time we hear a narrative that denies us [. . .] I want people to listen and give a chance to a different voice because in my view it has a truth, and anger seals the ears and the eyes shut. To a certain extent, however, I regret this since [I tell myself], "Why do I feel sorry for them at all—let them pay with their nerves, that's all." This is part of my dissonance—on the one hand I want to have channels of cultural dialogue, but on the other hand I am really convinced that the channels are actually blocked.[1]

Khaled Majdalawi's fear in the play and the moment this fear is conquered are two aspects of a particular phenomenon I investigate in this book—how Palestinians in Israel construct their collective memory and how they display it publicly. Similarly, Iyad's dilemma over what to include in the play and my own expected role in evaluating the possible reactions to the play, illustrate the interactive and relational nature of this process.

The encounters of Palestinians in Israel with the Israeli state apparatus and with Jewish Israeli citizens of Israel, as well as their political status as Israeli citizens, have driven them into three discernible modes of action: (1) caused them to disguise or carefully select their public displays of collective memory out of fear, (2) motivated them to contrast their narrative with the dominant narrative of Jewish Israelis as a form of protest, and (3) inspired a desire for a dialogue with Jewish citizens of the state. Hence, Palestinian commemoration in Israel is at the same time a practice of political protest, a subject of surveillance by the authorities, and a sphere of dialogue with, and defiance of, Jewish Israeli citizens and the state. The combination of these factors is reflected in cross-pressures that shape Palestinian commemoration in Israel as cautious and vigilant. Commemoration vacillates between commitments to pan-Palestinian solidarity, emphasizing the uniqueness of Palestinian citizens, as well as blatant defiance and a pacifying tone. While the narrative, historical references, and symbolism of this commemoration have been embedded in Palestinian and Arab contexts, its discursive boundaries have been defined to a large extent by the political status of its producers as Israeli citizens.

CITIZENSHIP AND COMMEMORATION

During the 1948 Arab-Israeli war and the subsequent mass expulsions that lasted until October 1950, approximately 85 percent of the Arab Palestinians who had lived in the areas of Mandatory Palestine that ultimately were subjected to Israeli sovereignty were driven outside the borders of the newly established state of Israel. In the process, hundreds of Palestinian villages were completely destroyed, and the larger towns and cities lost most, if not all, of their Arab populations. Between 700,000 and 800,000 Palestinian refugees took shelter in the remaining parts of Palestine still under Arab control (the Gaza Strip and the West Bank), as well as in the neighboring Arab countries of Lebanon, Jordan, Syria, Egypt, as well as elsewhere. These events are known in the Palestinian vocabulary as the Nakba (Arabic: catastrophe), and they constitute the key episode in Palestinian national history.

Those 156,000 Palestinians who remained under Israeli rule could not escape the dramatic consequences of the Nakba: about one-sixth of them came from nearby villages that were destroyed and depopulated. Subsequently they became internal refugees; many others lost their lands to Israeli state expropriations even though they remained in their villages; and families were torn apart never again to be reunited. Most Palestinians in Israel suddenly found themselves under strict military rule that dictated most aspects of their lives; and finally, they shared the drastic and sudden devaluation of their status from an established majority in the country to a subjugated and discriminated against minority.

While the Nakba has constituted the major anchor of contemporary Palestinian national identity, it has also created borders, both physical and mental, between Palestinians. Israel prevented the return of those Palestinians who fled or were expelled beyond the armistice line. Those who were able to secretly return were unsafe. After the first Israeli census in November 1948, and the distribution of Israeli identity cards or temporary residence permits, Israeli security forces conducted sporadic searches for Palestinians who, for various reasons, had not registered during the census and therefore were considered illegal aliens and were forcibly expelled across the border.[2] Hence, during the first years of the state's existence, an Israeli identity card (and later citizenship) provided crucial, even if imperfect, protection from expulsion beyond the armistice line. Gradually, expulsions stopped, but those without Israeli identity cards still faced difficulties in obtaining jobs, collecting government food rations, or legally marrying.[3] Under these circumstances an Israeli identity card became a valuable asset and a means of survival for a member of the Palestinian minority.

In 1966 the military government that had been imposed on Palestinians inside Israel was formally removed, only to be quickly exported to the West Bank and the Gaza Strip the following year after Israel's occupation of those territories. Since the beginning of the military occupation that began in 1967, more than half of the Palestinians in the world live under various segments of the "Israeli control system."[4] The territory under this control system, between the Mediterranean and the Jordan River, is ruled by ethnocratic principles that preserve Jewish domination while dividing Palestinians among various subgroups with different levels of civil rights, political rights, and economic opportunities.[5] This internal hierarchy places Palestinian citizens in an intermediate political status between Jewish Israelis and Palestinian non-citizens and ensures their relative benefits vis-à-vis their fellow Palestinians. To be sure, Palestinians in Israel suffer from blatant, systemic discrimination,[6] but compared to Palestinians who live in the militarily-occupied West Bank and the besieged Gaza Strip, they are far less vulnerable to arbitrary violations of their rights. As a result, differing existential conditions among the various Palestinian communities have led to a growing discrepancy in the collective self–image of both groups.[7]

Over the long term the salience of citizenship developed beyond merely existential instrumentalism. "In an endeavor to survive," observed the political scientist Amal Jamal, "Israeli Palestinians integrated components of their national and cultural identity with their new identity as citizens of the state."[8] Furthermore, Palestinian citizens have become part of a political community they share unequally with Jewish citizens. Palestinians in Israel also share various segments of the public sphere with Jewish citizens, albeit awkwardly, such as universities, hospitals, and soccer stadiums. Most adult Palestinians in Israel are bilingual and consume Hebrew media. In fact, a 2007–2008 survey of hundreds of members of the Arab elite in Israel (artists, authors, bankers, educators, civil activists, and university professors) found that 75 percent of them read both Arabic and Hebrew newspapers.[9] That figure is lower among a representative sample of the general population (survey from 2005), yet 63 percent of Palestinians reported that they read Hebrew newspapers at least irregularly.[10] Palestinian exposure to Hebrew radio and television broadcasts is also significant, further supporting that at both elite and popular levels, Palestinians in Israel are highly aware of, and keenly interested in learning, the Jewish Israeli perspective.

The main purpose for the consumption of the Hebrew press by the Arab public is not simply gathering information since respondents expressed a high level of distrust in the Hebrew media. Rather, it is based on the need to know what is happening in the immediate social and political environment, especially the positions and arguments developing among Jewish citizens.[11] At the same time, as the Palestinian intellectual Azmi Bishara has commented on the Hebrew language used by Arabs in Israel, "The tool has become a part of the person who uses it."[12] In other words, it is very difficult to draw a clear line between purely instrumental use of the language and its implications for identity.

These conditions have salient implications on both the content and form of Palestinian commemoration in Israel. First, because they have much more to lose, the level of self-censorship prevalent among Palestinians with Israeli citizenship far exceeds that of other Palestinians. As I explore in this book, this self-censorship has diminished in the twenty-first century, but it has not disappeared. Second, the close proximity and frequent exposure of Palestinians in Israel to the Jewish Israeli perspective makes Jewish Israelis a highly relevant audience for Palestinian commemorative discourse, whether it aims to confront or to engage. Jewish sensitivities have a direct effect on how Palestinians in Israel negotiate a public image of the past, and their familiarity with the Jewish Israeli internal vocabulary enables them to communicate with Jewish Israelis in ways that are unavailable to other Palestinians. The title *Herzl Said*, for example, refers not only to the founding father of the Zionist movement (which is common knowledge among Palestinians), but also to the Israeli version of the children's game Simon Says. The title is directed toward both Jewish and Arab audiences, conveying criticism of the authorities of the Jewish state for their expectations that Arab citizens be obedient subjects; at the same time it criticizes the common tendency among Arabs to fulfill this role.

POLITICAL CALENDAR AND MARTYRS

This book traces the various ways that Palestinian citizens in Israel have negotiated their collective identity—as both Palestinians and Israeli citizens—through development of historical remembrance, political calendar, and shared martyrology. Over the past two decades, dozens of scholarly books about the Palestinian citizens of Israel have been published. Most of them have focused on the political organization of the Palestinians or the policy of the state toward them;[13] others examined particular spheres including the economy,[14] education,[15] the media,[16] urban exclusion,[17] generational issues,[18] the role of intellectuals,[19] collaborators,[20] cuisine,[21] and sports.[22] Most of these books have referred to commemoration and collective memory sporadically but did not make it a central theme. This lacuna is significant because as I illustrate in this book, the creation of a political calendar that provides a cyclical structure for political mobilization and a distinct pantheon of martyrs that fuels political protest have both played a central role in the gradual process of post-1948 recovery and empowerment.

For Palestinians in Israel, the creation of a political calendar is a form of control over time—an especially valuable asset when control over public space is extremely limited. Furthermore, collective memory can transform historical events into political myths,[23] and a collective calendar has a decisive role in this transformation and in maintaining collective identities.[24] "As a cycle of holidays specifically designed to commemorate socially marked events," writes the sociologist Eviatar Zerubavel, "the calendar year often encapsulates the conventional master narratives constructed by mnemonic communities from their history. By examining which historical events are commemorated on holidays, we can identify the most sacred periods in a group's collective past."[25]

Let us examine, therefore, what is included in the particular political calendar of the Palestinians in Israel. Among the long list of dramatic events that shaped their history, four commemorations have been gradually canonized on the political calendar: the 1956 Kafr Qasim Massacre (the execution of forty-seven Palestinian citizens who were not aware of a curfew imposed on their village); Land Day in 1976 (a country-wide strike and protest against Israeli government confiscation of Palestinian land, during which Israeli police killed six Palestinians); the October 2000 killing of Palestinians in Israel, and the Nakba.

These four events share several characteristics. They have been commemorated annually, for at least fourteen years, with mass processions and extensive coverage in the local and regional Arabic media. All major political streams among the Palestinians in Israel—communist, nationalist, and Islamist[26]—take part. Finally, these events are commemorated either exclusively by the Palestinians in Israel or in a distinct manner within Israel.

Figure 1 illustrates the percentage of Arab citizens who have reported participating in commemorative events since 2003, showing a sharp increase in Nakba Day and Land Day events. In addition, the ratio between those who reported participation in commemorative events and those who joined a general political demonstration has also gradually increased, indicating that the mass participation in political demonstrations is overwhelmingly dominated by commemorative events.

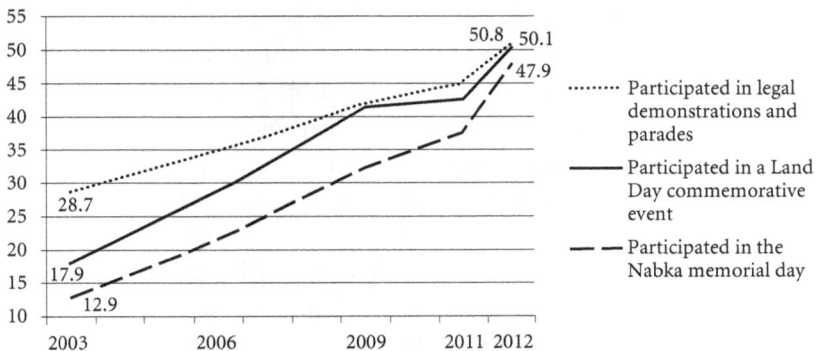

Figure 1. Percentage of Arab citizens who reported participation in political events by year, 2003–2012

WHAT IS COLLECTIVE MEMORY?

One of the theoretical underpinnings of this book is collective memory. The term "collective memory" has been used by different scholars to describe different phenomenon, and this terminological vagueness makes it necessary to clarify my own approach. My use of the term overlaps, in all or in part, with what was termed "historical memory" by Maurice Halbwachs,[27] "appropriated memories" by Karl Mannheim,[28] "cultural memory" by Jan Assmann and John Czaplicka,[29] and "popular memory" by the Popular Memory Group. Using Halbwachs's distinction between autobiographical and historical memory and the parallel distinction made by Mannheim between personally acquired memories and appropriated memories, it is important to emphasize that this book deals only with the latter, namely historical memory which was not personally acquired. A memory of an individual is 'collective' not because it is shared by every individual in her/his group but because it was acquired through certain social institutions (family, education system, political parties, etc.) which are identified with this group. The 1917 Balfour Declaration, for example, is not part of the autobiographical history of any of the Palestinians or Israelis who live today, but it is certainly part of the historical remembrance of many of them who learned about it as part of growing up as Palestinians or Israelis.

Assmann and Czaplicka distinguished between "communicative memory" which includes those varieties of collective memory that are based exclusively on informal, mostly personal everyday communication, and "cultural memory" transmitted through formal cultural formations (rites, monuments) and institutional communication (recitation, practice, observance). The events marked on the collective calendar of Palestinians in Israel are remembered in all these forms, but their mere anchoring in the collective calendar, their "monumentalization," or their inclusion in formalized curricula, is part of a conscious endeavor to include them in a long lasting cultural memory.

Most important, collective popular memory is a contested terrain in the constant struggle over hegemony.[30] This terrain is occupied by many actors with various agendas and diverse narratives who compete over the construction of the past. There are real processes of domination in the field of historical remembrance: at any given moment, certain representations achieve centrality, visibility, and prestige; others are marginalized or muted.[31] The apparatus of the State of Israel, the various Arab political parties and extra-parliamentary movements, the Palestine Liberation Organization (PLO), Arab local councils, Arab and Jewish Israeli non-governmental organizations (NGOs)—all these

actors, each with its own agenda, have competed over shaping historical remembrance and collective memory among Palestinians in Israel.

METHODOLOGY

My methodological choices are informed by the distinction made by the Popular Memory Group between the two main ways a sense of the past is produced:
through public representation and through private memory.[32] Similarly, the
sociologist Jeffery Olick distinguished between two approaches in the study
of collective memory: an "individualist" academic culture, which is based on
aggregated individual memories and a "collectivist" one that focuses on collective commemorative representations.[33] Although individual remembrance
and public representations of the past are partly autonomous, they are also
mutually dependent because the study of popular memory "is a necessarily
relational study."[34] Aggregated private instances of historical remembrance are
both products and reflections (even if as a mirror image in certain contexts) of
public representations. In this regard, I look carefully for the roads that connect the two.

Therefore, I am guided by a holistic approach that considers the production and reception of meanings as interrelated. I utilize diverse research
methods that examine different aspects of collective memory from different
angles and in various spheres with an emphasis on the struggle over meaning
between numerous actors. This combination diminishes the risk that methodological choices would overshadow the subtlety of the phenomena under
investigation.

In addition, I tried to avoid a common tendency to look at 1948 as the starting point of the history of the Palestinian citizens of Israel. The contemporary predicaments and challenges of the Palestinians in Israel are the results of
a long history, and its roots can be traced back at least to the early days of the
Palestinian national movement following World War I. Although Palestinian
citizens of Israel have developed a distinct repertoire of collective commemoration, this repertoire cannot be evaluated properly without a reference to its historical development since those days. Therefore, I researched the Arabic press
from the 1920s to the 1940s, diaries, memoirs, as well as secondary sources, in
order to understand the development of the Palestinian collective calendar and
martyrology under the British rule of Palestine (1917–1948).

Since the first commemoration on the national calendar of the Palestinians
in Israel is the *date* of the massacre at Kafr Qasim in 1956, I began my investiga-

tion of the post-state period from that year. I read the reports covering the four major anchors of the collective calendar in nine Arabic newspapers in Israel from 1956 through 2014, as well as other important dates on the calendar (for an outline of the other dates, see Chapter 6). This path of investigation is especially important from the early 1980s because newspapers in Arabic have been a key element of the independent Arab public sphere in Israel since that period.[35] With the beginning of the twenty-first century, the internet emerged as another major sphere of constructing historical remembrance and therefore I searched and followed the references to these events on numerous websites operated by Palestinian citizens of Israel with diverse political orientations. More sporadically, I followed the broadcasts of an Arabic radio station, reviewed memorial books published locally, and educational materials published by the Follow-Up Committee for Arabic Education (FUCAE). In addition, I watched three ceremonies in Kafr Qasim (in 1986, 1999, and 2006) recorded on film. To compare Palestinian historical remembrance inside and outside Israel, I also read two bulletins of Palestinian organizations and one private Palestinian newspaper published outside Israel.

While the newspapers and commemorative books provide much insight into the historical development of Palestinian commemoration, they cannot provide the point of view of the state apparatus attempting to suppress, manipulate, or contain it. This perspective can be found in the files at the Israel State Archive. I reviewed relevant correspondence of the Advisor to the Prime Minister for Arab Affairs, the Ministry of Education, and protocols and correspondences of Arab local councils. Obviously, I did not have access to many still-classified documents, and the most recently released relevant material available is from 1984. To understand contemporary modes of surveillance, I drew on my interviews with relevant functionaries and the protocols of the Knesset assembly.

A significant part of the investigation of more recent developments is based on face-to-face interviews. Between 2001 and 2014, I conducted more than ninety interviews with key Arab and Jewish "memory actors," namely, individuals who are directly or indirectly involved in the public struggle over historical remembrance. Among the interviewees were activists involved in organizing commemorative events and Jewish legislators who acted to ban these events; Arab educators who attempted to bring the Palestinian national narrative into public schools and functionaries in the Israeli Ministry of Education who sought to monitor and circumscribe these attempts; and local activists, mayors, journalists, directors of youth summer camps, artists, as well as others.[36] Most of these interviews took place at the homes of the interviewees, many others at their workplaces, and a small number in a café. In rare cases, I conducted the interview by phone. The length of most interviews ranged between one hour and two hours. Depending on the circumstances, some of these interviews were recorded and transcribed.

In addition, I attended commemorative events in various Arab localities— Land Day events in Sakhnin and Deir Hanna, the memorial procession in Kafr Qasim, al-Aqsa Day in Sakhnin, Memorial Day for the massacre in 'Aylabun, Memorial Day for the 2005 assault in Shefa'amr,[37] and the March of Return commemorating the Nakba. In 2009, 2011, and 2012, I visited youth summer camps run by two Arab political parties. I followed the production of national historical remembrance in these camps, as well as the governmental attempts to monitor them.

During my ethnographic work, as well as during interviews, I faced the challenge of gaining the trust of my direct interviewees or of other people around me. As a Jewish Israeli man who speaks Arabic—with this profile I could have easily been sent by the Israeli Shabak under the guise of an academic researcher[38]— some of my initial contacts with people was often met with suspicion. Many of my interviewees were public figures who are used to being interviewed (mayors, members of local councils, authors), a factor that made them less suspicious than the average person. However, in other cases, I had to be creative.

First, whenever possible I did not contact people directly but rather through mutual acquaintances with the help of Palestinian friends, some of whom I have known for many years dating back to our student days at the Hebrew University of Jerusalem. Palestinian social networks are very dense, and in many cases my distance from the actor I wanted to interview, including leaders of the Islamic Movement, was no more than one degree of separation.

Second, while contacting organizations I attempted first to gain the trust of the individuals at the top of the formal or informal hierarchy, hoping that they would open other doors for me. This was especially important in my ethnography at one of the summer camps, where one of the members of the camp crew protested my presence in the camp. The acting director who defended my presence won the argument by mentioning the name of a highly regarded person in the party who had invited me to visit the camp.

Third, I worked to establish my academic status early in any interaction: I presented myself at the first instance of contact as *Dr.* Tamir Sorek (Israeli culture is informal and I do not use my title in other contexts), used my business card, repeatedly referred to my American home institution, and provided copies of my published articles. In cases where I expected a high level of suspicion, I brought a copy of my first book in Hebrew to leave as a gift. Obviously, this mode of presentation was more effective when the interviewees themselves had some familiarity with the academic world, at least as students. Although hypothetically these tactics could have been used as well by the Shabak, I was surprised to find how well they lessened suspicion. The frequent interpretation of my publications as sympathetic to Palestinians in Israel in all likelihood was also helpful.

With time I learned not to display too much knowledge about their organizations to my interviewees. Although I gained this knowledge from the internet or from other interviews, sometimes it caused them to feel that they were under surveillance, and I learned to restrain my tendency to demonstrate my familiarity with the field. Nevertheless, the challenges of ethnographic research emphasize the need for additional channels of investigation and the examination of additional spheres.

Surveys with representative samples provide a bird-eye view of social phenomenon. In July and August 2008 I conducted a nation-wide, questionnaire-based survey of 530 Arab and 515 Jewish citizens in Israel through phone interviews.[39] The respondents constituted representative samples of their respective adult populations.[40] An individual-centered survey methodology allows for inquiry into how private remembrance correlates with certain social and political orientations, an issue highly relevant to the literature about the collective memory-national identity nexus that rarely has been investigated by this method. These correlations, if found, might be evidence of the replication, reflection, contradiction, or even dialogue between private remembrance and public commemoration. Beyond this survey I analyzed raw data from related public opinion polls conducted between 1996 and 2009 by the Guttman Institute at the Israel Democracy Institute, Modiin Ezrahi, and Dahaf Institute.

Finally, a comparison of the Palestinians in Israel to other cases is crucial for developing sociological insights. While this book does not present a systematic comparative analysis, it does reflect sporadically on the parallels and differences between the commemoration among Palestinians in Israel and similar cases. The important task here is to decide what constitutes a similar case. Looking for studies of ethno-national groups that face similar dilemmas and challenges led me to the conclusion that any attempt to classify the political status of the Arab-Palestinian citizens of Israel would have to acknowledge some of the extreme and even idiosyncratic characteristics of their condition. This makes a comparative discussion an especially challenging task. I suggest viewing the Palestinian citizens of Israel as located on the far margins of two categories of cases: "trapped" minorities and colonized peoples. In both categories they stand out as a particularly unique or extreme type. Many of the peculiar dynamics of the production of their collective memory and public commemoration can be understood by taking into consideration their location on this taxonomic juncture. Thus, it is crucial to explain these peculiarities before taking a closer look at this commemoration.

PALESTINIAN MEMORY IN ISRAEL AS AN EXTREME CASE

The anthropologist Dan Rabinowitz considers the Palestinians in Israel a "trapped minority":[41] a segment of a larger group spread across more than one state, citizens of a state hegemonized by others and whose political power is limited by their non-affiliation with the dominant ethno-national group. This category includes Kurds in Turkey, Turks in Bulgaria, Russians in the Baltics, Armenians in Azerbaijan, and many others. Implicitly, this concept echoes the sociologist Rogers Brubaker's "triadic nexus." Brubaker observed that the collective identities of certain minorities are frequently shaped by the combining influence of a nationalizing state under whose sovereignty they live, an external kin-state (or motherland), and the institutions of the ethno-national minority.[42] The Arab-Palestinians in Israel seemingly have several Arab kin-states around Israel (Egypt, Jordan, Syria, and Lebanon). The attachment to these states is mainly in the form of cultural affinity and expressions of solidarity in times of crisis, but it lacks a concrete political dimension. Since 1948 none of these states have seen the Palestinians in Israel as potential citizens as many kin states tend to do.[43] Like Kurds, Tamils, and other ethnic groups with sporadic, partial, or unfulfilled national aspirations, Palestinians in Israel do not have an external sovereign kin nation state as a subject of patriotic sentiments. They have been influenced, however, by a vibrant Palestinian national movement whose political, military, and myth-making activities since 1948 mostly have taken place outside the internationally recognized borders of Israel.

Looking at other cases of trapped minorities, the development of diverse collective self-images among Palestinians who live in different political contexts is not surprising because formal citizenship rarely remains merely formal. Even when such a minority is politically mobilized, maintaining citizenship is frequently part of the political vision. The geographer Oren Yiftachel defined this form of mobilization as "ethnoregionalism," which is "ethnonationalism in constraining political and territorial circumstances." It is distinct from conventional ethnonationalism by its lack of drive for ethnic sovereignty and by the tendency to reconcile ethnic and civil elements of identity. At the same time it is distinct from civil mobilization by its emphasis on the protection of a specific homeland territory and by its demands to restructure the ethnic foundations of the polity and not merely to redistribute its material resources.[44]

There are many examples of the far-reaching implications of formal citizenship on the collective identity and memory of trapped minorities. Basques in Spain and France, for example, have developed different orientations of identity;[45] the status of Hungarian communities as citizens of Hungary, Romania, and Slovakia has differential impact on the ways they commemorate the Hungarian national past;[46] the commemoration of Bloody Sunday in Northern Ireland has become a rhetorical battlefield between Irish Republicans and Catholic leaders supporting constitutional nationalism in Northern Ireland.[47] The narrative of the young generation of the Russian-speaking minority in Latvia regarding the Soviet conquest of the country is influenced by the official Latvian national narrative, indicating that these Russian-speakers gradually are moving away from the views of their contemporaries in Russia on the Soviet history of the Baltic States.[48]

Although Rabinowitz presented Palestinians in Israel as a prototypical trapped minority, if we follow his definition strictly, we would find that in multiple aspects they constitute an extreme case, and the peculiar combination of these aspects makes the Palestinians in Israel a unique case: the social boundaries between them and the majority society is particularly rigid; their national narrative is diametrically opposed to the state narrative; their territory is central to the national narrative of their trans-border community; they face an exclusionary nationalizing policy; they are part of a stratified system of an active colonial project; and they face the anxiety over the reversibility of power relations by the settler society. Each of these dimensions of exceptionality or extremity has direct implications on the production of historical remembrance.

First, the social boundaries between Arabs and Jews in Israel are exceptionally rigid, with almost no gray area. The number of individuals who would define themselves as both Arab and Jewish in Israel today is negligible. Even when it is done, usually this self-labeling is considered a political statement and is not socially approved. From 1949 until the late 1960s, approximately 900,000 Jews immigrated to Israel from Arab countries. There is a scholarly debate as to what extent the title Arab-Jews was relevant to this population before the immigration,[49] but there is no doubt that by now most of the third generation does not speak Arabic and firmly rejects the Jewish-Arab label. The combination Jewish-Palestinian is even less common.[50]

A crucial indicator for the social distance between Arab and Jewish citizens of Israel is the lack of intermarriage between them. While intermarriages affects approximately one in four ethnic Hungarians in Romania,[51] one out of ten Kurds in Turkey,[52] more than 40 percent of the ethnic Russians in Latvia,[53] and one out of ten couples in Northern Ireland at the end of the twentieth century,[54] the number of Arab-Jewish mixed marriages is negligible. Family is an important site for the production of vernacular national narratives, and when intermarriage is common there is more room for developing alternatives to "zero sum game" national narratives commonly produce by elite rhetoric. The diametrically opposed elite narratives in Transylvania, for example, are frequently not reproduced in the nuclear mixed Hungarian-Romanian families.[55] The almost complete absence of mixed families in Israel significantly diminishes the opportunities for the development of these alternative narratives.

Second, the level of alienation of the Palestinians in Israel from the official state narrative is incomparable to most other cases. Diametrically opposed historicization might characterize the experience of trapped minorities in general.[56] There is no other case, however, where the total contradiction and the zero sum game relations between the narratives are as extreme as in the Israeli-Palestinian case. In the common Palestinian national narrative, the creation of the State of Israel is the direct cause for the destruction of Palestine.

Although the creation of Northern Ireland was done against the will of most of the local Catholic population, it was not followed by the uprooting of 85 percent of them. Unlike the Nakba for the Palestinians, the Irish civil war is only one event in the long chain of Irish national history. Similarly, there is no existential contradiction between the founding mythology of Estonian and Russian nationalism. The disagreement is about specific historical episodes, not about the actual existence of the other nation. The Kurdish national movement in Turkey demands self-determination but does not consider the mere existence of the Turkish republic as a terrible injustice. Therefore, while the production of a counter-hegemonic memory by a trapped minority frequently has the potential to be perceived as challenging the very legitimacy of the state,[57] in Israel the production of this memory is seen frequently by Jewish citizens as an existential threat.

Furthermore, unlike Kazakhstan and Kyrgyzstan where the Russian minorities are either not allowed or are unable to form their own independent parties, Palestinians in Israel do have ethno-national parties represented in the parliament, but they lack any practical political power. Since the end of the twentieth century, parties representing the minority ethno-national groups in Northern Ireland, Romania, Slovakia, Serbia, Montenegro, Bulgaria, and other countries have been part of the ruling coalition at least part of the time. A parallel scenario in which an Arab party joins the Israeli government belongs to the realm of fantasy. Thus the inability to influence the allocation of material resources has pushed Arab members of parliament to overemphasize themes of identity and national narratives.

The third dimension of exceptionality of the Palestinians in Israel is the status of the territory they inhabit in the collective narrative of their national community. Trapped minorities differ in the relative importance of their territory in the canon of their kin state or their broader ethno-national community. There is a difference between minorities who live in territories with little importance to the core national narrative, such as Russians in the Baltic states, and Hungarians in Transylvania, a territory that has a respectable status in the Hungarian national mythology.[58] Here, again, Palestinians in Israel are located on the extreme edge of a continuum. Pre-1967 Israel is considered in the Palestinian vocabulary as the *dakhil* (Arabic: inside). In the Palestinian national canon of poetry and literature, this territory is *the* subject of longing and passion, especially among the secular elements that dominated the Palestinian national movement until the early 2000s. The location of the Palestinian citizens of Israel at the core territory of the Palestinian national mythology carries the potential for tense disputes with Jewish citizens.

Fourth, Israel has never attempted to assimilate Palestinians. Rogers Brubaker distinguished between assimilationist and differential nationalizing discourse and practice,[59] and Israel's policy toward its Arab citizens belongs to the latter category beyond any doubt. Palestinian citizens were even encouraged to maintain a separate education system in their own language (up to high school level), as long as the content was supervised by the state. In the long term, the reluctance of the state to truly "Israelify" its Arab citizens contributed to their alienation from the state and to the development of a separate national identity and collective memory.

Fifth, beyond being a trapped minority, the Palestinians in Israel can be considered an indigenous dispossessed colonized group, like Native Americans in the United States and Canada, aboriginal people in Australia, or Maoris in New Zealand.[60] As such, their collective memory is dominated by themes of dispossession and humiliation, themes that are tightly linked to concrete political demands in the present and that further intensify the struggle over the representation of the past. Here, again, the Israeli-Palestinian case is at the margin of the category. Israel is not a typical colonial project, since it lacks a metropole; economic gains were not an important drive for colonization; and the settlers shared a pre-existing proto-national identity. However, the most important distinction for analyzing the construction of historical remembrance is that the colonial element in Zionism is still active. Land allocation and investment in infrastructure by the state are still subjugated to the unilateral aspiration to strengthen the power of the settler community.[61] Under these circumstances the lines between protest over past and present dispossessions are especially blurred.

Furthermore, since 1967 millions of Palestinians who are not citizens live under Israeli military occupation, which by itself ensures the continuation of the colonizing project. Palestinians in Israel constitute a minority only if we consider Israel in its pre-1967 border as a separate political unit, an assumption which is increasingly challenged by scholars who suggest that between the Jordan River and the Mediterranean Sea there is one state in which Palestinians are dominated by different means.[62] The numbers of Arabs and Jews in this territory are roughly equal. Even if we do accept that this territory should be analyzed as a single political system, the numerical inferiority of Palestinians among Israeli citizens is meaningful and relevant for understanding their political discourse and practice because most of them do take seriously their Israeli citizenship. Therefore, the comparison to other trapped minorities is still pertinent. None of the other trapped minorities is embedded in such a fragmented and stratified system of control.

Finally, unlike native communities in the United States and Australia, Palestinians in Israel have to deal with the anxiety of the settler community over the reversibility of the demographic ration and the power relations. The Israeli sociologist Baruch Kimmerling argued that the Zionist settlement enterprise has been seen as a process that could go in only one direction—that of increasing control over territories. Decreasing control has been considered likely to initiate decolonization, in a manner similar to the "domino theory."[63] In the case of the remembrance of 1948 and the issue of Palestinian refugees, the concern of reversibility is even greater than in the case of retreat from a certain piece of land. Since actual return of the refugees would mean the end of Jewish dominance and control in Israel/Palestine, even the slightest symbolic gesture raises the fear of entering a slippery slope that would end Jewish national sovereignty. Therefore, while the celebration of the indigenous narratives that negate the "founding moments" of the nation can be tolerated or ignored by the dominant groups in the United States and Australia,[64] in Israel this Palestinian counter-narrative has been frequently followed by anxious reactions.

.   .   .

The year 1948 is both the time of the birth of the State of Israel and the year of Nakba, but it is also the time when "the Palestinian citizens of Israel" began to emerge as a political and social category. Their pre-1948 past has immediately become specific contested terrain: the state made an effort to disconnect its Palestinian citizens from their pre-1948 national history, and to make pre-1948 national martyrology and memorial days be forbidden knowledge. At the same time Palestinian intellectuals have tried to bring these elements back to the public sphere. Our journey begins, therefore, with exploring Palestinian national commemoration under British rule.

1 COMMEMORATION UNDER BRITISH RULE

ON 1 MAY 1921, a series of violent clashes broke out in the Jaffa and Tulkarm regions of Palestine and resulted in the death of hundreds of Jews and Arabs— the largest and most violent confrontation in the Palestinian-Zionist conflict to date. These clashes were the latest incidents amid the growing unrest after the Balfour Declaration of 1917 that promised Britain's support for the Zionist project and the subsequent British occupation of Palestine. In 1923 on the second anniversary of the Jaffa/Tulkarm riots, Palestine's leading newspaper at the time *Filastin* ran a front-page editorial with the headline "Martyrs' Day" (*yawm al-shuhada*), which read in part:

> It has been two years since the day pure blood flowed out of us, since the day pure souls passed. We were inattentive to what was going on until that day when we were awakened in the morning by the roar of bullets.
>
> Our revival was poor in all that other revivals are rich. Since that day, however, it became rich in martyrs, abundant with memorial days. One hundred brave sons of Palestine became martyrs (*istashhadu*) and they were not aggressors—and now Palestine considers them as having died for the sake of salvation. Martyrs are an inevitable component of the revival of nations. They breathe life into them. Memories, sweet and bitter, are another inevitable component, for they provoke reviving nations to action and renew their determination.
>
> And if days start to look alike and become forgettable, we have one guiding day that we will not forget, one day that is stained with blood, crowned with blackness. The memory of that day awakens in us all that went dormant; it restores what went lukewarm in our enthusiasm and pushes us forward. That day is 1 May, Martyrs' Day.

In his attempt to establish 1 May 1921 as a historic turning point in the Palestinian collective consciousness, *Filastin*'s editorialist was clearly aware of the political role of martyrdom and collective calendars in the creation of a national identity and was actively nurturing a Palestinian/Arab national identity under British rule.

The political boundaries imposed on the Palestinians following the dismemberment of the Ottoman Empire in the aftermath of World War I eventually were adopted as boundaries of political identity. These postwar boundaries came with a demographic threat, phrased in the Balfour Declaration, and resulted in the politicization of a Palestinian particularism. This emerging emphasis on Palestinian identity coexisted with other collective identities, such as religious and local identities, Ottomanism,[1] as well as Arab nationalism. Depending on circumstances and context, these identities can either complement each other or compete for importance and priority. Overlapping identifications were very common, and the boundaries between Arab and Palestinian nationalism were especially fluid. That said—various forces in Palestinian society gave differential weight to each element. Palestinian particularism refers here to the tendency to prioritize Palestinian solidarity over other identities, not an aspiration to substitute one for the other.[2]

The invention of modern nations frequently relies on pre-existing markers of identity such as religion, language, shared myths about the origins and history of the group, daily customs, or cuisine. The Arab inhabitants of Palestine did not share the same religion (most of them were Muslim, but there was a sizable and influential Christian population), and their language and daily culture did not differ much from the Greater Syria region in general. Pre-modern elements of Palestinian collective memory, such as the shadow of the crusades and the glory of Saladin's victory,[3] constituted only useful raw material for the production of a national identity. To transform Palestine from a regional category into a political category, requiring commitment and mutual solidarity, there was need for a more elaborated imaginative process. This is why calendars and martyrs had special appeal to Palestinian nationalists. These elements aimed to unify Muslims and Christians, villagers and urban dwellers, and diverse geographical regions, while at the same time nurturing a distinct Palestinian collective identity. Although martyrs and political calendars also serve to cultivate Arab nationalism or Islamic pride in Palestine, martyrs and the invention of new calendars were less crucial for nurturing these identities.

AN EMERGING CALENDAR

Following the British takeover of Palestine in 1918, about fifteen political clubs were founded by upper-class Muslims and Christians in the major Palestinian towns. These clubs were named the Muslim Christian Association (MCA), and they formed a national body, the Palestine Arab Congress, which opposed the Balfour Declaration and Zionist immigration. Although other organizations, such as the Literary Forum and the Arab Club took part in this opposition, the latter two were Palestinian branches that were part of a broader regional network whereas the MCAs were a local Palestinian phenomenon. In addition, the institutions established by the MCAs played a leading role in the political mobilization of Arab Palestinians. Therefore, some scholars consider these associations as the first manifestations of a national movement among the Arabs in Palestine.[4]

All three organizations, though, provided the stage for the first documented attempts by Palestinian elites to establish a national political calendar. Following the Arab revolt against Ottoman rule toward the end of World War I, Faysal al-Hashimi established a short-lived Arab government in Syria with British approval; and for a short time, leading Palestinian intellectuals saw the future of Palestine as part of this new political entity. In spring 1919, the author Khalil Sakakini suggested to the members of the Jerusalem chapter of the MCA that the date the anti-Ottoman Arab revolt was launched (9 Sha'aban in the *hijri* calendar) be celebrated annually as an independence day of the Arabs.[5] Sakakini, a Christian Palestinian, reported that he had to convince his fellow Christian members of the MCA that this was an event with national significance, which should concern not only Muslims. That year the MCA, the Literary Forum, and the Arab Club in Jerusalem celebrated Independence Day (which happened to be 9 May that same year). Sakakini, who attended the ceremony at the Arab Club in Jerusalem, reported that it included speeches, musical performances, and the singing of the Arab national anthem, which Sakakini himself had written (*Ayuha al-mawla al-'athim*). The British military governor of Jerusalem, Ronald Storrs, attended the event.[6]

Although the celebration of Independence Day did not become a long tradition, it is one example of many elite attempts to establish a political calendar during the British Mandate period. The dates on this calendar had diverse origins and fall into two main categories. One category includes those that grew out of the politicization and nationalization of traditional holy days. In this category only one attempt succeeded beyond regional and factional divisions: the

Nabi Musa festival. The other category includes those dates commemorating recent politically significant events. The most salient commemoration in this category is the annual protest against the Balfour Declaration on 2 November. Another relatively successful initiative was the Memorial Day for three Palestinians executed by the British authorities in 1930, a commemoration that was observed annually for four consecutive years.

Nabi Musa Festival

The Nabi Musa festival included a procession from Jerusalem to a shrine traditionally believed to be the tomb of the prophet Moses. Pilgrimages to the shrine have been recorded since the late thirteenth century,[7] but the Nabi Musa festival was fixed to the date of Easter in the Eastern Orthodox calendar and became an official, civic, public event only in the nineteenth century.[8] With the emergence of an organized political opposition to Britain's Jewish national home policy, it became an important site of protest. In 1920 the procession devolved into violent riots, in which five Jews and four Arabs were killed. Following these events, Sakakini wrote in his diary: "Until now the Muslim and Christian holidays were religious, but last year and this year they appear to be national holidays."[9]

Some scholars see the 1920 riots in Jerusalem as the first anti-colonial eruption in the history of the Zionist–Palestinian conflict;[10] however, at this point the struggle was defined in terms of opposition to British policy and Zionist aspirations and as displaying Arab national identification but not necessarily in terms of defending the nationalist idea of Palestine.[11] It was in subsequent years, especially between 1929 and 1936, that the annual festival gradually became an idiom of Palestinian national identity.[12] The "nationalization" of the Nabi Musa festival was reflected in the extension of the social groups that participated in the procession, both geographically and demographically. From an event that initially attracted participants from the greater Jerusalem area, it was extended to include a wider area of central and southern Palestine with participants from Jaffa, Ramleh, Lydda, Gaza, Nablus, and even from the Beersheba region.[13] In other words, the new participants came from different regions of Mandatory Palestine but not from neighboring Arab countries.

In addition, Christian participation expanded, a significant development given the popular association between the Nabi Musa holiday and the struggle against the crusaders. A popular tale circulated that Saladin had initiated the holiday in response to the large number of Christian pilgrims who visited Jerusalem for Easter ceremonies during the years of the Crusader control of the city

(1099–1187).[14] The increase in Christian participation, therefore, implies that the meaning of the holiday was reshaped to support Muslim-Christian solidarity. The presence of Christians and the absence of Jews marked the emerging socio-political division of the country—Arab-Palestinians against Jews. As historian Eddie Halabi writes: "For the Arabs who witnessed this procession, the image of Christians and Muslims marching in unison, singing patriotic anthems, served as a 'model for reality,' a discursive construct that portrayed the elite as leading a modern nationalist movement free of communal discord."[15] By the early 1930s the Nabi Musa banner itself had been transformed into a nationalist symbol, from a green cloth bordered in gold to a version of the green, red, black, and white Arab national flag,[16] with an embroidered Dome of the Rock[17]—a symbol that can represent both Palestinian particularism and Islam—at its center.

In addition to Nabi Musa, several other traditional holidays, pilgrimages, and events from Islamic history offered opportunities to politicize and nationalize the Palestinian calendar, most notably the Nabi Salih festival north of Ramallah and the birthday of the prophet Mohammad (Mawlid al-Nabi). The latter was celebrated especially in the Haifa region,[18] and the Haifa-based (Christian-owned) newspaper al-Karmil even "deconfessionalized" the holiday by having it commemorate "the birth of the honorable Arab prophet."[19] In 1936 Filastin explicitly called for the instrumental use of religious holidays to promote national socialization (arguing that this is what the Jews do) and suggested including Easter in the list of commemorations in addition to the Nabi Musa festival.[20] The Battle of Hittin (4 July 1187) in which Saladin defeated the crusaders was celebrated from 1932 to 1937 by the pan-Arab Istiqlal party (established in 1932).[21] The party presented the battle as a victory of the East over the West to include the Christian population in the national community. However, none of these commemorations ultimately had the resonance of the Nabi Musa festival, failing to gain relevance beyond specific regional or partisan boundaries or draw widespread participation from all over Palestine.

The increasing importance of Nabi Musa during the British Mandate period is not only a derivative of the religious and political centrality of Jerusalem. It is related as well to the relative power of Haj Amin al-Husayni, who was the most influential Palestinian leader during this period. His rise to power is directly linked to the Nabi Musa riots in 1920, where he delivered an anti-Zionist speech. In the aftermath of the riots, he fled to Damascus and was tried in abstention by the British authorities but later, in an attempt to co-opt him, they gave him amnesty and nominated him as the Grand Mufti, the foremost position of Islamic authority in Palestine.[22] In 1922 he was elected as president of the Supreme Muslim Council (SMC), an institution created by the British High Commissioner. The SMC enjoyed the control of considerable resources based on *waqf* assets,[23] which enabled al-Husayni to orchestrate the Nabi Musa celebration and to expand it from a local to a national event. In this way the annual pilgrimage became an instrument for establishing the leadership status in Palestinian society for al-Husayni and the SMC. These resources were unavailable for other political forces that competed over leadership.[24]

The SMC also benefited from the policy of the British authorities that tolerated many of its activities as part of its co-optation efforts. For fifteen years the SMC kept a delicate balance between mobilizing opposition to the pro-Zionist British policy and satisfying Britain by regulating this opposition. The balance ended during the Arab Revolt (1936–1939), during which British rule in Palestine faced a nationalist uprising demanding independence and an end to Jewish immigration. The revolt opened with a six-month-long general strike and devolved into armed rebellion. In 1937 British authorities terminated Amin al-Husayni's control of the SMC, and he fled the country before being arrested. In a parallel path, they imposed severe restrictions on the Nabi Musa pilgrimage and practically neutralized its nationalist character. The exile of al-Husayni, the dismantling of Palestinian political institutions, and later the food shortage during World War II had a detrimental effect on the festival,[25] and it was never celebrated again with the same magnitude.

Balfour Day

Writing in his diary during the Nabi Musa festival on 17 April 1919, Sakakini reflected on the difference between Jewish and Arab holidays. He noted that the former were "created as memorial days for tragedies" and resulted in "dulled" senses and "pain and sadness," whereas Muslim holidays are "exciting" and left the Muslim "full of enthusiasm and energy." He then added: "A nation whose holidays include only crying has no future."[26]

Sakakini could not foresee that Palestinians would soon accumulate many memorial days commemorating tragedies and death—the days of remembrance that constitute the pillars of their national calendar even today. In this regard, Ernest Renan's observation that "defeat and mourning have greater importance for the national memory than victories,"[27] diametrically opposed to Sakakini's, would seem more apt, given their effectiveness in mobilizing for struggle. Thus the incorporation of tragedies (which in the Palestinian case concerned recent events) into the collective Palestinian narrative was part of the discursive nationalization of Palestinian identity.

In arguing his case to the MCA for commemorating Independence Day, Sakakini noted that "the Jews are already celebrating their independence since the Balfour Declaration."[28] Indeed, from 1918 through World War II, the Zionists in Palestine had made 2 November, the date the declaration was issued, a national holiday.[29] For the Arabs of Palestine, the Balfour Declaration could only be a tragedy, and soon it became commemorated as such—the first of the tragic commemorations that have since marked their calendar. Although the protest against the declaration began shortly after its publication, the formalization of cyclical annual protest under the title Balfour Day did not begin until 1921.

The main choreographer of Balfour Day was the Arab Executive, a committee first elected by the third Arab Congress in 1920, which played a role in leading the Palestinian national struggle until 1934. Remarkably, although in 1919 "Independence Day" was celebrated according to the *hijri* Islamic calendar, Balfour Day—as other new memorial days suggested by Palestinian leadership in the mandatory period—was scheduled according to the Gregorian calendar.

Unlike the Nabi Musa festival, Balfour Day had no religious significance and was equally shared by Muslims and Christians. Therefore, it was more compatible with the cross-sectarian ideological orientation of the MCA and the Arab Executive. On Balfour Day 1923, for example, Jaffa's MCA organized an event where Christians were invited with Muslims to Jaffa's Great Mosque to celebrate the "participation of the Muslim and Christian brothers in the Jihad for saving the country."[30]

From 1921 until 1947, 2 November was marked by a general strike (though sometimes for as little as two hours). Shops were closed, newspapers were printed with black borders, and buildings were decorated with black crepe.[31] Press headlines announced the "Black Day of Palestine" and "The Declaration of Injustice and Tyranny." The British authorities opposed the Balfour Day strike and in some years even tried to prevent it. Partly as a result, the Arab Executive did not always announce it officially but even when it did not, there is evidence of spontaneous annual strike initiatives, for example, by students in Arab schools (sometimes disobeying their principals).[32]

Balfour Day was observed as well in neighboring Arab countries. Strikes, demonstrations, and riots took place in Syria, Lebanon, Transjordan, and Egypt. In this regard, Balfour Day was not only a Palestinian observance but an element in the calendar of pan-Arab solidarity. Protest demonstrations in Palestine, however, were not limited to the major urban centers but took place in smaller towns all over the country as well. No less important was the fact that these demonstrations were reported in the press and allowed Palestinians from different parts of the country to know that they shared the same experience, as Palestinians.

Integral to the Balfour annual protest was the concrete demand that Britain end its commitment to the Zionist project. Opposition to the Balfour Declaration required action, and the collective body that was expected to act was the imagined community of Palestinians. A page-wide, black-framed announcement in *Filastin* on 2 November 1929 captures this idea in nine lines: "**The Balfour Declaration:**/Outrageous injustice—shameful iniquity/A Blot of Shame in the 20th century's history/**Great Britain:**/Must efface this shame that harms its interests and contaminates its dignity/**The People of Palestine:**/Must actively work for this goal by:/(1) Not selling land to Jews/(2) Encouraging patriotic [*wataniyya*] commerce and production."

A similar message appeared on Balfour Day in 1931 in *al-Jami'a al-'Arabiyya*, the SMC's mouthpiece:

> O Palestinians! Remember the notorious Balfour Declaration on 2 November and unify your efforts . . . to abolish this abusive commitment and to achieve your liberty and independence [. . .] O Arabs and Muslims in East and West! Remember Palestine the martyr (*al-shahida*) and do not forget your sacred sites there and its history with many pages of glorious, dignified, and courageous battles.[33]

Again, Palestinians were called on to translate their remembrance into a collective action aimed at achieving their independence. Arabs and Muslims elsewhere are expected only to express solidarity.

This emerging political cartography was both verbally and visually highlighted by *Filastin* in the reports on Balfour Day in 1932. The main headline stated: "A general strike throughout the country in protest over the notorious Balfour Declaration and the ongoing colonial policy." The issue provided detailed reports on the protests in Jerusalem, Jaffa, Tulkarm, Haifa, Acre, Jenin, Lydda, and Nablus. There was also a brief report on the strike in Beirut and a strike of Arab students in Damascus.[34]

The sense of a Palestine united in simultaneous protest conveyed by these reports was reinforced by the cartoon appearing on *Filastin*'s front page, which portrayed Lord Balfour himself at the center of a map of Palestine holding his declaration (Figure 2). Arrows from the declaration lead to various scenes representing Zionism's gains achieved under the protection of British military force. These include arriving Jewish immigrants, Jewish factories and mechanized agriculture, the Department of Public Works,[35] and two major Jewish-owned concessions (the Rutenberg electricity project and the Dead Sea mining project). Also depicted are a Palestinian peasant family uprooted by Zionist land purchases and a group of urban Arabs heatedly arguing, presumably over British policy, instead of acting against it.

The Istiqlal party attempted to extend the circle of participants in Balfour Day in Palestine to express their pan-Arab nationalist ideology. During the first Balfour Day ceremony organized by the party in Nablus in 1932, delegations from Transjordan and Syria were invited. Sakakini, who attended the event, found this noteworthy and in a letter to his son he commented that the attendance of these delegations was unprecedented.[36]

During the 1936–1939 revolt in Palestine, political leaders were arrested, exiled, or fled. The Arab Higher Committee (AHC) that was established at the beginning of the revolt was outlawed seventeen months later and was practically paralyzed. The demoralizing effect of this institutional breakdown was worsened by the violent factional clash among Palestinians. Press censorship

Figure 2. Cartoon of Lord Balfour holding his declaration on a map of Palestine. Source: Filastin, 2 November 1932

became stricter after the beginning of the revolt and even more so during World War II. As a result, there was a drastic decline in the visibility of public formalized Palestinian commemoration in the 1940s. The public commemoration of Balfour Day was almost unnoticeable during most of the war years. Only with the re-establishment of the Palestinian Arab Party in 1944 were the commemorative patterns renewed.[37] In 1945, after the war, the country-wide strike was renewed. Facing reports of two international commissions of inquiry (the Anglo-American committee in 1946 and the United Nations Special Committee on Palestine [UNSCOP] in 1947) and the growing sentiment that a decision on the future of the country was imminent, Balfour Day's political relevance became particularly evident.

We can learn from press reports about the atmosphere on the Palestinian street (or at least the atmosphere desired by the Palestinian press) during Balfour Day, such as the following description of the strike in Jaffa in 1946 that appeared in *al-Difaʿ*:

> On the day of the notorious Balfour Declaration the city was striking completely. The strike included all the sectors and public movement stopped completely. Retailers, stores, and institutions were closed. The streets were emptied of cars, coffee shops and restaurants were closed, and people gathered in public places. Yesterday, the notorious day of remembrance, not a single person departed from the national consensus [. . .] the residents of the neighboring villages participated in the strike, transportation between them and the city stopped, and the villagers avoided coming to the city.[38]

NATIONAL MARTYROLOGY

Formulators of modern secular ideologies in the Middle East adopted a rich arsenal of Islamic symbols and concepts, such as jihad (utmost effort in a religious context),[39] and borrowed as well the concept of Islamic martyrdom.[40] Because Christian themes have pervaded Palestinian culture and the discourse of the literary classes, Christian images of martyrdom, and especially the crucifixion, also became part of the cultural tool kit of both Christian and Muslim Palestinians.[41]

The Ottoman Empire, which adopted European institutional and symbolic elements in the nineteenth century (e.g., civil courts, architectural style), was influenced as well by the growing importance of national martyrdom as an element in the construction of political identities.[42] In this context, the traditional meaning of sacrificing oneself for God was secularized, and the modern

shahid/şehit ("martyr" in Arabic and Turkish, respectively) was seen as sacrificing himself for the Ottoman nation.

Palestinian national martyrology was developed in these political-cultural
conditions. For the Arab inhabitants of Palestine in the first decades of the
twentieth century, the nation, for which the martyrs were supposedly dying
was fluid and changed with evolving political circumstances. For example, before World War I, national feeling in Palestine often took the form of Ottoman
patriotism,[43] for example, when Is'af al-Nashashibi, a young poet from a notable Jerusalem family, described those killed in the 1909 Ottoman counter-coup
against the Young Turks as *shuhada'* (martyrs) for the "Ottoman nation."[44]

During World War I, the emerging Arab national movement embraced as
martyrs those activists from Syria, Lebanon, and Palestine who were hanged by
the Ottoman military in 1915–1916.[45] Although their deaths appear to have been
less widely and enthusiastically commemorated in Palestine than in Syria and
Lebanon,[46] there is anecdotal evidence of commemoration there as well, even if
not as institutionalized as in Damascus. In March 1919, shortly after the first Palestinian Arab Congress (which considered Palestine part of Greater Syria), Jaffa's
Arab Club sponsored a play about the tyranny of Jamal Pasha. The play ended
with the actors waving the Arab flag in front of the corpses of the 1916 martyrs
and with the audience joining them in singing the Arab national anthem.[47]

While the commemoration of the 1916 martyrs was part of pan-Arab or
at least pan-Syrian emerging mythology, for some intellectuals in the same
period, Palestine had become a place worth dying for. In April 1918, five months
after the Balfour Declaration, a large map of Palestine was prominently displayed at the Rashidiyya School Club in Jerusalem, inscribed with the following lines of poetry: "The Blessed Land of Palestine / Is the land of the sons of
Ya'rub[48] / O the best land of all, do not despair / I have other love but you / We
shall sacrifice our souls for your sake. . . . "[49] Later, with the French occupation of Damascus in July 1920 and the end of the Greater Syria adventure, Arab
Palestinians (many of whom had been enthusiastic backers of Palestine as
southern Syria) increasingly articulated their political identity in more local
Palestinian terms.[50]

The inter-communal violence in early May 1921 provided the emerging Palestinian local patriotism with its necessary protagonists for building its own
martyrology.[51] The Muslim Christian Association in Jaffa looked after the city's
Arab victims and took the lead in organizing joint Muslim-Christian religious
ceremonies. Indicative of the conscious effort to reach beyond the localities

directly involved, the Jaffa chapter published a call for all MCAs throughout Palestine to collect donations for the injured and the families of those killed.[52] Besides the ecumenical religious ceremonies, which provided an opportunity to demonstrate Muslim-Christian fraternity, delegates from each community participated in the religious ceremonies of the other side. The speakers in these inter-religious visits emphasized the common fate of Christians and Muslims in the face of the Zionist threat.[53]

The adoption of the term "martyr" to describe those who died in the conflict was gradual. Immediately after the riots, for example, *Filastin* described the Muslim and Christian dead as *qatla* (those who were killed). On the fortieth-day commemoration,[54] the same newspaper used the terms *dahaya* (victims) and *shuhada'* (martyrs) interchangeably. On the first anniversary they were referred to as victims, but by the second anniversary (1923), as already noted, *Filastin* not only uniformly presented them as martyrs but advocated the creation of an annual Martyrs Day to commemorate them.

The 1930 Martyrs

Although *Filastin* in 1921 had created an early rhetorical link between martyrs commemorated and Palestine, it had not explicitly described them as patriots who died for *Palestine*. Moreover, no attention was paid to the martyrs' personal identities: their names were not even mentioned in the press. The individualization of martyrology, which allows a more focused glorification of the martyrs and greater emphasis on their motives, had to await the high-profile executions of three Palestinian men on 17 June 1930. On that day, Muhammad Jamjum and 'Ata al-Zir of Hebron, and Fu'ad Hijazi of Safad—the first "national Palestinian martyrs"—were hanged by the British for taking part in the massacre of Jews during *Thawrat al-Buraq* (the Buraq Revolt) in August 1929.[55]

One of those hanged, Fu'ad Hijazi, was quoted extensively in the Palestinian press for his explicit references to martyrdom. According to family members and prison cellmates, he had declared his intention to die for the nation. In his will, published the day after the hangings, he explicitly asked that "the day of my hanging should be a day of joy and cheers, and so should 17 June every year. This day should be a historic day in which speeches are delivered and anthems are sung in memory of our blood shed for Palestine and the Arab cause."[56] Hijazi used the same rhetoric in a letter he wrote to the vice-president of the Arab Executive, proclaiming that his "heart was full of joy and happiness since I will be hanged for Palestine, the beloved country."[57] The historian Yehoshua

Porath mentioned that a later letter to the same addressee, in which Hijazi denied the charges and begged the Arab Executive to lobby for his pardon, was not published at the time.[58] This selective publication of Hijazi's letters was part of the conscious production of a martyrological myth.

At the time, British authorities were aware of the potential political fallout of the commemoration and attempted to pressure Arab Executive members to restrict the event. In a telegram to the Secretary of State for the Colonies in London, the Officer Administering the Government of Palestine wrote that ". . . it is the declared intention of the Arab Executive to consider the holding annually of commemoration services and to erect a tomb to 'the Martyrs.' I am convinced that firm action now may lead the Executive to abandon any such intentions."[59]

However, the British authorities were not able to prevent this commemoration. After the men's execution, the Arab Executive announced that 17 June would be commemorated annually,[60] and it organized memorial rallies every year until it was disbanded in 1934.

The press also published poems dedicated to the new martyrs, the most famous of which at the time was "Bloody Tuesday" by the Palestinian poet Ibrahim Tuqan.[61] The pattern was repeated cyclically on 17 June for the next five years. The martyrs were glorified by newspapers across the political spectrum, from the MSC's *al-Jami'a al-'Arabiyya* to its rival *Filastin*, whose owner was affiliated with the opposition,[62] and irrespective of whether their ownership was Muslim or Christian. Even the Palestinian Communist Party, in spite of its universalistic orientation, celebrated the annual Memorial Day.[63] Furthermore, while the Buraq revolt itself was imbued with Muslim symbolism (as the name indicates), both Muslim writers and Christian writers utilized metaphors of martyrdom that were unmistakably Christian. In several newspapers (as well as in Ibrahim Tuqan's poetry), the word "crucifixion" was used for the executions.[64]

While the newspapers wrote that the executed men had died for the "nation" or the "homeland," sometimes the reference was to the Arab nation (". . . they are those who irrigated with their pure blood the roots of the tree of Arab independence"[65]) and other times to "the Arab nation in Palestine" (. . . "deep sadness" in the chest of "every member of the Arab nation in Palestine, men, women, and children"[66]). Following the fortieth-day ceremonies, *al-Jami'a al-'Arabiyya* wrote: "Yesterday Palestine marked the fortieth day for the martyrdom of three of her sons, Fu'ad Hijazi, 'Ata al-Zir, and Muhammad Khalil Jamjum [who were martyred] for her freedom and independence."[67] In *Filastin*, the most consistent voice of Palestinian particularism, their sacrifice was simply "for Palestine." The editorial published under the title "Martyrs' Day" on the first anniversary of the execution ended with the words: "For Palestine Hijazi, al-Zir, and Jamjum died, and for her they sacrificed their youth and power [. . .] For Palestine they devoted their blood and for them Palestine devotes her boundless tears."[68]

Even when the three were described as having died for the Arab nation, their identity as Palestinians was highlighted. On the fourth anniversary of the execution, the Jaffa-based newspaper *Al-Difaʿ* published an editorial clarifying that martyrs are the necessary price Palestine must pay for freedom: "Is it possible that Syria has martyrs, Iraq has martyrs, Egypt has martyrs—and every country that revolts against colonialism would have martyrs but Palestine, hit by colonialism, would not have martyrs?"[69]

After the execution, demonstrations and memorial ceremonies took place in all the major cities and towns of Palestine (Safad, Hebron, Jenin, Jaffa, Jerusalem, Nablus, Haifa, Acre, and Tulkarm), as did a general strike on the first anniversary. These same cities also sent condolence delegations to the ceremonies near the martyrs' graves in Acre on the first three anniversaries. But while there were protests over the executions throughout the Arab and Muslim world, there were no reports of delegations from abroad attending memorials inside Palestine or holding anniversary commemorations. A symbolic cartography was emerging, and the new martyrs were martyrs of Palestine.

In light of this emphasis on local Palestinian martyrs, the little attention given to Pan-Arab martyrs in the commemorative repertoire of the Palestinian press in the same period is indicative of the role of martyrology in developing Palestinian particularism. Remarkably, the Palestinian press showed little interest in commemorating the Day of Maysalun, a battle on 24 July 1920, whereby the French effectively ended Faysal's rule in Syria. This military defeat became a major myth of victimhood for Syrian and pan-Arab identities. Satiʿ al-Husri, the most prominent ideologue of pan-Arabism, considered it "one of the most important events in the modern history of the Arab nation."[70] Nevertheless, during the 1920s the battle of Maysalun earned only sporadic reference in the Palestinian press on its anniversary (July 24) but even then, the texts frequently referred to the fate of the "Syrian sister," not as part of the collective experience of Palestinian readers.[71] The Syrian national hero who was killed in the Maysalun battle, Yusef al-ʿAzma, was rarely referred to. Interestingly, in July 1930, shortly after the fortieth day of commemoration of the triple execution in Acre, *al-Jamiʿa al-ʿArabiyya* decided to mention the tenth anniversary of al-ʿAzma's martyrdom. It seems, however, that the importance of this reference is in its implicit message to take example from the Syrians in the way they remember their martyrs: "Every year on this day, the Syrians still visit en masse the martyr's tomb in Maysaloun where they put bouquets of flowers and pour tears of sorrow and pain."[72] The Palestinians are cast in this text as sympathetic outside observers, not the community that is expected to visit the tomb; for that, they have their own martyrs. Similarly, the Italian execution of 'Omar al-Mukhtar in Libya on 16 September 1931, which became another pan-Arab myth,[73] received scarce and minor references in the Palestinian press. *Al-Difa'* dedicated an editorial to the topic on the third anniversary of his martyrdom, but in most other newspapers the 16 of September passed without any reference to al-Mukhtar.

In the early 1930s Palestinian newspapers attempted to nurture the image of other Palestinian martyr-heroes. Palestinians who died in the context of struggle over land were especially important in this context. In one of these conflicts over agricultural land near Tab'un, a young Palestinian named Muhammad 'Alyan was shot and killed by Jewish settlers. *Al-Difa'* called upon Arabs to make pilgrimages to his grave and added, "We will make of your day what they [the Zionists] made of Trumpeldor day,"[74] referring to the elaborate Zionist commemoration of Joseph Trumpeldor (1880–1920), who was killed in the northern settlement of Tel Hai and subsequently became a Zionist national hero.[75]

However, 'Alyan, as other Palestinians who died in local land conflicts at the time, did not enter the pantheon of national martyrs like the 1930 martyrs. The symbolic resonance of these martyrs is clear in a flyer published on the fifth anniversary of their execution by an underground group from the Tulkarm/Qalqilya region named "The Red Palm," which called for the assassination of Palestine's British rulers in retribution for the execution and demanded that the martyrs be celebrated annually.[76]

Martyrs Day of 1935, however, was the last anniversary to be mentioned by the Palestinian press. By 17 June 1936, the Palestinian Revolt was already underway, and press censorship had greatly tightened. In any case, for the young Palestinian national movement, the 1930 martyrs would soon be overshadowed by the heroic image of the martyrs who fell during the revolt.

'Izz al-Din al-Qassam: Precursor to Revolt

Sheikh 'Izz al-Din al-Qassam, a Muslim preacher who called for armed struggle against British rule, was killed with four of his followers in a clash with British troops on 20 November 1935.[77] Two days after his death, *Filastin* published a testimony by 'Abd al-Ghani al-Karmi, a journalist who claimed to have seen al-Qassam on 17 June 1930, the day the three men were hanged: "I saw him with gloomy face, overcoming a tear, in his eyes a terrible spark, his body trembling with anger. He was almost unaware of his surroundings. I saw him hurrying to the mosque and I followed him. There he delivered a fiery sermon."[78] The accuracy of this report is less important than the evident attempt to construct a continuous martyrological narrative linking al-Qassam to the earlier martyrs. Similar linkage was emphasized by a delegation from Nablus, which on the fortieth day of al-Qassam's martyrdom went north to visit his grave, after first visiting the grave of the 1930 martyrs in Acre.[79]

Al-Qassam's funeral was massive. According to *Filastin*, it was attended by 30,000 people but very few political leaders.[80] There were reasons for this: the Muslim elite saw the populist/religious elements of al-Qassam's movement as a threat to their control,[81] while advocates of a more secular nationalism, who considered Islam as only one legitimizing element among others, feared that his religious activism would disrupt the balance among such elements.[82] By the fortieth day of his death, however, the indifference of the leaders had disappeared with their realization of the symbolic power of his image.[83] From then on, the various political parties competed in praising al-Qassam and in appropriating his martyrdom for their political agendas.[84]

In contrast to Haj Amin al-Husayni, a late adopter of al-Qassam, *Filastin* "immediately nationalized the religious leader, denuding him of any Islamic content."[85] The newspaper used what were reported to be al-Qassam's last words as the title of its coverage of his death: "We will not surrender—this is a jihad for Allah and for homeland (*watan*);"[86] In its extensive coverage of the funeral the following day, *Filastin* mentioned that delegations came from all parts of Palestine and highlighted the fact that the coffins were wrapped with the Arab national flag. Compared with the commemoration of the 1930 martyrs, *Filastin* adopted a more pan-Arab line, emphasizing al-Qassam's Syrian birth and the fact that he had previously taken part in the Syrian revolt against the French in 1919–1920. It is likely that 'Isa al-'Isa, *Filastin*'s Christian editor, used this rhetoric to reduce the impact of the martyred leader's religious message.[87]

The pan-Arab Istiqlal party was similarly eager to cultivate the emerging myth of al-Qassam's martyrdom. One of its founders, Akram Zu'aitar, was among the few known political figures to attend al-Qassam's funeral. On 6 February 1936 Istiqlal organized a ceremony in Haifa. In a report about the event, *al-Difa'* provided the names of speakers, as well as of those who sent telegrams and money to the families. The pan-Arab orientation of the party was evident in the inclusion of three speakers from outside Palestine (Jordan, Aleppo, and Hama) although most of the speakers were Palestinian. However, the reported financial donations came only from Hebron and Jerusalem, not from outside Palestine.[88]

The Great Revolt (1936–39) erupted five months after al-Qassam was killed, and according to both popular remembrance[89] and scholarly observation,[90] his death should be considered an early stage of the revolt itself. The revolt, in which thousands of Palestinians lost their lives,[91] added a significant layer to Palestinian martyrology. Sacrificing for Palestine became a virtue appreciated by the mainstream. The Palestinian historian 'Isa al-Sifri dedicated his 1937 book, *Arab Palestine: Between the Mandate and Zionism*, to "Those who were martyred / those who fill the prisons / those who were arrested, exiled, and persecuted / those who fought with faith / those who tasted the bitterness of life /—**for Palestine** [emphasis in the original]."[92]

The fascination of Khalil Sakakini with heroic martyrdom is evident in his glorification of Sami al-Ansari. Al-Ansari was killed by a British soldier after shooting a British police officer,[93] and according to Sakakini, before his death he told his brother: "Don't be sorry, I did my duty." Then Sakakini added:

> This is the hero who fell yesterday. He is indeed a great hero [. . .] Yesterday the nation went to the house of his father who brought to this world such a hero. They congratulated him rather than comforted him, he spoke with pride about his son—and he deserves to be proud. [. . .] Every day we hear about this heroism. It seems that the heroism that was revealed in Palestine in the past in the many wars that were imposed on the country and was latent until we thought it was dead—has been rediscovered."[94]

With the growing numbers of Palestinian casualties during the revolt, two of Palestine's main newspapers, *Filastin* and *al-Difa'*, each called separately for building a monument to the "unknown martyr" (*al-shahid al-majhul*). On the first anniversary of al-Qassam's death, *Filastin*'s editorial column suggested:

> Just as the West invented a symbol (*ramz*) of heroism and courage after the Great War, a symbol for the unknown soldier, the nation that is so brave in its jihad and its heavy sacrifices should invent an eternal symbol for the unknown martyr who fell in defense of his nation, his soul and his property.[95]

The editorial also notes that Jerusalem's National Committee had decided to build a memorial to commemorate the unknown martyrs.[96] Two weeks later, *al-Difaʿ* raised the same idea with a similar argument:

> Commemorate, O Arabs of Palestine, the unknown martyr. Commemorate the one who was martyred and was not known among you, except by his father and mother. Establish for him a symbol like the symbol that was established in different European capitals (the unknown soldier)[. . .] The body of this soldier will be buried in Balʿa, or Yaʿbad, or Bait Imrin.[97] Then a symbol for him will be established in every city, and delegates will visit it, children will see it on their way to school, and the people will surround it with memory and reverence.[98]

The discussion over establishing memorial monuments was probably common at the time. In his book from 1937, ʿIsa al-Sifri presents a sketch for a memorial monument that was planned to be built in al-Mintar Mountain to commemorate the martyrs of the Balʿa battle.[99] In the cases of all of the above-mentioned suggestions and plans to build monuments, it is unclear how close the goal came to being accomplished.

The nationalist motivation for cultivating unifying symbols would increase even as internal tensions between Palestinians grew. As of 1938, the revolt became mired in internal conflicts along class and political lines.[100] The partial overlap between class and sectarian lines (and the overrepresentation of Christians in government jobs) triggered sporadic anti-Christian rhetoric and violence, which at least some Christians perceived as a threat,[101] especially at a time when their relative weight in the Palestinian elite was declining.[102] Although the AHC was committed to Muslim-Christian solidarity, the decentralization of the rebel leadership sometimes led to anti-Christian propaganda by local rebels.[103] For the AHC, the Istiqlalists, and local Muslim and Christian leaders opposed to sectarianism, a shared martyrology may have been a way to support national unity at a time of crisis.

COMMEMORATION UNDER CENSORSHIP

The zenith years of commemorating Palestinian martyrs were from 1930 until the beginning of the revolt in 1936. The Palestinian press was a powerful tool in country-wide propagation of the national calendar and commemoration of martyrs. By 1930, there were ten Arabic dailies and weeklies in Palestine. According to the historian Ami Ayalon, *al-Difaʿ* (established in 1934) and *Filastin* each had a country-wide circulation of 7,000–10,000. More important than the individual subscriptions, however, is the fact that newspapers were read aloud in public places.[104] This meant that tens of thousands of people, from Gaza in the south to Nazareth in the north, shared the content and could imagine themselves as part of a community commemorating and protesting together, for example, the Balfour Declaration, or grieving over the death of 'Izz al-Din al-Qassam.

Furthermore, compared to the first years after World War I, Palestinian political institutions were more developed in 1930. Although the Arab Executive was not an elected body and did not have any legal authority, the fact that it united respectable Muslim and Christian figures from various parts of the country made it possible to foster country-wide, simultaneous, and cyclical commemorations for several years.

The public visibility of martyrological commemoration was closely related to the level of control imposed by British authorities, which fluctuated throughout the Mandate period. From the start of British occupation, the press was subjected to strict supervision by the Criminal Intelligence Department. This supervision gradually loosened over the years and was eliminated by 1928.[105] As the system of oversight underwent reorganization,[106] there was minimal press supervision. But in January 1933, a new, strict Press Ordinance was issued. Not coincidentally, the most elaborate martyrological rhetoric developed in the Palestinian press in the gap between these two dates.

The 1933 Press Ordinance was amended six times between 1936 and 1945, with the press regulations becoming progressively tougher.[107] The amendments and new regulations made possible the frequent suspension of newspapers during the revolt and stricter supervision during World War II.[108] Under these circumstances, expressions of national sentiments were relegated to seemingly apolitical sections like the sports column,[109] and explicit commemoration of national martyrs was not possible. Thus, whereas press commemoration of Balfour Day was tolerated, probably because the authorities considered it less "inflammatory," references to 17 June as "Martyrs Day" or glorification of al-Qassam disappeared from the Palestinian press from the beginning of the revolt until 1948.[110]

With the Arab Palestinian press unable to play a role in promoting the martyrology of the revolt, oral poetry became an important alternative. Poets such as Nuh Ibrahim, Ibrahim Tuqan, 'Abd al-Rahim Mahmud, and Abu Salmah all played an important role.[111] Especially important was Nuh Ibrahim, who wrote his poems in a colloquial Arabic accessible to the large circles of illiterate peasants who became dominant at the later stages of the revolt.

Ibrahim had a significant impact on the popularization of the myth of al-Qassam,[112] and with it he provided unifying symbols to peasants and urban Palestinians.[113]

Ibrahim, himself a student and follower of al-Qassam, constructed al-Qassam's image as an Arab Palestinian hero rather than a Muslim one, and the overriding sentiment expressed by his martyrological poetry is Palestinian national unity.[114] In his widely known poem "O What a Loss, 'Izz al-Din," he called al-Qassam "a martyr for all Palestine."[115] National unity and Muslim-Christian solidarity are also important elements in his poetry: "Say not 'Christian' and 'Muslim'; we all are brothers of blood," is a line from "The homeland is for all," one of his best known poems. He is also remembered for the famous poem "*Min sijn 'Akka*," (from the Acre prison) dedicated to the three prisoners executed in 1930. Nuh Ibrahim, killed in a battle near Tamra on 28 October 1938, became known as the martyr-poet.[116]

WHICH COMMEMORATIONS ENDURE?

Palestinian national identity emerged from the common experience of Arabs who faced the same colonial effort to dispossess them. Shared experience by itself, however, does not create a sense of shared identity without cultural processing and the creation of myths and symbols related to this collective experience. Political calendars and shared martyrology thus became important markers of identity and symbolic tools for political mobilization in Mandatory Palestine. They were especially important for the advancement of Palestinian particularism, which could not rely on a pre-existing common religion or a distinct language.

Because the creation of a stable political calendar requires the use of state or state-like mechanisms, the success in building it was very limited. Neither the Arab Executive, the SMC, or later, the AHC represented a sovereign state, and therefore they lacked the ability to mobilize sufficient resources or to establish hegemony-producing mechanisms such as a national compulsory education system. Still, their support for establishing a stable date on the calendar was necessary for the routinization of commemoration. Suggested dates for national holidays that did not enjoy the support of these institutions proved elusive or were limited to a certain region or political party. The collective political calendar of the Palestinians in Mandatory Palestine included only a few events that were embraced by the public: the Nabi Musa festival, Martyrs' Day commemorating the June 1930 executions, and Balfour Day. Balfour Day was the only one commemorated both at the beginning and the end of the British occupation. Its endurance is at least partly explained by the tangible political implications of the declaration, which were continuously visible to most Palestinians. Even the commemoration of the Balfour Declaration, however, shrank drastically after the revolt and its devastating impact on Palestinian institutions. The Nabi Musa festival gained its status as a national holiday because it was a political instrument of the SMC, which had the resources to maintain and expand it, and also had a structural interest in shaping its meaning as a distinct Palestinian national event.

Martyrological memory also depended to a large extent on institutional support. Before 1930 none of the martyrs were commemorated by an annual memorial day in Palestine. In the years following the executions of 1915–1916 and the 1921 clashes, Palestinian national institutions and the press did not exist, or they were not sufficiently developed. Similarly, annual memorial days for martyrs were not observed after 1935 because of the institutional breakdown during the revolt. The formalized calendar was also more vulnerable to the restrictions and censorship imposed by the British authorities. Commemoration of martyrs in less formalized ways such as oral poetry was a more successful and durable project.

Commemoration under British rule reflected and shaped the boundaries of an emerging Palestinian national identity. The demographic and geographic demarcation lines of this identity were defined both by the commemorating community that shared the political calendar and by the identity of commemorated martyrs. These boundaries included Muslim and Christian Arabs who lived within the political borders of Mandatory Palestine. After the Nakba, the division of this emerging imagined community between different political sovereignties led to the emergence of a variety of calendars, with little overlap between them. The emergence of the particular political calendar of the Palestinian citizens of Israel is the topic of the next chapter.

2 THE KAFR QASIM MASSACRE AND LAND DAY

FROM 1947 TO 1948 almost all Palestinian urban elites were exiled to neighboring Arab countries. Arab-Palestinian newspapers, libraries, theaters, colleges, and other institutions of national knowledge-production disappeared with them. The Palestinians who remained in Israel were disproportionately villagers, with a relatively low level of education and literacy. Until 1966 this defeated population lived under an Israeli military government that severely restricted movement, work, political organization, and freedom of speech.[1] Furthermore, the Palestinian population was scattered in various isolated "pockets" that survived the expulsions: the Galilee, the Triangle (a concentration of towns and villages adjacent to the eastern border of pre-1967 Israel), the Negev/Naqb (a desert region in the south of Israel/Palestine), and various previously Palestinian cities (Jaffa, Haifa, Acre, Lydda, and Ramleh) that became mixed cities with a Jewish majority. These new conditions had far reaching implications on the way Palestinians who remained under Israeli rule have preserved and produced their collective memory.

In 1948 Nabi Musa remained under Jordanian rule and in 1953 the Jordanian authorities abolished the Nabi Musa celebrations—perhaps not a great loss for Palestinians in Israel, given that the tomb had been inaccessible for Israeli citizens, including Arabs, since 1948 and remained so until 1967. During this same time period, the political relevance of the Balfour Declaration declined. The British no longer held power, and the actual physical destruction of the Nakba far overshadowed the earlier symbolic commitment of the declaration. Even if there were intentions among Arab citizens to commemorate the Balfour Declaration, the restrictions on movement and political organization imposed by the military regime limited public political commemoration. The political calendar that was developed during the British Mandate period had now almost vanished. When Palestinians in Israel became more organized in the late 1950s, new dates took their place in the collective calendar.

These new dates and the new martyrology nurtured around them have played an important role in the articulation of new competing definitions of collective identity for the Palestinians in Israel. In the long term, the power balance between the various actors involved in this competition has led to the dominance of a perspective that sees both Arab-Palestinian national identity as well as Israeli citizenship as two complementary and legitimate elements of identity. In the same way that the Arab Executive and Amin al-Husayni were the entrepreneurs of Palestinian particularism under British rule, this new identity had its own major entrepreneur: the Israeli Communist Party.

THE ISRAELI COMMUNIST PARTY

A new incarnation of the pre-1948 Palestinian Communist Party resulting from the merger of its pre-war Arab and Jewish factions, this party was the only organization that could legally and publicly politicize the memory and identity of Arab citizens under military rule. It attracted Palestinian Arab support because it was a legitimate political party, represented in the Knesset, and strongly defending the rights of Arabs and opposing Israeli positions in both foreign and domestic affairs, including demanding the return of Palestinian refugees.[2] Over the years the party has gone through many changes, and the official display of unity has masked deep controversies (which even led to a split in 1965).[3] However, the dominant voice in the party has always considered the Israeli citizenship of the Arabs in Israel as an important asset and aspired to develop it beyond its instrumental value.

Thus, aside from the explicit commitment of the Arab members of the party to Arab nationalism (and from the 1970s to Palestinian nationalism), the party attempted to develop a non-Zionist version of Israeli civic patriotism shared by Arab and Jewish citizens.[4] In the long run, and especially since the mid-1970s, this civic patriotism was replaced by a more subtle aspiration for being part of a shared Israeli public sphere, but Israeli citizenship remained an important element in the party ideology. In the 1970s and the 1980s, the party was by far the strongest among Palestinians in Israel.[5] Furthermore, it was a "workshop that produced the views of other forces in the Arab sector," since all other forces "have moved toward the idea of two peoples and two states, a concept of equality that focuses on closing gaps between Jews and Arabs, and struggle that remains within the confines of Israeli law."[6] Its key role in developing conscious-ness was related to its network of Arabic language publications, effective party organization, and financial support from the former Soviet Union.[7] For the party, the commemoration of key events was central to political mobilization. This chapter deals with the emergence of the two events that dominated the po-litical calendar from 1956 to 1998: the massacre in Kafr Qasim and Land Day.

WHY KAFR QASIM?

Kafr Qasim is an Arab village in the Triangle that was annexed by Israel follow-ing the 1949 Israeli-Jordanian armistice agreement. On 29 October 1956, a group of peasants from Kafr Qasim returned to the village from their fields, unaware that their village was under curfew. Forty-seven of them were executed by the Israeli Border Patrol troops.[8] The massacre triggered a long-term unifying po-litical protest that crossed regional, communal, and political differences—but mostly without crossing the political borders of the State of Israel.

The emergence of Kafr Qasim as a major political myth is not as self-evident as it appears to be. The policy of killing unarmed Palestinians as a method of controlling their movement was common at the time. The historian Benny Morris estimated that in the years from 1949 to 1956, between 2,700 and 5,000 Palestinians were killed by the IDF, police, and civilians along Israel's newly cre-ated borders, most of them unarmed refugees who tried either to return home or to harvest their crops.[9] Morris draws a direct line between this policy and the massacre in Kafr Qasim. Nor was the massacre of Kafr Qasim the incident with the single largest number of casualties in the 1950s. From 14 to 15 October 1953 Israeli troops attacked the village of Qibya in the West Bank, only ten miles away from Kafr Qasim, and killed sixty-nine Palestinian villagers, most of them women and children. In the case of Qibya the documented order to commit a massacre is much clearer and more explicit than in the case of Kafr Qasim,[10] but nevertheless, the remembrance of the massacre did not become a mobiliz-ing myth among Palestinians in Israel.

The massacre in Kafr Qasim was also not the only one committed in the very same period. It occurred only a few hours before Israel invaded the Sinai Penin-sula and the Gaza Strip in what became known as the Suez War. According to a UN report, on 3 November, during the conquest of Khan Yunis in the Gaza Strip, Israeli forces killed 275 Palestinians.[11] In the Gaza Strip this event is commemo-rated publicly: in 2009 the city hall of Khan Yunis established a committee that would develop ways to commemorate the massacre of 1956; subsequently some educational institutions in the city commemorated the event.[12]

According to the same UN report, on 12 November Israeli military forces killed 110 Palestinians in Rafah after the fighting was already over. The author of the UN report, R. F. Bayard, chairman of the Egyptian-Israeli Mixed Armistice Commission (UN observers), stated that among the victims in both events in the Gaza Strip "a good number of persons have been shot down in cold blood for no apparent reason."[13] According to the official Israeli version of the Rafah events, soldiers faced riots, including gun shots, and during their attempts to end the riots they killed forty-eight people.[14]

At least Knesset members of the Communist Party were aware of the Rafah event and tried, unsuccessfully, to initiate a discussion about it in the Knesset, as they had with the Kafr Qasim massacre. Regarding the massacre in Kafr Qasim, however, they were much more determined to make it public knowledge, against the government's attempt to block information.[15] Al-Ittihad, the Communist Party's newspaper, gave much less attention to the killing in the Gaza Strip. During the first decade after 1956, al-Ittihad did link the Suez War and the Kafr Qasim massacre in its commemorative rhetoric, including a reference to both events in the main headlines on their anniversaries, but the reference to the specific massacres in the Gaza Strip was brief and uncommon. These massacres did not become a subject of commemoration by themselves, nor were they grouped with the massacre of Kafr Qasim to constitute one episode ("the massacres of autumn 1956," for example, in the same way that the series of expulsions in 1948 is remembered as one event, the Nakba).

Interestingly, when representatives of eleven Arab states submitted a letter to the President of the General Assembly of the UN in December 1956, they protested the "inhuman treatment of the Arabs who live in Israel, the Gaza Strip, and the Sinai Peninsula [. . .] Hundreds of Arab men, women, and children have been ruthlessly murdered in cold blood."[16] In this protest the various 1956 massacres constituted a *single episode*. Similarly, *al-Difaʿ*, the formerly Jaffa-based journal that after 1948 was published in Jordanian-ruled East Jerusalem, reported on the communists' protest in the Knesset against the Rafah events and mentioned the massacre in Kafr Qasim as a side note in the same report.[17] Later on the newspaper reported briefly on the Israeli Prime Minister Ben Gurion's announcement in the Knesset about the Kafr Qasim massacre.[18]

The selection of Kafr Qasim from a series of concurrent massacres and the endurance of its commemoration are related to the political status of the victims and those who commemorated them outside Kafr Qasim—Israeli citizens—unlike the victims of the massacres in the Gaza Strip or in Qibya. Similarly, what distinguished the Kafr Qasim victims from the thousands of Palestinians who were killed while trying to cross the armistice line is that the victims were Israeli citizens, who were on their way home from work, not refugees on their way back home who tried to cross a recently-created international border.

As historian Shira Robinson has pointed out, in the first years of the state's existence citizenship became a "category of exclusion" that enabled Israel to legalize Palestinian expulsion and prevent Palestinian return. When Israel started to issue Israeli identity (ID) cards in late 1948, the criteria for eligibility were shaped by the drive to minimize the number of Arabs in the state. Similarly, when the Citizenship Law was legislated in 1952, its parameters were shaped to a large extent by the motivation to exclude the maximum number of Arabs from citizenship, while keeping a universalistic language and the appearance of a liberal inclusive citizenship.[19] In these formative years, not having an Israeli ID card or Israeli citizenship significantly increased the likelihood that a Palestinian would be deported beyond the state's borders. This policy divided Palestinians between those who did not have ID cards (and later citizenship), and therefore were likely to be exiled or remain in exile, and a minority who received Israeli ID cards and was allowed to stay and, in some cases, even allowed returning after expulsion.

As Hannah Arendt argued, human rights can be better protected if articulated as civil rights.[20] Palestinians in Israel did not have to read Arendt in order to develop these insights. By the end of 1950 Israel stopped en masse expulsions of Palestinians from its territory; its demographic policy instead focused on preventing Palestinians from returning by blocking the armistice line. Since then there have been plans to "relocate" the remaining Palestinians,[21] and even some contingency plans to expel them,[22] but at the end of the day, citizenship has protected most of them from further expulsion.

Therefore, while Palestinian writers in Israel frequently analyzed the massacre of Kafr Qasim in the wider context of the Arab struggle against colonialism,[23] classifying violence against Palestinians as a violation of civil rights was even more frequent. This emphasis has been the most rational path for protecting them from further expulsion or arbitrary killing. At the same time, since commemoration of this violence has been seen by the authorities as a threat, Palestinians have been carefully monitored and a subject of aggressive attempts to discipline commemoration. This, in turn, added the additional drive to highlight citizenship in order to protect the commemoration itself. Hence, the selection of events into the canonic political calendar and the selection of martyrs to the pantheon frequently have been shaped by the need to *highlight Israeli citizenship*. This emphasis on citizenship was also highly compatible with the ideology of the Communist Party, the dominant voice of Arab opposition in Israel at the time of the massacre in Kafr Qasim.

Tawfiq Tubi, a prominent communist leader, and a Member of Knesset (MK) played a crucial role in disseminating information about the massacre to the public, bypassing the heavy censorship. He was also the first to articulate the political lessons of the massacre. An article he published in *al-Ittihad* on 31 December 1956, titled "After the massacre," is an early expression of the major themes that would dominate the commemorative rhetoric for the next few decades. First, Tubi demanded an investigation as to "who gave the order," suggesting that the government itself bore responsibility, not only the troops on the ground. Second, he argued that the massacre reflected a broad racist ideology. This ideology led to various massacres since 1947/48, which Tubi listed, including the massacre in Rafah (tellingly, the reference to this massacre appeared as a passing remark, not as the focus of protest). For Tubi, the Kafr Qasim massacre was one extreme act among many violations of the rights of the Arab citizens of Israel, including: discrimination, the subjugation to military regime, land confiscation, dispossession of Arab peasants, and administrative arrests. Tubi repeatedly referred to the massacre's victims as well as to the Palestinian public in Israel as "citizens" (*muwatinun*). Furthermore, Tubi argued that the massacre was not a particularly Arab affair, and the protest against it should come (and indeed came) from Jewish citizens as well. In his view, the massacre was not only a crime against the Arabs but also against "the real interests of Israel." Finally, Tubi asserted that the only way to prevent the reoccurence of the tragedy was by uprooting the roots of national oppression.[24]

In later years, the demand to investigate was complemented by a statement that the massacre was part of a broader plan to expel the residents of the Triangle. This plot failed because the residents stuck to their village (common in the local Kafr Qasim narrative)[25] or because the Communist Party uncovered the conspiracy and published the massacre (common in the communist narrative). It is noteworthy that a plan to relocate the residents of the Triangle during wartime did exist. Although the existing evidence suggest that it was not intended to be activated that same evening,[26] given Palestinian memories of the Nakba and their awareness of the state's aspiration to reduce the number of Arabs in the country, the centrality of the expulsion theme in the commemoration is not surprising.

The emphasis on the Israeli citizenship of the victims is intimately related to the fear of expulsion and was initially driven by the need to ensure legal protection. It is not a coincidence that the first mass country-wide protest took place the day of the opening of the trial of the perpetrators (6 January 1957), expressing the hope to obtain justice through the Israeli judicial system. The two-hour general strike announced that day united Palestinians from the Triangle, the Galilee, and the mixed Arab-Jewish cities across Israel[27] and distinguished them from Palestinians living beyond the armistice line. Despite the Military Government's aggressive attempts to prevent gatherings on 6 January, some small-scale meetings were held, and in these meetings the memorial ceremonies were only a prologue for protesting the broader context of dispossession and life under military rule.[28]

This emphasis on the judicial process is expressed as well in what has become an iconic symbol of the massacre—a coin of one cent (*agora/qirsh*) symbolizing the extremely light punishment imposed on the brigade commander Colonel Issachar Shadmi for his responsibility in the massacre. "Shadmi's *kirsh*" has been referred to in every annual commemoration, and portrayals of an *agora* appear in several art works commemorating the massacre. One of them was chosen as the first object in the entrance to the commemorative museum established in Kafr Qasim in 2006, and another was chosen to form the backdrop on the stage during the main ceremony on the fiftieth anniversary that same year. The insultingly inadequate punishment of the perpetrators (none of them remained in jail after the end of 1959) had not changed the importance ascribed to the judicial process, but only focused the protest against this lenient penalization. This emphasis on state-citizens relations is indicative of the main line of commemoration that has been shaped in the decades since the massacre—a protest of citizens against their state, rather than a revolt of a national movement.

There is also another aspect to the separation of Palestinian citizens from non-citizens. Arab and Palestinian scholars and politicians outside of Israel by and large ignored the massacre of Kafr Qasim,[29] especially during the first decade after the massacre. I reviewed every issue of the bulletin *Falastinuna*, the monthly mouthpiece of the Fatah movement that was published from 1959 to 1964 in Kuwait and Beirut. *Falastinuna* commemorated other massacres committed by Israel, such as the 1953 Qibya massacre and the Deir Yasin massacre in 1948.[30] I did not find, however, a single reference to the Kafr Qasim massacre. *Falastin al-thawra*, the PLO bulletin published from 1972, made only passing references to the massacre, usually not as the topic of an article. The massacre certainly did not become an element in the bulletin's main calendar as the Black September events in Jordan did.[31] The movie *Kafr Qasim* (1975), directed by the Lebanese director Borhane Alaouié, appeared almost two decades after the massacre and is noteworthy as a rare representation of the massacre in art created outside of Israel. In other words, in the same way that the annual commemoration of the 1930 execution overlapped with the political boundaries of Mandatory Palestine, the commemoration of the Kafr Qasim massacre overlapped with the concentrations of Arab population inside the State of Israel. Again, martyrological commemoration was the tool through which political boundaries shaped collective identities. Paradoxically, the massacre of Kafr Qasim became a landmark in the construction of Palestinians as Israeli citizens.

On the first anniversary of the massacre, thousands of Palestinian citizens from various regions inside Israel (and only inside Israel) were united in simultaneous memorial processions, strikes, and meetings.[32] This was the beginning of a political tradition and the first anchor in their political calendar. Until 1976, the annual commemoration of the massacre was the most important platform for Palestinians in Israel to display political protest.

LAND DAY AND THE BIFOCAL CALENDAR

If there was any Palestinian hope for turning back the wheels of history, it was based on the promising pan-Arab momentum in the 1950s and 1960s, during which Egyptian leader Gamal Abdel Nasser promised to politically unite the Arab world and confront Zionism. These hopes, however, were shattered with the Arab defeat in 1967. In this war, Israel captured the Sinai Peninsula and the Gaza Strip from Egypt, the West Bank from Jordan, and the Golan Heights from Syria. Following the war, the Palestinian national movement, led by the PLO, reemerged as a focus of collective identity and pride, but it did not represent a viable political option for the Palestinians in Israel. The 1967 war also clarified that Israel was not going to disappear soon, and as a consequence, the Palestinian citizens of Israel gradually turned to the Israeli political sphere to cope with their predicament.[33]

These integrative tendencies were enhanced by the comparison made by Palestinians in Israel between their improved economic conditions and that of their fellow Palestinians under occupation in the West Bank and the Gaza

Strip.[34] In the first decade after the 1967 occupation, the Israeli economy profited immensely from the influx of cheap Palestinian labor from the West Bank and the Gaza Strip.[35] The Palestinians in Israel, although at the bottom rank of this economy, were part of it.

By the early 1970s the dramatic rise in the level of education of the Palestinians in Israel enabled the development of a new educated stratum that constituted the human potential for wider circles of political leadership.[36] In addition, new political institutions were established: in 1974 the Israeli government established the Committee of Arab Mayors, but very soon the committee gained independent political power. In 1975 the Communist Party established the National Committee for the Defense of Arab Land (here after, the Land Committee), which was seemingly non-partisan but was dominated by the communists. This committee focused on confronting the on-going confiscation of private Arab land.[37]

The most notable expression of the above-mentioned sociopolitical transformations was the ability of Palestinian citizens in Israel to organize the general strike known as Land Day.[38] Following the decision of the Land Committee on 30 March 1976, Palestinians in Israel took part in a popular country-wide strike and participated in demonstrations against a plan to confiscate land from Arab owners in the Galilee. The rallies turned into violent clashes between the demonstrators and the Border Patrol troops who used live ammunition, killing six Palestinians and injuring seventy.

The day after Land Day, the main headline in *al-Ittihad* utilized the already established political status of the Kafr Qasim massacre to grant legitimacy to a new emerging myth: "A second Kafr-Qasim massacre in the Galilee and the Triangle." This headline became a self-fulfilling prophecy. For the next two decades the calendar of Palestinian political commemoration inside Israel would become bifocal.

However, Land Day quickly replaced the Kafr Qasim massacre as the major temporal focus of political mobilization. After 1976 the parallel between the massacre in Kafr Qasim and Land Day became less blatant, since such a parallel would have impaired the efforts to constitute Land Day as a historical turning point. As historian Yael Zerubavel has indicated, "The choice of a single event clearly provides a better opportunity for ritualized remembrance than a gradual process of transition does. The master commemorative narrative thus presents these events as *turning points* that changed the group's historical development."[39] "Land Day," therefore, "became a watershed in political consciousness and protest methods."[40]

The annual commemorative ceremonies of Land Day extolled the ability and readiness of the Palestinian citizens of Israel to carry out a country-wide organized struggle for their rights as well as to pay the price with blood.[41] The dominant commemorative narrative has highlighted three aspects of transition symbolized by Land Day. The first aspect is psychological. Land Day has replaced Kafr Qasim as the starting point of Palestinian resistance. Land Day symbolized a transition from the humiliation of 1948 and the military government to collective self-assertion and pride, and from "false consciousness" to a "true consciousness." This aspect is especially evident in the discourse of people from the towns directly involved in Land Day: "Land Day equipped people with courage, and definitely toppled the barrier of fear which the authorities tried to establish for decades";[42] "Land Day is the dividing line between the frightened Israeli Arab and the Arab Palestinian who is a citizen of Israel";[43] or "Land Day is the real expression of the sentiment of belonging. It broke the false consciousness. Before Land Day people were celebrating Independence Day and they stopped after it."[44] "The end of fear" of the military government is the same motive that local leaders in Kafr Qasim emphasize in their own narrative of local resistance,[45] but it seems that assigning this role to Land Day is more popular.

The second aspect of the change is political. Land Day has been presented as an uprising against the Israeli government's "divide and rule" policy and a shift from sectarian politics to Palestinian national unity. On the tenth anniversary of Land Day in 1986, *al-Jadid,* the literary bulletin of the Communist Party, emphasized this aspect:

> On Land Day the racist policy that divided us into "denominations," "clans," "Muslims, Christians, Druze and Bedouins," "Arabs and Druze"—failed. All the people were fused in a melting pot and were forged in the shared national fire . . . Land Day reflected the failure of [our] national oppression and in this sense Land Day was the eruption of the sacred anger not only against the looting of 20,000 dunams in the al-Battuf region, but against all the governmental policy toward the Arab-Palestinian minority in Israel.[46]

It is noteworthy that *al-Jadid* did not list the division between Palestinian citizens and non-citizens. We will return to this point later.

The third aspect of Land Day's function as a turning point is social. Palestinian activists and Arabic media have presented it as an event that undermined internal hierarchies among Palestinians in Israel and therefore extended political participation to wider circles. The "horizontal fraternity" and suspension of differences between individuals is a dominant feature of nationalist rhetoric,[47] and the presentation of Land Day as a historical moment of flattening hierarchies is one element in its construction as a national day. This image of Land Day as an historical equalizer suited the political rhetoric of both communists and nationalists. The communist author Salem Jubran, for example, wrote that:

> Land Day was a milestone in our national democratic struggle. Since then, as a result of many factors, very wide popular circles which had been afraid, indifferent, or negatively neutral in the past, approached the struggle. The working class, the peasants, the intellectuals, the merchants, the students, men, and women, all launched the struggle together."[48]

Similar rhetoric is evident in individual memories. 'Omar Sa'id from Kafr Kana who was a high school student and a member of the Alliance of the Israeli Communist Youth (hereafter Communist Youth) in 1976 told me in 2001:

> The teachers changed. Teachers who were formal became closer to the students. Society in general became less hierarchic. Only after Land Day could a person like me have been elected to the Student Council. Land Day brought people from the periphery of society to the center. It gave opportunity to small families. Local groups could emerge under this new atmosphere.[49]

This is beyond mere rhetoric. Under the new circumstances marginalized elements in the Arab villages, like small families, started to gain relative power. In the four local elections after Land Day, from 1977 to 1989, there was a gradual shrinking of the power of familial lists.[50]

There also seems to have been a change in gender balance. In the Kafr Qasim ceremonies we have no evidence of female participation in the preparations or as speakers at the time (even in the ceremonies that took place outside of the relatively conservative village). In the first Land Day annual ceremony in Kafr Kana, however, a local girl named Lutfia Khatib spoke and linked the Land Day martyrs with Amina Dakduk from Kafr Kana, whom she described as the first martyr of 1936.[51] Women also joined the committees that prepared the Land Day commemorations in the Galilee. The leading role of the relatively secularized Galilee in the commemoration probably contributed to this change.

Another tangible repercussion of Land Day was the growing involvement in the Israeli political system. New parties emerged as participants in the election. In the year following Land Day, the Communist Party joined several other

Jewish and Arab organizations to establish the Democratic Front for Peace and Equality (DFPE) in an attempt to extend the circle of supporters beyond its traditional constituency. In 1983 nationalist activists who considered the DFPE as an "Israelified" party, as well as a puppet of the Soviet Union, joined a group of non-Zionist Jewish activists to establish a new party, the Progressive List for Peace (hereafter, Progressive List). Although it was based initially on an Arab-Jewish alliance, the party adopted a blatant Arab-Palestinian nationalist orientation, and by 1988 most of the Jewish members left it. In 1988 the first exclusively Arab party, the Arab Democratic Party, took part in the Knesset election and gained one seat.

In the same period there were further institutional developments. In 1982, Arab mayors, Arab parliament members, and representatives of extra-parliamentary Arab organizations, established the Follow-Up Committee (FUC) to coordinate the collective action of Palestinians in Israel. Since 1988 the FUC has been the major forum for making decisions about nation-wide strikes and demonstrations. Its decisions have been widely followed by the Palestinian public in Israel. Unofficially, in some instances Israeli authorities even recognized it as a leadership body for coordinating and negotiating strikes and rallies. The FUC also has some sub-committees; one of them, the Follow-Up Committee for Arab Education (FUCAE), has been especially active (see Chapter 8).

The improved organizational ability of the Palestinians and the removal of the military government made Land Day commemorations more coordinated than the early commemoration of the massacre in Kafr Qasim. Until the late 1980s the major entrepreneur of this commemoration was the Land Committee. Since 1979 the geographical spread of this commemoration reflected the emerging ethno-regional cartography that set the Palestinians in Israel apart from other Palestinians: beyond many local events, there was a central event for each of the major regions of the Arab population—the Galilee, the Triangle, and the Naqb. *Al-Ittihad* highlighted this structure both before the events and after them with headlines aimed at nurturing cross-regional solidarity such as: "From the heights of the Galilee to the Naqb through the Triangle: the Arab masses prepare to commemorate Land Day."[52] These ceremonies were covered in detail, with a great deal of attention to every speaker. Land Day events beyond the Green Line, such as strikes, rallies, conferences, and leaflet circulation were reported briefly and in a separate section.[53]

No less important was the audience that was exposed to this coverage in the formative years of the Land Day myth. Until 1983 *al-Ittihad* was the major media through which Palestinian citizens could have learned about the ceremonies in various parts of the country—and it was distributed only inside the Green Line. On the other hand, East Jerusalem newspapers, which gave much more attention to West Bank events, were not sold inside the Green Line, except in Nazareth.[54]

BETWEEN PALESTINIAN UNITY AND CIVIL EQUALITY

Unlike Kafr Qasim, Land Day has been commemorated as well by Palestinians outside Israel and even in the wider circle of non-Palestinian Arabs. The international network of communist parties enabled the DFPE to export Land Day to countries beyond the Arab world, where it usually has been celebrated by communist parties. From the beginning, though, there has been some tension, although not necessarily a contradiction, between the Palestinian nationalist and the universalistic meaning of Land Day.

On Land Day, the Israeli state treated its Palestinian citizens with the same disregard for human life that characterized its policy in the territories occupied in 1967. For some political actors this theme served as a starting point for emphasizing the unity of Palestinians regardless of their political status. For others, it was an impetus for reemphasizing their particular status as citizens to prevent further erosion of their rights. Therefore, the rhetoric around Land Day has been characterized by highlighting both the unity of Palestinians everywhere and a demand for civil equality as citizens of Israel.[55] In the first two decades after Land Day, a major source of tension was the relative weight that each element should receive in the commemoration.

What clearly helped to present Land Day as a unifying Palestinian symbol was its early adoption by Palestinian leaders outside Israel. From the declaration of the general strike on 6 March, 1976, the PLO was active in supporting the strike and attempted to extend it to include Palestinians everywhere.[56] The PLO also incorporated Land Day into its official ethos and has commemorated it annually in its publications and with organized rallies. The first years following Land Day were years of rapprochement between the PLO and the communists in Israel, with an intensification of their contacts and the publication of mutual compliments in their official publications.[57] Later, Land Day was declared an official holiday by the Palestinian National Authority (PNA), which was established in 1994.

Therefore, Land Day as a symbol of Palestinian unity was common in the rhetoric of both communist and nationalist Palestinian leaders in Israel. Before the first anniversary, Saliba Khamis of the DFPE, who played a pivotal role in organizing the Land Day strike as the founder of the Land Committee, wrote:

> [W]e emphasize that what happened to the Arab people [in Israel] is, in a microcosm, the Zionist aggression against the Palestinian people wherever it is. The aggression shattered the claim of the dominating Zionist leadership that they consider the Arabs as Israeli citizens, even if of a second class [. . .] All the Arabs, in Israel's eyes, are enemies. There is no difference between those who reside in the Green Line and those outside of it.[58]

At the same time, the communists were careful not to let the PLO take too much credit on Land Day and according to Nabih Bashir, they even marginalized the role of the PLO on Land Day.[59] Keeping Land Day as the "property" of the Palestinians in Israel was also a matter of prestige within the Palestinian sphere. Saliba Khamis epitomized this attitude on the fourth Land Day anniversary (1980):

> Each part of the Arab-Palestinian people has its own day, and we, the part of this people in Israel have our day, during which we remind the rulers of Israel that we are a living people that will not give up its rights and its national dignity.[60]

In addition, following Land Day the communists had faced the growing challenge of nationalists, who now dared to confront them publicly and to accuse them of hijacking the struggle and denying the Palestinian national identity of the Arabs in Israel.[61] The most vocal organization representing this tendency in the 1970s was the Sons of the Village (*abnaa' al-balad*), a secular nationalist movement founded in 1972 in the Triangle calling for the abolishment of Israel's identity as a Jewish state. In 1976, on the twentieth anniversary of the Kafr Qasim massacre (following Land Day), its members used the anniversary for distributing fliers attacking the communists.[62] This emerging challenge pushed some communist leaders to clarify their position on the question of identity and its relation to Land Day.

Tubi was especially explicit in drawing a clear distinction between Palestinians inside Israel and other Palestinians and stating that Land Day was a distinct symbol of the former. In a long essay published in April 1978, he repeatedly argued that Land Day is a symbol of the steadfastness of the *Arab people in Israel*. He clarified that the Arabs in Israel belong to the Arab Palestinian people, but "they participate in their own particular way, stemming from the circumstances in which they have been living throughout the last thirty years." He explicitly blamed the Sons of the Village for fracturing the unity and argued that those who use the slogan:

> "The Galilee and Hebron—one battle, one fate" . . . push this people into an impasse . . . In this way of struggle the fate of the Galilee would be like the fate of Hebron and not the other way around. The dream of Begin[63] and the supporters of the Greater Land of Israel will come true together by causing a complete paralysis of the Arab masses in Israel.[64]

Three decades earlier Tubi had highlighted Israeli citizenship in order to prevent the expulsion of Palestinian ID holders from the newly established State of Israel.[65] The same calculated approach is echoed in this text—too much identification with the Palestinians who are not citizens might downgrade the rights of the citizens and make them similar to the diminished rights of the non-citizens. Only a decade later, slogans of Palestinian unity in Land Day ceremonies, such as "from Khan Yunis to Jenin, one people who won't give up!" and "From Sakhnin to Beirut, one people who won't die!" would become unquestionable, but at this early stage prominent leaders attempted to confront them.

Later, the official announcement of the Land Committee before Land Day stated that "this day is a national holiday of the masses of the Palestinian people in Israel,"[66] a text that most likely reflected a compromise between various perspectives on the desired level of distinction of Palestinian citizens from non-citizens.

Nationalists criticized communists for what they considered to be blurring the national meaning of Land Day. On the tenth Land Day anniversary in 1986, the poet Fawzi 'Abdallah published a column in *al-Watan*, the Progressive List bulletin, where he wrote:

> It has become clear that the struggle over Land Day is a struggle over the essence of the lives of the Arabs in this country (*diyar*). What is at stake is whether the Arabs in this country will be Israeli sectors without a distinct national identity, or will they be Palestinians courageously demanding all their national rights. [67]

Until 1987 the annual commemorations were guided by the Land Committee, so the communist activists who dominated the committee could dictate its line. They attempted to monitor the slogans in the central rallies, to ensure the exclusion of what they called *muzayadat* (exaggerations). This term referred to illegal actions but frequently also to slogans that too explicitly blurred the Green line. The Committee of Arab Mayors, in which the nationalist Progressive List and the Sons of the Village were marginally involved, backed up the decisions of the Land Committee. Its support was crucial because Arab mayors had the resources and facilities to maintain the commemorations. The Progressive List was represented on the Land Committee but failed to influence its decisions; therefore, in some years in the mid-1980s the party organized separate Land Day ceremonies. However, these separate ceremonies were not very successful because even the Sons of the Village participated in the events organized by the Land Committee.

In the same period the communists attempted as well, with significant success, to impose a ban on Palestinian flags. The opposition of the communists to the flag was not ideological but tactical. When demonstrators in the West Bank and the Gaza Strip raised Palestinian flags, *al-Ittihad* reported this information with much pride. Inside Israel the Palestinian flag was outlawed in 1980, and the insistence of the DFPE on limiting itself to legal protest led to various flag-related, violent confrontations between the DFPE and nationalist activists.[68]

A related controversy was also a tactical one—whether to strike or not on Land Day. The DFPE tended to be very careful with the strike weapon while nationalists tried to turn the strike into a tradition. At the preliminary meeting of the Land Committee in 1979 to plan Land Day, a controversy about the strike deteriorated into physical violence between communists and nationalists. During Land Day itself that same year, there was a brawl in a high school in Umm al-Fahm between supporters of a strike and its opponents.[69]

Beginning in 1988, decisions about central Land Day commemoration were made by FUC, which served as an umbrella organization and included the Committee of Arab Mayors, the Land Committee, and other elements. In 1989 the relative power of the communists in FUC was undermined after they suffered losses in several municipalities in the local elections; their almost absolute power to shape the commemoration was weakened.

One might ask who the winner was in the communist-nationalist controversy. There is no doubt that in the long term the national stream has been tremendously successful in embedding symbols of Palestinian national identity and slogans of Palestinian national solidarity in Land Day commemorations. The elements of Palestinian national identity and solidarity dominate the contemporary Land Day ceremonies. At the same time, the aspiration of Tubi to make Land Day a distinct political myth of the Palestinians in Israel also has been successful. While Land Day commemoration is practiced by Palestinians inside and outside Israel, the scale of popular participation of Palestinians inside Israel is significantly larger and incomparable to other locations. In addition, whereas for Palestinians in Israel, Land Day has been the major date on their political calendar since 1976, for Palestinians in the West Bank, the Gaza Strip, and Lebanon, it has been only one day among a long list of memorial days.

Furthermore, Land Day has become a major expression of the strategic choice that enjoys a wide consensus among Palestinians in Israel—to fight for their rights in a non-violent, popular political struggle within the parameters of Israeli law. For Palestinians living under military rule in the West Bank, Israeli law is not a source of legitimate authority and, as non-citizens, acting from within the Israeli political system is not an available option. Furthermore, while inside the Green Line the ability of the authorities to restrict commemoration was somewhat limited by the rule of law, in the occupied territories, the military authorities could easily ban even peaceful gatherings, which they did on several occasions.[70] This difference had been especially evident in Land Day events during the two Palestinian uprisings in the occupied territories (1987–1993 and 2000–2004). Whereas the West Bank and the Gaza Strip were usually under curfew and violent clashes resulted in death and injuries, inside the Green Line, demonstrations were held in full coordination with the police. Nadim Rouhana illustrated this gap in the following description, referring to the 1989 commemoration of Land Day inside the Green Line:

> Parents, confident that no clashes with police would ensue (organizers often encourage the police not to interfere or even to remain outside the Arab town in order to avoid tension), carried their children on their shoulders. While Arab and Jewish speakers gave speeches, participants could buy drinks, coffee, sandwiches, and barbecued meat, giving the event a coloring of a festive "happening."[71]

Here again the paradox of Palestinian commemoration in Israel surfaces—the rhetoric of Palestinian unity is challenged by the difference in political status that dictates the form of commemoration. Rouhana's description implies yet another element that distinguishes Palestinian commemoration inside and outside Israel and was especially evident in both the Land Day and Kafr Qasim commemorations until 2000: the visible presence of Jewish Israelis as organizers, speakers, and a potential audience.

JEWISH CITIZENS IN ARAB COMMEMORATIONS

The inclusion of Jews in commemorative ceremonies of the Kafr Qasim massacre was visible from the very beginning of commemoration. Latif Dori, an Iraqi-born Jew and a member of the Zionist *Mapam* party, who was the first

to enter Kafr Qasim after the massacre, has spoken in the commemorative ceremonies since the first anniversary and has frequently taken part in planning
them. In 1996, during the fortieth anniversary ceremony, he was declared an
honorary citizen by the local council of Kafr Qasim.

As an Arab-Jewish party, the Communist Party has been the major supporter
of joint politics. This partnership was rooted in the universalistic communist
ideology and, possibly, the Jewish-Arab characteristic also gave the Arab members psychological assurance against the disaster of becoming refugees like their
fellow Palestinians.[72] Some of the Arab party leaders were personally invested in
Arab-Jewish partnership since they were married to Jewish Israeli women (Emile
Toma, Saliba Khamis); others had indirect family relations with Jews (Tawfiq
Tubi's daughter-in-law is Jewish). Accordingly, the presentation of the commemoration as a joint civic project of progressive Arabs and Jews in the communist
press was common.

Before the tenth anniversary of the massacre, Saliba Khamis wrote in an editorial in *al-Ittihad*:

> We, and all the aware democratic masses, do not commemorate to inflame na-
> tional grudges and hatreds. No. We want a joint action, Jewish, Arab, for the
> tenth commemoration of the massacre. This action should be a joint struggle
> and joint invitation for democratic life based on equality, peace, brotherhood of
> peoples, and respect of mutual rights.[73]

Following Land Day in April 1976, Tubi made a similar declaration:

> The events of 30 March proved that the Arab masses are not alone in their
> struggle against the policy of national oppression and in support of their le-
> gitimate rights. They received the support and encouragement from the Jewish
> democratic forces, and this element has great importance for the resistance
> against the racist Judaization policy.[74]

Following the Kafr Qasim ceremony in 1976, *Al-Ittihad* reported an especially
visible presence of Jewish participants. Joseph Algazy, a prominent Jewish member of the Communist Party who was among the ceremony organizers, hypoth-
esized that the brutality of the police during Land Day shocked certain circles in
the Jewish Israeli left who had come to express their solidarity in Kafr Qasim.[75]

The Hebrew daily *Davar* reported that when a Land Day rally was first organized in the Naqb/Negev in 1979, one-third of the 700 participants were Jews.[76]
Such a high proportion has probably never reoccurred, but Jewish speakers

have been included in the annual Land Day rallies since 1977. In addition, in the 1980s and 1990s Jewish citizens were seen as a major audience of the commemoration. Before each Land Day, the Land Committee organized a regular press conference in Tel Aviv for the Hebrew media.

The ceremonies of the thirtieth anniversary of the Kafr Qasim massacre were prepared by a special committee of fifteen people, three of them Jewish. The 1986 central ceremony was recorded on film, which offers insights on the significance of Jewish citizens as participants, as well as a target audience. Three out of the twelve invited speakers at the event were Jewish. The mayor, 'Abd al-Rahim 'Isa, who was the emcee of the event, frequently translated his words into Hebrew. He read many telegrams of sympathy sent by Arab and Jewish organizations and celebrated the fact that even the right-wing Herut Youth sent such a message. When 'Isa declared that a press conference would take place after the ceremony, he said it in Hebrew, implying that he expected members of the Hebrew media to attend.

'Isa also took the opportunity to read a report from the Hebrew newspaper, *Yediot Aharonot*, which mistakenly reported that Fatah activists who killed an Israeli soldier were from Kafr Qasim. "They made us a village of murderers!" He protested in Hebrew, "This village extols co-existence of peace and equality, Jews and Arabs live here together and will have to continue to live here together!" The mayor's anger over the association of his village with the armed struggle, and his insistence on keeping a safe distance from the struggle, was a common pattern of the commemorative repertoire of the Palestinians in Israel. Needless to say, calling the Fatah activists who killed the soldier "murderers" is an impossible scenario in a major Palestinian commemorative event outside Israel.

Almost all Arab speakers thanked the Jewish organizations and individuals who came to express their solidarity. Muhammad Mi'ari, the Progressive List leader, complained that Jewish parties did not publish any announcement for the thirtieth anniversary and also that the Hebrew newspapers did not mention it, a protest that indicated his interest in the perspective of the Hebrew media.

Especially remarkable was the closing speech by the founder of the Islamic Movement, 'Abdallah Nimr Darwish[77]. Darwish, who was born in Kafr Qasim in 1948, was convicted of "membership in a terrorist organization" in 1981. After his release from prison in May 1985 as part of a prisoner-exchange deal, he adopted a consistent line of opposition to the use of violence by Palestinian citizens of Israel and called on them to use only legal means. Speaking at his home base in front of a highly supportive audience, Darwish delivered a seventeen-minute-long speech. Five minutes of his speech were delivered in Hebrew. He called on Jewish Israelis to reject the policy of Greater Israel, to support the establishment of a Palestinian state, and to agree to the return of the Palestinian refugees.

There was one blatant exception to this trend: the rising star of the Islamic Movement, Ra'id Sallah from Umm al-Fahm, who read a poem he authored. In his words, Jews were only a target for a threat: "Ho, tribe of Moses [*qawm musa*], your house is heading to disaster—if you keep supporting war and aggression!" Sallah did not consider Jewish citizens as partners in the same political community, but as a separate tribe, living in their own habitat.

The thirtieth anniversary was a precursor of two important processes. The enthusiasm with which Darwish and Sallah were accepted by the crowd was just one more sign of the mounting power of the Islamic Movement that would take over the local council in Kafr Qasim in 1989. In addition, the extra attention given by Darwish to a dialogue with his Jewish audience and the cold shoulder given by Sallah were a precursor to the split in the movement. In 1996 Sallah led the northern faction of the movement that refused to take part in the Knesset election,[78] and more broadly, withdrew from a common public sphere with the Jewish citizens of Israel. When Sallah spoke two decades later on the fiftieth anniversary of the Kafr Qasim massacre (2006), he was already a leader of a powerful mass movement that led the deemphasizing of Israeli belonging among Muslim citizens.

Under the spiritual leadership of Darwish, Kafr Qasim and the commemoration of the massacre kept its integrative orientation. During the 1990s there was a surge of commemorative activities in Kafr Qasim itself.[79] Several commemorative books were published, various monuments were established, and a documentary movie was produced—but there was no change in this orientation.

In the introduction to a 1999 poetry collection dedicated to the massacre and published by the Kafr Qasim municipality, mayor Sami 'Isa (of the southern faction) delineated a list of demands to the State of Israel. Before his call for a just peace based on the establishment of a Palestinian state and respect for the Right of Return, 'Isa outlined concrete local demands that appeared in one way or another in the annual commemorative rhetoric throughout the 1990s and the 2000s:

> We do not resent and we do not look for revenge. We look for justice and equity and we demand from the state to make justice with this injured village, and the sign of this justice will be that the state would recognize its sin and the

government would apologize to the martyrs' sons, their grandchildren, and the people of their village, and that it would remove its hand from our lands which it unjustly and aggressively looted[80] [. . .] and that the massacre would be incorporated into the school curriculum of both the Arab and the Jewish sectors in order to warn the generations from the repetition of this horrible massacre.[81]

The demand for a governmental apology and the call to educate both Arab and Jewish students came from within the discursive boundaries of Israeli citizenship, and they are based on the assumption of an existing shared citizenship between Arabs and Jews. The demand for apology was repeated in a second introduction authored by 'Abdallah Nimr Darwish.[82] Darwish also highlighted the shared citizenship when he promised to get back the confiscated lands by "a peaceful, legal, civilized, and conscious struggle, with the participation of the honorable citizens of this state, Arabs and Jews."[83] In his own poem included in the collection he used a clear pacifist expression: "Our martyrs are the soldiers of peace."

The integrative orientation of the Kafr Qasim commemoration peaked in the late 1990s when government ministers were included among the speakers in the ceremonies: Moshe Katsav in 1997 and Yossi Beilin in 1999. Katsav, who was then the Minister of Arab Affairs, was invited by the local council and represented the right-wing government on the podium. This was too much even for DFPE activists who protested his presence vocally.[84] Mayor Ibrahim Sarsur (the future leader of the southern faction of the Islamic Movement) explained his decision to invite Katsav:

> The residents appreciate very much the minister's readiness to participate in the ceremony and they hope that, as a result, the authorities would stop referring to the victims of the massacre as "victims of a work accident" as the National Insurance Institute does, but as war victims for every purpose.[85]

Sarsur revealed some of the implications of the dominant role of a local council in the commemoration: aside from their relative autonomy that allowed the politicization of commemoration, pragmatic and instrumental local considerations frequently gained much weight in shaping the public display of memory. These considerations have not fully overlapped with a national ideological agenda. Local leaders were more likely to highlight their Israeli citizenship to optimize their ability to gain resources from the central government.

Although public protest against non-Zionist Jews has been extremely rare at Land Day ceremonies, not everyone welcomed the presence of Jewish speakers from Zionist parties on the stage. At the 1990 Land Day ceremony, the inclusion of Zionist speakers faced a protest from some Son of the Village activists who interrupted the speech of Haim Oron (then a member of the Zionist *Mapam* party). These activists called out: "Zionists go home; we don't want to see Zionists here."[86] The event devolved into a fist fight between Son of the Village activists and other members. Oron's participation was part of his struggle for the rights of Bedouins in the south, and Land Day was for him just another opportunity to express public support for their civic struggle. For the protesters against him, his participation challenged their attempt to shape Land Day primarily as a Palestinian national day. In 1994, a member of the Knesset (MK) of the Labor Party Shmuel Avital joined Oron to speak at a commemorative Land Day rally in Rahat.[87] 'Abd al-Hakim Mufid, a journalist who previously had been a member of the Son of the Village and then moved to the Islamic Movement, wrote about this occurrence: "Is there something sadder than speakers of the Labor Party climbing the stages of Land Day to 'congratulate' the masses on their 'holiday'?"[88] Mufid's protest was an expression of the gap between local activists with a concrete agenda of protecting their lands and ideologically motivated activists who insisted on contextualizing the local struggle within the broader national narrative.

COMMEMORATION AND THE RELIGIOUS-SECULAR DIVIDE

While nationalists and communists usually have been divided about national versus civic aspects of Land Day, these two secular groups have been united against the attempts of the Islamic Movement to "Islamize" the commemoration of Land Day.

There are different perspectives on the historical relation of the Islamists to Land Day. The common communist narrative is that the Islamist activists were antagonistic to Land Day commemoration, whereas the common narrative among Islamists denies antagonism. However, the lack of publications by the Islamic Movement until the mid-1980s makes it difficult to accurately narrate the evolution of the movement's relation to Land Day. The first mayor of the Islamic Movement, Kamal Rayan from Kafr Bara, participated in the Land Day mayors' preliminary meeting of the Triangle region in 1984.[89] The movement's representatives started to deliver speeches in local Land Day rallies (or in separate Land Day events) in the late 1980s. Interestingly, however, in the movement's monthly magazine *al-Sirat* that appeared between 1987 and 1989, Land Day was not mentioned even once (while the massacre of Kafr Qasim received much attention). It is possible that this ambiguous picture reflects the diversity inside the Islamic Movement at the time. Only beginning in the early 1990s did the Islamic Movement's adoption of Land Day become unquestionable.

The communists have highlighted their leading role in initiating the original Land Day and considered it not only a national achievement but also an achievement for the party. As a result, after the Islamic Movement fully adopted Land Day, a frequent theme in its commemorative rhetoric was refuting the link between Land Day and the communists. The Islamic Movement argued repeatedly that Land Day was a spontaneous collective act that was not organized by any party.[90] In 1995 'Abd al-Hakim Mufid wrote that Land Day was a failure of the "Israeli Communist Party" because it expressed the national belonging that this party opposed.[91] Because of its policy, he argued, "Land Day died on the day it was born."

The entrance of the Islamic Movement to the field of Land Day commemoration led to frequent confrontations around its character. The use of Islamic religious slogans in rallies antagonized the communists. Many of them saw these slogans as contradicting both the principle of cross-confessional Palestinian national unity, as well as Arab-Jewish partnership—both central to the communist view of Land Day.

For the Islamic Movement, the mixed-gender crowd on Land Day was an undesirable phenomenon. In Kafr Qasim, they did not have the same problem because the Islamic Movement controlled the local council starting in 1989, and the council oversaw the ceremonies. Even before that, though, as evident from the film of the 1986 ceremony, women and men were separated. However, secular forces have been more influential in shaping Land Day commemoration, and the repetitive demand of the Islamic Movement to separate men and women in the central rallies was rejected. The issue of women's inclusion was especially controversial in the Galilee where the population is more secular. In 1993, the tension led to a violent clash in the ceremony in Deir Hanna that was followed by police intervention, ending the rally prematurely. On the following day, the main headline in *al-Ittihad* was the slogan: "National unity: the boys with the girls."[92] In the following year *al-Ittihad* dedicated a long article to the role of women in Land Day, who "demonstrated heroism, responsibility, and awareness no less than the men."[93] This religious-secular conflict shapes the way Land Day is remembered. The list of traditional Land Day heroes of the DFPE, who had been almost exclusively male, was extended to include women.

LAND DAY LEADS TO THE COMMEMORATION OF NAKBA

Until 1998 Land Day and the Kafr Qasim massacre anniversary were the two focal points of temporal commemoration by the Palestinians in Israel. Like the commemoration of the Kafr Qasim massacre, Land Day became a platform for protest on various political issues as well. It seems that Land Day itself provided the confidence needed for the public discussion of the Nakba. The Majd al-Kurum events in 1977 are one early sign of this process.

On 10 November 1977 Israeli authorities destroyed an unlicensed house in Majd al-Kurum. During the protest riots that broke out in the village, a young Palestinian named Ahmed Masri was killed. In the same way that *al-Ittihad* promoted the myth of Land Day by relying on Kafr Qasim, now Land Day was used to emphasize the political relevance of the Majd Al-Kurum events. The main headline in *al-Ittihad* on the following day was "A seventh Land Day martyr fell in Majd al-Kurum."[94] Covering the densely attended funeral, *al-Ittihad* mentioned: "The general form was a copy of the annual memorial day for the land martyrs and the twentieth memorial day of the massacre of Kafr Qasim, as implied by the slogan carried in front of the coffin: "The martyr of Majd al-Kurum embraces Land Day martyrs."[95]

The coffin was brought to the Spring Square in the middle of the village where ten thousand people gathered. On 5 November 1948, in the exact same square, IDF soldiers had executed five men as a form of collective punishment for what the soldiers considered to be a reluctance to hand over the remaining arms in the village.[96] Both on the funeral day and on the fortieth-day ceremony, speakers at the stage made reference to the 1948 massacre and linked the new martyr to the past martyrs.[97]

These references constituted an early and significant sign of the emerging drive to carve out a public space for the commemoration of the Nakba, as well as to emphasize the historical continuity of the Palestinian struggle and sacrifice. Public expressions by internally displaced Palestinians (persons who were expelled from their lands in 1948, but who remained within the area that became the state of Israel and became citizens) longing for their villages appeared even earlier, but references to the 1948 massacres were much less common and were considered more risky.[98] In addition, as early as the early 1980s, the commemorative repertoire of Land Day included organized visits to the ruins of depopulated villages. From the moment that the Nakba began to find a place in a formal public commemoration, its weight was too significant to remain only a secondary topic.

The Nakba entered the canonical political calendar of Palestinians in Israel from the back door, but in 1998 it eventually appeared as an independent subject of temporal commemoration. Soon after this development, the killing of thirteen Palestinians by the Israeli police in October 2000 signaled the emergence of the fourth date on the political calendar. The developments of these last two foci of temporal commemoration and their implications for the commemoration of the first two dates are the topic of the next chapter.

3 THE POLITICAL CALENDAR IN THE TWENTY-FIRST CENTURY

THE TWO MOST RECENT ADDITIONS to the canonized political calendar represent two major tendencies in Palestinian commemoration in Israel. First, the addition of the Nakba to the political calendar was an important step toward a growing similarity between the commemorative repertoire of Palestinian citizens and non-citizens. The events of October 2000 (al-Aqsa Day), on the other hand, are commemorated exclusively by Palestinians inside Israel. The commemorative rhetoric on this day is certainly embedded within the broader Palestinian national narrative, but it includes a strong emphasis on redefining Israeli citizenship—not necessarily denying it. Both developments have become evident in all four memorial days on the political calendar.

THE EMERGENCE OF A MEMORIAL DAY FOR THE NAKBA

The late addition of the Nakba to the political calendar of the Palestinian citizens of Israel stands in contrast to the continuous commemoration of the date by Palestinians elsewhere. As early as 1949, one year after the establishment of the State of Israel,[1] 15 May was marked in several West Bank cities (under Jordanian rule) by demonstrations, strikes, the raising of black flags, and visits of the graves of the 1948 martyrs. These events were organized by worker and student associations, cultural and sports clubs, scouts clubs, committees of refugees, and the Muslim Brotherhood. The Palestinian newspaper *al-Difa'* (now published in East Jerusalem), provided detailed reports on this protest. The speakers in these gatherings blamed the Arab regimes and the Arab League for failing to save Palestine. *Al-Difa'* reported a very emotional atmosphere, of demonstrators who were crying and swearing to "return the wheels when an opportunity will come up."[2] By the late 1950s, the 15th of May would be known in the Arab world as Palestine Day, mentioned by the media in Arab and Muslim countries as a day of international solidarity with Palestine.

The reviving Palestinian national movement of the late 1950s included 15 May on its calendar. Every year the Fatah bulletin, *Falastinuna*, dedicated detailed analytical texts dealing with the meaning of the day and the lessons of the 1948 disaster. Since the late 1960s, with the emergence of other commemorations celebrating the armed struggle and the revolutionary spirit (See Chapter 6), 15 May was temporarily somewhat marginalized. Still, in the West Bank, the Gaza Strip, and in refugee camps in Lebanon, 15 May continued to be commemorated by demonstrations and strikes.

Inside Israel, none of these occurred until the 1990s. This was due to two main factors: the disciplinary power of the Israeli state authorities and the ambivalence of the Communist Party toward this commemoration. The disciplinary mechanisms used by the state are crucial for explaining the delay, and they are discussed in detail in Chapter 7. At this point, though, it is important to elaborate on the historical ambivalence of the Communist Party. As the dominant power in mobilizing national sentiments among Palestinian citizens, the boundaries of politicized commemoration set by the communists until the 1980s were very influential, and they were reflected as well in the controversies over the commemoration of the Nakba in 1998.

The Communist Party has never avoided dealing with the Nakba per se. There is no doubt that the party did raise the issue of Palestinian refugees from a very early point—in the middle of the expulsion campaigns themselves, as well as in following years.[3] However, the party avoided a temporal commemoration of the Nakba. Any meaningful choice of date would have been interpreted as mourning the mere existence of the state, whether it was 15 May, 2 November, or Israel's Independence Day (celebrated according to the Hebrew lunar calendar, in the second half of April or the first half of May). Although the party accepted Israel's right to exist, its leaders differed in their views on whether this was an a priori right to exist or an ex post facto right. Following the acceptance of the 1947 UN partition plan and the subsequent outbreak of violence, Jewish leaders of the party (belonging to the then-Palestinian Communist Party) encouraged party members to join the Jewish militia, the Haganah. Some Arab leaders of the party (belonging to the National Liberation League) tried to organize military opposition to the Haganah.[4] Meir Vilner, the general secretary of the party from 1965 to 1990, even signed the Israeli Declaration of Independence.

The Soviet Union supported the partition plan, and the Communist Party was known to be extremely loyal to the Kremlin.

Significantly, until the 1980s the presidents of the State of Israel were invited to the general congress of the party, and the Israeli flag was raised at its annual conferences until the 1990s. These symbolic aspects were part of the party's attempts to promote a civic, secular form of non-Zionist Israeli patriotism shared by Arab and Jewish citizens. A shared calendar for Arabs and Jews could have supported this civic identity. While these efforts focused on 1 May, the international socialist workers' day, this day was not an official public holiday in Israel.

As the most important official public holiday in Israel not rooted in Jewish religious tradition, Independence Day was considered to have a higher potential for cross-confessional inclusion if reinterpreted to fit a universalistic ideology. In addition, at least until the late 1980s, the party made a significant effort to appeal to their Jewish constituency,[5] which gradually, but consistently, abandoned it, and the adoption of Independence Day might have been part of this effort. Accordingly, until 1987, the party did not reject the celebrations on Independence Day but instead tried to de-Zionize the day both by reshaping its meaning as a civic holiday and by presenting the 1948 war as an anti-imperialist war rather than a Zionist war. This rhetoric did not change even after the 1965 split in the party that left *al-Ittihad* in the hands of the faction that was considered to be closer to Arab nationalism. Before and after 1965, *al-Ittihad* published the party's warm congratulations for Independence Day:

> In these days the people of Israel celebrate the twentieth anniversary of the establishment of the State of Israel. Independence Day is a sacred holiday in every people's life. We remember the sons who fell in the battle for the independence of Israel, for disconnecting the people of Israel from the colonialist countries and making it free in its homeland. The best sons of the Jewish and Arab people [sic] in Palestine fought against the foreign British rule of our country, for the liberation of the two peoples and their national independence. For those who cherish the future of our country, the Day of Israel's Independence symbolizes the love of the homeland and the hope for its development, prosperity, peace, and security.[6]

It is noteworthy that *al-Ittihad* published these texts as formal announcements of the party, but none of the writers of *al-Ittihad* ever signed his or her name. In the 1970s these congratulations were sarcastically criticized in public by the communists' political rivals,[7] and their enthusiastic tone significantly dwindled in the same decade.

Furthermore, for many years 15 May was not included among the dozens of memorial days celebrated in *al-Ittihad*. The first time a direct editorial reference to the date appeared (as opposed to reports on demonstrations in the 1967 occupied territories) was in 1986. In a short article the editor explained that 15 May had become a day of international solidarity with the Palestinian people because this was the day two states were supposed to be established, but the establishment of one of them, the Arab state of Palestine, was prevented by imperial forces.[8] In other words, *al-Ittihad* did not protest the UN partition plan, but rather its incomplete implementation. By this unconventional justification, *al-Ittihad* adopted 15 May without questioning Israel's legitimacy. Still, this was a low key reference, not an inclusion in the canonic political calendar.

The Battle over the Date

With the relative relaxation of the Israeli public sphere since the 1980s (See Chapter 7), public reference to the Nakba became more common in communist publications, as well as in publications of other emerging political forces. This development, however, did not include the marking of a specific date on the calendar for the Nakba. The establishment of the PNA in 1994, as part of the Oslo process, created the state-like mechanisms that are so important for the creation of a stable, institutionalized political calendar. The Palestinians in Israel, although not part of the PNA, were influenced by this process. The decision of the PNA to commemorate Nakba Day in 15 May 1998 inspired Palestinians in Israel to take another step in the formalization of the memory of the Nakba and to include it on their political calendar. It is likely as well that the preparations for the high profile celebrations of Israel's fiftieth Independence Day were a contributing factor.

Among the four major events commemorated in the Palestinian political calendar, however, the Nakba is the only one that has not yet gained a stable and agreed upon date. Since 1999 the PNA has commemorated Nakba Day on 15 May (in 1998 it was commemorated on 14 May), but inside Israel this date usually has been observed only by local or partisan events. In most years since 1999, the central commemorative event of the Palestinians in Israel has been the March of Return, a mass procession during Israel's Independence Day to the ruins of a depopulated village.

The choice of date was controversial from the beginning, but the main reasons for the controversy have changed. In March 1998, the FUC met to discuss ways to commemorate the Nakba. At this meeting the members disagreed on the desired relation to the celebrations of Israel's fiftieth anniversary. The disagreements focused on whether the Nakba commemoration should be presented as a "mirror image" of the independence celebrations (emphasizing Israeli responsibility), or should the commemoration avoid intentional emphasis on this linkage so that the choice would not be seen as provocative.[9] The atmosphere during the discussion was tense. Rafiq Haj Yahya, the mayor of Taybeh who was also a member of the Zionist Labor Party, even attempted to prevent the discussion about the Nakba commemoration, arguing that "there are more important issues."[10] Later MK Walid Sadiq Haj Yahya, another Taybeh resident and member of another Zionist party (Meretz), said on an Arabic television talk show that while he was not opposed to commemorating the Nakba, he was concerned about the timing—referring to the implicit linkage between the fiftieth anniversary of Israel's independence and the commemoration of the Nakba.[11] On the other side of this controversy, Raja Ighbariya from the Sons of the Village directly stated in a discussion about the Nakba commemoration on a Hebrew talk show: "Your Independence is our Nakba," a statement that, slightly modified, would be adopted as the March of Return's main slogan in the post-October 2000 era.

Although in the 1998 FUC meeting it was decided that the central event would take place on 15 May, in the following years, 15 May was overshadowed by the March of Return on Israel's Independence Day. In fact, only twice, in 1998 and 2012, was 15 May celebrated officially in a unified ceremony shared by all political forces represented in the FUC.

Since October 2000, however, the common arguments in favor of each date have changed, both because the objection of the DFPE (the "communists") to direct confrontation with the mainstream Jewish public has eroded and because the power of Zionist parties among the Palestinians in Israel has shrunk drastically.[12] In the post-2000 controversy, both sides usually do not deny the importance of commemorating the Nakba on both dates, but since it is impractical to organize two mass events of tens of thousands of people twice within days or weeks, every political movement or organization should decide on its own as to which one of the two dates to commemorate.

The supporters of commemorating the Nakba on Israeli Independence Day have highlighted the need to contrast the Palestinian and the Zionist narratives and to confront the state and the hegemonic Israeli view of 1948. In addition, they argue, many Palestinians who were socialized in the Israeli education system were accustomed to celebrating Independence Day until the late 1970s, and therefore commemorating the Nakba on the same day is an "antidote" to this false consciousness. A third argument is practical: since Independence Day is an official holiday in Israel anyway, it is easier to mobilize a large number of participants who have the day off from work and school.

Those who advocate for 15 May, on the other hand, argue that this is the date adopted by Palestinians everywhere, and the Palestinians in Israel should express their belonging to the Palestinian people by sharing the same calendar. Some of the 15 May advocates are concerned that adopting a date sanctioned by the State of Israel implicitly recognizes its legitimacy.[13]

The March of Return and the Religious-Secular Divide

Beyond these explicit arguments, however, at the end of the first decade of the twenty-first century, the bifurcation of the Nakba's temporal commemoration has become related mainly to an uncompromising struggle regarding the role of Islam in the national struggle and the place of women in it. To understand this conflict we should go back to the early 1990s when personal memories of the Nakba started to gradually gain a politically organized shape.

This transition was expressed by publications of personal memories in newspapers and books, but above all it had a spatial dimension: family pilgrimages to the depopulated villages became institutionalized in a process named by the social scientists Efrat Ben Ze'ev and Issam Aburaiya as "middle-ground politics" that bridges the gap between "Palestine as an abstract notion and the concrete daily concerns of the Palestinians."[14]

Several grass roots organizations were responsible for this transformation, but two of them have had the most tangible impact. The first is the National Committee for the Defense of the Rights of the Uprooted in Israel (hereafter, Committee of the Uprooted), an umbrella organization of the internally displaced Palestinians. The second central actor in the field has been the Islamic Movement through its financial arm, the Al-Aqsa Institute. While these two actors operated in cooperation in the 1990s, in the twenty-first century their differences have become an important factor that affects the Nakba commemoration. This collision reflects a broader division between secular and religious Arab NGOs, which the political scientist Amal Jamal has described as "almost completely separate, parallel civil societies."[15]

The most significant actors responsible for the cultivation of public memory of 1948 are the internally displaced Palestinians. These are Palestinians who were uprooted from their villages in 1948, but who remained in Israel and became Israeli citizens. The continuous attempts of Israeli governments to efface the refugee identity of the internally displaced failed,[16] and instead the second generation became politically active and assertive. The adoption of the two-state solution by the PLO in 1988, as well as the Madrid-Oslo processes, raised concerns that their issue would be sacrificed.[17]

Since 1992 internally displaced citizens established numerous local committees and in 1995, these committees were united under the Committee of the Uprooted. The name of the committee intentionally include the title "uprooted" rather than "refugees" to distinguish the internally displaced Palestinians from other Palestinian refugees.[18] The Committee of the Uprooted has worked both at the local and national level by organizing community activities, using local media, and encouraging volunteers to maintain the buildings and sites that remain in the depopulated villages. One clear indication of the relative importance of Nakba commemoration among the uprooted is the finding from the 2010 survey conducted by sociologist Sammy Smooha: two-thirds of the interviewees who belonged to uprooted families reported participating in the Nakba demonstration compared to only one-third of other interviewees.[19]

In a parallel path, since the early 1990s the Islamic Movement started to organize its activists for restoration of cemeteries, shrines, and mosques, which frequently were the only remnants of depopulated villages.[20] While the northern faction of the Islamic Movement would become the most popular party/movement among the internally displaced Palestinians,[21] this political orientation has not been reflected in the composition of the Committee of the Uprooted. Although the committee defines itself as nonpartisan, its founders and central members have been affiliated with secular movements and parties, and so far none of its members has been publicly identified with the Islamic Movement. The Committee of the Uprooted accompanied its pilgrimage and restoration activities with a rhetoric focused on the Right of Return, whereas the Islamic Movement emphasized the religious sacredness of the sites. The partial overlap of goals between the two created a temporary but productive cooperation between them.

The most vital contribution of the Committee of the Uprooted is the annual March of Return. The march emerged as an intersection of two traditions, the first of which was the practice of private family visits to the destroyed villages. Under military rule Israel's Independence Day was the only time that refugees and their families were allowed to visit the sites of their old homes. To a certain extent the March of Return is an institutionalization and popularization of these private traditions.[22] This institutionalization was a gradual process that had started already in the early 1980s.

In November 1984, for example, hundreds of people marched from the entrance of the depopulated village Kafr Bir'im to the church in its center to commemorate the thirty-sixth anniversary of their expulsion. Representatives of the DFPE and the Progressive List delivered speeches in which they contextualized the Kafr Bir'im case in the broader issue of the Palestinian refugees. Leaders of the Kafr Bir'im community were more cautious and referred to their particular demand to return to their village. This orientation enabled them to gain the sympathy of mainstream Zionist parties. Three of them, Mapam, Ratz, and Shinuy, as well as the Peace Now movement greeted the participants by telegram.[23]

The second origin is the diversification of the commemorative practices of Land Day, which already in the 1980s had begun to include organized visits to depopulated villages. On Land Day 1995 the Committee of the Uprooted organized a rally in the depopulated village of Ghabisiyya in the western Galilee. At the rally, the elders of Ghabisiyya told the participants the story of their expulsion. The organizers hung on the wall of the village's mosque the names of dozens of depopulated villages along with signs with a clear demand to implement the return, such as: "We will not forget" and "The Right of Return is a sacred right." However, being aware of Jewish Israeli sensitivity to the issue, the demand to return was mixed with a pacifist message: "The road to peace will pass through our village," "The meaning of peace is the return to the land and home," "The land is wide enough for everyone," and "We demand the implementation of the Supreme Court decision from 1950."

The last slogan is especially important for understanding the cautious tactics of the Committee of the Uprooted. The fact that the March of Return tradition started in Kafr Bir'im and Ghabisiyya is also indicative of a broader pattern of cautious commemoration. In both cases the Supreme Court ruled that the residents should be allowed to return, but in both cases the state has never respected the court's decision.[24] In other words, in these cases the Palestinian claim was backed by an Israeli court decision and therefore they easily could have been framed within the discourse of civil rights, which is less threatening for a Jewish audience. In 1995, the pacifying tone of the Committee of the Uprooted might have been related as well to the expectation that the civic struggle of Kafr Bir'im and Iqrit communities would bear fruit soon, since at the same time, in spring 1995, a committee appointed by Rabin's government was in the process of examining a possible return.[25]

The rally in Ghabisiyya on Land Day was repeated in the next three annual Land Day commemorations, and representatives from all Arab political parties, including the Islamic Movement, addressed the rally. In 1998 the event was entitled "March of Return," while Nakba Day was observed separately on 15 May by a mass rally in the ruins of the village of Safuriyya. Since 1999 the March of Return has marched to a different depopulated village every year, and it is conducted on Israel's Independence Day, usually as the central rally *instead of* Nakba Day. The number of participants seems to be growing consistently.[26]

In 1998, when the FUC decided to mark Nakba Day on 15 May at a mass rally, the two factions of the Islamic Movement took part in it, but the Islamist leaders left the event when the female singer Amal Murqus went on stage.[27] The Islamic Movements also organized their own events. Because in 1998 the celebration of the Islamic new year fell close to Nakba Day, the two factions of the Islamic Movement called on their supporters to attend "the festival of migration (*hijra*) and return." These events gained much more attention in the Islamist press than the Nakba Day organized by the FUC.

Compared with the southern faction, the northern faction has been much more assertive and ready to confront the secular movements, especially on gender issues. Since 2009 these tendencies of the northern faction have led to an open conflict with the Committee of Uprooted. Unlike the central rallies of Land Day and al-Aqsa Day (see below), which are coordinated by the FUC, the March of Return is organized by the Committee of Uprooted. Although the preparations for the march are coordinated with the FUC, the committee has remained independent in making decisions about the details. Because the Islamic Movement gained relative power at the FUC, it has been able to influence the character of the central ceremonies of Land Day and al-Aqsa Day, but it failed to achieve the same influence on the march.

Therefore, the March of Return has kept a blatant secular character, including a mixed male-female crowd, *debka* dancing, and songs by unveiled female performers. Martyrs have been cherished by a moment of silence, but without Qur'anic verses as is the custom in the other three major dates on the political calendar. The events of Land Day and al-Aqsa Day are much less centralized with many local rallies whose content is defined by the local political balance of power, and therefore they have a broader range of political character. The March of Return, in contrast, is a single unified event, and the Islamic Movement refuses to tolerate its secular orientation.

The mixed-gender crowd is probably the main concern of the movement, which has had to face a rapid social change in this respect. In 1975 *al-Ittihad* reported that for the first time women participated in the commemorative procession in Kafr Qasim. In a 2012 survey, on the other hand, an almost equal number of men and women reported at least one-time participation in Land Day or Nakba commemoration.[28] In the case of the March of Return, this mixing has been organic to its historical roots because it emerged as a tradition of family activity. The northern faction has also grown dissatisfied with the list of speakers, which includes Jewish and unveiled female speakers. Anti-Jewish Islamist slogans were heard more than once from the ranks of the Islamic Movement at national events while a Jewish speaker delivered a speech.[29]

For all these reasons, it is clear that the northern faction has adopted a reserved attitude toward the march. Islamist participation in the march has been relatively marginal, and the event has been covered lightly by the print and internet Islamic press. For the movement the march is only one event commemorating the Nakba, not the central one. Since 2008 the northern faction has commemorated the Nakba on 15 May separately in a mass event (leaders of the southern faction attend the event as guests). This is in addition to a separate event for Muslim women, the Festival of Return, which began in 2006 and is held shortly before 15 May. At this event modestly dressed women address the crowd.

In 2011 and 2012 the Committee of the Uprooted made a compromise and agreed to separate the "political" part from the "artistic" part of the march, to enable the Islamists to leave the march before unveiled female performers begin their concert. Later on, however, encouraged by the seizing of power by the Muslim Brotherhood in Egypt in summer 2012, the Islamic Movement's leaders gained further confidence and toughened their insistence on their principles. The Committee of the Uprooted reacted by intentionally positioning women in all key roles at the 2013 March of Return. In 2013 and 2014 the northern faction decided not to call its supporters to participate in the march and its media did not report on it. Practically speaking, then, the movement boycotted the event. 'Aida Toma-Suleiman, a DFPE member and the first woman member of the FUC, analyzed the reasons for this boycott:

> In recent years the northern faction of the Islamic Movement raised more than once and on several occasions two issues: its wish to prevent the mixing of men and women in public events and the participation of progressive Jewish forces in the general national events [. . .]. The March of Return remained the only

collective national event whose character the northern faction of the Islamic Movement has not succeeded in dominating and has been unable to subjugate to its customs and world view, especially in that which concerns the status of women and their active participation [. . .] Over the past three years, the scene of the movement's leaders leaving the events while a woman went up to the stage is more an embarrassment to the movement than to the march organizers."[30]

Publicly, the movements' leaders deny that their non-participation in the march is related to these issues, and they consistently justify their reservation for merely procedural reasons, arguing that the event is not organized by the FUC. They did raise these concerns, however, in closed meetings of the FUC.[31]

. . .

As in the case of Land Day, disagreements in the present shape the way the Nakba is remembered. The leaders of the Committee of the Uprooted began to argue that discrimination against women made a decisive contribution to the Palestinian defeat in 1948. In a radio debate about the absence of the Islamic Movement from the march, Wakim Wakim, the founder of the Committee of the Uprooted who played a central role in establishing the March of Return tradition, said: "The marginalization of women, and their distancing from the national leadership, political leadership, and sporting activity in the organizations and institutions of civil society is one of the reasons of the Palestinian Nakba."[32]

The withdrawal of the northern faction of the Islamic Movement from the march further emphasized the march's role as a major stage for displaying secular nationalism. In the 2014 march, the book booth that was located near the central gathering location included only secular literature and scholarship. I have noticed very few veiled women among the thousands of participants. Indeed, activists of the Islamic Movements published angry Facebook posts, referring to the "immodest" appearance of women at the march. While the organizers of the march have always considered the number of participants as an indicator of the development of Palestinian national consciousness, from 2013 they have seen it as well as an indicator of the power of secular nationalism.

The Uniqueness of the March of Return in the Palestinian Sphere
Like Land Day, the temporal commemoration of the Nakba looks very different on each side of the border. Nakba Day in the West Bank has been part of the continuous struggle against Israeli military occupation. It frequently has

been characterized by violent confrontations, including throwing stones and burning tires. In 2014 an IDF sniper killed two demonstrators. In 2011 the confrontational method of protest-commemoration was adopted by Palestinians in Lebanon and Syria who approached the border fence and tried to cross it; the IDF killed nine of them.

In contrast, by 2014 the March of Return has already turned into a family-friendly and peaceful festival with ice cream trucks, free supplies of bottled water, souvenir booths, and a book-selling booth. It is orderly and organized, fully coordinated with the police who prevent Jewish Israeli provocateurs from approaching the participants. Palestinian solidarity, though, is clearly manifested at the symbolic level. Along the path of the march in 2014, the organizers hung large photos of Palestinian refugees and their descendants in the diaspora with accompanying text that stated their names and their villages of origin.

The March of Return traditionally begins with the singing of "Mawtani" (my homeland). The political fragmentation of the Palestinian national movement is reflected in the parallel existence of several songs considered as national anthems and, therefore, the choice of any of them has political meaning. The lyrics of "Mawtani" were written by the poet Ibrahim Tuqan, and since the mid-1930s it has been considered an unofficial Palestinian national anthem. During the golden age of pan-Arabism, an Egyptian national song (that would become the official Egyptian national anthem in 1979) "Biladi, Biladi" became popular among Palestinians and was incorporated into the canon of the Fatah movement, but the lyrics were modified to fit the Palestinian context and the revolutionary spirit of Fatah. Soon after, the PLO decided to officially adopt another song as the national anthem—"Fida'i" (the one who sacrifices himself).

Following the communist victory in the Nazareth municipal election in 1975, the poet Samih al-Qasim authored new lyrics for "Biladi Biladi,"[33] in which patriotic statements were mixed with praise for the party. Since then, the song has been used at many party events, such as conferences and summer camps, as if it was a national anthem. The National Democratic Assembly (NDA) party, established in 1996, has used "Mawtani" for the same purpose. The PNA, established in 1994, officially adopted the PLO anthem, "Fida'i"; however, none of the Arab parties in Israel ever adopted "Fida'i." Until the establishment of the PNA, the rejection of "Fida'i" might have been related to the tendency to keep a safe distance from the armed struggle. Later, however, the lack of popularity of the PNA among national activists (who see it as a tool of the Israeli occupation) might have added another reason for this rejection. In any case, the choice of "Mawtani" reflects the strength of the national stream among the organizers of the March of Return.

At the same time, much more than Palestinian commemoration elsewhere, Palestinian memory in Israel is constructed against Jewish Israeli memory. Since 2004 the March of Return has been organized around the title "Their Independence—Our Nakba," a title that epitomizes the aspiration for contrast. This title has not appeared in Nakba Day events outside the Israeli context. The number of Jewish Israelis who participate in the march is negligible, but some participants still aspire to convey their message to a Jewish audience (see Figure 3).

Figure 3. Palestinian activist at the March of Return in 2014 wrapped in a Palestinian flag with a sticker in Hebrew that states: "Nakba, let's talk about it!" Source: Photo by the author.

Jewish Israelis play the role not only of the bearers of the counter narrative, but since 2003 a Jewish Israeli representative always is included in the list of speakers, a list carefully crafted in advance by the Committee of the Uprooted. In 2014, when the planned Jewish speaker (Ilan Pappé) was stuck in traffic on the way to the march, the organizers asked another Jewish participant to replace him. In some years a Jewish Israeli representative also was present in the preliminary organizational meetings. This is another expression of the autonomy of the Committee of the Uprooted, which acts independently from the purist forces that gained influence in the FUC and among Palestinians elsewhere. At a time when Palestinian activists in the West Bank increasingly reject cooperation with Jewish Israelis out of concerns of "normalization," this consistent and public inclusion of Jews in the commemoration has become another significant distinctive marker of the March of Return.[34]

AL-QUDS AND AL-AQSA DAY

During the same years in which the tradition of the March of Return was established, the fourth anchor of the calendar was added. In early October 2000, at the beginning of the Palestinian uprising known as Intifadat al-Aqsa, riots spread inside the Green Line, and the country witnessed a wave of demonstrations, stone-throwing, and police gunfire against demonstrators that killed thirteen Palestinians. Since 2001, 1 October became an annual day of commemoration in which thousands participate in memorial processions. These processions have become another major stage for displaying Palestinian national symbols, including a sea of Palestinian flags and the collective singing of "Mawtani." The various memorial monuments that have been erected since 2000 (see Chapter 5) serve as the starting or ending points of these processions. In many Arab schools where the staff is confident enough, teachers discuss the events of October 2000 and their meaning with students. In some years a general strike takes place as well.

A central thread in the commemorative discourse of most political forces is the anger and frustration over the fact that Israeli citizenship did not protect the October 2000 victims. This discovery was translated into a reexamination of the meaning of citizenship that led to two distinct patterns of political discourse and practice—both of these patterns are evident in the commemoration of October 2000.

The first reaction is a growing tendency to demand collective national rights, the strengthening of autonomous Palestinian institutions inside Israel, and the elimination of the ethnocratic elements of the Israeli political system. These are demands to redefine the meaning of Arab citizenship in Israel. Although this orientation is mostly identified with the NDA, it is evident as well in the discourse of other parties, including the DFPE, and to a certain extent in the rhetoric of the southern faction of the Islamic Movement. The second reaction is a complete withdrawal from the Israeli political field and from the discourse of citizenship. The northern faction of the Islamic Movement, which adopted this orientation as its raison d'être after the 1996 split, intensified it following October 2000.

An article epitomizing the first approach was published by Nadim Rouhana in *Fasl al-maqal* on the first anniversary of the October 2000 events:

> Regardless of the different views, many Palestinians in Israel understand that the basis of their relations with the state has changed. There is a need to redefine their citizenship, which constitutes the basis of their relation with the state, in a way that would take into consideration their history and the history of their people.

This approach would become the basic principle of the Future Vision Documents published in 2006 and 2007.[35] As evident in Rouhana's text, this political reaction is far from being a withdrawal from the Israeli political game, but a call to change its rules. Accordingly, the commemorative discourse has repeatedly emphasized that the October 2000 victims were citizens. *Fasl al-maqal*'s editorial on the third anniversary, for example, blamed the state's military apparatus for killing "the souls of the thirteen citizens who demonstrated in protest processions, without any weapon except the justice of their demands and cause."[36] This approach was accompanied by the demand to give real meaning to this citizenship.

Accordingly, the annual announcements published by the FUC emphasize that the memory of the October 2000 martyrs enables the renewal of the struggle for the defense of Palestinians' "national and civil rights," two demands that are clearly presented as complementing each other. Indeed, aside from the unambiguous visibility of Palestinian flags in the annual processions and the rhetorical commitment to the unity of the Palestinian people, the particular demands of the Palestinians in Israel as Israeli citizens are evident. For example, every year the demand that the government find and punish the individuals responsible for the killing is repeated (though so far not a single criminal charge has been submitted).

Palestinian commemoration outside Israel is rarely interested in the identity of the particular individuals who pulled the trigger. If any attempts to bring perpetrators to trial are made, they are not made in Israel but at the international level, and they target political leaders or senior officers. The demand of Palestinians in Israel that the Israeli government exercise its power to bring justice is a demand articulated from within the boundaries of Israeli citizenship. Accordingly, even though Hebrew has a much weaker presence than in past commemorations, it is not absent from the slogans heard during the annual October procession. For example, in the 2011 procession, some of the Arab participants called in Hebrew: "Barak, Barak, the minister of defense, how many children have you killed so far?" (The slogan commonly has been used by Jewish leftist activists against various ministers of defense.)

Memorial books published following the events expressed unambiguous protest against the government but not against the idea of a shared citizenship with Jewish citizens. The memorial book for Walid Abu Salih and 'Imad Ghenayem, published only weeks after the events by the local branch of the Islamic Movement (southern faction) in Sakhnin, included thirty pages of press coverage of the events and their aftermath. Five of these pages dealt with condolence visits by Jewish citizens to the grieving families. The book's editor Masu'ud Ghenayem later became a Knesset member in 2009.

The growing popularity of the idea that Palestinians need to build their own institutions raises the question of Jewish participation in the commemoration. Under these circumstances, the DFPE, which is an Arab-Jewish party, found itself on the defensive. Following the first anniversary, Ahmad Sa'ad wrote in *al-Ittihad* that "our masses declared their national vow to continue their just struggle against the unjust politics of national oppression and racial discrimination by the authorities, and for their right for full equality and full citizenship in this shared homeland."[37] Then Sa'ad highlighted the participation of Jewish demonstrators in the commemorative events and emphasized the importance of the joint Arab-Jewish struggle. As in the March of Return, Jewish Israelis are among the speakers in the annual October 2000 ceremonies.

The northern faction of the Islamic Movement is an exception to the common use of civic discourse (some elements in the Sons of the Village have a similar approach, but their political weight seems to be negligible). Whereas the secular movements and the southern faction of the Islamic Movement use the memory of October 2000 to mobilize a struggle for national and civic rights, the northern faction interprets al-Aqsa Day literally, as a day dedicated to the al-Aqsa mosque. During the mass processions the supporters of the Islamic Movement frequently shout the slogan: "By spirit, by blood, we will redeem you, al-Aqsa!" Similarly, *Sawt al-haq wal-Hurriyya* conducted an interview with the movement's deputy chair Kamal Khatib before the eleventh anniversary, in which he stated: "After eleven years from the eruption of the al-Aqsa uprising, the plan to destroy al-Aqsa and build the so-called temple continues."[38] This statement was used as the title of the interview. Khatib criticized the secular commemoration of the event that marginalizes al-Aqsa: "There are those who want to strip the religious and national dimension from this uprising, and there are people who talk about 'the October uprising.' They do not want to name things by their name, but to disconnect our issues from our noble history." Khatib did not say it explicitly, but "the elephant in the room" was almost explicit in the text: unlike the Land Day martyrs, all the martyrs of October 2000 were Muslim.

The reference to the title of the day is part of a controversy that has accompanied the commemoration from its very beginning. The day gained different titles that varied according to the secular/religious divide. While blatant seculars prefer the term *habbat Octobir* (the October eruption), the Islamic Movement prefers *habbat al-aqsa* or *yawm al-aqsa* (al-Aqsa Day), referring to the event that triggered the uprising—the high profile visit of then leader of the opposition Likud party Ariel Sharon to the Haram al-Sharif/Temple Mount. The FUC adopted a compromise to make the title inclusive of Christian Palestinians—*yawm al-quds wal-aqsa* (the Jerusalem and al-Aqsa Day). This recent term gradually has been adopted even by the secular parties and media, which by 2008 almost abandoned the term *habbat Octobir*. The giant illustration of the al-Aqsa and 'Omar mosques that was set as background to the stage in the central rally in 2013 is evidence of the power of the Islamic Movement to shape the content of the al-Quds and al-Aqsa Day. Beyond any doubt, however, the 1 October commemorative events are shared by all political forces of the Palestinians in Israel, regardless of its title.

While the commemoration of the Kafr Qasim massacre in the twenty-first century became dominated by the Kafr Qasim local council and the March of Return is dominated by the Committee of the Uprooted, the dominant actors in shaping the October 2000 commemoration of the victims are the FUC and the families of the victims. The families established a committee to coordinate their efforts and have had a strong influence on the content of the annual commemoration. Their representatives are invited to the preliminary meetings of the FUC before the annual commemoration, and they have gained high public visibility. In the almost annual controversy over whether a general strike should be announced, the families have always supported the strike and protested when the FUC did not adopt their stand.

In contrast, the families of the Land Day victims never even came close to having such an influence. As a result, while Land Day's commemorative discourse has focused on political dynamics, and the identity of the martyrs was marginal, the identity of the October martyrs became a central element in the commemoration. The image of the thirteen martyrs in the front row of the annual procession has no precedence in Land Day commemorations. Similarly, some of the participants in the march carry with them large photos of individual martyrs. In contrast, in the first years after Land Day, pain over individual loss had already been marginalized, and the emphasis was directed instead to collective prowess rather than to collective mourning.

IMPLICATIONS OF THE EVENTS ON THE
COMMEMORATION OF KAFR QASIM AND LAND DAY

With the addition of two major commemorations to the Palestinian political calendar, it became crowded. It seems that because of its growing localized orientation, the memory of the Kafr Qasim massacre beyond Kafr Qasim itself was especially vulnerable to this development, and there has been a long-term decline in its centrality as a national mobilizing myth.

In 2008, the DFPE Secretary Ayman 'Odeh complained that:

Secretly, the massacre of Kafr Qasim is commemorated, and this is being called "commemoration." Without a country-wide gathering, without the Follow-Up Committee, without consultation and media, without parties, without private or general invitations—the people of Kafr Qasim, alone, commemorate the massacre of Kafr Qasim. With the persistence of localism the procession begins at 8 a.m., nobody hears about it until it ends, except by word of mouth. When the procession takes place in the middle of the week, it will not find its share in the weekend press, while the Hebrew newspapers are not getting reports and do not report [. . .] This situation did not exist twenty years ago. Before that the massacre was a national event for all the sons of our people and many of the democratic Jews.[39]

'Odeh's description might be exaggerated. Representatives of all Arab political movements are present in the annual commemoration, and every Arabic media, electronic or print, continues to refer to the massacre on its anniversary. There is a growing gap, however, between the intensity of the reference to the massacre by different political forces. The newspaper of the elitist NDA, Fasl al-Maqal has given little attention to the ceremony in recent years. In 2012, for example, it covered the ceremony only by a brief report on page 13 of the issue. The southern branch of the Islamic Movement—Kafr Qasim is its strongest base—continues to dedicate a great deal of space to the massacre in its newspaper, al-Mithaq. Similarly, while in the twentieth century the massacre was commemorated in numerous locations throughout the country (if not every year, at least on the twentieth, thirtieth, and fortieth anniversaries); in the twenty-first century commemorative gathering outside Kafr Qasim has become rare.

One final and decisive indication for the decline of the Kafr Qasim massacre anniversary as a central date on the political calendar is the lack of power struggles around the event. The list of speakers, the approved slogans, or the exact title of the event, are not issues on which the various political forces would clash. Although the lack of public conflicts until the mid-1970s can be easily explained by the weakness of the national and Islamic streams at the time and the almost monopoly of the Communist Party over organized commemoration, their absence today stems from the little potential political capital that could be accumulated through the commemoration. This is very different from the dynamics that have characterized the other three events on the calendar.

Land Day has remained a major date on the political calendar and the increase in the number of people reporting participation (see Introduction) is a good indication of that. The number of participants is similar to the number of participants in the Nakba commemoration. In addition, the rate of participants among supporters of major parties and movements is similar: in a 2012 survey supporters of the DFPE, NDA, and the northern branch of the Islamic Movement reported similar levels of participation in Land Day (63, 67, and 69 percent, respectively, reported participation at least once).[40] The different rhetoric of party leaders, however, reflected the gap in the level of relative importance they ascribed to Land Day and al-Aqsa Day. The Communist Party was the only viable political force in 1976, and its leaders insist that Land Day's importance far exceeds that of October 2000. The leadership of the NDA, established only in 1996, tends to ascribe equal importance to the two events.[41] Since the Islamic Movement makes an effort to present itself as the defender of the al-Aqsa mosque (supporters of the leader, Ra'ed Sallah, named him "Shaykh al-Aqsa"), its leaders try to turn al-Aqsa Day into the central pillar of the political calendar.

In both Land Day and Kafr Qasim ceremonies, Jewish citizens are still included among the speakers, although in the case of Land Day this participation is not consistent anymore. Remarkably, the frequent use of Hebrew by Arabic speakers in the central ceremony in Kafr Qasim that was so evident in 1986 has almost vanished. As a general tendency the status of Jewish Israelis as an audience for the commemoration is in decline, a process that reflects a broader tendency of Arab citizens to withdraw from the common Israeli public sphere. Still, in 2014, for the first time, an Israeli president (Reuven Rivlin) took part in a memorial ceremony for the victims of the massacre in Kafr Qasim, which gained much attention from the media.[42] Similarly, it is remarkable that the relative power of the political forces that are the most vocal and explicit in their demand to abandon this sphere is still limited.[43]

· · ·

One particular aspect of the commemoration of the four events has not been discussed in detail yet: the establishment of memorial monuments. Unlike the political calendar that emerged gradually from the late 1950s with two of its anchors already well established by the early 1980s, memorial monuments for martyrs first appeared only in the mid-1970s and have become widespread only in the twenty-first century. The reasons for this delay and its sociological and political meanings are discussed in the next two chapters.

4 MEMORIALS FOR MARTYRS, I (1976–1983)

"Um Hassan said that she passed there on her way to al-Kweikat and saw
among the village's ruins a burned-out bus and a destroyed armored car.
The Israelis built a monument for their dead on the site.
'And we, what shall we build there?' I asked her.
'What shall we build?' she wondered.
'I mean, after the liberation,' I said.
She looked at me with half-closed eyes as if she didn't fully understand
me, and then she laughed."

Elias Khuri, *Bab Al-Shams*

ALTHOUGH SINCE THE 1930s forces within Palestinian society have been calling for the establishment of memorial monuments for martyrs, we have no evidence that such a monument was built under British rule. Palestinians in Israel first built a memorial for their martyrs only in 1976, in memory of the victims of the Kafr Qasim massacre. What could explain this delay?

When the editors of *Filastin* and *al-Difaʿ* suggested building a monument for the unknown martyr in 1936, they identified secular martyrological monuments for national warriors with "the West." They adopted a common view that war memorials are a "visual sign of modernity"[1] and that Palestinian modernity should be based on a Western model. Their use of this argument might imply that, compared with other forms of commemoration, martyrological monuments were less deep-rooted in the local cultural legacy. However, the cultural argument supplies only a marginal explanation because even if we consider the martyr monument as foreign, the indigenization of foreign cultural forms was already prevalent in Mandatory Palestine. During the first half of the twentieth century, Palestinians adopted various ideologies and institutions of European origin, from the nation-state to communism, as well as diverse cultural forms including clothing and leisure habits. Furthermore, prominent Palestinian intellectuals, such as *Filastin*'s editor ʿIsa al-ʿIsa and the historian ʿArif al-ʿArif held senior positions in the short-lived Syrian kingdom under Faysal that led an intensive spatial commemoration of secular national martyrs from 1919 to 1920.[2] These intellectuals were surely aware of this commemoration if not active contributors to its production. Furthermore, in 1933 a monument was established in Haifa to commemorate King Faysal al-Hashimi who had died in Switzerland

and whose body passed through Haifa on its way back to Iraq. Although Faysal was not considered a national martyr, his monument illustrates that this kind of commemoration was already practiced by Palestinians, not only discussed among intellectuals.

The antagonism of the British and later Israeli authorities was probably the major reason that different plans to build Palestinian national monuments did not materialize. Building monuments that commemorate national martyrs is a major practice of constructing national consciousness in the modern era.[3] These monuments enable the nation-state to construct space as a national landscape and to crystallize national identification for its citizens by placing the hegemonic national narrative in public space,[4] creating a concrete representation of its sovereignty, providing validity and legitimacy to a political claim for a territory, and mobilizing future sacrifice for the nation. Not coincidently, following the end of a colonial rule, former colonies were quick to remove, alter, or relocate memorial monuments built by the colonizers.[5] Thus, a main obstacle for erecting memorial monuments by a national minority is the potential interpretation of these monuments by various social actors as part of the national set of symbols, like the national flag. Since a nationalist discourse assumes that there is room for only one national sovereign, and since commemoration of national martyrs is so central in legitimizing national ideologies, by building monuments for their victims of the conflict, Palestinians are interpreted as defining a certain territory as Palestinian national territory and, by that, questioning the legitimacy of Israeli sovereignty.

A noticeable example (although somewhat unique) of the concerns of Jewish Israelis regarding memorial monuments could be found in the saga of the improvised memorials built in East Jerusalem shortly before the first anniversary of the 1967 occupation to commemorate Arab combatants who were killed in the battle. Since East Jerusalem was officially annexed to Israel after the 1967 war, it was not subjected to military rule like the rest of the West Bank, and therefore the method of Israeli control had to be compatible, at least in appearance, with the rule of civil law. On the other hand, unlike Palestinian citizens of Israel, Jerusalemite Palestinians did not live under military law for two decades and did not internalize the system of bans and restrictions on politicizing public space. The memorial monuments emerged from this crack in the control system. The anniversary memorial processions that took place in the city in June 1968 marched toward these new monuments and participants put flowers on them.[6] The city hall of Jerusalem objected to the existence of the improvised memorials but in the negotiations between the *waqf* administration and the city hall, it was agreed that the improvised memorials would be removed and in their place three permanent memorials would be authorized. However, the agreement was criticized in Hebrew press editorials, in Knesset discussions, and in the government. According to a public opinion poll, two-thirds of the Jewish residents of Jerusalem opposed the Arab memorials. Following this public turmoil, Israeli authorities withdrew their consent and agreed to leave in place only a single memorial whose establishment had already begun.[7]

In contrast, the first wave of memorial monuments inside Israel, which began to emerge following Land Day, appeared inside Arab localities, far away from the eyes of most Jewish Israelis, and did not cause any public uproar. Still, the Israeli authorities watched this process closely. The removal of the military government in 1966 had relatively and gradually liberalized the means of protest and commemoration available to Palestinians in Israel, but it took years until this relative liberalization was internalized by both the functionaries in the state apparatus, as well as by Arab citizens. The Land Day events and the emergence of new, local martyr-heroes broke a mental barrier and enabled a growing boldness in appropriating space for national memory. One expression of this growing collective self-confidence was the establishment of six monuments for martyrs within seven years (1976–1983). In all these cases both the content and the process of construction embodied the cautious nature of commemoration at the time. The Appendix presents a comprehensive list of the monuments for martyrs that are discussed in this chapter and in the following chapter.

In this first wave of monuments this caution was expressed by locating monuments in cemeteries rather than in central visible locations, by inscribing a sanitized text on the monument that did not identify a perpetrator, by including Jewish citizens as creators or commemorated subjects, by avoiding explicit contextualization of the commemoration in the broader Palestinian national narrative, and by emphasizing loyalties that were considered less political such as local, religious, and communal identities.

THE FIRST MONUMENT IN KAFR QASIM: SANITIZED LANGUAGE

Although some improvised signs at the site of the Kafr Qasim massacre existed after the massacre took place, the first initiatives by local activists to build a permanent memorial in the 1960s failed when the military government, with the assistance of its local agents, prevented the allocation of a land tract for a monument.[8] The local commemoration committee that was established in

Kafr Qasim in preparation for the tenth anniversary publicly demanded that the local council of the village establish a memorial monument.[9] This demand was raised repeatedly in the following years,[10] but in vain. Fear of the authorities probably played an important role in toning down spatial expressions of commemoration. After his visit to Kafr Qasim in summer 1969, Emile Habibi reported that the graves were not in good shape. "When we asked the people: 'Why don't you build them?'" wrote Habibi, "They said that the families of the victims were concerned that they might face the anger of the authorities if they do so."[11]

The reluctance of the local council to adopt spatial commemoration is related to the use of the local council as a tool by the military rule in its attempts to depoliticize the ceremonies. Therefore, in the first years after the massacre, the center of gravity of the politicized commemoration, led by the Communist Party, had been outside Kafr Qasim. During the 1970s, however, the formal removal of military rule, the emergence of Arab local councils as relatively autonomous actors, as well as personal changes in the local council brought the council to adopt a more assertive line and to take the lead in commemorating the massacre as a political event.[12]

The acceptance of the repeated demands of the Commemoration Committee to establish a memorial monument was part of this process. *Al-Ittihad* reported that donations for building the monument came from throughout the country. The monument, located at the same spot where most of the victims were executed, was unveiled during the twentieth anniversary of the massacre in 1976. According to the then-Kafr Qasim mayor, 'Abdallah Sarsur, Israeli authorities placed innumerable obstacles to prevent the construction of the monument and used their agents in Kafr Qasim to put pressure on him.[13]

Other sources, however, depict a slightly different story. The protocols of the local council meeting from October 1976 (two days before the unveiling ceremony), refers to the monument and states that: "the work that was done will be supported by the Prime Minister's Office."[14] In other words, there was probably a tacit agreement between the local council and the Advisor to the Prime Minister for Arab Affairs (hereafter—Arab Affairs Advisor) who gave his consent and even supported the cautious and dull text that was inscribed on the tablet, in which the event is described merely as a "painful tragedy" without mentioning who was responsible for it. Throughout the meeting protocol, the expression "painful tragedy" substituted the word "massacre," which was completely absent from the discussion. The uniformity and compatibility of the vocabulary used in the meeting and on the monument suggests that the local council avoided deviating from a text pre-approved by the Arab Affairs Advisor. Sanitized language is a form of cultural violence,[15] but here this language not only is used against the victims, but they are forced to adopt it in their own voice. This adoption is evidence that the power dynamics and mechanism of control used under Israeli military rule remained intact years after its formal end. In contrast, the plaques and monuments erected in the 1990s are much more explicit in pointing fingers. For example, a memorial plaque installed on the wall of a mosque in that later period states that the victims "were murdered by the IDF in cold blood."

Regardless of the dull wording, the marble plaque immediately gained the social recognition of a memorial monument. Since then it has served as a starting point for the annual memorial processions, and in the first years following its establishment, visitors in organized tours to the village used to stop near the monument for a moment of silence.

THE LAND DAY MONUMENT: A JOINT ARAB-JEWISH PROJECT

Two monuments were built following Land Day. One of them, and the more famous of the two, is dedicated to all six martyrs and located in Sakhnin.[16] Three months after the unveiling of this monument in 1978, the journalist Ibrahim Malik suggested that married couples should adopt a custom common in the Soviet Union and Poland: to visit memorials for national martyrs before their wedding ceremony.[17] This custom, argued Malik, is compatible with the main text inscribed on the monument: "They died as martyrs (*istashhadu*) for us to live . . . thus, they are alive." There is no evidence that anyone adopted Malik's suggestion, but the idea itself reflects the enthusiastic welcoming of the monument, at least among intellectuals. Another monument, much less famous, was established in Taybeh to commemorate Rafat al-Zuhayri from the refugee camp Nur al-Shams, killed in Taybeh during Land Day.

Although in the story of the Land Day monument in Sakhnin we can find a higher level of daring than in the case of the Kafr Qasim monument, it is still a cautious project. Shortly after Land Day, the Land Committee and the local committees of commemoration established in Sakhnin and 'Arabeh decided to create a memorial monument. They financed it from donations and by selling copies of a poster designed by a Palestinian painter from Ramallah, Suleiman Mansur, depicting the six martyrs.[18] The poster itself is one example of the fact that unlike Kafr Qasim, the Land Day myth was immediately adopted by Palestinians outside Israel.

The artist chosen for this task was 'Abed 'Abdi, a thirty-four-year-old Palestinian from Haifa who had returned recently from art studies in East Germany
and worked as an illustrator for *al-Ittihad.* 'Abdi asked his friend, townsman, and
member of the same party, the Jewish Israeli sculptor Gershon Knispel, to join
him in co-creating the monument. 'Abdi and Knispel knew each other long before their joint project, they shared a similar world view, and 'Abdi had much
appreciation for Knispel's artistic work and technical skills. Knispel was already
known for his commemorative memorial for fallen IDF soldiers, with a pacifist
message. 'Abdi ascribed also a political declarative importance to establishing a
memorial monument together with a Jewish Israeli artist.

Without underestimating the importance of these considerations, 'Abdi was
concerned also that he might confront the state's authorities. "I did not receive
any threats, but I felt threatened. It was in the air,"[19] he told me. These concerns
were not baseless. For example, while the monument was under construction,
Mayor Jamal Tarabiyeh of Sakhnin was interrogated by the police and was accused of "illegal construction."[20] Therefore, the inclusion of Knispel, the Israeli
Jew, had the potential of conveying a non-nationalist message and reducing
the risk of confrontation. The participation of a creator of Zionist memorial
monuments, who had served in the Israeli army in 1948, in a project that commemorates the most important heroic myth in the history of the Palestinian
citizens of Israel might be considered ironic. This participation, however, embodies in microcosm the complicated status of the Palestinians in Israel, as well
as the hesitant and cautious path they had to choose in the field of political
commemoration.

The need to be cautious is reflected as well in the text inscribed on the monument that avoids any explicit nationalist tone. The bilingual text inscribed on
the back wall of the monument calls for co-existence and rapprochement between the two peoples. This is a sharp contrast to the combatant slogans that
accompanied the Land Day victims' funerals, such as "In blood and spirit we
will redeem you, Galilee,"[21] and the explicit contextualization of Land Day in
the Palestinian national struggle in *al-Ittihad*'s rhetoric at the time.[22]

At the same time, the text on the monument is more than a simple cautious tactic, and must be considered as well a genuine expression of its creators'
worldview. It reflects also the aspiration of the Palestinian communist activists
to emphasize both Palestinian and Israeli affiliations. In its pacifying and universalistic message, the monument strikingly resembles the monument built
in 1974 to commemorate Bloody Sunday in Derry, Northern Ireland.[23] In both

cases the commemorating agents (communists in Israel, Northern Ireland Civil Rights Association in Northern Ireland) articulated the grievance of a trapped minority in universalistic and non-violent vocabulary. At the same time, and given the stricter surveillance and the shadow of Israeli military rule, Palestinians in Israel had to be much more careful than Irish nationalists, and therefore, unlike the Derry monument, the Land Day monument avoids pointing fingers at state authorities.

The monument's location was also prudently chosen. Originally, its creators wanted to locate it at the western entrance of 'Arabeh, east of Sakhnin. However, they faced the objection of the private owner of the land at the desired location. In addition, there was a concern that the proximity to the main road would enable the Israeli authorities to use the pretext of public safety for removing the monument. After consultation with the Land Committee, it was decided to locate the monument in the Muslim cemetery in Sakhnin. This decision was motivated by the hope that the government would refrain from sending demolition and security teams into the cemetery.[24]

SABRA AND SHATILA: COMMEMORATING A JEWISH CITIZEN

In June 1982 Israel invaded Lebanon in an attempt to uproot the PLO infrastructure in the country and to establish an Israeli-friendly puppet regime led by Christian Maronite forces.[25] In September the Lebanese Phalanges, sent by Israel to the Sabra and Shatila refugee camps in Beirut to capture Palestinian fighters, massacred at least 800 Palestinians and Lebanese citizens. The event triggered the establishment of two additional monuments. In Kafr Kana in the Galilee, the local branch of the Sons of the Village built a memorial in the old Muslim cemetery. One of the activists involved in this initiative was interrogated by the police and accused of "illegal construction."[26] Remarkably, this monument is almost unknown among the residents of Kafr Kana today.

In addition, in the (then) unrecognized Bedouin village of Laqiyya in the south of the country, a local NGO established a modest monument in memory of the victims. As a cautionary measure, another monument was built nearby to commemorate Emile Grunzweig, a Jewish Israeli peace activist who was killed by a grenade thrown at an anti-war protest in Jerusalem in 1983. Nabhan al-Sani', a young activist in Laqiyya, supported the establishment of this second monument. According to al-Sani', when members of the NGO board questioned the necessity of this monument, he answered: "The Emile Grunzweig monument will protect our monument."[27] Unlike in Sakhnin, this time a

Jewish citizen was included as an object of commemoration, rather than as a co-creator of the monument, but in both cases this inclusion was at least partially driven by the need to protect Palestinian monuments.

'AYLABUN: LOCAL AND CHRISTIAN IDENTITY

Although thousands of Palestinians were killed during the 1948 war,[28] there is no evidence that Palestinians in Israel established monuments to commemorate them before 1983. It is possible that compared with the relative ephemerality of the printed medium, establishing commemorative monuments would have served as a physical acknowledgement of the loss of Palestine, akin to building a grave for a missing person whose family is still waiting for her/his return. In the words of James Young, "It is as if once we assign monumental form to memory, we have to some degree divested ourselves of the obligation to remember."[29] Death, therefore, became a relatively marginal motif in the Palestinian commemoration of the Nakba. The public commemoration crystallized mainly around the expulsion, loss of lands and homes, the dignity of the owners who suddenly became refugees or a subordinated minority, and the determination to return. It is not a coincidence, therefore, that the first monument commemorating 1948 martyrs was establishment by a community in which the inclusion of its particular tragedy in the Palestinian collective narrative is questioned. This first monument also demonstrates that, at this point, denationalization and de-Palestinization of the Nakba's memories facilitated their representation in a public space.

On 30 October, 1948 the IDF conquered the 500-person Christian village of 'Aylabun in the eastern Galilee. After occupying the village the soldiers executed fourteen men and expelled the other residents to Lebanon. In the days following the massacre, the IDF fought against the Mawasi Bedouin tribe (the largest tribe in the Galilee before 1948) who were herding sheep on neighboring land. On 2 November they captured a group of Mawasi men, collected their arms, and later executed fourteen of them.[30] Most of the tribe was chased across the border into Syria.[31]

At that point, the people of 'Aylabun took advantage of their connections with European clergy to mobilize international pressure on Israel. In a rare move, the Israeli government approved the return of the villagers to their homes. Later, in the 1950s, several Bedouin families, remnants of the Mawasi tribe who remained in Israel, were settled in 'Aylabun as part of a government policy to sedentarize the Bedouin population. As a result, 'Aylabun became a mixed Christian-Bedouin village (according to the 2008 census, 70 percent of the population was Christian).

The Christian residents of 'Aylabun conducted annual memorial ceremonies for their victims beginning with the first anniversary of the massacre.[32] Unlike the rallies commemorating the Kafr Qasim massacre that became national political demonstrations, the memorial ceremonies in 'Aylabun maintained a local, familial, and religious character for decades. Until the 1990s no political speeches were delivered at these ceremonies.[33] In view of that fact, the commemoration referred only to the Christian dead and excluded the Bedouins.

The memorial monument established on the external wall of the village cemetery reflects this spirit. This monument was created by a young artist from the village, Naif Sam'an, trained at the Jewish-Arab club of Beit ha-Gefen in Haifa. According to Sam'an, at Beit ha-Gefen he had assisted the Jewish artist Shalom Dorner in creating a memorial monument for Holocaust victims, and from that point on he was determined to create a similar monument for the victims in 'Aylabun. In 1983 he succeeded in creating the monument, financed with the help of a local friend.[34]

Sam'an created a metal embossment depicting a mother holding her dying son, blood pouring from his gunshot wounds, especially from his head and chest. This image powerfully echoes the famous *Pieta* icon, one of the most familiar images in Catholic iconography, in which Mary holds Jesus after he was taken down from the cross. While the crucifixion metaphor is not rare in Palestinian art, such an explicit spatial reference of it cannot be found in any of the other Palestinian memorial monuments.

The names of the Christian victims are inscribed on a marble tablet with the title: "'Aylabun's victims, 30/10/1948." The heroic discourse, which could already be detected on the Land Day monument, and the purpose of death ("they gave their lives so we could live" as stated on the Land Day monument) are completely absent. True, the combination of gunshot wounds and the year 1948 is sufficient for providing the national context for every Palestinian observer, even without explicit statements. Still, the fact that the text neither contextualizes the massacre among other events in Palestinian history, nor does it invoke the word "Nakba" is significant. In addition, even though the victims were called "martyrs" (*shuhada'*) as early as 1949 (in the invitation to a memorial ceremony written by the village priest), Sam'an preferred the use of the term "victims" and with that further blurred the national context of the monument.

Hence, the local dimension of collective memory in 'Aylabun was emphasized against Palestinian national identity and not complementary to it. To a
certain extent the Christian identity of the victims and their community played
a similar role: after all, it was only by making their case unique, unrelated to the
fate of other Palestinians that the people of 'Aylabun were able to return to their
homes in 1949.

NATIONAL, LOCAL, AND COMMUNAL IDENTITIES

The list of martyrs on the Land Day monument is compatible with the aim of
those who aspired to construct the event as a breaker of internal boundaries—
it includes both Muslims and Christians, both men and women, as well as
individuals from different localities and regions. From a Palestinian national
perspective, the 'Aylabun monument that excludes the Bedouins is a step backward. Indeed, the rhetorical commitment to national unity and cross-sectarian
solidarity has not been enough to overcome the social reality that has encouraged various dimensions of divisions.

Highlighting non-national identities in order to depoliticize self-presentation
in front of the state authority or Jewish citizens is a form of a cautious measure
that would remain noticeable even later, beyond the first phase of memorial
monuments. For this reason it is important to examine it closer.

Local Identity as a Cautious Measure

By depoliticizing daily interactions through emphasis on identities considered
in Israel as apolitical, Arab citizens can avoid the potential threats attached to
either Israeli identity (being considered as subversive by Palestinian nationalists) or Palestinian identity (being considered as the enemy within by Jewish
Israelis). These "non-political" belongings either can be communal-religious
identities,[35] communal-cultural identities,[36] local identities,[37] or even loyalty to
a soccer team.[38] The emphasis on localism and communalism, therefore, has
specific instrumental aspects. Since building memorial monuments is related
to struggles over public space, the development of local identity (which is based
on spatial distinctions) is especially relevant for our discussion.

Although local communities played an overriding role in defining Palestinian identity even before 1948,[39] the new political circumstances in which the
Palestinians in Israel were trapped has strengthened the status of local identity.
Under the watchful eyes of military governors, Arabs in Israel faced difficulties
in traveling from one town to another as well as in organizing country-wide

supra-local frameworks.[40] Even after military rule was removed in 1966, because of their limited access to the state's political center, local politics became
the main sphere where Arab public leaders could exert power.[41] Most important however, is the fact that unlike Jewish citizens who control the common
space and landscape, Palestinians have no Arab common space outside of the
Arab localities.

Furthermore, Palestinians in Israel suffer from a lack of urban centers that
are collectively recognized as a symbolic or unifying cultural center. Jerusalem
as a religious-cultural center is outside their control, and the modern pre-1948
Palestinian cultural centers, Haifa and Jaffa, were destroyed in the 1948 war and
are now under Israeli control and Jewish hegemony. In struggles over spatial
commemoration in these mixed towns, Arab residents can protest but usually
cannot carve their collective narrative in the shared space.[42]

In the sense of a cultural, political, and economic center, a Palestinian urban
national center does not exist, and even Nazareth, the largest Arab city in Israel,
is far from qualifying since it does not have central institutions like a university,
national library, national book publishers, and so on.[43] Therefore, almost every
cultural production, and certainly those that shape space, necessarily acquires
a clear local character. Sometimes this local character coincides with national
identification, but in other cases, like in the 'Aylabun monument, localism over-
shadows national connotations.

Regarding martyrological commemoration, local identity is strategically
mobilized in two different ways: as part of the national narrative or against it.
First, most studies of local identity and commemoration tend to emphasize
the co-production and mutual enhancement of local and national identities in
commemorative practice.[44] In the Palestinian nationalist sphere, local martyrs
enable residents of a certain village or town to present themselves as possess-
ing a higher rank in the imagined hierarchy of Palestinian national importance.
Local pride in the Land Day martyrs from their own localities is an example
of that. In addition, against the collapse of the urban centers and a large number of Palestinian villages in 1948, local narratives of war developed among the
villages that survived and gave meaning to the survival. Accordingly, people
in Kafr Qasim, Sakhnin, and other places formulated local myths of heroism
that ascribed their non-expulsion to their unique steadfastness,[45] not necessarily to Palestinian prowess or solidarity.[46] The expression of this pattern in
commemorative practices is the interweaving of local martyrology with the national narrative and presenting the contribution of the local martyr to national

success (e.g., both Sakhnin and Kafr Qasim are named in certain contexts— *Balad al-Shuhada*—the Martyrs' Village, referring respectively to Land Day and the massacre in Kafr Qasim in 1956).[47] Indeed, some survey analyses found positive correlation between local identification and Palestinian national identity among the Arab citizens of Israel.[48]

Local martyrology, however, is sometimes strategically mobilized to distance oneself from Palestinian national identity since the latter is perceived by many as potentially detrimental to their status as Israeli citizens. Hence, interactions with Jews tend to be accompanied by emphasizing institutions with a clear local identity. Therefore, in the same way that the tremendous popularity of local Arab soccer teams and the local-patriotic rites that evolved around them stem in part from their potential to provide a warlike, masculine, and competitive pride that does not contradict "Israeliness," commemorating the dead in a local context rather than a national one might reduce the potential for a conflict with Jewish Israelis. The local character of the commemoration in 'Aylabun is a case in point.

Religious and Sectarian Identity as a Cautious Measure

The frequent emphasis of religious identities has a similar strategic purpose. The Palestinians in Israel belong to different religious communities—about 84 percent are Sunni Muslim, 8 percent are Druze, and 8 percent are Christians. Although these distinctions and the conflicts related to them are older than the State of Israel, they have been sustained and nurtured by governmental authorities striving to prevent the emergence of a unified national consciousness.[49]

Christian Palestinians, who once stood at the forefront of the Palestinian national struggle, had to face the accelerated Islamization of this struggle in the West Bank and the Gaza Strip,[50] the emergence and salience of the Islamic Movement inside Israel since the 1970s, which undermined Christian self-confidence,[51] and more specifically, the growing role of the Islamic Movement in shaping Palestinian national commemoration in Israel.[52] Accordingly, Muhammad Amara and Izhak Schnell found that Christian Arabs in Israel are much more likely to see the term "Palestinian" as irrelevant to their identity repertoire than Muslims (28 percent and 11 percent respectively).[53] On the other hand Christian Palestinians seem to be more active in national commemoration: Christians are over-represented in Nakba commemorative activities[54]; Christian activists were dominant among the founders of the Committee of the Uprooted; and institutions affiliated with the Christian Orthodox community, such as the Orthodox College in Haifa and the Orthodox Events Center in Nazareth, have made some pioneering contributions in bequeathing the memories of the Nakba to the younger generation (see chapters 8 and 9). The marginalization of Christians in the Palestinian sphere seems to push them in different directions. For some it might be an incentive to politicize their Palestinian identity, whereas for others, this marginalization meets their frequent need to deemphasize their Palestinian identity as citizens of Israel, and therefore their Christian identity is used to depoliticize social encounters.[55]

This phenomenon is evident in the following finding: in the open-ended self-description in my 2008 survey (for details, see the Introduction), Christian interviewees who used their religious affiliation to describe their identity were far less likely to choose the Nakba than other Christians as one of the most important events in the history of the country.[56] This does not mean that Christian Palestinians ascribe less importance to the Nakba, since overall Christians in this survey were the religious group that mentioned the Nakba more than any other. What it does mean is that those who tend to *highlight their Christian identity* tend also to stay a safe distance from the Nakba (Druze identity, which plays a similar role but in a much more extreme way, is discussed in the next chapter). This finding is compatible with the explicitly Christian monument in ʿAylabun that both excludes non-Christians and avoids explicit reference to the Nakba.

Finally, about one-fifth of the Arab Muslims in Israel are Bedouins. Unlike most Muslim Arabs, Bedouin men are allowed to volunteer for military service in the IDF (one of the rare channels of employment for Israel's Bedouins, the country's least-educated Arab population) and came to be viewed within Jewish Israeli society as a separate, non-Arab minority group loyal to the state,[57] or at least as "'good Arabs." Furthermore, past surveys have shown that Bedouins were more ready than other Arabs to accept their "separate but equal" status in the Jewish state.[58] My own 2008 study found that the likelihood of Bedouins to self-identify as Israelis was more than twice that of other Palestinians in Israel.[59]

There is, however, significant difference between those Bedouins who live in the south of the country (about two-thirds) and those who live in the north. It seems that the "de-Arabization project" among the southern Bedouins failed,[60] while the Bedouins in the north show a greater readiness to accept the Jewish-Zionist character of the state and a weaker Palestinian identification.[61] The southern Bedouins also face a more aggressive policy of the state on land issues, and therefore they have become extremely over-represented in the commemoration of Land Day. In a 2010 survey, 63.5 percent of Bedouin reported participation in at least one Land Day event, compared with 37.2 percent in the entire sample; the northern Bedouins were extremely underrepresented (8 percent).[62] Accordingly, the northern Bedouins provide most of the IDF Bedouin conscripts, and military service is common among 'Aylabun's Bedouin residents. In other words, their distance from the mainstream Palestinian narrative is even more pronounced than that of their Christian neighbors. Their absence from the 1983 monument in 'Aylabun is not only a reflection of their exclusion by their Christian neighbors, but also an expression of the tendency to keep their 1948 memories out of the all-Palestinian narrative.

The Bedouin inhabitants in 'Aylabun have commemorated their victims separately. Immediately after their deaths, the bodies were buried in a cave adjacent to the place where they were killed. In the 1950s, the Israeli National Water Project was dug through the cave, and the Mawassi people took the bones to another cave. During the 1980s, presumably influenced by the monument built for the Christian victims, the bones were moved to a common grave in the small Muslim cemetery in 'Aylabun. A tombstone was erected that records only the date of the deaths. The tomb of an IDF soldier from the Mawassi tribe, located several feet from this grave, is a sharp reminder of the severance of the northern Bedouins from the Palestinian national narrative.

·   ·   ·

The first wave of monuments reflects both the growing self-confidence following Land Day, as well as the caution shaped by governmental surveillance that did not disappear with the formal removal of the military government. This caution is expressed in diverse ways, including the highlighting of "apolitical" affiliations, such as local and religious identities, which contradicts the tendency to shape the commemoration as a display of Palestinian national solidarity. As the next chapter illustrates, only the events of October 2000 triggered a surge of assertive monuments in Arab localities, but commemorating the massacres and battles of 1948 would still remain a sensitive issue that many Palestinian citizens would prefer to avoid.

5 MEMORIALS FOR MARTYRS, II (1998–2013)

IN MARCH 1998, the FUC was looking for ways to commemorate the fiftieth anniversary of the Nakba. The FUC nominated a Nakba and Steadfastness Committee, chaired by the writer Muhammad ʿAli Taha. Among the various initiatives of the committee, one garnered particular attention in the Arabic media, which reported on it in front-page headlines: the call to Arab municipalities to establish memorial monuments for the Palestinian martyrs of 1948.[1]

The decision to commemorate the Nakba provoked implicit and explicit threats from the Israeli government. The then-Minister for Arab Affairs Moshe Katzav (elected as Israel's president two years later), described the FUC's decision to commemorate the Nakba as "dangerous and might damage Jewish-Arab co-existence."[2] The Minister of Interior Eli Yishai threatened to cut the governmental funding of local authorities that financed the commemoration of the Nakba.[3] A televised debate about the proposed Nakba commemoration—between Taha and a Likud MK, the late Gidʿon ʿEzra (a former chief deputy of the General Security Service)—deteriorated into name-calling and mutual shoving.[4]

At the same time, Taha's committee had no independent resources, no authority to implement its plans, and was wholly dependent on the cooperation of Arab local municipalities.[5] In fact, most of the Arab municipalities, which were expected to carry out the initiative, avoided giving high priority to the monument project or investing money from their scarce resources. There was no public pressure on them to implement the committee's decisions, nor was there any public enthusiasm to contribute money, materials, or labor.

Given these unfavorable starting conditions, Taha's expectation that at least fifteen local authorities would positively respond to his request (in particular those villages and towns where a battle or massacre had taken place)[6] were not met during the first thirty months after the decision. It was only after the events of October 2000 that memorials mushroomed in many Palestinian towns and villages in Israel. These later memorial monuments commemorate Palestinian martyrs from various periods since 1936.

Broadly, the story of the establishment, non-establishment, or destruction of these memorial monuments epitomizes many of the dilemmas and contradictions inherent in the production of collective memory by Palestinian citizens of Israel. Palestinian memorial monuments in Israel have been located at the junctures of several societal tensions: first, between the Palestinian citizen and the state; second, between members of intellectual and political elites whose social and occupational status make them more self-confident and ready to defy the state, on the one hand, and larger circles of insecure, suspicious, and cautious publics who prefer to keep "risky" memories private, on the other; and third, between different religious and ethnic groups within Palestinian society.

THE CROSS-CONFESSIONAL MONUMENT IN 'AYLABUN

The fact that an established commemorative tradition for the 1948 massacre already existed in 'Aylabun (see previous chapter) paved the way for the local council to accept the FUC's call to build a memorial monument to the Nakba victims, unlike most other localities However, from a Palestinian national perspective, the 1983 memorial had a noticeable flaw—the exclusion of the Bedouin residents of 'Aylabun.

Therefore, in 1998 the mayor of 'Aylabun, Dr. Hanna Sweid (a member of the DFPE), considered a new inclusive monument an opportunity to strengthen Palestinian national consciousness in 'Aylabun, as well as to tighten the ties between the Christian and Bedouin segments of the village. Presumably, the upcoming local elections and the traditional role of Bedouin votes as the deciding factor was an additional drive for his support of the monument. The monument was unveiled on 30 October 1998 in a ceremony commemorating the massacre's fiftieth anniversary, which included a speech by Mayor Sweid, in which he stated: "In this project, we share the fiftieth memorial day of the Nakba with our Palestinian people, and by building the monument we confirmed the unity of 'Aylabun."[7] The monument was created by reshaping a brick wall near an old church where IDF soldiers had executed some of the victims. Copper tablets bearing the victims' names, Christians and Bedouins alike, were installed on the wall. A few spotlights under the wall were supposed to illuminate it at night.

It is unclear, however, how many of the Bedouin residents shared the mayor's view regarding the need to contextualize the commemoration in the Palestinian national narrative. According to Elias Srur who took part in the preparations for establishing the monument, even though the families of the Bedouin victims cooperated with the municipality in building the memorial monument, only a handful of the Bedouin residents showed significant interest in it.[8]

In any event, the monument had a short existence. The copper tablets with the martyrs' names gradually disappeared from the wall. It might have been simply a case of metal theft, which had become common in the country during that same year. It is noteworthy, however, that the nearby metal cross on the roof of the church remained untouched. In other words, the martyrs' names did not gain enough respect to protect them. As a result, less than five years after the unveiling, the 'Aylabun Nakba memorial monument looked just like another wall. Above it the new ground floor of a private Christian-owned home was built. In a visit to the town in December 2006, I asked the owner of this home about the monument that once stood there. His blatant answer was another example of the way many residents of 'Aylabun chose to present themselves before a Jewish audience: "We are Christians here. They put here the names of Bedouins. Nobody wanted it, so some children came and removed it. We don't want Bedouins here. Fuck them! Next thing they will start to pray here and will ask to build a mosque here." I asked him if he knew who the people commemorated by the memorial wall were. "Of course I know," he answered. "My father-in-law died here. But it was a long time ago."

The Bedouin residents with whom I discussed the issue were unaware that the monument had been virtually effaced, since they rarely visited that area of the village. In any case, they did not seem to care. A decade after its establishment, the former mayor Sweid presented his own perspective on the destruction of the monument:

It is no secret that among some circles in the village there was an attempt to play down—not to hide but to play down—this issue [. . .] This is a political concern—maybe the authorities would take revenge. People have personally experienced punishment in the form of preventing employment or their daily needs. So people were just worried. I'd say that it even has lasted to current days. People do not want to make a national story out of it. They are satisfied with it being a local story, that this is a tragedy that occurred here in the village. Part of the population thinks that it is inappropriate and not worthwhile to weave it

together with the Nakba in general. We have this mindset among segments of
the public here in ʿAylabun. There is a gap even between the very cautious way I
handled this matter and the sentiments of parts of the public here in ʿAylabun.[9]

The case of ʿAylabun sharply illustrates the gap between a political leadership
that strives to promote a Palestinian nationalist discourse and the wider social
circles that are not always enthusiastic about it. The mayor intended to nurture a cross-communal local pride in ʿAylabun, and this localism was supposed
to be interwoven with the Palestinian national narrative. However, this idea
was incompatible with the aspirations of significant segments of the Christian
population, and local identification can replace Palestinian national identity
rather than enhance it. In fact, unlike the destroyed joint monument of 1998, the
manifestly Christian monument from 1983 is still in good shape. It has a clear
local and religious character, and it is not oriented toward the construction of a
unified Palestinian identity common to Christians and Bedouins. Every year the
people of ʿAylabun commemorate the massacre near the 1983 monument. On
their way to the monument, they pass by the wall that once was a monument.

SHEFAʿAMR: THE BATTLE OVER THE MONUMENT

The first Arab municipality to decide on the establishment of a Nakba memorial
monument was that of the mixed Muslim-Christian-Druze town of Shefaʿamr.
On April 1, 1998, the municipal council decided unanimously to build a monument in the traffic circle near the municipality to commemorate Shefaʿamr's
victims of the 1948 war.[10] The year 1998 was also a municipal election year. The
town mayor, Ibrahim Nimr Husayn (Abu Hatem), had ruled since 1969 and
had served as the chair of the FUC since its establishment in 1982. Since 1983,
Abu Hatem had led a coalition that comprised all three religious communities
but faced growing dissatisfaction from the Christians,[11] who felt excluded from
most positions of power.[12] Abu Hatem assumed (mistakenly, as it turned out)
that a monument might improve his undermined local political status.[13] The
municipality and the Nakba and Steadfastness Committee published a call to
Shefaʿamr inhabitants to assist the project by collecting the names of victims
from Shefaʿamr and the neighboring villages Hawsha and Khirbat al-Kasair,
which were destroyed by Israeli forces in 1948.[14]

In July 1998 a monument was erected, consisting of a vertical marble tablet with copper embossments of people wearing traditional Palestinian peasant clothing. A second marble tablet angled at the base of the main tablet bore

the victims' names. However, the monument was never officially unveiled. In the elections, Shefa'amr's residents, fed up with Abu Hatem's three-decade-long authoritarian rule, rejected him, and elected by default the other main candidate, his son-in-law 'Orsan Yasin. Although the ruling right-wing Zionist Likud party unofficially supported Yasin, his election did not reflect an ideological shift but rather, communal and familial struggles and interests. Although a Muslim like Abu Hatem, Yasin enjoyed widespread support from Shefa'amr's Christians, who found in him a suitable means for ousting his father-in-law.[15]

After Yasin's election, his pro-Zionist line was emphasized. It became clear that Yasin represented the view that to be considered "good citizens," Arabs in Israel should refrain from identifying themselves as Palestinians and should distance themselves from the Palestinian national narrative. Although this perception is not rare among Arabs in Israel, Yasin's formulation was extreme. His aspirations to gain greater resources from the government for his city were articulated in a cynical strategy that included hanging Israeli flags near the municipality far beyond what is required by law, making pro-Zionist declarations in the media,[16] and actively opposing strikes organized by the FUC.

Yasin's main move in this context was the reshaping of the Nakba monument in such a way that its commemorative national aspects disappeared. Under the (unnecessary) protection of the Israeli police, the main marble tablet was plastered over and decorated with embossments of flowers, and a turret-like structure was attached to it. The small square around the monument was turned into a pool with fountains in such a way that the victims' names were submerged under water. The voices of protest by the monument's supporters, mainly members of the DFPE and the NDA, were ineffective. Yasin's deputy, Ahmad Khatib, sent him a letter of protest asking to convene the municipal council for an emergency meeting.[17] Ahmad Hamdi, a city council member representing the DFPE, sent a letter to Yasin in which he warned that "Shefa'amris would punish those who try to assault their sacred values sanctities."[18]

Yasin was not impressed by the protest; and by the following summer, the site had become an unofficial bathing pool for the town's children. Yasin, who was previously a member of the council that unanimously approved the construction of the memorial, sarcastically explained his decision to a reporter from the Hebrew newspaper *Haaretz*: "What do they want? That I allow an ugly tomb in front of the municipality? I made a renovation, so everyone feels good under the water."[19] Later the water was drained because of safety considerations, and the empty pool became an improvised garbage dump. In the local election held in October 2003, Yasin's opponents attempted to use the reshaping of the monument in their campaign, but in vain: his victory was clear cut.

In my visit to Shefaʿamr in December 2006, I found the monument covered with commercial ads, signifying the complete failure of the town's attempts to maintain it as a commemorative site. I asked some local residents what they knew about this monument. Here, like in ʿAylabun, the answers reflected the caution of ordinary Arab citizens when they address a Jewish visitor. H., a fifty-year-old man active in the local Christian Scouts club (located approximately 100 yards from the monument), told me: "There was a monument here for those who died a long time ago—but we should move forward, go ahead. The world is changing, people progress. There is pain, but it was a long time ago—who needs that?"

Later, when several scouts and guides gathered around us, I asked them if anyone knew why the monument was built. Everyone said that they had no idea, except for M., a twenty-four-year-old student at the University of Haifa, who said confidently that the monument was built to commemorate the victims of October 2000 and was later distorted. Although misinformed about the monument's history, M. thought there was a need for this kind of monument because "every group in society should be able to express its identity." When I insisted that nobody had seriously resisted its distortion, he replied: "People are afraid. Although we seemingly live in a democracy, people's minds are still shaped by many years of surveillance, and they prefer not to get into trouble. For example, if someone is employed by a Jewish employer, he doesn't want to annoy the boss, so he distances himself from political issues."

In 2008 a new mayor, Nahed Hazem, was elected. Hazem was supported by the DFPE, which had objected firmly to Yasin's distortion of the monument. To the surprise of many, including members of his municipal coalition, Hazem not only avoided restoring the monument's commemorative character, but he destroyed it even further. He reactivated the fountain and as part of his renovation, part of the original text was covered not only with water but also with cement and stone. Unlike Yasin who proudly justified his action by his objection to the political meaning of the monument, Hazem described his actions only as a "transitory phase." In 2014, only a very close scrutiny of the monument enhanced by previous knowledge could reveal that it had been once a memorial for the Nakba victims.

It seems that beyond Yasin and Hazem's short-term political motivations, the transformation of the commemorative monument into a water playground or garbage dump was facilitated by its feeble status among the town's residents. Shefaʿamr's residents did not do all they could, to say the least, to defend the monument. It is likely that only a minority of Shefaʿamr's residents adopted the FUC's view regarding the need for a memorial monument. ʿAbed ʿAnbetawi, the FUC secretary and a former member of the Shefaʿamr municipality who tried to organize the opposition to the monument's destruction, told me: "We felt alone in the battle." In his view, this had something to do with the collective character of Shefaʿamr: "We did not have a militant opposition. The public in Shefaʿamr is different from the public in Sakhnin or Umm el-Fahem. It is not a city where the nationalist atmosphere reigns."[20] ʿAnbetawi's complaints are clearly borne out in Ibtisam Ibrahim's study, which ascribes the primacy of religious allegiances over Arab-Palestinian identification in Shefaʿamr to the successful "divide and rule" policies of Israeli authorities.[21]

The Druze Monument

The position of the Druze residents of Shefaʿamr on the commemoration of 1948 is especially interesting given the peculiar history of this community. Before 1948 the majority of Druze in Palestine were largely indifferent to the Zionist-Arab conflict and adopted a position of neutrality.[22] However, the dynamics of the 1948 war forced some of them to choose sides. In late March 1948 a battalion composed of Druze volunteers affiliated with the Arab Salvation Army arrived from Syria to Palestine and set up base in Shefaʿamr.[23] On 12 April the battalion was deployed in the nearby Hawsha and Khirbat al-Kasair villages and over the next four days it lost dozens of fighters in a fierce battle against the Haganah. The result was a decisive Arab defeat and the occupation of Hawsha and Khirbat al-Kasair.

Following the battle, the officers of the battalion reached an agreement with the Haganah forces and returned to Syria. Some battalion officers and soldiers, however, remained in Palestine, joined the Haganah, and later recruited the first Druze soldiers to the IDF.[24] The end of this battle is considered by many as a crucial landmark in the emergence of the alliance between the traditional Druze elite in the country and the Zionist establishment. A second important milestone was the fall of Shefaʿamr to Zionist hands in July, which happened in coordination with the town's local Druze inhabitants.[25] After the state was established, Israeli governmental efforts to shape a separate Druze identity disconnected from Arab and Palestinian nationalism have been largely successful.[26] To be sure, opposition to the pro-Zionist orientation of the traditional leadership has existed, especially among secular supporters of the Communist Party, but it has remained marginal. As a result, only a small minority among the Druze in Israel define themselves as Palestinians.[27] Typifying this relationship, the first memorial ever built in Israel to commemorate Arab fighters was established in 1974 in the Druze cemetery in Hurfeish to commemorate fallen Druze IDF soldiers. *This* monument, obviously, is not considered by anyone as a Palestinian national memorial.

In the first decade of the twenty-first century, opposition to de-Arabization began to emerge from among the ranks of religiously educated Druze. In 2003 three hundred of them established a new organization, Lajnat al-tawasul al-Durziyya (the Druze Networking Committee—DNC), which aimed to improve the connection of Druze citizens in Israel with other Druze communities in the region and with the broader Arab world. In 2013 the DNC initiated the establishment of a memorial plaque to commemorate the Druze soldiers who fell in the Hawsha and al-Kasair battle near their mass grave in Shefa'amr. The initiative alarmed elements in both the Druze spiritual leadership and the political leadership (the Druze mayors).[28] To contain the commemoration and inoculate it from any anti-Zionist connotation, those leaders hurried to establish the memorial themselves.

The result was a commemoration full of internal contradictions. Members of the DNC wanted the memorial to mention that the martyrs fell while "defending Palestine,"[29] but the actual text avoids contextualizing the battle as part of Arab or Palestinian national history. Under a decoration of the five-colored star (a symbol of the Druze religion) and a Qur'anic verse referring to martyrs, the tablet reads: "The collective grave of the Druze martyrs who fell in the battle of dignity, defending the land and the honor, from Shefa'amr, the Druze Mountain, and Lebanon. The battle of Hawsha and al-Kasair 12–16 April 1948." The unveiling ceremony was attended by Mayor Nahed Hazem, as well as senior Druze political and religious public figures, including the spiritual leader Shaykh Muwaffaq Tarif, and Hamed 'Amar, a Druze member of the Knesset from the extreme right-wing (and frequently anti-Arab) party, Yisrael Beiteinu. At the time, 'Amar served as Deputy Speaker of the Knesset as well. An Israeli flag and the Druze flag were held by children of the Druze scouts who stood behind the stage.[30] The DNC members who initiated the memorial did not attend the ceremony.

In the ceremony, Mayor Hazem typically turned to localism to avoid any reference to the nationalist connotation of the battle by paying tribute to the martyrs who "fell defending the land of our dear city."[31] Shaykh Tarif praised the historical standing of Druze against various oppressors, including the occupation of Ibrahim al-Basha (in the 1830s), Ottoman rulers in Lebanon, French colonialism, and the Syrian President Adib al-Shishakli[32] (who brutally oppressed Druze opposition in Syria in 1953). Both Shishakli and the Druze soldiers commemorated on the memorial, however, had belonged to the Arab Salvation Army and had fought on the same side in the 1948 Arab-Zionist war, a relevant piece of information not mentioned in the ceremony. Needless to say, there was no reference to the identity of the opponent in the battle commemorated by the monument. In that way, the memory of fighters who fought as part of a pan-Arab effort to prevent the establishment of the State of Israel was neutralized from signs of Arab nationalism. Instead, Druze communal identity was emphasized to enable their inclusion in the narrative of a continuous Druze-Zionist alliance.

The Monument for the 2005 Assault

In August 2005 an IDF deserter killed four Shefaʿamr residents in an attempt to prevent the withdrawal of Israel from the Gaza Strip. Immediately after, two members of the local council demanded that a memorial monument be established to commemorate the victims.[33] This time, eager to satisfy the angry Arab public and prevent the recurrence of the October 2000 events, state authorities even participated in financing a monument. However, Mayor Yasin and the victims' families disagreed about the text that should be inscribed on it. The families, supported by the municipal council member of the NDA party, wanted to contextualize the commemoration in a broader political struggle, whereas the mayor insisted on a personal and apolitical framing.[34] Following the appointment of Nahed Hazem as mayor in 2009, the city completed the monument with a relatively apolitical text, referring to "the pure martyrs of the Shefaʿamr massacre."

Shefaʿamr is the only Arab locality to establish three memorial monuments for three separate events. In all three cases, however, pressures to disconnect the memorials from Palestinian national history have been effective.

KAFR KANA: THE SUCCESSFUL MONUMENT

Of the three monuments built following the FUC's call in 1998, only the one in Kafr Kana has survived. Unveiled in September 2000 a few days before the eruption of the al-Aqsa Intifada, the Kafr Kana monument was built at the main

entrance of the village near the new mosque. Since its establishment, it has functioned as a gathering point for events with national significance: Land Day ceremonies, ceremonies to memorialize the events of October 2000, and political
demonstrations like those held against the American invasion of Iraq in 2003.

The monument was built as a round plaza with a wall on its eastern side
and a stone column in its center. The martyrs' names are listed on the wall.
Although a secular-dominated municipality promoted the monument, the
power of political Islam in Kafr Kana in 2000 is evident in its structure and content. Human figures are absent, not only as a result of a purely artistic decision.
Mayor Wasel Taha explicitly asked the artist Abed 'Abdi (who co-created the
1978 monument in Sakhnin that included human figures) to "respect Islamic
and Christian sensitivities."[35] Although two of the village's dead were Christians, the list of names is headed by the *BismAllah* Islamic opening and the
most famous Qur'anic verse on martyrs (3:169): "And reckon not those who are
killed for Allah's way as dead; nay, they are alive."

The poem of the Palestinian poet Ahmad Dahbour, on the square column
in the center of the plaza, ensures the necessary balance by conveying Christian
and secular elements. Its title, "We Died for Kafr Kana to Live," can be read as a
secular answer to the religious phrase ("died for Allah") on the nearby wall. The
poem paraphrases the reference to Kana in the New Testament: "Our name is
a symbol and a meaning / And our death is a birth / We are the wedding of the
Galilee / And the holidays / We are the plain of wheat." The reference to a wedding has a nationalist connotation: wedding festivities occupy a special place
in the Palestinian national imagination for after 1948 these festivities became
one of the principal means by which Palestinians could expressed their national sentiments.[36] The last lines of the short poem bound national and local
pain and pride: "This monument begins from us / We wrote our motherland by
wound." The "Brotherhood of Peoples" that appeared in Hebrew on the Land
Day monument created by 'Abdi twenty-two years earlier disappeared. The dim
nationalist discourse at the monument in Sakhnin became explicit here.

The salience of the local-national nexus is a very significant feature of the
monument in Kafr Kana, which later would be the model for memorial monuments in other localities. Although the original intention of the FUC was to
commemorate the Nakba, the monument in Kafr Kana commemorates all the
martyrs of Kafr Kana since 1936. Hence, instead of taking part in constitut-
ing national memory through a common supra-local experience, Kafr Kana's
municipality chose to emphasize the status of Kafr Kana in the Palestinian na-

tional experience by a multi-generational monument that binds together the dead from the rebellion of 1936–1939, the Nakba in 1948, and Land Day. After a local boy, Muhammad Khamaysi, was killed during the October 2000 events, his name was added to the list.[37]

In this way, the monument in Kafr Kana became the first multi-generational memorial. It was preceded by the multi-generational exhibition of martyrs in Sakhnin that has been held every Land Day since 1999 and similar memorial books produced by several villages in the Galilee, such as ʿArabeh and Kafr Manda. Multi-generational commemoration is also a common practice of Zionist commemoration (following a similar European pattern). In Israel there are more than 300 monuments of this kind, and they are particularly common in rural Jewish settlements where there is proximity between the dead and the commemorators.[38] Indeed, like the creator of the monument in ʿAylabun, the person who initiated the monument in Kafr Kana (Mayor Wasel Taha) argued that he was inspired by Zionist memorial monuments: "I was travelling with my son to Tiberias and at the entrance to the city we saw a monument in memory of the soldiers who conquered Tiberias. My son asked me 'What is this?' so I explained it to him. Then he asked: "Daddy, why don't we have such a monument for our dead?"[39]

LONG-TERM TRENDS

Several weeks after the establishment of the central monument in Kafr Kana, the Second Intifada erupted, and inside Israel thirteen Palestinians were killed in what will be later termed "the events of October 2000." The post-October 2000 monuments reflect long-term trends in Palestinian society in Israel. Although all of these changes were visible even before October 2000, the killing of citizens that autumn certainly played a role in accelerating them.

The first trend is a limited decline in caution. By the end of September 2000, only three municipalities had followed the FUC's call to build memorial monuments (ʿAylabun, Shefaʿamr, and Kafr Kana). A fourth municipality, ʿAylut, decided to build a memorial monument to the victims of the 1948 massacre in the village,[40] but the foundations for the monument were built only a decade later. Furthermore, two of these monuments, in Shefaʿamr and ʿAylabun, not only failed to become a pilgrimage site or a gathering point for political rallies, but were literally destroyed after a short time by local residents.

The political earthquake of October 2000 made an important contribution to removing some of the self-imposed barriers. The unbearable ease with which Arab demonstrators were killed by the Israeli police in conjunction with the indifference to the police brutality of the frightened Jewish public caused popular anger and a sharp awareness of the fragility of the civil and political rights of Arabs in Israel. In the first years after the 2000 events, the risk taken by nationalizing public space seemed suddenly less frightening. If, in the past, the establishment of monuments was hesitant because of its potential to be perceived as threatening to Jewish citizens, after 2000 it became a necessary form of protest—probably because it was considered defiant. This trend is expressed most of all by the exponential increase in the number of monuments. The number of monuments for national martyrs built in the first three years after October 2000 is approximately equal to the number of monuments built from 1948 to September 2000.

This process also expresses a growing popular recognition of the political role of historical remembrance and the production of specific autonomous "sites of memory" as a possible strategy of struggle. This trend is broader than the commemoration of martyrs. Monuments commemorating prominent Palestinian and Arab figures have been established in some localities—for Gamal Abdel Nasser in Abu Snan, for the poet Mahmoud Darwish in Makr and in Sha'b, for the poet Abu 'Arab in the depopulated village of Shajara, and for the soccer coach 'Azmi Nasar in the 'Aylut stadium. As a side note, it should be mentioned that this quantitative transformation is related as well to the gradual incorporation of memorials as a broader commemorative practice beyond the context of national commemoration: after October 2000 memorials were built also for Arab victims of car accidents.

Another indication of declining caution among Palestinians in Israel is the "migration" of monuments from the cemeteries to the town square. Cemeteries had been considered safer not only because they are less visible than a town square but also because they are organized on a religious basis, and the religious context can dim a nationalist connotation. Therefore, half of the six monuments in the first wave (1976–1983) of monument building were located in cemeteries. In contrast, none of the twenty national memorial monuments built since 1998 are located in cemeteries. Eighteen of them are located at a central site that cannot be missed by occasional visitors to the towns.

Still, none of the surviving memorial monuments is located outside of the jurisdiction of Arab municipalities. The appearance of monuments inside Arab towns and villages is indicative of the relatively autonomous power of the Arab local authorities, but at the same time their absence from the interurban space and the mixed Jewish-Arab cities is an indication of the inability of Palestinian citizens to appropriate these spaces even symbolically. The local orientation of the monuments is expressed as well by the absence of a central monument for the October 2000 events. Every municipality and some of the victims' families took care of the commemoration of their own martyrs, while the other twelve dead were occasionally mentioned on some monuments—but none of the monuments were built as a result of supra-local coordination. The Committee of the October 2000 Martyrs' Families initiated the development of a central commemorative site and the municipality of Kafr Manda even allocated a tract of land in its jurisdiction for the project, but there has not been any further progress.[41]

Another long term trend is the shifting relations between the local and the national. There is still an ongoing contest on the meaning of local identity, between aspirations to frame local pride as an aspect of national pride and the attempts to use localism as a protective measure from the state's antagonism to Palestinian national identity. As a general trend, however, there is a mildly growing tendency to frame local pride as an aspect of national pride. The monuments built following October 2000 are the best examples of this process.

One of the main controversies preceding the building of a monument in almost every locality was related to the question of who should be commemorated. Should the monument commemorate only the local victims of October 2000? Should it mention all the local victims in the history of the conflict? Or should it commemorate the thirteen Palestinian youngsters who were killed in Israel in October 2000? Some of the monuments are the results of private initiatives by the victims' families, and in these monuments there is a tendency to prefer contextualization of the death in the al-Aqsa Intifada, together with the other Arab citizens who were killed. Most of the memorials, however, were built by municipalities, which tended to prefer the multi-generational local pattern, namely, highlighting the historical sacrifice made by the town/village, like in Kafr Kana.

The creators of the monuments of this latter category seem to have used the commemoration of the October 2000 victims to compensate for the local commemoration "deficit." Namely, this was an opportunity to commemorate all the dead in conflict-related events from the same locality. An example of that is the memorial monument built by the Kafr Manda municipality that mentions all the martyrs of Kafr Manda from 1936 until Hasan Bushnaq, who died in October 2000. In contrast, the private memorial monument built by the

Bushnaq family at the junction where their son was killed refers to all thirteen martyrs of October 2000, but not to other Kafr Manda martyrs. In Sakhnin, after some controversy, it was decided to commemorate the thirteen martyrs together, partly because Land Day martyrs already had their own monument and the other dead from 1948 and 1936–1939 are commemorated in an annual memorial exhibition. The monument in 'Arabeh commemorates all thirteen victims of October as well as the village's victims since 1936 and other Palestinians killed in 'Arabeh as part of the conflict. In Kafr Kana, the name of Muhammad Khamaysi, killed in October 2000, was added to the central monument, but the family also initiated a separate monument on the site of his killing dedicated to their son, "The martyr of the al-Aqsa Intifada." Only in one locality, Umm al-Fahm, were the local victims of October 2000 commemorated alone, without the martyrs from other localities.

The two patterns, the diachronic local commemoration (referring to all local martyrs since 1936) and the synchronic supra-local commemoration (referring to the martyrs of October 2000 country-wide), following the model of the Land Day monument), do not necessarily represent an ideological schism. At times the October 2000 commemoration movement triggered pressure from family members of past martyrs who had not been commemorated by a monument,[42] while at other times there was not always sufficient documentation of past martyrs available to facilitate a longer historical framing.

As part of the growing convergence between local and national pride, since 2000 activists in many localities where memorials had not been established yet started to look back at their local past searching for local martyrs who should be commemorated spatially. Demands to establish memorials for these martyrs were made by local activists in Tamra, Majd al-Kurum, Lydda, Tarshiha, and other localities, and the success of these initiatives depended on the readiness of each local authority to join the trend.

The third long-term trend is the Islamization of monuments, which is an outgrowth of the growing importance of Islam as an element in the political identity of the Arabs in Israel, as well as the Islamic spirit of the Second Intifada. This tendency is expressed in the religious texts inscribed on the monuments, the absence of human figures, and icons like the image of the Dome of the Rock mosque. Two exceptions are the monument commemorating 'Abd al-Nasir in Abu Snan, which includes an etching of his image, and the memorial monument built in the village of 'Arabeh, which has a human sculpture in its center. In 'Arabeh the Islamic Movement withdrew from the local popular committee that was established to commemorate October 2000, partly because of the significant involvement of women. As a result, secular forces had more freedom in shaping the monument.[43]

In Nazareth the Islamic Movement demanded to build a copy of an iconic Iranian memorial monument at the entrance to Nazareth. The city hall, dominated by secular parties, rejected this proposal. The formal reason was transportation-related technical obstacles, but according to Mahmoud Yazbak (who was then-chair of the Committee of the October 2000 Martyrs' Families), the main reason was the concern that the monument might upset both the Christians in Nazareth and the Jewish public in Israel.[44]

THE LIMITS OF CHANGE

The declining caution of Palestinian commemoration in Israel as well as the transition toward merging local and national pride on monuments is evident, but they do not constitute an overarching change. These elements are expressed unevenly across different localities, and the old prudent tactics are still practiced—especially around monuments referring to 1948. Significantly, the only two monuments that were both dedicated exclusively to martyrs of 1948 and were based on cross-confessional inclusivity (in 'Aylabun and Shefa'amr) were effaced or distorted. In these same localities the two surviving 1948 monuments are based on communal exclusivity (for Christians in 'Aylabun and Druze in Shefa'amr). These monuments are respected and remain in good shape. In these cases the use of communal rather than national discourse is mobilized to counter the sensitivity of the Palestinian narrative of 1948 in the Israeli sphere.

Furthermore, regarding 1948, it seems that not only monuments for martyrs face objections. In May 2014 a local party in Nazareth, Shabab al-Taghyir (The Youth of Change), built a monument in the memory of the Nakba—a twelve-foot high statue of a key—and located it in the middle of a square in a residential area of Nazareth (without getting municipal permission). The statue was vandalized the following night.[45] Whether it was an independent initiative of local residents or "agents" sent by the Israeli authorities, as implied by the monument builders, memorial monuments for the Nakba are more likely to be vandalized than monuments commemorating most other events.

And yet, the Nakba commemoration project has been successful in some realms, with the March of Return as a major example. However, the failure of the Nakba monuments stands in contrast both to other forms of the Nakba commemoration, as well as to memorial monuments for other events.

To explain this exceptionality, we should first recognize the centrality of memorial monuments to Israeli national identity.[46] It is likely that Israel has the world's highest ratio of monuments per victim,[47] most of them built by Jews to commemorate their victims in the Arab-Israeli conflict. As discussed earlier, some of my Palestinian interviewees attributed their motivation to establish a memorial partly to their desire to challenge Zionist commemoration. Naif Sam'an from 'Aylabun related it to his impression of memorials for Holocaust victims, and Wasel Taha from Kafr Kana stated that he was influenced by his son's question about the IDF memorial in Tiberias. 'Abed Anbetawi, secretary of the Shefa'amr municipality in 1998, considered the monument only a first step on the way to building a larger commemorative center that would include a research institute, museum, and archive. When I interviewed him, he named this future center "Yad La-Banim" (which is the name of the official organization for the memorialization of IDF fallen soldiers).[48] Regardless of whether Palestinians are intentionally aspiring to challenge Zionist commemoration, this is how the Israeli state authorities interpret their commemoration. Since Jewish Israelis utilize monuments as objects that legitimize and validate Israeli sovereignty as well as the ultimate spatial representation of patriotism,[49] the use of monuments by Palestinians to commemorate their victims is deemed threatening, and the authorities react accordingly. Therefore, many Arab citizens still are not enthusiastic to adopt this challenging practice.

It is noteworthy in this context that pan-Arab heroes who are unpopular in the Jewish Israeli collective memory might be widely popular among Palestinian citizens of Israel, but they are rarely commemorated by a monument. The image of former Iraqi president Saddam Hussein might appear on invitations to weddings,[50] but never on a statue in the public sphere. At the same time, Palestinians who are not Israeli citizens commemorated Saddam with monuments in Kafr Thulth and Bir Zeit in the West Bank. The one exception was for the most popular Arab leader in the twentieth century, Gamal Abdel Nasser, who was commemorated by one low-key statue established in Abu Snan in the western Galilee in 2011. The monument was vandalized soon after its establishment.

The uniqueness of the commemoration of the Nakba as compared with other events concerns the way Jewish Israeli anxiety about the Nakba memory is interpreted and processed by Palestinians. Unlike the other events I have discussed, since 2000 only commemorations of the Nakba have continued to elicit tangible threats from the Israeli authorities (see Chapter 7). For the intellectual elite who promoted the commemoration project, a symbolic challenging of the legitimacy of the State of Israel is a motivating factor. Among wider circles of citizens, however, this same challenging is still playing an inhibiting role as they fear the negative impact on their rights.

Significantly, even in those contexts where Palestinian belonging is emphasized, it is done simultaneously with a reminder of the Israeli citizenship of the victims: the identity of those commemorated in Palestinian monuments in Israel draws the geographical boundaries of a national minority within a state. Only two low-key monuments have ever been dedicated to Palestinians killed beyond Israel's borders (the monuments for the Sabra and Shatila massacre discussed earlier); they are not well known among Palestinians in Israel, and one of them, in Kafr Kana, is even unknown to most of the local residents. The Green Line, the pre-1967 borders of Israel, has a tangible impact on the monuments. It conveys a consistent distinction of the Palestinian citizens not only from Jewish Israelis but also from other Palestinians. In the next chapter we turn to the marginal status of Palestinian non-citizens in Palestinian commemoration inside Israel.

6 ON THE MARGINS OF COMMEMORATION

ALTHOUGH THE RELATIVE IMPORTANCE of the four major dates on the political calendar of Palestinians in Israel keeps changing, they are easy to identify in the second decade of the twenty-first century. Beyond the canonic events and the martyrs commemorated at recurring annual, mass processions, the historical remembrance of Palestinians in Israel includes many other dates and events, situated in various degrees of distance from the core of the canon. What makes them marginal might be one or more of the following: they have been commemorated mainly locally, without cross-regional participation; they have been commemorated mainly by a specific party or movement; the commemoration has been limited to press coverage, and the memory was not embodied by mass rallies; or the embodied commemoration in the form of mass rallies did not last more than a decade.

Some examples of local annual commemoration with a national connotation but with limited participation were mentioned in previous chapters, for example: the people of Kafr Bir'im have commemorated their expulsion by a parade or an art festival; there are annual commemorations of the massacres of 1948 in 'Aylabun and 2005 in Shefa'amr. Other examples include: the "Sandala" massacre in September 1957, referring to the death of fifteen school students from the explosion of an IDF live shell that was left in a field near the village. More than fifty years after the actual event, the people of Sandala organized an annual memorial ceremony, which has taken place for several years. The Committee of Prisoners (a sub-committee of the FUC) sanctioned the memorial service in 2013, but only leaders of the two factions of the Islamic Movements came to speak. In another example, in September 1961 Israeli soldiers killed five Palestinian citizens from Haifa, Sakhnin, and Umm al-Fahm who were at-tempting to cross the border into the Gaza Strip. Tens of thousands of Palestin-ians attended their funerals, and for several years after the event *al-Ittihad* made reference to the anniversary of the killings. Gradually, the protest over the event was absorbed into the Kafr Qasim commemoration, and in most years memo-rial ceremonies were attended primarily by family members. A more politicized event took place on the fiftieth anniversary of the event at the Midan theater in Haifa, but only several dozen people attended the memorial evening.

Among Palestinians in Israel there are various examples of partisan events on the political calendar, spanning the breadth of the ideological spectrum. Given the prominence of the Communist Party among Palestinian intellectuals until the 1970s, foremost on this political calendar were International Workers' Day (1 May), an important day of political mobilization characterized by mass dem-onstrations, the anniversary of the 1917 Soviet revolution (6 November), and the celebration of the Soviet victory in World War II on 8 May. In the late 1960s and 1970s, *al-Ittihad* dedicated to these three socialist holidays much more space and special graphics (photos, large red headlines) than the space and visual ef-fects dedicated to the Kafr Qasim massacre anniversary. In general, *al-Ittihad* has been obsessed with memorial days. Throughout the years one could find annual references not only to major communist dates, but also to many minor events, such as the birthdays of Marx and Lenin, the day of Rosa Luxembourg's assas-sination, the day the atomic bomb destroyed Hiroshima, the Cuban revolution, the 1958 revolution in Iraq, the centennial celebration of the commune in Paris in 1870, and others. With the rise of pan-Arabism, the Free Officers' revolution in Egypt (23 July 1952) began to be celebrated by editorials in secular newspa-pers and later in summer camps of the NDA (see Chapter 8). The anniversary of Abdel Nasser's death has received similar attention in the secular press.[1]

Since the entrance of the Islamic Movement into the sphere of national politics, the movement has tried to use elements from Islamic history for po-litical mobilization within a national framing. From 1985 until the early 1990s, the movement organized a mass rally to commemorate the Battle of Badr, a key event in early Islam that is remembered as a decisive victory and a turn-ing point in the power balance between the prophet Muhammad and his op-ponents. After the 1996 split of the Islamic Movement, the battle was celebrated only in low-key local events. Instead, from that year on the northern faction of the movement has organized a mass festival every fall with tens of thousands of participants under the title "Al-Aqsa is in Danger."

None of the above mentioned commemorations, though, are characterized by the combination of consistent country-wide attention, cross-party support, and cross-confessional participation—as the four major anchors of the political calendar do. While the marginal status of these dates and martyrs might be circumstantial, there are three dimensions of a more systematic pattern of marginalization. First, temporally—the period of the British Mandate is certainly part of contemporary Palestinian collective memory, but the events and martyrs who had great importance then did not gain a tangible presence on the political calendar, nor are they widely commemorated by monuments. The second dimension is thematic: as a general tendency, Palestinians in Israel have remained a safe distance from the armed struggle, especially when it targeted civilians. Therefore, they have rarely officially commemorated persons or themes related to the armed struggle. Third, and perhaps most important, is the geo-political dimension. Palestinian non-citizens of Israel have been represented in an extremely marginal way in public commemoration by Palestinian citizens of Israel. The second and third dimensions clearly distinguish the commemoration practiced by Palestinian citizens of Israel from that of other Palestinians. They clearly illustrate the power of citizenship to shape consciousness, even when this citizenship is truncated and keeps its carriers in constant subordination, and even when the collective narrative of the group is diametrically opposed to the official narrative of the state.

THE MARTYRS OF THE 1930S AND THE GREAT REVOLT

As discussed in Chapter 1, elaborating a distinct martyrology was an important tool in the discursive delineation of the boundaries of Palestinian particularism under British rule. The martyrs of the mandate period did not disappear from the popular memory of Palestinians in Israel. The leading role of the peasants in the revolt and the role of popular poetry in nurturing the martyrs' memory partially protected this memory from the effects of the collapse of the Palestinian urban centers. The reemergence of a militant Palestinian national movement in the late 1960s helped revive Palestinian interest in the 1936–1939 revolt and its martyrs.

The Communist Party (under its various titles), which had unquestionably dominated the Palestinian discourse in Israel in the 1970s and the 1980s, shared with the PLO an anti-colonial perspective and the Arab-Palestinian national narrative. It shared as well the socialist vision of the Popular Front for the Liberation of Palestine (PFLP, a Marxist organization affiliated with the PLO) although the political status of communist leaders in Israel oriented them toward less revolutionary rhetoric and practice. Two emerging intellectual leaders, Ghassan Kanafani (1936–1972) in Lebanon and Tawfiq Zayyad (1929–1994) in Israel, belonged to the same generation who were too young to take part in the Great Revolt or in the dramatic events that preceded it, but who nevertheless absorbed the related mythology from their social environment. In fact, both men helped to canonize a 1930s martyrology.

Kanafani published a seminal work about the revolt[2] and contributed to the endurance of its mythology, particularly the myth of 'Izz al-Din al-Qassam. This publication was part of the particular tendency of secular and leftist Palestinian groups to adopt al-Qassam's image as a role model.[3] Zayyad, a poet and one of the emerging leaders of the Communist Party in Israel, formalized the remembrance of the martyr-poet Nuh Ibrahim[4] as well as other poets of the revolution.[5] Zayyad explained the political importance of his project: "The popular poem of the Palestinian rebel 'Awd, one of the heroes of our people in 1936, while on the scaffold in the Acre prison, has the ability to instill in the human soul sacrifice and self-denial more than thousands of lectures, speeches and poems."[6] In the late 1970s, the Damascus-based music band, Firqat Aghanı al-'Ashiqın (founded in 1977), performed Nuh Ibrahim's poem about the three 1930 martyrs, "Min sijn 'Akka," as a song. This recording revived the popularity of the poem, and it has been played at Palestinian weddings.[7]

Land Day events in 1976 provided further momentum to martyrological commemoration. Two years later, in July 1978, al-Ittihad published an elegy commemorating the thirtieth anniversary of the death of 'Abd al-Rahim Mahmud, a prominent poet during the Great Revolt who was killed in battle in 1948;[8] it published another article on the thirty-fifth anniversary of his death. Around this time nationalist activists established the al-Sawt publishing house in Nazareth, which decided to collect and publish Mahmud's poems and to erect a tombstone on his grave.[9] To a large extent this decision was an attempt to join a broader Palestinian trend: books dedicated to Mahmud had been published earlier in Beirut (1974) and in Nablus (1975). The "Israeli" collection of poems was finally published in 1985 by the Center for the Renewal of Arab Heritage in Taybeh, and the tomb was officially unveiled in 1986.[10]

The commemoration of Mahmud was part of a growing renewed interest in the 1936–1939 revolt. In April 1986 al-Ittihad dedicated its editorial to the fiftieth anniversary of the revolt. That same year the local branch of the DFPE in Tamra worked with the town council to establish a committee for commemorating

Nuh Ibrahim, who was buried in the local cemetery. The committee collected testimonies from elders who remembered the revolt and the circumstances of Ibrahim's death and initiated the publication of a book in his memory.[11]

Compared with the commemoration of the revolt, the reference to the three Palestinians executed in 1930, required more caution. From a mainstream Jewish-Israeli perspective, this commemoration was outrageous: the three men had been sentenced to death for their part in the massacre of Jews in Hebron and in Safad/Tsfat in August 1929, an event which became a constitutive myth of victimhood in the Zionist narrative. Residents of Acre continued to visit the graves of Hijazi, Jamjum, and al-Zir even after 1948, and these tombstones have remained in good shape.[12] The awareness of the way Jewish Israelis remember the 1929 events, however, must have played a role in their omission from the political calendar and from high–profile, embodied commemoration. Interestingly, the three rarely have been mentioned by *al-Ittihad*, even during the renaissance of 1930s remembrance in the 1980s.[13] Only the post-October 2000 era enabled public commemoration of the execution. In 2005 the Tawfiq Zayyad Center (unofficially related to the Communist Party) organized a one-time commemorative parade on the seventy-fifth anniversary of the execution. About 150 people participated in the parade, but it was not repeated in the years that followed (see Chapter 7).

Similarly, reference to ʿIzz al-Din al-Qassam in the press became more common. By the mid-1980s both the communist *al-Ittihad* and the nationalist *al-Watan* began dedicating articles to al-Qassam around the anniversary of his death. It is noteworthy that during the first Intifada in the West Bank and the Gaza Strip, the United Leadership in the territories announced a general strike on the anniversary of al-Qassam's death, a sharp contrast to his low-profile commemoration inside Israel. Al-Qassam's grave has been a contested site for years. It was vandalized even before 1948,[14] but the escalation in the Israeli-Palestinian conflict since 2000 and frequent reference to al-Qassam in the media gave his memory increased public attention.[15] The result was more cases of vandalism and more clean-up and renovation campaigns led by the Islamic Movement. A related development was the 2012 intention of the Israel National Roads Company to install a sewer line on the Muslim cemetery that houses al-Qassam's tomb.[16] Protests by the Islamic Movement and Arab Knesset members from other parties prevented the tomb's destruction, and the Islamic Movement used the threat to further mobilize activists to maintain and protect it.

While reviewing this list of local and partisan initiatives, one should ask to what extent this martyrology serves as a mobilizing force for continuous cross-confessional and cross-party popular political action, as in the case of the commemoration of the martyrs of Kafr Qasim, Land Day, and October 2000. The number of documented public commemorative events in memory of the 1930s martyrs among the Palestinian citizens of Israel since 1948 is small, and they usually took the form of low-scale gatherings for poetry reading. In fact, the number of participants in all these events combined does not reach the number of participants in one annual event of any of the four anchors of the political calendar.

The results of my 2008 survey point in a similar direction. When asked to choose the most important three out of seven events suggested to them, only 12 percent picked the Great Revolt. This figure constituted about half of those who picked the second least-mentioned event, the Oslo Accords (23%), chosen far less than the Nakba (74%), the Kafr Qasim massacre (46%), October 2000 (40%), Land Day (39%), and the 1967 war (39%). This low frequency cannot be ascribed only to what cognitive psychologists call the "recency effect" since the Oslo Accords were signed only fifteen years prior but this event was not included in the choices of 77 percent of respondents. In addition, the second- and the third-oldest events (the Nakba and the Kafr Qasim massacre), were the first and the second most commonly mentioned events, respectively.

The low frequency of mentioning the revolt is both the reason and the result of its exclusion from the political calendar. Although Palestinian intellectuals have attempted to revive the legacy of the revolt as a mobilizing heroic political myth, as described earlier, they have not included it in the annual commemorative cycle. In addition, they did not have a compulsory education system that would support the memory of the revolt (See Chapter 8). Another possible reason for the weak status of the revolt in contemporary Palestinian collective memory is that the dramatic effects of the Nakba effaced or blurred many of its traces. The implications of the 1967 war, for example, are highly relevant to contemporary politics. As a result of all these reasons, the revolt that resulted in more than five thousand Palestinians deaths, was more comprehensive in its geographical scope than any past or future Palestinian uprising, and left a rich legacy of martyrological poetry, nevertheless remained marginal in the historical remembrance of Palestinians in Israel. Elite efforts to maintain this remembrance through alternative education channels are discussed in Chapter 8.

A SAFE DISTANCE FROM THE ARMED STRUGGLE

In the mid-1990s anthropologist Ted Swedenburg described the popular memory of Palestinians who live under Israeli rule as a battlefield between a state apparatus that attempted to suppress nationalist remembrance and the efforts of the PLO to forge a "national-popular" past by recalling memories of unified national struggle. Since the PLO lacked the apparatus of state power, it was particularly dependent on the support and goodwill of the Palestinian masses.[17] While I do not deny the important role of these two actors and the analysis of the dynamics between them, Swedenburg's analysis omits one element of the "triadic nexus" of nationalizing state, national minority, and external homeland (which in the Palestinian case is an external, national, institutional infrastructure).[18] In this particular case, the Palestinian citizens of Israel are a vital group of actors who have been playing in this contested terrain and developing their own political institutions, including political parties and movements, as well as cross-partisan leadership organizations. These actors, each with their own agendas, are no less important than the Israeli state or the Palestinian nationalist leadership in shaping Palestinian popular memory inside Israel. In the 1970s and the 1980s, nowhere was the distance between the PLO and the Palestinian institutions inside Israel more pronounced than in their relation to the armed struggle. Following the Oslo Accords and the establishment of the PNA in 1994, the gaps between the two sides was narrowed but it is still evident.

Inside Israel, Palestinian political leaders have adopted a very careful treatment of the armed struggle and have tended to avoid the inclusion of military myths in the political calendar or on memorial monuments. This cautious rhetoric has been projected backward to the 1948 war and earlier, as evidence by the marginalization of Jamjum, al-Zir, and Hijazi, the three men tried and hanged by Britain for their role in the 1929 riots. Another example is 'Abd al-Qadir al-Husayni, the charismatic military leader killed in battle in1948, who is commonly glorified by both PNA- and Hamas-affiliated media,[19] but rarely by the Arabic media inside Israel. In 2008 a statue of al-Husayni was placed in the West Bank village of Bir Zeit, but inside Israel there is no memorial monument dedicated to him. This absence might be explained partly by the fact that the Husaynis have no representation among the Palestinians in Israel. However, the rare attempts to include al-Husayni in the martyrology of the Palestinians inside Israel do not seem to be very successful. In 1986 the nationalist Progressive List bulletin, *al-Watan*, published an article that commemorated the thirty-eighth anniversary of his martyrdom, and a delegation of the Progressive List visited his tomb as part of the party's attempts to display a greater loyalty to Palestinian national mythology than the communist-led DFPE.[20] Notably, the memorial pilgrimage did not become a tradition. In my 2008 survey (see Introduction), when interviewees were asked to mention four persons whom they consider to be the most important in the history of the country in the last one hundred years, not a single one mentioned al-Husayni.

Furthermore, during the heyday of plane hijackings and the first PLO attacks on Jewish Israeli civilians in the late 1960s, al-Ittihad condemned them unambiguously.[21] The coverage in al-Ittihad of the massacre of eleven Israeli athletes during 1972 Munich Olympic Games was very similar to the line adopted by the Hebrew media. By extension, the Communist Party has carefully avoided adopting the broader military martyrology of the Palestinian organizations. Since 1969 the Fatah movement, the main faction within the PLO, has celebrated 7 January as "Martyrs' Day." The PFLP has its own Martyrs' Day on 9 March, commemorating the killing of its leader Muhammad al-Aswad (known as the Che Guevara of Gaza), who was killed by Israeli soldiers on that date in 1973. Although individuals inside Israel have participated sporadically in the 7th of January ceremonies in PNA territory since 1994, neither the 7th of January nor the 9th of March have become a component of the political calendar of any Palestinian party inside Israel.

Another crucial example in this context is a battle that took place in the village of Karameh ("honor" in Arabic) in the Jordan valley on 21 March 1968 between the Israeli army and the Jordanian artillery, supported by some Fatah fighters. The event became a pivotal myth in the emergence of a new Palestinian political identity, and for years afterward, the event was celebrated by the Fatah movement as the Battle of Karameh, as an incredible triumph and a turning point in Palestinian history.[22] The Karameh myth-creators emphasized self-sacrifice, the superiority of spiritual over physical power, and an independent, self-reliant Palestinian resistance in sharp contrast to the humiliating defeat of the Arab armies nine months earlier in the 1967 war.

Even when the myth was at its political zenith in the 1970s, however, and even with rapprochement between the PLO and the communists in Israel in the middle of this decade, there is no evidence that the latter commemorated Karameh in any form. The Palestinians in Israel were not active in this chapter of Palestinian resistance and had relatively narrow exposure to the glorifying rhetoric that followed the event. At the same time, this does not mean that the story itself was unknown. A single reference to Karameh in al-Ittihad in 1975 is evidence that the reporter assumed a previous knowledge of Karameh among his readers.[23] During an Israeli attack on Palestinian armed organizations in south Lebanon in May 1975, the newspaper titled the resistance: "Karameh instead of Black September," implying that this time the Arab fighters would be victorious. Interestingly, the only further reference to Karameh in the report appears in the subtitle where the current fight is described as similar to the **Jordanian** Karameh battle. This is significant because the Fatah tendency at the time was to downplay the role of the kingdom's artillery units and to over-emphasize the role of the Palestinian fighters. *Al-Ittihad* expressed satisfaction with Israel's failure but avoided giving the credit to the PLO, either because of self-censorship or because of a latent competition with the later.

In 1985 *al-Ittihad* published a weekly column called "Memorial Days" in which it listed major historical dates for the following week. Between 20 March, dedicated to the Tunisian Independence Day, and 22 March, dedicated to the foundation of the Communist Party in Laos, 21 March remained blank (similarly, *al-Ittihad* skipped 17 June—the day of 1930 executions). The next reference to Karameh in *al-Ittihad* was on the nineteenth anniversary of the battle in 1987. This time, in a minuscule sixty-four-word report, the newspaper described the battle as a Palestinian achievement.

Land Day, which occurred at the time when the Karameh myth was most powerful among Palestinians elsewhere, was crucial for the Palestinians in Israel. This event helped them to acquire a collective self-image with a solid component of heroism, and afforded them a place of honor in the internal Palestinian and Arab hierarchy without risky association with the armed struggle. It is noteworthy that the six Palestinians who died on Land Day were not the only Palestinians killed by Israel during this period. The ten months that preceded Land Day were very tense along the border with Lebanon, and thirty-one members of Palestinian guerilla organizations were killed during various operations on or beyond the border inside Israel. Although many of them were glorified by the PLO's *Falastin al-thawra*, they received little attention in *al-Ittihad*. Whenever Israeli civilians were killed in those operations, the communists were quick to condemn them. During the same period, a similar number of Palestinians were killed in Israeli retaliation attacks on Lebanese territory.[24] None of them has ever been publicly commemorated inside Israel.

Between 1972 and 1979 Israel assassinated more than thirteen senior leaders of Palestinian organizations. *Al-Ittihad* gave little attention to their memory with only two exceptions. Ghassan Kanafani (assassinated on 8 July 1972) and Kamal

Nasir (assassinated in May 1973). *Al-Ittihad*'s adoption of the two most likely stems from the fact that the two were writers and intellectuals who took no part in attacks against Israeli civilians. After Land Day the paper eulogized Kanafani on some subsequent anniversaries of his assassination, and the municipal theater of Nazareth organized annual cultural gatherings in his memory.

In contrast to the Communist Party's extreme caution, during the 1980s the Progressive List and the Sons of the Village consistently attempted to unify the collective memory of Palestinians in Israel and elsewhere. *Al-Watan*, the Progressive List's bulletin that was published from 1985 to 1987, commemorated some "forbidden" dates, such as Black September and 1 January, referring to this date in 1965 when Fatah launched its first armed-struggle operation (known as *yawm al-intilaqa*, Launching Day). *Al-Ittihad*, however, ignored this date until the 1980s, and even then it provided only minimal coverage of the celebrations in the occupied territories. The only time *al-Ittihad* dedicated an op-ed column to Launching Day was in 1984, following the establishment of the Progressive List and likely as a result of the pressure of this political competition. Still, that exceptional text was not signed by any of the editorial board members, but by the obscured nickname "Abu 'Adi."[25] *Al-Watan* also commemorated the anniversary of the death of 'Abd al-Qadir al-Husayni in 1948 and of PLO leaders such as Fahd Qawasma.

Later, *al-Raya*, the bulletin of the Sons of the Village movement, commemorated the first anniversary of Israel's 1988 assassination of Abu-Jihad (Khalil al-Wazir), a PLO leader and a symbol of the armed struggle. As evident by this commemoration, *al-Raya* did not keep a safe distance from the armed struggle, and in early 1989 it was shut down by the Israeli government. However, neither the Progressive List nor the Sons of the Village were able to turn their rhetorical commemoration of Palestinian fighters into mass demonstrations attended by thousands of marching bodies, such as the form the commemorations took in Kafr Qasim and on Land Day.

Another prominent example of a safe distance from the armed struggle is the reference in the Palestinian press in Israel to suicide attacks, which began inside Israel in the mid-1990s. In sharp contrast to Palestinian newspapers in the West Bank and the Gaza Strip, Palestinian newspapers in Israel usually did not refer to the perpetrators as *shuhada'* (martyrs), a label that is accorded to any Palestinian who dies as a result of the Israeli Occupation. Indeed, the Palestinian press inside Israel consistently avoided this language if the individual in question attacked civilians (as opposed to soldiers),[26] but it applied the title without hesitation to Palestinian citizens who were accidental victims of sui-cide attacks. For example, following the first such attack against Israeli civilians in 'Afula on 6 April 1994, which *al-Ittihad* labeled a massacre, it pointedly re-ferred to the Palestinian accidental casualty, Fadia Shilbi, as a "martyr," and the Jewish casualties as "victims." Furthermore, unlike Palestinian newspapers in the occupied territories, the paper also listed the names of the Jewish victims of the attack and printed personal details about each of them.

Yahya 'Ayyash, the chief bomb maker of Hamas, known for planning the at-tack in 'Afula as well as several other deadly suicide attacks before being killed by Israel in 1996, became a national hero among Palestinians in the West Bank and the Gaza Strip, with several streets and squares in Palestinian cities named after him. 'Ayyash, however, is absent from the pantheon of martyrs of Pales-tinian citizens inside Israel, and it is uncommon to find public praise of him.[27] 'Ayyash is viewed differently by Palestinians on the two sides of the Green Line, and his positive image among occupied non-citizens became a divisive issue in the relations between them and their fellow Palestinians in Israel.

This divide is reflective of a deeper cleavage between Palestinians inside and outside Israel about the history and ongoing question of armed struggle. The former have overwhelmingly rejected violence as a potential means to gain their rights. In a 2012 survey of the adult Palestinian population within the Green Line, only 16.6 percent of the respondents agreed or tended to agree that they and their fellow citizens should use all means, including violence, to im-prove their conditions. While this figure was a significant increase from a simi-lar survey conducted in 2003 (5.4 percent), non-violent legal means were still much more popular in 2012, including: general strikes (81%), protest abroad (71%), boycotting the parliamentary elections (41.3%).[28] In addition, the histo-rian Hillel Cohen, in his comparison of attitudes of Arab education students in Israel and in the West Bank, found that the Palestinian students in Israel were significantly more likely to view Palestinian violence in a negative light and to agree with both statements, that Palestinians (in addition to Israel) have com-mitted war crimes and that force will not solve the Israeli-Palestinian conflict.[29]

Another comparative project that revealed this gap was conducted by three Palestinian groups inside and outside Israel.[30] In 2008 these groups joined to-gether to produce a booklet entitled "Sixty Years from the Nakba, Sixty Terms on the Nakba." The editors solicited 150 terms related to the Nakba from Palestin-ian high school students in Israel, the West Bank, Syria, and Lebanon. As a proj-ect aiming to bridge the distance between Palestinians, the booklet makes no mention of the differences between the perspectives of students from different countries. However, the booklet editors did observe a significant difference in the terms chosen by the students surveyed, depending on their location. Those from the refugee camps in Syria and Lebanon focused on the armed struggle and the Right of Return. Those from the West Bank tended to refer more to the destroyed Palestinian villages. Finally, Palestinian students from Israel focused on cultural aspects and tended more to refer to poets and authors.[31] This variance reflects fundamental differences in the political and educational experiences of Palestinians in different contexts; unlike Palestinian refugees or occupied Palestinians, for the Palestinian citizens of Israel, a civic-political struggle is still available as an option.

To be sure, as in other areas, since 2000 there has been a noticeable change in the way armed struggle is treated in Palestinian commemorations. Land Day 2014, for example, focused on "security prisoners" who are Palestinian citizens of Israel. Sa'ada Ighbariyya, the mother of two brothers from Mushayrifeh who took part in the killing of three IDF soldiers in 1992, was among the speakers on the podium. Flashing backward to the 1986 commemoration of the Kafr Qasim massacre in which the mayor assertively distanced his town from a similar operation (see Chapter 2), the far-reaching rhetorical change is evident.

EXCLUDING PALESTINIANS WHO ARE NOT ISRAELI CITIZENS

In Chapter 2 I referred to the exclusion of Palestinians killed in the 1956 Gaza Strip massacres from the commemorations of Palestinians inside Israel. Years later, however, the Communist Party used the memory of these massacres for political purposes, but to delegitimize a political rival, and not as a unifying national myth. In the 1984 elections, when the Progressive List emerged as the first non-Zionist electoral challenge to the communists, *al-Ittihad* attacked the military record of Matti Peled, a peace activist and senior candidate of the Progressive List who had served as the IDF military commander of the Gaza Strip in 1956–1957.[32] The editors awkwardly tried to connect Peled to the massacres, ignoring the fact that he was appointed as military commander of the region only after they had occurred. After Peled withdrew from political life in 1988, *al-Ittihad* ceased to express any interest in the Gaza Strip massacres. However, this temporary mobilization of the 1956 Gaza Strip massacres in the context of inter-party rivalry illustrates that their memory has been available for political use, and therefore we must acknowledge that their omission from the commemorative repertoire of Palestinians in Israel is an active political choice.

Another prominent relevant exclusion is the massacre of thousands of Palestinians in Tal al-Za'tar (Lebanon) by Syrian forces and their allies in August 1976,[33] only four months after Land Day. Together with the Sabra and Shatila massacre, Tal al-Za'tar came to dominate Palestinian national history, at least in Lebanon.[34] The two massacres, however, certainly do not dominate the history of the Palestinians in Israel. *Al-Ittihad* extensively covered the battle in Tal al-Za'tar immediately after its occurrence, and glorified it as "the symbol of sacrifice and steadfastness."[35] By the second anniversary, however, *al-Ittihad* only republished a short report on the commemoration of the event in Lebanon that had been published previously in the PLO bulletin. Furthermore, Tal al-Za'tar failed to gain an embodied commemoration such as rallies or processions, and in the long term the event remained outside of the commemorative repertoire of Palestinians in Israel.

In contrast, the footprint of the Sabra and Shatila massacre in September 1982 lasted longer. Following the massacre the Land Committee decided to establish an annual memorial day. On the first anniversary a general strike was announced, three thousand people participated in a parade in Nazareth, and some smaller memorial parades took place in other villages and towns in the Galilee. A similar pattern characterized the second anniversary. From the third anniversary, the memorial rallies took place on a low scale. On the third anniversary, *al-Ittihad* reported on the general strike and mass demonstration in Lebanon, but to illustrate the participation of Palestinians in Israel, the newspaper used an archive photo that was taken right after the massacre, three years earlier. The minor memorial gathering continued until the early 1990s but since then, the massacre has been commemorated mainly textually by the press.

The difference between the relative endurance of the commemoration of Sabra and Shatila and the silence regarding the Tal al-Za'tar massacre indicates once again that Palestinian commemoration in Israel is first of all a form of protest of citizens against their state. In Sabra and Shatila Israeli responsibility was much more evident, and accordingly the event was followed by large-scale protest in Israel, far beyond the boundaries of the Palestinian public. The massacre was adopted by left-wing Jewish activists, both Zionists and non-Zionists, as a symbol of the moral bankruptcy of Ariel Sharon, Minister of Defense who planned the war, and the ruling Likud party. The hundreds of thousands of Jewish Israelis who came to Tel Aviv to protest the war following the massacre legitimized the commemoration of the massacre in the Israeli public sphere. *Al-Ittihad* explicitly mentioned this 1982 mass demonstration in an editorial protesting the high fine imposed on an Arab boy wearing a shirt with the words "Sabra and Shatila" during the second anniversary of the massacre. This demonstration was presented as proof that protesting the massacre was a legitimate act in the Israeli public sphere.[36] Small-scale commemoration of the event among Jewish Israelis continued for several years, and on the fifth anniversary of the massacre, a small commemorative rally took place in Tel Aviv. Furthermore, a popular 1980s Hebrew song commemorates the massacre ("Emtsa September," written by Astar Shamir). This public legitimacy to protest the massacre is probably a major reason for its exceptional status as the only event that took place outside of Israel that was almost included in the canonized political calendar of the Palestinians inside. Furthermore, unlike many other cases of large-scale killing of Palestinian non-citizens, the victims of Sabra and Shatila are the only ones commemorated by monuments as two monuments in their memory were established in Laqiyya and Kafr Kana (see Chapter 4).

The distinction between expressions of solidarity and long-term inclusion in politicized commemoration is evident as well in the case of the martyrs of the first Palestinian Intifada. This Intifada was mostly unarmed in its initial stages, and Palestinian victims gained much attention from the Palestinian media in Israel. Newspapers counted the dead, published their photos, told their stories, glorified them, and took part in the pan-Palestinian project of myth-making. *Al-Ittihad* even dedicated a daily column to personal stories of martyrs, publishing one story of a martyr per day. The terminology used in *al-Ittihad* in this coverage was virtually indistinguishable from that used in the occupied territories.[37] In 1988 the conventions of at least two Arab parties, the Progressive List and the Arab Democratic Party, opened with a moment of silence in the memory of the "martyrs of the Intifada."[38] These immediate expressions of solidarity and sympathy were adopted by other parties, but they did not leave any traces on the Palestinian political calendar and spatial commemoration inside Israel.

Especially telling in this context are the riots that broke out in the square at the Haram al-Sharif/Temple Mount in Jerusalem on 8 October 1990, during which Israeli police killed between seventeen and twenty-three Palestinians. The victims were commemorated on a stone slab at the entrance to the Muslim cemetery near the Lions' Gate in East Jerusalem. Inside the Green Line, however, there is no spatial commemoration of the event, and the date was not included on the political calendar.

Significantly, however, one of the victims of the Haram al-Sharif massacre, 'Adnan Khalaf Mawasi from Tamra, was an Israeli citizen. With the proliferation of memorial monuments since October 2000, his family demanded that the Tamra local council establish a memorial monument for him. When the mayor was unsupportive, the local branch of the NDA adopted the martyr, and in 2009 the party started a campaign to commemorate him. A major argument in the campaign was that Tamra deserved to have its own martyr like other towns. The martyr's brother stated: "In the last parade in 'Arabeh [referring to the commemorative parade for the October 2000 events] I heard a conversation between the town's youth wondering: 'Why don't we have a martyr in our town?' [. . .] and I cannot understand why the martyrs are commemorated in the other towns except in Tamra."[39] Clearly, since the commemoration of Al-Aqsa Day refers to the events that occurred inside the Green Line in October 2000, "the other towns" are those towns inside pre-1967 Israel commemorating their martyrs, who presumably gain much prestige by this commemoration. The justification for building a memorial, then, was primarily the potential benefit for Tamra in the internal competition of prestige, whereas the motivation to commemorate the massacre of 1990 (as opposed to the individual martyr) is marginal.

The 1994 massacre in Hebron is another case that illustrates once more the difference between empathy and solidarity, on the one hand, and the active inclusion of martyrs in a repertoire of political commemoration. On 25 February 1994 an American-born Jewish settler entered the mosque in the Tomb of the Patriarchs in Hebron and killed twenty-nine Palestinians with an automatic weapon. The PNA, Fatah, and Hamas media has commemorated the event annually by retelling the story of the massacre and interviewing eye witnesses and relatives of the martyrs. Except in the first years after the massacre, the Arab media in Israel was less outspoken in relation to the massacre.

In the riots that took place outside and inside the Green Line immediately following the massacre, nineteen Palestinians were killed, including one Israeli citizen from Rahat, Muhammad Abu Jami'. A year later, *al-Ittihad* reported that the Rahat municipal council commemorated his death with a popular procession to his grave and the planting of an olive tree in the cemetery.[40] That same year, commemorative demonstrations for the massacre itself were reported in various locations in the West Bank (Hebron, Na'alin)[41] but not anywhere inside the Green Line. In Hebron thousands of Palestinians have participated in the annual commemorative prayer every year. Inside Israel, the only institutional commemoration of the event refers particularly to the martyr from Rahat. In 1998, following his family's request, the Rahat local council established a memorial pillar near the Rahat city hall to commemorate him. The text on the pillar mentions that he was martyred following the massacre in the Tomb of the Patriarchs, but there is no reference to other Palestinians killed in the massacre itself or in the riots that followed it.

If the singling out of the martyrs in Tamra and Rahat might be explained simply as local bereavement and pride and not as a marker of the socio-geographical boundaries of a trapped minority, the monuments commemorating al-Aqsa Day provide unmistakable visual representation of this socio-geographical cartography. The monument in Figure 4 is one out of ten memorials that Palestinian citizens of Israel built to commemorate the martyrs of October 2000. It is located in Jat, a Palestinian town in the Triangle. At first glance, the memorial seems to convey only an unambiguous and overarching commitment to Palestinian nationalism. The map of British-Mandate Palestine, the colors of the Palestinian flag, and the drawing of the Dome of the Rock are all well-known icons of Palestinian national identity. The red text underneath (not on the frame) reads "Palestine"; the red text in the middle indicates the monument's title: *The Martyrs of the al-Aqsa Intifada*. The names of the thirteen martyrs are written in black and green, and an arrow leads from each name to the location of the person's death on the map (which with the exception of one case is also the town or village where the martyr was born and raised). What is most significant about this monument, however, is its omissions. During the exact same time frame, forty-seven other Palestinians were killed by Israeli security forces in the West Bank and the Gaza Strip.

Furthermore, the events of late September and early October 2000 were only the beginning of the al-Aqsa Intifada, in which more than 3,300 Palestinians were killed over the course of four years. It is clear that the meaningful dividing line between the martyrs commemorated on this monument and the other Palestinians killed in the Intifada is their Israeli citizenship. All the monument's martyrs were killed within the internationally recognized borders of Israel, and all but one were Israeli citizens. The exception, Muslih Abu Jarad, was a resident of the Gaza Strip who worked in Umm al-Fahm. He was among three Palestinians killed there and, thus, was included on the list of martyrs. Other victims, like Mahmud Musa'ad who died two days later and only eight miles away but beyond the Green Line, were left off the monument in Jat (and, as we shall see, every other monument inside Israel). In other words, according to this monument, the killing of Palestinians in Israel constituted a single event while the killing of other Palestinians—even though occurring on the same days—are considered as other, separate events.

Figure 4. Memorial monument, including the names of those killed in October 2000 inside the Green Line, entitled *The Martyrs of the al-Aqsa Intifada*, in Jat. Source: Photo by the author.

The monument in Jat is only one example of monuments built to commemorate the Palestinian martyrs of October 2000. By referring only to the victims who died inside the Green Line while ignoring the forty-seven Palestinians who were killed beyond it on the exact same days, these monuments delineate the Green Line as the relevant boundary for political identification. Even the familial monument commemorating Hasan Bushnaq in Kafr Manda, which refers to the victims as martyrs who died in the al-Aqsa Battle (indicating solidarity with the uprising of Palestinians in the West Bank and Gaza Strip), includes only the thirteen victims who died inside the Green Line. In other words, even a private monument, which is relatively free of the pressures applied on a state-dependent municipality, and even when the text explicitly expressed solidarity with Palestinians elsewhere, still creates distinctions between Palestinians in Israel and other Palestinians.

THE SIGNIFICANCE OF OMISSION

The significance of this phenomenon is two-fold. First, the culture of martyrological commemoration among Palestinians in Israel is related to the emergence of a political identity with strong affinity to the Palestinian struggle outside Israel but with distinct characteristics and agendas. Palestinian martyrological commemoration inside Israel, from the massacre in Kafr Qasim to October 2000, is part of a struggle for civic equality, and therefore Palestinians who are not citizens are usually excluded from it. The Future Vision Documents, published by Arab intellectuals and NGO activists in Israel in 2006 and 2007, reflect this political orientation: Israel within the Green Line is considered a *fait accompli*, but its character as a nationalizing Jewish state is challenged.[42] The exclusion of other Palestinians from Palestinian commemoration inside Israel is exclusion from the process of the public politicization of death, not from emotional sympathy or national solidarity. It does not mean that Palestinians in Israel are "less Palestinian" or are indifferent to Palestinian victims. This exclusion does mean, however, that internal boundaries among Palestinians, created by the separation imposed by different political realities, are very meaningful and shape diverse collective imaginations and diverse forms of struggle.

Second, Palestinian commemoration inside pre-1967 Israel is part of an attempt to confront, as well as to dialogue with Jewish citizens and the Israeli state. Muhammad 'Ali Taha, the Nakba and Steadfastness Committee chair, unambiguously acknowledged that the Nakba commemoration project aimed to target both Palestinian and Jewish-Israeli audiences.[43] While Israel denies its responsibility for Palestinian suffering, when the victims are Israeli citizens the denial becomes more complicated since it contradicts both Israel's claim to sovereignty and its aspiration of being considered a liberal democracy.

The exclusion of Palestinian non-citizens and themes of armed struggle are aspects of cautious commemoration practiced by Palestinians inside Israel. This caution necessary partly due to the strict official and unofficial surveillance imposed on Palestinian commemoration in Israel. The mechanisms of this surveillance and its historical development are the topic of the next chapter.

7 DISCIPLINING PALESTINIAN MEMORY

IN 1987 an Israeli military band won the first prize in the Israeli Songs Festival. The winning song, "A Dove with an Olive Branch," became a hit. The popular military radio station Galei Tsahal, however, initially refused to broadcast it, most likely because of the fourth line in the lyrics:

> I have a picture at home of a dove with an olive branch.
> Above it the wheel sun, on its feet the ravages of war
> The dove of peace
> **On the ruins of another nation**
> Perfect picture, a dream within a framework.

Only after the composer, Talma Alyagon-Roz, agreed to provide a second version in which the fourth line was replaced by the words "it is painted by a master hand," and after a new version was recorded, did the station remove its objection. The song is still popular in Israel today, but few are familiar with the original text. The modified lyrics of "A Dove with an Olive Branch" are symptomatic of both the common anxiety among Jewish Israeli citizens regarding a public discussion of the 1948 events and the consistent denial of the existence of a thriving Palestinian community before that war. The psychologist Tova Buksbaum has argued that the parallel existence of the two versions of the song is a metaphor for the simultaneous existence and non-existence of the Nakba in Israeli collective consciousness.[1] Researcher Noga Kadman has described the depopulated Palestinian villages as existing on "the margin of consciousness" of Jewish Israelis.[2] The historian Anita Shapira has written that the Israeli Jewish remembrance of the expulsion of Palestinians "continues to hover in the twilight zone between the conscious and unconscious, between repression and recognition."[3] This borderline nature is what allows both a military band to sing "on the ruins of another nation," as well as the demands for the subsequent "correction" of the lyrics. These lyrics were a reminder of an inconvenient truth: it was not only the war that established the Jewish state, but the uprooting of hundreds of thousands of Palestinians that enabled the creation of a stable Jewish majority in Israel in its pre-1967 borders.

The sensitive status of the remembrance of 1948 memories is expressed as well in public opinion polls. The Jewish Israeli public tends to be relatively supportive of Arab-Jewish equality in many spheres. In a 2008–2009 survey conducted by the Dahaf Institute (Figure 5), more than half of the Jewish Israeli interviewees supported legislation that would guarantee that Arab citizens receive their

Statement	Agree or tend to agree (%)
The State of Israel should acknowledge its share of responsibility for the Nakba of the Palestinian people	18.8
The state should give Arab citizens appropriate expression in its symbols, flag and anthem	26.6
The State of Israel should be a state in which Hebrew and Arabic have equal status	37.6
I would support a plan to narrow the gaps between Jews and Arabs even if it would harm me	39.3
Israel should be a state of the two peoples, the Jews and the Arabs	43.3
The State of Israel should recognize Arab citizens as a national minority and as part of the Palestinian people	47.7
There should be a law that guarantees appropriate representation for Arab citizens in all state institutions	54.9
The state should be committed to narrowing the gaps between Jews and Arabs as it is committed to narrowing the gap between Ashkenazi and Mizrahi Jews	56.6
A law should guarantee that Arab citizens receive their appropriate share in the state budget	57.7

Figure 5. Support among Jewish Israelis for policies to increase equality between Jews and Arabs, 2008–2009. Based on a survey imitated by Sikkuy and conducted by the Dahaf Institute between December 2008 and April 2009 with a representative sample of Jewish Israeli citizens aged 25 to 50 (N=550). Dataset provided to the author by Sikkuy (Association for the Advancement of Civic Equality Report).

appropriate share in the state budget and appropriate representation in all state institutions. But where respondents showed reluctance was over questions of symbols and identity, while the most extreme objection was related to history. The only statement that was supported by less than 20 percent of the Jewish interviewees was one related to the past: "The State of Israel should acknowledge its share of responsibility for the Nakba of the Palestinian people." In other words, Arab and Jewish citizens are divided about the past much more than they are divided about the present. The growing importance of the past, especially the 1948 war, in the political culture of the Arabs in Israel both reflects and explains the deterioration of Arab-Jewish relations since the late 1990s.

Undoubtedly the reluctance of Jewish Israelis to accede to the demand to acknowledge Israeli responsibility for the Nakba is its connection to two related and common anxieties of the Jewish Israeli public: the anxiety over the legitimacy of the Zionist project and the anxiety over reversibility.

The 1948 war is remembered by most Jewish Israelis as the War of Independence, a constitutive redemptive moment. It is commemorated as the heroic defensive fight of a small and poorly armed community that, with its back against the wall, defeated seven Arab armies against all odds. For many years the producers of the hegemonic Israeli-Zionist collective memory delegitimized public discussion about the tragic price the Palestinians paid for the establishment of the Jewish state, the fate of Palestinian refugees, and the drastic change in the country's landscape following the war.[4] Acknowledging responsibility might be interpreted as recognition that Israel was born in sin. This is much more than taking responsibility over a crime, as it might undermine the moral justification for the existence of Israel and Israeli national identity.

The concern of Jewish Israeli anxiety over legitimacy can be illustrated by comparison to another country. In both Israel and Turkey the authorities deny the state's responsibility for the collective tragedy of the "other." In both cases, as well, this denial is fundamental to the legitimacy of the state. The expulsion of the Palestinians is considered a pre-condition for the establishment of a state with a stable Jewish majority. Similarly, some scholars argue that the elimination of ethno-religious minorities in the late Ottoman Empire and early Turkish Republic (the Armenian genocide and later the forced "population exchange" of Greeks) was necessary for the establishment of a relatively homogenous, ethnic Turkish nation-state.[5]

As a result, Turkish authorities restrict the commemoration of a long list of atrocities against ethnic and religious minorities.[6] More specifically, the Israeli

"Nakba anxiety" is similar to the sensitivity of the Turkish state to the commemoration of the Armenian genocide. Numerous Turkish intellectuals have faced trial for "insulting Turkishness" because they acknowledged that what happened to Armenians in 1915 amounted to genocide.[7] Spatially, although there is still a tiny Armenian minority in Turkey (about 70,000 people) and despite the fact that about 140 memorial monuments commemorating the Armenian genocide have been built in twenty-five countries, not even one of them was built in Turkey.[8]

Israeli sensitivity, however, has another crucial element that does not exist in Turkey or, for that matter, in other cases of mass catastrophe imposed on indigenous people like in North America or Australia. Commemoration of the Nakba is related to the most sensitive controversy over the Right of Return for the Palestinian refugees, recognition of which is considered by Zionists as an existential threat that would bring about the end of the Jewish state. Therefore, whereas in recent years official Turkey has made some tiny reconciliatory gestures, including offering "condolence,"[9] even these sorts of minimalistic steps are unlikely to be seen soon in contemporary Israel. Remembering the Nakba is perceived by state agencies as challenging the legitimacy of the State of Israel and, therefore, attempts to commemorate it by Arab-Palestinian citizens of Israel are carefully monitored.[10] This monitoring and disciplining by the state extends as well to the commemoration of other events that could potentially contribute to Palestinian national political mobilization.

"MILITARY RULE" IN THE 1970S AND 1980S

Probably the most difficult task for Israeli authorities in their attempts to efface Palestinian remembrance of the Nakba is dealing with the personal memories of internally displaced Palestinians whose attachment to their depopulated villages was unmediated. For the approximately 25,000 initial internal refugees in Israel, Israel's policy since 1948 aimed to disconnect them from their original villages and to prevent the development of a "refugee identity."[11] This policy included physical restrictions on their access to their former lands (including establishment of new Jewish villages on these lands), providing reparations or alternative housing, obliterating the names of the abandoned villages from state maps, removing the internal refugees from United Nations Relief and Works Agency (UNWRA) figures, registering them in the Israeli Population Registry as inhabitants of their host villages rather than their original ones, and excluding the abandoned villages and the refugee problem from the school curriculum, including that used for Arab pupils.[12]

Another major area of state control has been the political calendar itself. For the military government officers and the Shabak in the 1950s and 1960s, the celebration of Israel's Independence Day was the ultimate test of Palestinian loyalty, a litmus test that enabled the state to rank Arabs according to their levels of obedience. Every year, all state institutions in Arab towns and villages were required to perform festive ceremonies and raise the Israeli flag.[13] Police informants received detailed instructions to report on the atmosphere in their villages on Independence Day. Negative attitudes, such as removing or vandalizing flags and pictures of leaders, or speeches that referred to the "tragedy of the Palestinian people," were followed up with police investigations and arrests.[14]

Similarly, the politicization of the memory of the 1956 Kafr Qasim massacre through cyclical commemoration was strictly monitored and restricted by the military government. This monitoring included "preventive arrests" of local and regional activists before the annual memorial days, as well as physical blocking of the entrance to Kafr Qasim.[15] Military governors, through their loyal appointees in the local council of Kafr Qasim, tried to contain the commemoration and shape the annual anniversary as a religious rite and personal expression of mourning. In some years, the local council published an announcement before the anniversary calling the residents of Kafr Qasim to "limit themselves to reading surat al-Fatiha [the opening chapter of the Qur'an, commonly read in Islamic memorial services]."[16] Controversy over this constrained commemoration led to severe inter-generational tensions in the village between young politicized activists and a very cautious council that represented the careful approach of the older generation.[17]

Interestingly, the end of the military government in 1966 did not immediately change these policies and methods. Although since the 1970s Arab citizens have not been forced to celebrate Israel's Independence Day and the Kafr Qasim massacre has been commemorated more freely, state authorities continue to express strong concerns for how Palestinians in Israel construct their political calendar.

Regarding Land Day, it is evident that state authorities were well aware of the mobilizing potential of its commemoration. The first Land Day anniversary in 1977 took place in 'Arabeh. Those who arrived to participate in the commemorative rally faced a police checkpoint where policemen wrote down their ID numbers and tried to convince them not to participate in the rally. Israel's main bus company, Egged, as well as some smaller bus companies, refused to rent buses for the event.[18]

Some of the military government's tactics of surveillance of Palestinian commemoration survived during the 1980s as well. "Preventive arrests" of activists before the annual Land Day commemoration were common. Some of the participants in Land Day rallies who waved a Palestinian flag or uttered Palestinian national slogans were jailed, sometimes for months.[19] In 1982 the mayor of Umm al-Fahm was tried in court for his decision to close schools and the local council of Umm al-Fahm on Land Day.[20] As late as 1988, following the eruption of the Palestinian uprising in the occupied territories and the growing Israeli concern over its spreading into the Green Line, Prime Minster Yitzhak Shamir decided to shut down *al-Ittihad* from 25 to 31 March, to prevent "incitement" around Land Day events.

A classified letter sent before the eighth anniversary of Land Day in 1984 by Binyamin Gur Arieh, the Arab Affairs Advisor to Prime Minster Shamir, outlined the preemptive actions taken to "calm down the atmosphere." These actions included: meeting with "moderate" Arab mayors to coordinate the discipline efforts; postponing more land confiscations until after Land Day; instructing journalists for Arab affairs in the Hebrew media to tone down their reporting on Land Day; warning the imams regarding the content of their mosque sermons on Friday, 30 March (the warning was made through their employer, the Ministry of Religious Affairs to guarantee its effectiveness); and warning school directors not to join the one-hour strike planned for Thursday, 29 March (again the warning was made through their employer, the Ministry of Education).[21]

The need to warn school directors was related to the growing confidence of some Arab local councils following Land Day. Since high school teachers are employed by the local councils, which control the school facilities as well, in the years following Land Day some of the more daring local councils attempted to extend the commemoration into the state education system. School directors found themselves under cross-pressures from the local council and the Ministry of Education.[22]

Commemorative initiatives that alarmed the state authorities came not only from teachers but from students as well. In the mid-1980s the Association of Arab High School Students initiated the dedication of one regular teaching hour for discussing Land Day in Arab schools every year on 30 March, in addition to a moment of silence in memory of the martyrs,[23] and later extended this initiative to the Kafr Qasim massacre memorial day. According to a letter sent in December 1986 from the Office of the Minister Responsible for Minority Affairs to the Ministry of Education, they did it "presumably with a considerable success," and the event "already became a tradition." The letter's author was concerned that "... it is possible that the association would 'decide' soon on mentioning other memorial days and events inside the schools (the 1st of January is coming soon ...)."[24]

While the local Arab authorities played a crucial role in organizing commemoration ceremonies, they also served as an effective way for the state authorities to monitor the commemoration events. This dynamic was much more blatant under military rule in the case of the Kafr Qasim commemoration,[25] but the dependency of local authorities on the government ensured its continuation in later decades, although in a more subtle way. Local authorities remained financially dependent on the state in many areas, especially in education and welfare. In the early 1980s, the relative share of government funding for the expenditures of all local authorities in Israel was approximately 70 percent.[26] Most of the money transferred to the local authorities was based on transparent criteria, but government ministries still had a wide range of maneuvering, and therefore mayors had structural interests in keeping good relations with the government.

In addition, since both the state authorities and the mayors shared interests in maintaining stability, they frequently coordinated their efforts. Before the eighth anniversary of Land Day in 1984, for example, the chief of the northern region of the police, Meir Sadeh, attended a meeting at the 'Arabeh city hall with all three mayors of the "Land Day Triangle" (Sakhnin, 'Arabeh, and Deir Hanna). The protocol of the meeting sheds light on the relations between the local authorities and the police. It is noteworthy that the protocols were required to be submitted to the Ministry of Interior, and therefore their content reflects to a large extent the impression-management practiced by local governments toward the central authorities.

'Arabeh's mayor at the time, Muhammad Nassar of the DFPE, declared a collective commitment to uphold public order. The police chief declared his commitment to allow the commemorative event to take place, and moved on to define the allowed parameters of commemoration. He reminded the members of the local council that the Terrorism Law forbids waving the Palestinian flag and that in the previous year the police had to exercise force to remove a flag. He also warned them that there was no permission to block the main road. In his response, one of the council members, Ahmad Na'amna, praised the cooperation between the local council and the police in the past and emphasized the commitment of the three local councils to maintain order and to prevent any illegal slogans or waving the Palestinian flag. He argued that those who "violated the order" in the past came from outside of 'Arabeh, and he specifically blamed the Matspen movement.[27] Mayor Nassar added that the local slogans have always been legal and promised to prevent the appearance of any "illegal slogans" in his town's commemorations.[28]

The cautious tone of the members of the local council of 'Arabeh, a town considered to have a leading role in Land Day commemorations, illustrates the limited protest that could be exercised by local authorities. Since their own status is defined by Israeli law, local councils are unable to cross the line of legality, even if the law forbids the mere expression of their national sentiments and belonging.

DECLINING SURVEILLANCE

Since the late 1980s, however, the state's motivation and ability to discipline Palestinian memory have rapidly waned as a result of several interrelated sociopolitical processes in the region, the state, and within both Jewish and Arab societies. First, the strengthening of the liberal discourse of citizenship and the increased power of the Israeli Supreme Court, which defended this discourse,[29] created a wider range of freedom of speech. As early as 1984, in a discussion about government policy toward the National Committee of Arab Mayors, Nahman Tal of the Shabak complained that "in 1964 it was possible to outlaw al-Ard,[30] but today it is much more difficult to outlaw a movement."[31]

Furthermore, among certain elements of the Jewish Israeli academic elite and related circles, publications of the "New Historians"[32] partially legitimized public discussion about Israel's responsibility for the Palestinian tragedy.[33] The exclusion of Egypt from the Arab-Israeli military conflict after the Camp David Accords in 1978 and the dismantling of the Soviet Union—the major strategic ally of Israel's enemies—also reduced the siege mentality in Israel by abating existential anxieties and increasing the collective self-confidence of Jewish society. Later on, the Oslo process, which became public in September 1993, intensified this dynamic and temporarily introduced some "post-conflict" attitudes among parts of the Israeli elite, who conveniently adopted the view in the late 1990s that the conflict had virtually ended.

At the same time, Palestinian society in Israel gained confidence with the emergence of new circles of educated elites and a formalized leadership in the form of the FUC and its sub-committees. Moreover, Arab local governments gradually gained more autonomy from the government.[34] By 2005 the relative share of government funding in the expenditures of all local authorities in Israel had shrunk to 40 percent.[35] This was especially significant in the field of high school education because, as mentioned previously, local councils nominate teachers for these schools and pay their salaries. Another crucial development was the emergence of an independent profit-driven Arabic press in the 1980s.[36] Because historical writing attracts the attention of a wider social circle than other social sciences, "history is also business."[37] The profit-driven newspapers played an important role in the production of the cultural memory of the Nakba, especially in the 1990s.

This empowerment of Palestinian citizens and the decline in the legitimacy of the unrefined, coercive disciplining of Palestinian commemoration was reflected in a heated debate that took place in the Knesset assembly on 9 December 1992.[38] The debate dealt with a proposal to outlaw Campus, the Arab students' association at the University of Haifa. One of the major concerns of Gonen Segev, the MK from the right-wing Tsomet party who initiated the discussion, was a calendar distributed by the student organization. The calendar referenced key dates in the Palestinian national narrative. Segev protested:

> Some of the dates mentioned in this calendar: the anniversary of the Palestinian revolution; Land Day; the Deir Yasin massacre; the partition plan; the anniversary of the trauma of 1948 (and I know this is the day when the war of liberation of my people erupted) [. . .]; the Balfour declaration is mentioned there as well and also the Intifada anniversary. The anniversary of the Palestinian revolution and Palestinian Independence Day—the day is mentioned at the University of Haifa as a holiday.
>
> Honorable Speaker, Knesset members, I am talking about students at the University of Haifa and not about students at Bir-Zeit or al-Najah [Palestinian universities in the West Bank—T.S.]. I am talking about Arab students born in Israel in its limited pre-1967 borders. You call them Israelis. They call themselves first of all Palestinians. They mention the dates of the Palestinian people and make our national holidays days of mourning. This is the main problem.
>
> MK Tawfik Zayyad [DFPE]: There is no contradiction.
>
> Segev: The day when the state was declared is considered by them as a day of mourning. [. . .] Yesterday a sticker was distributed at the University of Haifa that says: "Today is the fifth anniversary of the blessed Palestinian Intifada." On the same day three victims of the Intifada were buried. [. . .]
>
> Zayyad: Send them to jail. What do you want?

Segev: If we will not bash the head of the snake while it is still young, a latent intifada will erupt among the Arab Israelis, and we will not know how to stop it. I am calling on the Minister of Education to impose order on the chaos that prevails in the institutions of higher education and in schools. I would like to remind everyone that we live in the Land of Israel, in the home of the Jewish people. I demand that Campus be outlawed and that the activity of Campus members in the universities in Israel be forbidden.

The proceedings of this parliamentary session were symptomatic of the evolving atmosphere in Israel in the 1990s. It seems that for some Jewish politicians the mere existence of the Palestinian narrative was a surprise, while for others its public appearance was a threat. Segev himself was worried as well about the similarity between the Campus calendar and the calendar of the Palestinian national movement outside Israel. The sarcastic reaction of MK Zayyad (i.e., "jail them") clarified that the arsenal of legitimate methods to confront this narrative was by then limited. The Knesset voted against Segev's demand,[39] and for the next nine years there was no recorded attempt by legislators to clip the wings of Palestinian national commemoration inside Israel.

NEW MODES OF DISCIPLINING MEMORY

The change described above does not mean that during the 1990s Palestinians in Israel were completely free to write their own narrative or to commemorate their national past without interruption. The Shabak was still involved in nominating employees in the education system, and Arab formal education continued to be strictly monitored (see Chapter 8). Organized visits to the ruins of Palestinian villages in the 1990s sometimes faced police interference, and violent confrontations took place. Officials of the Israel Land Authority embarked on a large-scale operation of fencing off abandoned Arab structures and erecting large signs that warned against trespassing.[40] The decision of the FUC to commemorate the Nakba spurred threats from the Israeli government.

Having said that, before the eruption of the al-Aqsa Intifada in 2000, these public threats were vague and relatively minor in their tone. This dynamic prevailed, however, only as long as it was accompanied by a decline in the level of existential anxiety on the Jewish side. The events of October 2000 and the Second Intifada, on the other hand, quickly interfered with the gradual processes of strengthening Jewish Israeli self-confidence. Historian Tom Segev, who celebrated post-Zionism in a book published shortly before the Intifada, wrote after its eruption: "Palestinian terrorism seems to push Israelis back into the Zionist womb,"[41] and the "Zionist womb" opposes Palestinians commemorating their tragic past. Indeed, the dominance of the Zionist ideology among Jews in Israel, which has always been high, increased in the first decade of the twenty-first century.[42] At the same time, it became impossible to restore the old state practices of disciplining memory, which were blocked by a combination of several sociopolitical developments.

During the 1990s Palestinian civil society inside Israel grew and rapidly became institutionalized to create a strong web of self-confident civil activism.[43] This development was part of a global process of the accelerated development of civil society organization in different countries.[44] Many organizations directly or indirectly dealt with establishing the public presence of a Palestinian national narrative,[45] and these organizations developed effective skills in obtaining the protection of the Israeli legal system. This development has been accompanied by a generational change. The demographic weight of the generation whose consciousness was shaped under the strict disciplinary power of the military rule has been decreased and toward the beginning of the twenty-first century, Palestinian citizens with no biographical memories of the period of military rule have been gradually occupying key positions in political parties, NGOs, and municipalities. This generation carries a different generational "habitus" and demonstrates a greater readiness to defy the authorities.[46]

In addition, the Internet and satellite TV have made the flow of information more difficult to control by the state and have strengthened the links of Palestinians in Israel to the Arab world.[47] In my 2008 survey I asked respondents to identify the main source of their historical knowledge. Among Arab respondents, 24 percent mentioned television, and 16 percent mentioned the Internet;[48] among Jewish respondents, only 14 percent mentioned television and 6 percent mentioned the Internet. These gaps suggest that for Palestinian citizens, new technologies were especially important given their mistrust of the state-sponsored school system and highlight as well the greater potential of this media to cross the borders between Israel and its neighbors.

Furthermore, in 2008 the Qatar-based Arab satellite TV, al-Jazeera, was much more popular than any Israeli channel,[49] and this development is meaningful: a 2009 survey conducted by Smooha revealed a clear-cut association between watching the satellite channel al-Jazeera and participating in commemorative events. Among those who said that they watch al-Jazeera "every day" or "frequently," 49 percent reported participating at least once in an event commemorating the Nakba, and 46 percent reported participating in Land Day events at least once. Among those who watch al-Jazeera "seldom" or "almost never," the numbers were 21 and 24 percent, respectively.[50] Obviously, these numbers are not evidence of causality, but they do suggest at least an elective affinity between the content of al-Jazeera and the sphere of Palestinian national commemoration.

The following story illustrates the inability of the old state disciplinary mechanisms to deal with these new developments. As mentioned earlier, a major source of power of the Palestinian community in Israel is the relative autonomy of local councils that support and sometimes initiate commemorative events. In Israel, when a local council or mayor fails to run their town or city, the Minister of Interior is authorized to dismantle the council or to dismiss the mayor and to nominate a temporary committee and a temporary mayor. Only Jewish temporary mayors have been appointed so far to run failed Jewish councils whereas in failed Arab localities, most temporary appointees are Jewish as well.

On 25 December 2007, due to the complete failure of the local council of Kafr Kana, the Minister of Interior nominated a temporary mayor. Five months later in May 2008 the local branch of the Islamic Movement planned to celebrate the birthday of the prophet Muhammad and to commemorate the Nakba at the same event in the local soccer stadium. They submitted a routine request to the local council and to the police. They received police approval but were astonished to receive a negative answer from the state-appointed council. According to the council, "this is a political event and it is forbidden by the law."[51] A popular committee in the town organized a protest and called on residents to boycott Ilan Gavrieali, the appointed temporary mayor, who was Jewish. A flyer the committee distributed stated, "We will not allow the military government to return to Kafr Kana." The committee members also appealed to the district court in Nazareth to overrule the council's decision. The appeal was accepted, and the event took place as planned.

THE DISCIPLINING CIVIC GAZE

The court's decision in favor of the Kafr Kana Islamic Movement was a stark illustration that the old methods used to discipline Palestinian memory, namely, arbitrary decisions by state functionaries that are not necessarily backed by the rule of law, had lost their legitimacy. However, certain forces in Israeli society have been trying to reinstate the undermined disciplinary power of the state. These attempts have been carried out by an increasingly present voluntary "civic gaze" of ordinary citizens backed by new legislation and public intimidation by certain functionaries in the legislative and executive branches.

For Michel Foucault, the gaze imposes disciplinary practices that inscribe identities upon docile bodies.[52] Foucault's original thesis referred to specific agents and specific kinds of surveillance modes, which direct their scrutinizing gaze to specific individuals. Foucault's panopticon metaphor, which symbolizes this ever-present institutional gaze, certainly fits the reality of the military government. Furthermore, the military government's long shadow, although fading, still deters many Palestinians in Israel from attacking sacred cows of the Zionist ethos.[53] The Jewish civic gaze on Arab public behavior, however, is much less institutionalized, and its sources are only vaguely identifiable. This civic gaze should not be confused with the phenomenon of self-appointed informers, namely, citizens who voluntarily report to the security services about other citizens. Instead, the agents of this civic gaze themselves act to correct the subject's behavior. In addition, the civic gaze is not focused; rather, it is a consistent, random scrutinizing of the public sphere without pre-determined attention to specific individuals. Nevertheless, it is still effective as a disciplinary mechanism.

The Jewish civic disciplinary gaze is as old as the state of Israel, and it has functioned from the very moment Arabs met Jews under the post-1948 imbalance of power. However, because of the effectiveness of state-controlled disciplinary practices in the specific field of political commemoration, most Jewish citizens never encountered commemorative events organized by Arab citizens. Palestinian political commemoration has taken place almost exclusively inside Arab towns and villages, with the exception of events held in mixed university settings. Since 2000, though, because Palestinian political memory has become increasingly public and more determined to broach topics sensitive for Jews in Israel, Jewish citizens gradually and increasingly have paid attention to these events and have expressed a readiness to correct "diversions" from the dominant Zionist narrative. Until 2005, this Jewish civic monitoring and opposition was located mainly in the universities, where sporadic clashes between Arab and Jewish students occurred.[54] In recent years, however, confrontations between Arab commemorators and Jewish counter-demonstrators occurred in other contexts.

On 17 June 2005, about 150 people, most of them Arab-Palestinian citizens, marched from the old prison in Acre to the Muslim cemetery in the city. They were commemorating the seventy-fifth anniversary of the execution of Hijazi, Jamjum, and al-Zir by British authorities (See Chapter 1).[55] On the way to the cemetery, some Arab merchants played the song "Min sijn 'Akka," based on the lyrics of the Palestinian poet Nuh Ibrahim. After entering the old city, the participants were surprised to encounter a group of Jewish Israeli yeshiva students waving Israeli flags and holding large signs bearing the word "traitors." Subsequent short reports about the march in some Hebrew news websites sparked furious reactions from Jewish readers,[56] who interpreted the commemoration as praise for the massacres for which the three men were executed.

The protest in Acre was an important landmark because it reflected two important processes in Jewish-Arab mixed cities. First, since the turn of the twenty-first century, religious Zionist groups have made efforts to settle these cities, with an explicit agenda to Judaize and de-Arabize them. Clashes between them and the local population have been frequent.[57] Second, due to the growing confidence of Palestinian activists, Palestinians are increasingly undertaking events of national commemorations in these cities, and conflicts with Jewish citizens around these commemorations have become common.

In recent years, even the Nakba has been publicly commemorated in mixed Arab-Jewish cities. The modest event organized in Lydda in 2006 faced a Jewish counter-demonstration organized by some right-wing members of the local council under the banner "Flags for Israel." One member wrapped in an Israeli flag addressed the participants and warned that: "Commemorating the Nakba by the Arabs of Israel is a denial of the mere existence of the State of Israel, and whoever denies our right to live in peace and security cannot complain that we do not accept him for a job, cannot complain that he is not allowed family unification, cannot be surprised that we check him from head to toe when he enters the bus, and should not be surprised if he is not welcome to live near us."[58] Interestingly, every element in this multidimensional threat has been identified by the sociologist Areej Sabbagh-Khoury as deterring Palestinian citizens in Israel from protesting against issues considered taboo by Jewish Israelis: the economic dependency on the Jewish side, the tendency to give priority to issues concerning their daily lives, and finally, the fear of another expulsion, shaped by the remembrance of the Nakba.[59]

"Domination Is Not a Nice Word"

The social anthropologist Paul Connerton has noted that commemorative ceremonies are frequently "re-enactments of the past, its return in a representational guise which normally includes a simulacrum of the scene or situation recaptured."[60] The Palestinian March of Return discussed in Chapter 3 is an example of the exact opposite: the creation of a mirror image of the past, where the commemorative practice embodies a reversal of the event that is commemorated, namely, the expulsion. The Jewish Israeli anxiety over this reversal can explain much of the reactions among Jewish citizens to the annual march.

From an early stage, the march had the potential for friction with the Jewish public and the state. This friction became inevitable both spatially and temporally. Spatially, many Jewish settlements were established on the ruins of Palestinian villages (sometimes with the intention of preventing the return of dispossessed residents). Temporally, the choice of Israel's Independence Day for the march has been perceived by many Jewish Israelis as a provocation.

In 2007, for the first time, a group of Jewish citizens came to confront the March of Return. The group, identified in the Arabic press as "right wing activists,"[61] came to one of the gathering points at the beginning of the march and confronted the participants with their own slogans. An Arab journalist who photographed them was attacked and his camera was broken. The police intervened before further escalation took place.

The following year, shortly before the planned annual march, Danny Danon, the chair of World Likud (the international branch of Israel's ruling party), sent a letter to the Israeli Minister of Interior demanding that he ban the march.[62] During the march itself, which took place on 8 May 2008, a group of Jewish activists organized a counter-demonstration. At the invitation of a new organization named Ha-Shomer he-Hadash (the new guardian), several hundred people came to a massive picnic at the Jewish cooperative settlement of Tsipori that had been established in 1949 on the land of the depopulated village of Safuriye. The route of the march was thereby obstructed because on its way to Safuriye, it was slated to go through Tsipori.

Ha-Shomer he-Hadash was founded in early 2008 by Jewish ranchers from the Lower Galilee who felt that the state had failed to protect them against trespassing and looting. Although their point of departure seems to be related to mere protection of private property, their struggle is articulated in the typical ethno-nationalist discourse of a settler society, and it is consciously contextualized in the history of the Israeli-Palestinian conflict. Their name echoes the name of the pre-state para-military organization, Ha-Shomer, founded to "conquer"[63] the jobs of Arab guards in the Jewish settlements. Symbolically, their first country-wide meeting was scheduled for Land Day (30 March 2008). At this meeting, the chair, Yoel Zilberman, said: "An all-out war is managed every day and every hour over the national land of all of us; there is a need to return to national pride, patriotism, and Zionism, and to make sure that the ranchers will learn to be courageous and proud."[64]

Several weeks later, Ha-Shomer he-Hadash organized the protest against the Nakba commemoration in Tsipori. The event itself was not officially defined as a protest but as a counter-celebration, and the official title was "Celebrating independence—in the face of the Nakba events." The event itself deteriorated into a violent confrontation between the Arab participants and the police. There were injuries on both sides, and thirty-one Arab demonstrators were arrested (all of them were released later without trial). The police interrogated some of the organizers of the march for about an hour including the chairman of the Committee of the Uprooted Wakim Wakim and the spokesman Suleiman Fahmawi.

In subsequent years, the police were careful to create a safe distance between the two sides. In 2009 the March of Return marched to the remnants of the village Kafrin, and the celebration of Ha-Shomer he-Hadash was made on an adjacent hill. The two camps were close enough to see each other but distant enough to avoid any direct confrontation. I went back and forth between the two events interviewing participants on both sides until the police stopped me from doing so.

The title chosen for the 2009 counter-celebration by Ha-Shomer he-Hadash was "Celebrating Independence—Without Fear." This is an ironic title because from my conversations with the organizers and participants, fear, and the anxiety of being perceived as fearful, emerged as a major, driving sentiment. "Silence means fear," Yoel Zilberman, the movement's founder and a resident of Tsipori, told me in justifying the need to counter-celebrate. "A march of fifteen thousand into Tsipori—we evaluated it as the beginning of an intifada, as a very clear statement [. . .] this is a statement that this village was an Arab village and it will be again. [. . .] There is a silent intifada in the Galilee. Just a week ago there was a conference here and they talked there about 'a state of all its citizens' and Arab autonomy in the Galilee. They talk about it as a self-evident reality."[65]

The participants in the 2009 counter-celebration who answered my questions about what drove them to participate in this organized practice of collective civic gaze reverberated this fear: "We are here because we fear losing this country"; "I fear that one day we won't be able to come to these regions." One of the participants, a 19-year-old boy, told me that he was there to "demonstrate presence." "Why is it so important that they see you?" I asked. "It is a sort of showing domination . . . " he answered but after a short pause, he added, "well, not domination; domination is not a nice word. It is to show a counter-action." His words represented the dilemma of the post-2000 era—the fear that led to the drive to dominate, which in its turn meets awareness that "domination" is not politically correct anymore.

This sensitivity of Jewish citizens is taken into account by the organizers of the March of Return. Through preliminary meetings each year, the organizers invest great effort in disciplining the expressions of protest to ensure that the slogans and signs will not put the march in danger of being interpreted as a provocation or in violation of any law.[66] From the organizers' point of view, an event like the burning of an Israeli flag (which did occur once, in 2001) might jeopardize their entire project. In addition, the mapping of the exact path of every annual march is dictated partly by the desire to avoid potential conflicts with Jewish residents of the existing settlement built on the village's lands.

As a case in point, one of the founders of the Committee of the Uprooted, 'Abed Nimarnah, has refrained so far from taking the march to his own village of origin, Mi'ar. The reason is his reluctance to risk the positive relationship that he has been able to establish with residents of the Jewish settlement of Ya'ad that exists today on Mi'ar's land. In 2003 Nimarnah and other descendants of Mi'ar's uprooted residents were alarmed by a plan to expand Ya'ad into areas of Mi'ar that included the village cemetery. Together with a group of Ya'ad residents and the Zochrot organization,[67] they appealed to state authorities. In February 2004 the Regional Building and Planning Committee partially accepted the appeal. Subsequently, the assembly of the Ya'ad residents decided not to build in areas beyond the new boundaries defined by the regional committee, and they agreed to build a fence around the cemetery as well. These events triggered a continuous dialogue between the people of Mi'ar and Ya'ad. Nimarnah said that he was "not willing to risk the achievements. The vision of thousands of Arabs marching with Palestinian flags and shouting slogans might scare the people of Ya'ad."[68]

This is not the only case where Jewish sensitivities influenced the path of the march. In 2011 there was a controversy between committee members regarding the location of that year's march. In a press interview two months before the march, the committee's spokesman, Suleiman Fahmawi, said that the destination that year would be the emptied village of Hittin in the eastern Galilee.[69] This plan was later rejected by Chairman Wakim Wakim, who argued that it might bring the participants in confrontation with the residents of the Jewish village of Kfar Hitim, or even with the residents of a Druze village in the area.[70] In the end the march proceeded to the remains of destroyed villages al-Damun and Rweis, located far from any main road or Jewish locality. Even then, the discussion in the Committee of the Uprooted in preparation for the march revealed the concerns of some of the members. One member said: "In the previous march in Damun and Rweis, a masked person came and burned a flag of the State of Israel. We should protect ourselves from all these things. In Birweh [where the march took place in 2002] similar things happened. In my opinion, the program that will be distributed [should state]: 'If you want to come [to the event as it is presented] welcome, if you don't want—you shouldn't come. This is the program.' This person should not come to create provocation inside the demonstration."[71]

PUBLIC INTIMIDATIONS

In some contexts, the civic gaze can be effective only if everyone involved is aware that it represents the interests of the state, which is, for its part, ready to use its own disciplinary mechanism. In the post-2000 years, Palestinian citizens increasingly have been seen by the Israeli security services as an existential threat to the Jewish state. The level of anxiety was manifested in the description of the current processes in Arab society in Israel as the "real strategic danger in the long term." This quote comes from a closed discussion of Shabak senior advisers with Prime Minister Ehud Olmert in 2007 and was carefully chosen for release to the press.[72]

Nevertheless, the post-2000 modes of disciplining memory are not necessarily part of an organized and coordinated plan. Their main characteristic is their public visibility. Politicians, whether in office or aspiring to office, make public declarations that have the potential to deter Palestinian citizens from organizing or participating in commemorative events. Sometimes these declarations are explicit threats, but the intimidator cannot always follow through; therefore, their main, potential effect is in creating an intimidating public environment.

For example, in May 2001, before the first Independence Day anniversary after the eruption of the al-Aqsa Intifada, the newly-appointed Minister of National Infrastructure, Avigdor Lieberman, instructed the ministry's functionaries to avoid any contact with public figures who participated in Nakba commemorations. The Ministry of National Infrastructure has a large budget, and being denied access to its resources could seriously impede Arab municipalities. Lieberman justified his decision by a need to "punish public figures who turn Independence Day into a Day of Holocaust."[73] Three months later, the Minister of Education, Limor Livnat, declared that she was considering making the allocation of bonuses and extra funding to schools conditional on

the schools being "loyal to the state." Livnat explained that "schools that commemorate Nakba Day, or raise the Palestinian flag and celebrate after terrorist
attacks, should not receive bonuses."[74] Livnat went to the media with her new
ideas before consulting the ministry's legal advisors.[75] In both cases, the legality
of the newly-declared policies was dubious,[76] and there is no evidence that either policy was officially implemented. However, the importance of these statements is mainly in the atmosphere they created.

Although Lieberman and Livnat were the most explicit in linking commemoration of the past to the distribution of resources in the present, their attitude
represents a wider spectrum of the carrot and stick policy frequently articulated
by Israeli cabinet ministers. In March 2001, Israeli authorities were especially concerned about Land Day events because of the ongoing Palestinian uprising. To
the surprise of many, Prime Minister Ariel Sharon agreed two days before Land
Day to approve a full implementation of the development plan for Arab towns,
including a general survey of future needs—a step that several previous Israeli
governments had refused to approve. Some observers estimated that this decision
prevented confrontations during Land Day itself.[77] Seven years later in 2008, as
part of the preparations for the celebrations of Israel's sixtieth Independence Day,
the Israeli government made efforts to convince Arab municipalities to take part
in the celebrations. Arab political leaders were promised that the "celebrations
will include financial investment in the infrastructure of the Arab localities."[78]
Although we could classify this promise as a "carrot," the poor infrastructure of
most Arab towns and the desperate need for funding for public projects should
have given them high priority on the government's list of supported projects in
any case. Therefore, making the support they deserved conditional on obedient
political behavior should be seen as another form of "stick" (i.e., a threat).

Although the FUC leadership publicly rejected these attempts to "bribe"
Arab mayors, in some municipalities the carrot and stick policy seems to be effective. 'Orsan Yasin, mayor of Shefa'amr from 1998 to 2008, organized an official Independence Day celebration in his town. Yasin explained his instrumental
political philosophy on several occasions: "I had enough of the extremists. We,
the moderates, will overpower them. I expect that the Prime Minister will support the moderate Arabs more significantly."[79] In another interview with the
Hebrew media he complained:

This is our state and we should be part of it. The FUC positions only hurt
our lives. We have to find a good way to educate the children to be part of the

state [. . .] The problem is that in spite of what I am doing for the state, I am not being backed up. The attitude [of the government] to Shefa'amr is like [its] attitude to Umm el-Fahm. We should receive different treatment so that everyone will go in my direction.[80]

Yasin might have been unique in his overt instrumentalism, but it is possible that he could also represent a wider phenomenon. After all, the government was able to recruit two Arab Muslim mayors to sit on the advisory board of the sixtieth anniversary celebration (Sami 'Isa from Kafr Qasim and Talal al-Qirnawi from Rahat).

Some public intimidations inhabit the twilight zone of bizarre politics and potential crimes against humanity. On 3 December, 2007, the Israeli Knesset gathered for a special festive session to celebrate the sixtieth anniversary of the UN decision to partition Palestine into Jewish and Arab states. Arab MKs boycotted this event, provoking furious reactions from some Jewish MKs. Two days later, the FUC chair, Shawqi Khatib, informed the Israeli government that Arab municipalities would not take part in the celebrations of Israel's sixtieth Independence Day. "We are not part of these festivals," he stated. "The State of Israel was founded on the ruins of the Palestinian people."[81] Following this decision the Minister of Public Security and former head of the Shabak, Avi Dichter, declared, "Whoever cries about the Nakba year after year shouldn't be surprised if they actually have a Nakba eventually." He called on Israeli-Arab leaders to reconsider their decision not to take part in the celebrations. In the same context, the minister attacked the mere use of the term "Nakba," and argued that it harms the Arab public: "From the Nakba they will not get any better education, from the Nakba they will not get better economic opportunities."[82] These threats were made before an Arab audience at the opening ceremony of the first Arab branch of the Kadima party in a non-Jewish locality, in Shefa'amr. The municipal official turned scholar Meron Benvenisti opined in *Haaretz* that "only paranoia and a repressed feeling of guilt could produce" this kind of statement.[83]

Only eight years earlier, in 2000, Ami Ayalon, Dichter's predecessor in the Shabak (1996–2000), recognized that "their [the Palestinians'] Nakba accompanies them as a trauma in the same way that the Holocaust accompanies us," an empathic statement diametrically opposite to Dichter's approach. Although the difference between these two statements is related to differences in personalities and politics, it might capture as well the changes in the level of "Nakba anxiety" in Israel's main surveillance agency since 2000.

OUTLAWING COMMEMORATION

When Turkish authorities are interested in silencing voices that describe the 1915 mass atrocities against the Armenians as genocide, they can use an existing clause in the penal code that forbids "insulting Turkishness."[84] In Romania, on the other hand, the attempt of the nationalist Romanian mayor of Cluj to ban the public celebration of the 15 of March Hungarian national holiday in his city failed,[85] since such a ban was incompatible with post-communist Romanian law. Israeli politicians who have tried to restrict Palestinian commemoration of the Nakba since the beginning of the twenty-first century might be anxious like the Turkish authorities, but like the Romanian mayor, they have not been able to find a clause in the penal code to support a ban. Thus, recognizing that the authorities' ability to discipline commemoration of the Nakba is restricted by the rule of law, Israeli politicians have been involved in recurrent legislative attempts to outlaw Nakba commemoration.

In July 2001, four Jewish MKs from different right-wing parties submitted a bill aimed at amending the Independence Day Law. According to the proposed amendment, a person who commemorated Israel's Independence Day as a day of mourning would be jailed for one year or fined 100,000 New Israeli Shekels. The bill was rejected by the Knesset Assembly, and in the following years it was resubmitted and rejected several times. In 2009, however, the government adopted a softened version of this legislation, which was approved by the Knesset in March 2011 and became known as the Nakba Law. According to the amended bill, the Minister of Finance is authorized to halt public funding for organizations (read: Arab municipalities) who support the commemoration of "Israel's Independence Day or the day of its establishment as a day of mourning." Note that the law is phrased in such a way that even the commemoration of Nakba Day on 15 May (rather than on Independence Day) would justify punishment.

Some of the legislators who initiated this law genuinely believed that they had the power to shape the collective memory of the Palestinians in Israel. One of them, MK Alex Miller (Yisrael Beiteinu), a Russian-born politician who immigrated to Israel in 1992, told me:

> I want to change by this law the way that people, citizens in this state, think [...]
> At the end of the day if you remove the big events from the agenda, the thought would begin to change. From the moment that young people are not part of it and do not participate in those things, they think differently [...] There is an entire population that every year on a certain day commemorates a catastrophe

of this state [sic]. It's time to put an end to it and I think that this is the way [. . .] I do not think that all the young Arabs who participate in the Nakba events understand what the whole turmoil is about. Are their conditions so bad that it is such a disaster? They should look at their neighbors, their families who live on the other side, how successful they are and how well they live.[86]

Miller seems to be unaware of the irony in his argument—it is exactly when Palestinians in Israel look at their families on "the other side" that they are reminded of the expulsions of 1948 that split families irreparably. Although he is aware of the tremendous importance of the Internet and satellite TV, he still believes in the urgency to "disconnect the opinion of the former [generation] from the generation that replaces it," as well as in his ability to impose this disconnection.

To what extent was this legislation effective in deterring Arab citizens from commemorating the Nakba during Independence Day? It is difficult to isolate the peculiar influence of each mode of discipline, especially since the old disciplinary mechanisms have not completely disappeared.[87] Still, the sharp decline in the presence of Arab mayors at the March of Return in the four years following the initial governmental adoption of the Nakba Law in 2009 suggests that this legislation has had at least some impact already. In fact, only one Arab mayor participated in the March of Return in 2010, and the visible absence of the rest provided the main headline of the Arabic newspaper *Kul al-'Arab*. The newspaper even explicitly commented that the mayors were concerned with losing state funding for their councils.[88] The absence of Arab mayors was noticeable again in 2012 and 2013 and was again highlighted by Arabic newspapers.

At the same time, there is no evidence of a decline in the number of participants in the march, and many members of various Arab municipal councils do participate in the annual march. Furthermore, the preparatory committee of the march in 2010 convened at the city hall of Tira, signaling that this local mayor was not concerned about the potential consequence of defying the new law. After the March of Return in 2011, the Jewish mayor of Natseret 'Ilit (a settlement near Nazareth where 13 percent of its residents are Arab), Shim'on Gapso, demanded that the two Arab representatives in the city hall resign following their participation in the march.[89]

THE CHANGING MODE OF DISCIPLINE

The anxiety of the state authorities and the Jewish public regarding the public appearance of a Palestinian national narrative has led to continuous attempts to discipline the public display of Palestinian political memory and to contain it. In the first decades after 1948, this discipline was imposed mainly by strict monitoring by the security services and even by forcing Arabs to publicly adopt the Zionist narrative. As the Jews' siege mentality abated and Arab self-confidence and organizational ability increased in the 1980s and 1990s, elements of the Palestinian national narrative gained more public visibility. The Second Intifada reversed the direction of abating Nakba anxiety, but it was too late to restore the old modes of disciplining memory. Instead of strict monitoring by the security services, however, Palestinian memory in Israel is monitored by the watchful civic gaze of ordinary citizens and its bearers are subject to public intimidation by government officials and to restrictive legislation. These modes are not completely ineffective but they are far from pushing national historical remembrance back to the private sphere.

There is one sphere, however, where the shadow of the military government is still more evident: the formal education system. Palestinian parties and organizations in Israel have looked for creative ways to bypass, alter, or confront it. This is the topic of the next two chapters.

8 THE STRUGGLE OVER THE NEXT GENERATION

SEVERAL WEEKS after the tenth Land Day anniversary in 1986, the lawyer Tawfiq Abu Ahmad, chair of the Parent Committee in Nazareth, sent a letter to the general director of the Ministry of Education, with a daring request: To commemorate Land Day in all Israeli schools on 30 March every year. Abu Ahmad justified his request: "Land Day has become a symbol of the just struggle of the Arab citizens of Israel for equal rights and freedom, democracy, patriotism, and above all, peace between the two peoples in this land. The education for these values would contribute, beyond any doubt, to reducing tension, social harmony, and co-existence in mutual respect between the two peoples."[1]

Abu Ahmad was walking on a very fine line. The compulsory education system has been a major sphere of struggle over identity and historical remembrance between the State of Israel and its Palestinian minority. Arab or Palestinian national narratives have been excluded from the official curriculum, and the job security of teachers and directors has been dependent on keeping a safe distance from this narrative.[2] His presentation of Land Day as a symbol of peace between the two peoples might have genuinely reflected his view, or it might have been merely a tactical move aimed to introduce the Palestinian national narrative into the official curriculum. Anyway, there is no doubt that he knew that only by disconnecting Land Day from any association with Palestinian nationalism could he expect to find listening ears in this Ministry of Education. This careful approach did not help. Four weeks later he received a very short response from Eli'ezer Shmueli, the general director: "I do not find the idea in your letter compelling, and I do not believe that there is a chance to implement it."

Abu Ahmad's initiative represented an emerging tendency, gradually developing since the late 1970s. Palestinian parents, educators, NGOs, and political parties, advanced diverse initiatives and developed various tools aimed at bypassing, altering, or confronting the curriculum of the formal education system. The authorities, on their part, developed their own strategies to monitor, discipline, or contain these initiatives. In general, states tend to be reluctant to give up their control of public education. As the sociologist Ernest Gellner noted years ago, none of the modern political ideals (such as an independent judiciary, freedom of speech and assembly, and so forth), are taken as seriously by states as the principle of universal and centrally guaranteed education.[3] Although Gellner attributed this uniqueness to the need of industrial societies for a generic and standardized form of education, there is substantial evidence that mass public education serves the interests of political domination as well.[4] As several Gramsci-inspired scholars have pointed out, public education is a crucial tool in establishing political hegemony, a form of domination achieved by making the existing social order seem like common sense.[5] In that vein, Arab public education in Israel aimed at making the State of Israel, as well as the separation of the Palestinians in Israel from other Palestinians, part of an unquestionable reality.

Unlike the "nationalizing states" of central Europe,[6] the State of Israel has never been interested in assimilating or "Israelifying" Arab students. Because inclusion in the Israeli nation was conditioned on Jewishness, Israel did not try to impose education in Hebrew on its Arab citizens, and the need for separate public education in Arabic was self-evident. At the same time, the existence of a separate Arab educational system required a highly elaborated system of surveillance and monitoring. Through the Ministry of Education and the security services, successive Israeli governments implemented a centralized monitoring of the curriculum and the employees of the Arab schools.

Most significantly, in the particular field of teaching history, the Israeli state's policy in the first years after 1948 can be described as an attempt to reset historical consciousness. During those years, the Department of Arab Education (DAE), which was established within the Ministry of Education, completely purged all teaching materials that existed prior to the foundation of the state and then forced Arab students to study from state-approved books only.[7] Tens of thousands of copies of school books captured by Israeli forces in Jaffa and Haifa were shredded.[8] The DAE organized retraining courses for Arab teachers whose main field of focus was teaching history.[9] From the authorities' point of view, those teaching Arab history and culture to Arab students had to be careful not to contribute to the development of Arab national sentiments. This dilemma is epitomized by a sentence that appeared in 1957 in an internal correspondence of the Ministry of Education regarding the goals of Arab education: "Instruction of history—to give the students knowledge of Arab history and culture accompanied by the feeling that they are not one people."[10]

After the end of military rule in 1966, Israeli state institutions continued to monitor Arab formal education. Despite the introduction of some changes in the 1970s, the official curriculum still ignored the Palestinian national narrative,[11] and the security service was still directly involved in hiring and firing teachers and directors. Since the late 1980s, neo-liberal policies and practices in Israel introduced a certain degree of decentralization and privatization in the educational system. At the same time, however, the state has increased its involvement in educational affairs by dictating the goals of education; setting uniform standards of scholastic achievements; and most important for our discussion, by imposing a national value system intended to produce loyal citizens.[12] Although this policy affects the entire Israeli education system, it has been especially evident in Arab schools where the surveillance of the Ministry of Education continues to be coordinated with the Shabak. During the 1990s, three education ministers from the left-wing Meretz party attempted to reduce the Shabak's involvement in authorizing nominations of teachers and school directors, but they had only limited success.[13]

The fact that during the relatively liberal 1990s, the state still was reluctant to reduce surveillance or to release its centralizing and monopolizing grip on Arab public education further encouraged Palestinian parents, educators, and activists to fight over the curriculum or to suggest alternatives to it. In this struggle over education, all sides assume that the formal education system is an important sphere for shaping the historical remembrance and identity of the younger generation. Hence, before discussing the struggle itself, let us take a look at some indicators of the validity of this assumption.

WHAT IS AT STAKE?

In my 2008 survey I asked the interviewees to state what they considered to be the main source of their historical knowledge. While among Jews "school" was ranked at the top with 22 percent who considered it their main source of historical knowledge, among Arab interviewees it was ranked only fifth with 13.4 percent, lagging behind television, Internet, books, and family (Figure 6). Similar results were found when the interviewees were asked to list all of the sources of their historical knowledge. Among Jews, 53.5 percent mentioned school, while among Arabs only 28.7 percent mentioned it. These results clearly confirm that Palestinian citizens have markedly little trust in the Israeli education system, a fact that no doubt reflects the overbearing state policies discussed above.

These numbers, however, do not mean that schools are not influential in shaping the historical remembrance of Palestinians in Israel. Although a causal relationship is impossible to prove in this context, Figure 7 suggests that school attendance might be associated with certain kinds of historical remembrance. In the survey, interviewees were asked to name as many as four persons that they considered as most important in the history of the country. I classified the answers into categories. The two largest categories were Zionist figures and Arab figures.

I found that 58.3 percent of those Arab interviewees who selected "school" as the main source of their historical knowledge mentioned at least one Zionist figure (most commonly, Yitzhak Rabin, Ariel Sharon, and David Ben Gurion). Among the rest of the Arab sample, the ratio was significantly lower, 44.5 percent ($p<0.05$ in χ^2 test). This is also higher than the frequency of naming Zionist figures among those who selected Internet, television, print media, books, or family as the main source of their knowledge of history. Selecting "family" as a main source of historical knowledge, on the other hand, was negatively

| Jewish sample | | Arab sample | |
Main source of knowledge	%	Main source of knowledge	%
1. School	22.0	1. Television	23.9
2. Books	18.6	2. Books	19.0
3. Television	13.6	3. Internet	16.4
4. Family	12.9	4. Family	13.9
5. Print media	12.8	5. School	13.4
6. Internet	5.9	6. Print media	8.0

Figure 6. Distributions of answers of Jews and Arabs to the question: "Among the following, what is the main source of your historical knowledge?"

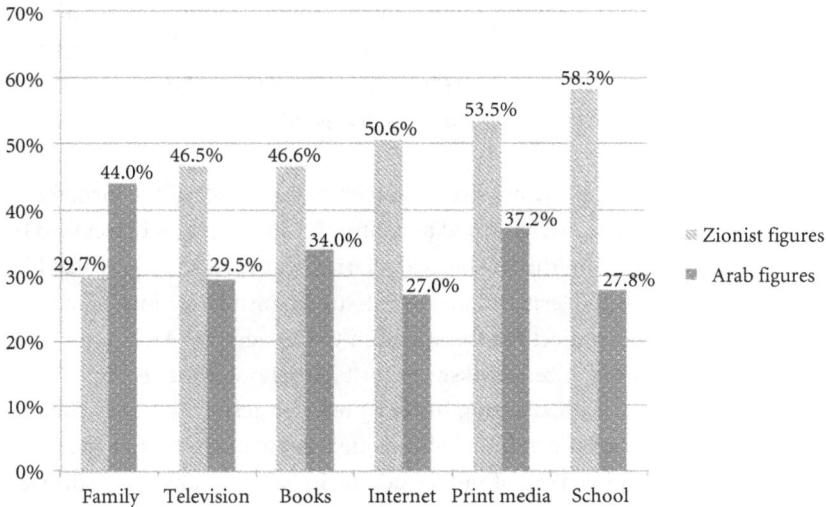

Figure 7. Percentage of respondents who mentioned Zionist and Arab figures by their main source of historical knowledge

associated with naming Zionist figures (29.7 percent among those who mentioned family, 48.9 percent among the rest of the Arab sample, p<0.01 in χ^2 test).

On the other hand, family was associated closely with recalling important Arab figures. Among interviewees who mentioned "family" as the main source of their historical knowledge, 44 percent mentioned Arab figures (most commonly Yasser Arafat, Hasan Nasrallah, and Gamal Abdel Nasser). Among the rest of the interviewees, only 30 percent mentioned Arab figures (p<0.05 in χ^2 test).

From these figures, it is clear that school and family are associated with diametrically opposed forms of historical remembrance. While school seems to play the role assigned to it by the state and is associated with "approved knowledge," the private sphere is associated with the counter-hegemonic "forbidden knowledge."[14] In fact, a prominent feature of the collective memory project led by Palestinian intellectuals, educators, and politicians since the mid-1990s is the attempt to extend the presence of personal memories with national relevance into the public sphere. In many cases, the carving out of new spaces for national memory in the public sphere (such as press reference or including the names of martyrs on monuments) has involved the active encouragement of individuals to tell their private stories, especially stories about the Nakba. Arabic newspapers have launched testimony projects and have published series of private testimonies. A prominent example is a series of articles published in *Kul al-ʿArab* in 1998 and later republished as a book.[15] The educational initiative of Palestinian activists I discuss in this chapter should be viewed as another sort of attempt to increase congruence between memories discussed within the family and public memory.

The survey results above are also indicative of the power of the formal education system that these activists had to confront.[16] In Chapter 6 I discussed the project "Sixty Years from the Nakba, Sixty Terms on the Nakba," in which high school students selected terms related to Palestinian history for inclusion in the booklet. As part this project the Ibn Khaldun Center and the Arab Association for Human Rights organized workshops for high school students aimed at assisting each student with selecting his/her preferred terms. For Dr. Mohanad Mustafa, the editor of the volume who guided the workshops, the encounter with Palestinian students (all of them studying in Israeli schools) constituted a sharp reminder of the necessity of the project:

> I was exposed to the lack of consciousness and awareness of Arab high school students regarding the historical memory and the basic elements in Palestinian history. For example, I asked one of the groups about Haj Amin al-Husayni. Almost nobody knew who he was. I knew beforehand that the situation was severe, but I did not know it was so severe. And we are talking here about organized groups who are supposed to be informed by other institutions—so what does this say about the rest of the Arab students? I was astonished. I did not think [that this is the case]. I thought that after the increase in the national consciousness among the Palestinians in Israel and the strengthening of the status of the Arab parties, it would influence their historical consciousness. [. . .]
>
> If you ask them, everyone would tell you "we are Palestinians." They wear the Palestinian *kuffiya*, or a shirt with a picture of a Palestinian poet or Handala.[17] He would tell you "I define myself as a Palestinian," but he does not know his history. He knows about the Palestinian-Israeli conflict, and about the Nakba. They know that the Jewish forces expelled the Arabs in 1948—but only that—not the small details, nor the big details.

The "Sixty Terms on the Nakba" project is only one example of the various institutionalized strategies developed by Palestinian intellectuals in Israel to shape the historical remembrance of Palestinian children and youth. In the next sections I discuss other strategies, as well as the reactions of the Israeli state apparatus to them. Some of these strategies aim directly at influencing the curriculum of the public education system, others at developing alternative channels of education outside the public education system, and others combine these two modes.

PRIVATE SCHOOLS

In Israel there are twenty-eight private Arab elementary schools and twelve private Arab secondary schools,[18] all of them belong to different Christian communities.[19] About 10 percent of the total number of Arab students study in these schools,[20] but the percentage increases dramatically when we look at the private secondary schools alone: almost one–third (about 30 percent) of Palestinian students in Israel study in private high schools.[21] In part this is because some of these secondary schools are considered elite and because of their prestige, they attract many Muslim and Druze students as well. By the second decade of the twenty-first century, at least in some of these schools, the Muslim students constitute the majority.[22]

Although Israel abolished the autonomous status that private schools enjoyed under Ottoman and British rule,[23] due to both international considerations and attempts to co-opt the Christian minority, it also initially refrained from actively interfering with their activities.[24] These schools were allowed relative autonomy in curricular development and employment; in fact, some of the teachers who were fired from the public education system because of their political views were subsequently employed by these private schools.[25]

However, the potential of these private schools to strengthen national consciousness among Arab students remained a source of concern for Israeli governments,[26] and in late 1957 the state decided to recognize them and subject them to the supervision of the Ministry of Education. For their part, Christian schools were ready to give up some of their autonomy in exchange for financial support, better professional training for their teachers, and better compatibility between their curriculum and the Israeli higher education system—a process that took place during the 1970s.[27]

Since 1978 these schools have been considered "recognized, unofficial educational institutions." Their legal status is determined by the Order of Education, which states that "the superintendent [of the Ministry of Education] is not allowed to demand changes in the curriculum or the internal administration of the school."[28] This statement, however, is qualified by another clause that allows the minister to impose his authority "at the level needed in order to maintain public order and proper administration."[29] State financing accounts for between 70–90 percent of their maintenance budget and teacher salaries, which is a significant portion but still lower than state financing for public schools.

The relative financial autonomy of the Arab private schools as well as the self-confidence of the teaching staff and administration have been reflected in the activities in some of these schools, especially the most elite among them, such as the Arab Orthodox College in Haifa, St. Joseph High School in Nazareth, and the Mar Elias College in Iʿblin. In these schools even graduation ceremonies are sometimes imbued with Arab and Palestinian national symbolism.[30] Usually, however, "political" content (namely, content that is unlikely to be approved by the ministry) has been included in informal activities such as activities organized by the student councils, the student papers, or guest lectures. For example, the Students' Council at St. Joseph High School in Nazareth was involved in organizing lectures and disseminating written material about Land Day in the late 1980s.[31] It is noteworthy that this tactic has been adopted by some public schools as well in cases where the local council supports such activity.[32]

These fertile conditions for national ideological education have some implications in the political sphere. The graduates of these private schools are overrepresented among the Palestinian intellectual and political elite in Israel, and have significant input on public political discussions. The most prestigious Christian school in Israel, the Orthodox College in Haifa, is a leader in this regard. Unlike other schools belonging to religious communities, since its establishment in 1952, the Orthodox College has focused on nurturing Arab identity rather than a communitarian Christian Orthodox identity.[33] As the chair of the Nakba and Steadfastness Committee (discussed in Chapter 5), Muhammad Ali Taha, himself a Muslim graduate of this high school, said at the graduation ceremony of the fortieth class in 1995: "We are a college whose goal is to create a person who is proud of his national, geographical, and human belonging [. . .] Do not forget that you are the sons and daughters of this great people and this beautiful homeland."[34] The college has been consistently involved in Nakba memorialization and education to such a degree that shortly after the Knesset legislated the Nakba Law in 2011, the alumni association appealed to the Supreme Court against this legislation out of concern that the government would cut its public funding. The appeal was rejected.[35]

Despite this exceptional example, the potential for political education provided by the relative autonomy of these private schools is far from being fully exploited. In part, this can be explained by the strong and growing emphasis on academic excellence in these schools, which involves harsh competition between the private schools themselves and subtracts from the readiness of administrators to invest resources or take risks in favor of ideological education.[36] Therefore, to find a tangible challenge to the formal education system's curricula, one should look elsewhere.

ATTEMPTS TO INFLUENCE THE CURRICULUM AT PUBLIC SCHOOLS

The letter that Tawfiq abu-Ahmad sent to the Ministry of Education was part of a broader Zeitgeist among Arab activists in the 1980s, who attempted to influence the curriculum at public schools. As early as February 1979, when the Land Committee met to discuss preparations for Land Day ceremonies, it called on Arab students and high schools to dedicate one hour of study on 30 March to commemorate Land Day.[37] This decision marked the beginning of a process over the next thirty years that gradually resulted in a highly organized and institutionalized challenge to the Ministry of Education. The FUCAE, established in 1984 as a sub-committee of the FUC and serving as the professional body addressing the educational and pedagogic issues that pertain to Palestinians in Israel, has been an important actor in this field. Its board includes Palestinian mayors, academics, pedagogues, heads of education departments in local councils, representatives of teachers' organizations and unions, school principals, the National Union of Arab Parents' Committees, and the National Union of University Students. Although officially the FUCAE is non-partisan, it has been dominated by representatives of the DFPE, and as a result it has attempted consistently to act from within the Israeli political system and has aspired to gain state recognition for its actions. Government officials were even invited to its inaugural event in 1984, but they decided to boycott it.[38]

Because neither the FUC nor the FUCAE have the legal authority or the direct power to shape the curriculum in public schools, to promote their initiatives they have needed the cooperation of the local councils, and even then they are limited to high schools. The resulting close relationship between the FUCAE and the local councils is highly relevant for understanding the FUCAE's modus operandi and, therefore, requires some elaboration.

In Arab communities in Israel more than in Jewish ones, municipalities are the locus of significant political, social, and economic power. As we have already seen, a primary reason for this is that Arab citizens have limited access to the political centers of power on the state level, which turned the municipality into a default sphere of direct political influence.[39] Another reason for the relative importance of Arab municipalities is the weak economic infrastructure in Arab towns and villages, which turned the municipality into the largest employer in most Arab localities.[40]

Unlike in the elementary and intermediate schools where teachers are employed directly by the Ministry of Education, high school teachers receive their salaries through the municipalities. This control over personnel in secondary schools, as well as the school facilities, gave local governments significant power in shaping cultural and educational policy. This observation was valid already in 1990,[41] but it has become even more noticeable in the decades since then.

The series of FUCAE educational initiatives since 2000 is a good example of this dynamic. Although during the 1990s the FUCAE called Arab schools to dedicate teaching time to Land Day in its anniversaries, it was only toward the end of the decade that a comprehensive program was launched. In 1999/2000 the FUCAE, led by Dr. Hala Espanioly, issued the first organized challenge to the curriculum of the Ministry of Education. Using funding from the Ta'awun Fund,[42] the FUCAE developed a new curricular program aimed at enhancing the Palestinian national identity of high school students. The new curriculum included chapters about the Nakba, the Kafr Qasim massacre, and the wars of 1967 and 1982. Visits to depopulated villages were an integral part of the Nakba component of the program. That year a pilot program was implemented in seven Arab high schools, without the approval of the Ministry of Education.[43] Some municipalities mediated between the FUCAE and schools so the FUCAE would not be accused of unauthorized intervention in the curriculum. However, this cautious tactic did not help: after related reports appeared in the Hebrew press, the Ministry of Education (under Minster Zevulun Orlev from the National Religious Party) banned the implementation of the full program scheduled for the following year.

Since then, the FUCAE and other Arab organizations have continued to produce educational materials and to send them to Arab high schools, especially before major events in the four major anchors of the collective calendar of the Palestinian citizens of Israel. Sometimes, following special events like the deaths of Yasser Arafat and the poet Mahmoud Darwish, additional materials were sent to schools. To avoid legal complications for violating the authority of the Ministry of Education, the guidelines letter written by the FUCAE opened with an explicit reference to the circuitous method of transmitting the information. This letter addresses "the honorable directors of the departments of education in the Arab municipal councils, and through them to the honorable school directors."[44]

Over the years the reaction of the Ministry of Education has fluctuated depending on the personal proclivities of the Minister of Education and the broader political atmosphere, alternating between clear-cut bans of these materials and attempts to negotiate over them. During the first years of the term of Limor Livnat as Minister of Education (2001–2006), ministry administrators communicated intensively with the FUC and the FUCAE. In November 2001 there was even a joint meeting between ministry administrators and three FUCAE members to discuss several aspects of Arab education. In the end, however, the Ministry of Education did not authorize the program and the teaching tools developed by the FUCAE, and instead developed a tactic of containment—developing its own teaching guidelines for the controversial events, as described below.

An especially turbulent dispute between the Ministry of Education and FUCAE has been the commemoration of the October 2000 events at Palestinian schools. Since the first anniversary in 2001, the FUCAE has called on school directors to commemorate them by dedicating teaching time to discussing the events and their significance. It even disseminated very detailed and specific guidelines for teachers. With little variation, the proposed plan every year since then has been a discussion of the topic in class for two hours according to the following scheme:

> 1) What happened in October 2000 (including the reasons for the demonstrations; the police reaction; number of martyrs, injured, and arrested); the students' feelings; the need to commemorate the events; the best ways to commemorate national events in general. 2) The Or Commission[45]—what was its mandate? What were its recommendations? Were those responsible for the killing punished? 3) Conclusion.

These annual initiatives presented the Ministry of Education with a dilemma. On the one hand, the ministry was witnessing the process through which the October events were to become a cornerstone in the emerging national commemorative calendar of the Arabs in Israel, a process they were determined to exclude from schools. On the other hand, the wounds among Palestinians in Israel were still fresh, and the ministry's administrators understood that preventing any discussion was an unrealistic goal. The result was an attempt to contain the discourse and to convert it from national commemoration and civic protest, into a psychological-therapeutic course of action. Along these lines, a day after the 2004 guidelines were sent by the FUCAE to Arab school directors, the director general of the Ministry of Education Ronit Tirosh sent a letter in Arabic to all the directors of Arab schools. The letter included the following warning:

> We support and cherish the freedom of expression of feelings, thoughts, opinions, and positions, within clear boundaries, according to the state's rules and laws. We will absolutely not allow anyone without professional authority to act in schools or to direct instructions and guidelines concerning this activity, which is under the ministry's authority. I ask every director to allocate two hours next week to discussing the October events and to giving the students the opportunity to express their feelings and thoughts in civilized pedagogic ways.[46]

Two months later, however, this relatively appeasing message was replaced with a harsh rebuking tone in an explicit ban on the implementation of the FUCAE guidelines. The second letter was sent after the FUCAE disseminated guidelines for classroom activities following the death of the president of the PNA based in Ramallah, Yasser Arafat. As a result, the new letter included the warning that "a director of an educational institution who is found to abide by these [the FUCAE's] guidelines, would be reprimanded and face a disciplinary hearing for violating a director general circular."[47]

In 2006 the Ministry of Education extended this containment tactic to Land Day. In early March of that year the ministry published a program entitled: "The Thirtieth Land Day Anniversary: Equality and Mutual Understanding between the Two Peoples." The fact that the program was intended for Arab schools only is evidence that the explicit aspiration for "mutual understanding" was no more than a cover for a calculated containment tactic. In the introduction, the new director general, 'Amira Haim, wrote to teachers and school directors:

> [T]his unfortunate event brought much sorrow and pain to the hearts of all of us and made us stand in solidarity with the bereaved families and the injured. We stand in the belief that all the citizens of this state are one family linked by daily co-existence and common destiny, a desire to build a bridge of mutual understanding and tight cooperation between all the forces, and [a desire] to reach a peaceful coexistence.

This was another attempt by the Israeli Ministry of Education to depoliticize Palestinian commemoration in Arab schools, presenting the killing of Palestinians by the Israeli police as an unfortunate incident that took place between two parties with seemingly equal power, detached from the broader context of the Israeli-Palestinian conflict. The letter repeated the ministry's commitment to "freedom of expression" within "clear boundaries" and included an implicit warning to Arab teachers to ignore the FUCAE's guidelines.

The following year in 2007 when Yuli Tamir (Labor Party) was Minister of Education, four joint FUCAE-Ministry of Education committees were created to examine the needs of the Arab education system in different areas. While three of these committees were able to submit their recommendations in the time allotted, in one of the committees the two sides were unable to reach an agreement. Unsurprisingly, it was the committee that dealt with the content of the educational curriculum.[48]

Despite these interventions, over the last twenty years Arab teachers and school directors have become gradually more confident in teaching unapproved materials. According to Hala Espanioly, the FUCAE chair between 1995 and 2000, in this early period only a negligible number of teachers adopted the materials provided by the FUCAE.[49] In most cases, school directors did not even distribute the materials to teachers. By 2008, however, the general director of the FUCAE, 'Atef Mu'adi, estimated that in the majority of Arab high schools, major Palestinian national events such as the Nakba, Land Day, and October 2000 were commemorated (although not necessarily by using the FUCAE materials), and the Ministry of Education has had little control over the actual content. Leading private schools such as St. Joseph in Nazareth even dare to publish the FUCAE program for commemorating October 2000 on their website.[50] Every once in a while, a director or a teacher has been warned by the ministry, but so far the ministry has avoided penalizing educators for including certain themes in class.

At the end of day the FUCAE is dependent on the readiness of individual directors and teachers to adopt their programs. It seems that there are three main factors that determine the decision of teachers whether to diverge from the approved line of commemoration. First, as mentioned earlier, high school teachers are less vulnerable than elementary school teachers and, therefore, are more likely to defy the official guidelines. Second, where the local authority is actively supportive of this political education, teachers are even encouraged to commemorate the various memorial days. In cities and towns like Nazareth and Sakhnin with a tradition of political activism, teachers have strong institutional support for deviating from the official line of the Ministry of Education. Finally, because universities are important sites of political socialization, the educational background of school teachers is a crucial factor as well. A series of interviews with female Arab teachers revealed that those who qualified through

a university degree (as opposed to those who qualified through teacher training colleges) were more prone to include ideological messages outside of the
instruction required by the curriculum.[51]

School Strikes

The FUCAE and politically-motivated teachers and directors have tried to
include Arab students in Land Day and October 2000 commemorations, especially in those years when the FUC declared a general strike. As with other
aspects of defying the policy of the Ministry of Education, the responsibility for
closing schools is taken by local municipalities instead of by individual school
directors who are more vulnerable. In some Arab cities and towns, the municipal council locks the school gates on certain memorial days, a step that allows
school directors to present themselves to the ministry as helpless.[52]

Before the ninth anniversary of the October events in 2009, the FUC called
for a general strike, including a strike in Arab schools. The Ministry of Education immediately announced that all schools would operate as usual. While
most Arab schools located in Arab towns effectively joined the strike (the directors opened the schools but teachers and students did not attend), Arab schools
in mixed cities had a more delicate position. Several days later, the director of
the Haifa district sent a letter to school directors in the city demanding that
they provide the names and ID numbers of teachers who were absent.[53]

Later, this threatening tactic was extended to Arab localities as well. Since
Land Day 2011, as part of the growing tension surrounding Palestinian commemoration, the Ministry of Education has become more pro-active in its attempts to prevent Arab pupils and teachers from participating in Land Day
rallies. That year, teachers in several schools in Lydda reported that ministry officials conducted surprise visits in the morning and noted which teachers were
absent.[54] In the north since 2011, the director of the Northern District, Dr. Orna
Simhon, has sent a letter to all school principals in her district demanding that
they provide a list of the teachers who were absent from work that on Land Day.
The ministry then subtracts the missing day from the salary of those teachers.
According to Simhon, this has discouraged Arab teachers from missing work
on days of subsequent commemorative events.[55]

The Pedagogical Council

In the hopes of centralizing and revamping Arab education in Israel, in 2008
the FUCAE established a professional pedagogic council for the Arab education

system, tasked with the proactive guiding of curricular policies. The launch of the council was funded by a grant from the European Union; and the council, comprised of leading figures in the field of Arab-Palestinian education, officially began its work in July 2010.[56] The FUCAE hoped to receive government recognition, and called on the Ministry of Education to grant the council an official status. However, the ministry was reluctant to do so even under the relatively liberal minister Yuli Tamir (2006–2009) and has ignored the initiative. As a result, the council works independently. On October 2011 its members prepared a document specifying the objectives of Arab education and circulated it among Arab and Jewish activists and scholars soliciting feedback. Although no noticeable progress has been achieved since that time, it might be too early to assess the influence of the council. Its establishment seems to indicate an intensification of the collective effort of Arab educational leaders to influence the curriculum in the formal education system.

Developing Pedagogic Material

On the eve of Land Day 2011, for the first time, the FUCAE published a guide for Arab teachers, entitled *al-Hawiyya* (identity). According to the editor, Raja Zaʿtra, the intention was to produce a document with the potential to be approved by the Ministry of Education. The booklet includes three parts: (1) short outlines of selected historical events and periods; (2) short biographies of major Palestinian intellectuals and artists, such as Khalil Sakakini, Fadwa Tuqan, and Edward Said; and (3) guidelines for pedagogical tours in the country through which students would learn about its nature and history.

The booklet does not present any maps, but judging by the sites suggested for tours and the focus on the particular history of the Palestinians in Israel, the relevant boundaries for the students are the pre-1967 lines. None of the sites is in the West Bank, and the booklet does not even include the major iconic sites of Palestinian nationalism in East Jerusalem. This geographic selection reflects, first, the recognition that Palestinian citizens of Israel have their own identity that differs in some respects from other Palestinians. It reflects, as well, the dominance in the FUCAE of the communist-led DFPE. Unlike other parties and movements (such as the NDA, the northern faction of the Islamic Movement, or the Sons of the Village), the DFPE is still very consistent in its support of the two-state solution, based on the pre-1967 borders.

For most of the sites the accompanying text provides the names in both Arabic and Hebrew. For some of them the guide suggests teaching students about the Arab villages that preceded the Jewish towns or villages built on their lands. Among the recommended sites are the cemetery in Acre, where the three Palestinian martyrs executed in 1930 were buried, and the cemetery in Kafr Qasim. The FUCAE submitted the booklet to the Ministry of Education, requesting that it be adopted as an official study unit, and through the municipalities, it distributed thousands of copies to Arab high schools.[57] The ministry reacted by threatening to take strict disciplinary measure against any school director who distributed the booklet.[58]

The FUCAE is only one actor among several NGOs involved in developing alternative pedagogic materials. In 2003 the Ministry of Education headed by Limor Livnat (Likud) developed "The 100 Terms Program in Heritage, Zionism and Democracy" designed for grades seven to nine, and in 2005 it published another version adapted for Arab schools. The difference between the lists aimed at Jewish and Arab schools was mainly in the "heritage" parts. The heritage terms designed for Arab schools referred almost exclusively to the different religious heritages of Muslim and Christian students. There were only a few terms referring to Arab history, and the only three figures from Arab history were from the middle ages.[59] The list did not include any important figures from modern Palestinian national history.

The program was harshly criticized for various reasons beyond the Arab-Jewish divide and beginning in 2009, it was removed from the curriculum. Before it was cancelled, however, the Ibn Khaldun Center and The Coalition against Racism in Israel produced an alternative list of terms.[60] As'ad Ghanem, the director of Ibn Khaldun and a political scientist at the University of Haifa, justified the urgency of reacting to the Ministry of Education with the concern that "younger generations of Palestinians in Israel suffer, in general, from a weak national identity, politically and culturally, to the point of the loss of national strength."[61]

The alternative list was constructed by a team of eighteen academics, authors, and journalists and published as a booklet entitled "Identity and Belonging." Sixty-five thousand copies of the booklet were printed. Some copies were sent to directors of Arab schools, but only four of these directors instructed teachers to use them.[62] The Ministry of Education reprimanded these directors and banned the use of the booklet. However, the book was distributed in alternative channels, by organizing regional workshops and conferences for teachers and parents, or through local community centers (*matnasim*),[63] which are controlled by municipal councils and not by the Ministry of Education. It is difficult to estimate how many teachers tacitly adopted the booklet following these efforts.

The alternative list included terms and figures related to Jewish and Zionist history such as the Holocaust, the Jewish National Fund, Theodor Herzl, David Ben Gurion, and Yitzhak Rabin—suggesting that the editors saw this project within the context of supporting a shared Israeli citizenship. However, unlike the list provided by the Ministry of Education, it also included several events from Palestinian history such as the Nakba, the Battle of Karameh, and Black September, as well as cities, including those beyond the Green Line, such as Jerusalem and Gaza. The list included Palestinian national figures as well, some of whom were active before 1948, such as Haj Amin al-Husayni, 'Izz al-Din al-Qassam, and the poets Ibrahim Tuqan and Nuh Ibrahim.

This return to pre-1948 history was an active attempt to counteract decades of omitting Palestinian national history from the state sanctioned curriculum. In my 2008 survey, for example, when asked to mention the most important figures in the history of the country, only 2.9 percent of the Arab interviewees mentioned Palestinian figures whose public activity occurred mostly before 1948. The founder of the modern Zionist movement, Theodor Herzl, was mentioned more frequently alone than all the pre-1948 Palestinian figures combined—4.1 percent. In contrast, among the parallel Jewish sample, 13.5 percent of the interviewees mentioned pre-1948 Jewish figures. These numbers validate the concern raised by the creators of the alternative list about the feebleness of Palestinian national-historical remembrance among the younger generation.

.   .   .

One major weakness of the various extra-mural, alternative pedagogic tools developed by Palestinian activists is that usually they are not presented to a captive audience. There is, however, a period of time when the formal education system is suspended and Palestinian political activists have the opportunity to expose students to alternative historical narratives for a relatively long period of time: summer time. The important role of summer camps for children and youth in nurturing Palestinian historical remembrance is the topic of the next chapter.

9 POLITICAL SUMMER CAMPS

BEFORE THE 2003 PARLIAMENTARY ELECTION, Israel's attorney general, Elyaqim Rubinstein, submitted to the Central Election Committee a request to disqualify the NDA from participating in the election. To his request he attached a review of the Shabak that described the worldview of the party and its leaders. Interestingly, the review included quotes from a youth summer camp organized by the NDA.[1] These quotes are evidence that the Shabak has been following closely the activity in these camps. Indeed, in the following summer, the police raided an NDA summer camp, arrested the director, and confiscated Palestinian flags and pictures of Gamal Abdel Nasser (they were later returned). In the same summer the police also raided a summer camp organized by the Sons of the Village, confiscated materials, shut it down, and arrested the organizers who were accused of incitement.[2]

If the Shabak experts are concerned about the potential of summer camps for enabling an efficient "un-authorized" socialization, they are probably right. The power of youth camps to nurture national identities has been illustrated in different contexts.[3] The structural setting of a "total institution"[4] is ideal for this purpose. In such settings, children or youth are gathered for several consecutive days, sometimes sleeping at the camp, where they create a "small world" that cuts them off from their regular environment, parents, and routines. It is an intense context, highly controlled by often charismatic camp counselors. Under these circumstances even routine activities might gain charismatic meanings and inspire ideological devotion.[5] In addition, summer camp is considered a form of informal education (outside of a standard school setting) and, as such, it is relatively difficult for authorities to monitor and discipline it.[6]

Camps for children and youth began in Europe and the United States in the late nineteenth century due to concerns about the potentially negative consequences of the urban, modern way of life and the romanticization of nature that grew out of these concerns. They also represented a solution to the question of children's socialization in modernity as traditional systems of socialization, especially the family and the community, became less powerful in shaping young people's lives.[7] In the United States, where summer camps achieved their greatest success, they drew on longstanding national ideologies and iconography, especially the idea of forging communities in frontier (or at least rural) conditions.[8] In the Soviet Union the Young Pioneer camps were established in 1925 and were instrumental in socializing children to socialist values.[9] In Palestine, summer camps were adopted enthusiastically by various branches of the Zionist society then established in Palestine that was at the same time a frontier society that idealized nature *and* a population that was highly influenced by Soviet socialism. The Arab Palestinian scout movement during the British Mandate organized occasional camps or hiking trips for several days, which included Arab nationalist content and encouragement to confront Zionism.[10]

The Israeli Communist Party adopted this practice as well, and the confrontation with the authorities around the issue started as early as July 1949. *Davar* reported that a joint Jewish-Arab youth camp organized in the western Galilee was relocated by order of the military government.[11] Over the years the Israeli government also tried to use summer camps to promote its own agenda among Arab citizens: from 1963 to 1973, the Arab Affairs Advisor's office initiated Jewish-Arab youth camps in Acre supervised by the Ministry of Education.

Following the split in the Communist Party in 1965, the faction that was closer to Arab nationalism remained in charge of the Alliance of the Israeli Communist Youth (hereafter Communist Youth), the youth wing of the party intended for ages fifteen to twenty-two. From 1968 until the early 1980s, the number of local offices of the Communist Youth doubled in number from thirty-six to seventy-three, a much sharper increase than the increase of party offices.[12] This development was related to the growing inclusion of youth in political activity and the importance ascribed to its political socialization among Arab citizens. In the same period the Communist Youth supported the establishment of Arab student committees at the local and district level, and in 1971 it was involved in the establishment of the country-wide Arab Student Association.[13] In the 1970s and the 1980s a delegation of the Communist Youth was sent to a summer camp in the Soviet Union.[14] The extension of this activity to local summer education soon followed.

As in other spheres, the emergence of summer activities for youth as a tool for developing Palestinian national consciousness and historical remembrance gained momentum after Land Day. This tendency was compatible with the de-hierarchization spirit of the post-Land Day era and the growing importance given to including youth in political practice. On 6 August 1976 *al-Ittihad* reported on a two-day long "glorified historical meeting" between communist youth from the Nazareth and Triangle regions that had taken place a week earlier in the Triangle. *Al-Ittihad* dedicated much attention to their visit to Kafr Qasim, where the participants marched from the entrance of the village to the cemetery "accompanied by the appreciation of the village people and slogans like 'O martyr, do not worry, we will continue the struggle!' Near the victims' tombs they stood for a moment of silence and heard the story of the massacre from the chair of the Commemoration Committee.[15]

THE NAZARETH WORKING CAMP

Later that same summer, a work camp of youth and university students opened in Nazareth. Until 1975, Nazareth, the largest Arab town in Israel, was ruled by Arab mayors who represented the interests of the Israeli government. The election of the communist leader and poet Tawfiq Zayyad as mayor that year alarmed the authorities, and the Ministry of Interior attempted to sanction Nazareth by not approving its budget (and therefore, depriving it of crucial public funds from the government). As a result, the municipal council of Nazareth, with the help of fourteen youth, women's, and students' organizations, initiated a summer work camp for "A beautiful and clean Nazareth." Beyond serving immediate municipal needs, Mayor Zayyad ascribed to the camp a much broader ideological meaning.

In his speech at the opening ceremony, he named the camp "the wedding of work and dignity." Among the other speakers at the opening ceremony was a young student named Azmi Bishara, who later would become the intellectual figure most identified with the idea of collective national rights for the Arabs in Israel. Over four days, 450 volunteers from the Galilee and the Triangle, who came to express solidarity with Nazareth, took part in cleaning streets, paving new roads, installing new sewage pipes, fixing equipment in schools, and planting trees. At the end of every work day, they listened to lectures about social and political issues and participated in cultural activities—dancing, singing, and sports competitions.[16] Cultural activities loaded with deep ideological significance, usually performed by the youth, are very common in the curriculum of youth movements,[17] and their inclusion is an indication of the pedagogic orientation of the work camps.

Al-Ittihad's reporter, Samih Ghanadri, wrote enthusiastically about the working day: "The men hit the ground and the ground is shaking. And suddenly, the anthem is rising: *mawtani! The youth will not tire* [a line from the Palestinian national anthem]."[18] For the reporter, the meaning of the camp went far beyond the immediate improvements in Nazareth: "The energy that exploded in the working camp proved that nobody can block the road of life and development in our society."[19] In a report summarizing the event, Ghanadri mentioned that the participants felt that they "provided a national service (*khidma watani-yya*) to their people in its struggle for achieving its rights."[20]

Being aware of its historical significance, the organizers started to name the camp "the *first* volunteer camp," implying that it was only the beginning of a new tradition. Indeed, the 1976 work camp was the start of an annual tradition that lasted fourteen years. In his opening speech at the 1977 camp, Mayor Zayyad was even more explicit about the pedagogic goals of the camp: "We will come out from this camp more united and organized, not only in the battle for development and construction but also for knowledge and culture. Let our camp be a festival of work and dignity in the morning and a festival of culture in the evening."[21] Subsequent camps included volunteers from the Triangle, the Naqab, the West Bank, and the Gaza Strip, as well as Jewish Israeli participants and delegations from several European countries. By the mid-1980s the number of volunteers reached the thousands and the number of participants in the opening ceremonies numbered in the tens of thousands, according to the reports in *al-Ittihad*. The opening ceremonies became major stages for displaying national pride, and in the 1980s they opened with the singing of "Biladi, Biladi" with Samih al-Qasim's modified lyrics (see Chapter 3).

The opening speeches of Mayor Zayyad and the reports about the camps in *al-Ittihad* accentuated and highlighted the participation of both Palestinians from the 1967 occupied territories as well as Jewish Israelis. Even this camp, though, exposed the gaps between Palestinians from both sides of the Green Line. In 1980, for example, volunteers from Nablus and Ramallah brought Palestinian flags with them, which they wanted to raise; in addition, they demanded that Israeli flags, commonly raised by the Communist Youth and the Arab Scouts, not be raised. In the opening ceremony two volunteers from

Nablus attempted to wave a Palestinian flag (which the Israeli government had outlawed that same year) in front of the visible presence of the Israeli police, but Mayor Zayyad approached them personally and gently folded the flag. On the following day, 150 volunteers from Nablus returned home in protest,[22] and Zayyad was condemned by Palestinian organizations in the West Bank.[23]

Another controversial aspect of these camps was related to gender relations. Inspired by European volunteers, adolescent girls and boys were able not only to work together in these camps but also to sleep in sleeping bags in the same location. For many Palestinians, especially old people and the religiously conservative, such a development was shocking and provoked much antagonism.[24]

The summer work camp model initiated in Nazareth was adopted subsequently by many other localities, and these other camps followed the pattern of combining urban improvement with celebration of national identity. For example, the major project in the 1986 camp in Tamra was installing a tomb on the grave of Nuh Ibrahim. Another important connection of summer camps to Palestinian collective memory has been the tradition of volunteer work camps at the depopulated village of Kafr Bir'im starting in the early 1980s.[25] Since 1987, the Kafr Bir'im community has organized a summer camp for their children in the de-populated village.[26]

In 1985 the Communist Youth began to organize local summer camps for younger children without incorporating the practical role of cleaning and renovating a city. Many of these camps were organized in partnership with the Movement of Democratic Women in Israel, a feminist Arab-Jewish organization affiliated with the Communist Party. From this point on, political socialization was the explicit raison d'être of these camps, not only a byproduct. There is a direct link between the successful first-generation work camps and the subsequent establishment of summer camps for younger children, as the latter were organized by the same local communist activists.[27]

The first Communist Youth summer camp for children organized in 1985 was a common camp for the children of Sakhnin and 'Arabeh, two of the "Land Day villages." In the following years communist branches in Tira, Tur'an, Shefa'amr, Makr, and Judeida joined the trend. In those camps children were divided into various groups, carrying names with clear national connotations, such as "Abdel Nasser," "Ghassan Kanafani," and "al-Ard" (the land). Frequently, singing, "Biladi, Biladi" was part of the camp program.

In the following summers, camps were opened in additional localities and before long, smaller movements and NGOs established their own summer camps, such as the Sons of the Village, the Orthodox Events Center in Nazareth, the Muslim Initiative Association in Haifa, and an association of the descendants of the uprooted residents of Kafr Bir'im. In 1987 each group in the children's summer camp of the Orthodox Events Center was named after a village depopulated by Israel in 1948. The *al-Ittihad* reporter who covered the camp commented that "there is no doubt that this topic is not even mentioned in the curriculum of the Ministry of Education, which is trying to distance our Arab students from every topic related to their national belonging."[28] The camp included visits to the remains of some villages and study sessions about their history.

Beginning with the first Palestinian Intifada in late 1987, displays of solidarity at Palestinian summer camps with the Palestinian uprising in the West Bank and the Gaza Strip were followed by the Hebrew media and Israeli authorities with great concern. In the summer of 1989 the Israeli police raided several communist camps and one camp organized by the Sons of the Village, confiscated some educational materials (including a photo of Charlie Chaplin), and in some cases arrested the organizers and accused them of "incitement." In Shefa'amr the police waited near the camp and raided it whenever "Biladi, Biladi" was sung, and later detained four of the organizers for twenty-four hours. Two MKs of the Likud party demanded that the government deprive the organizers of their Israeli citizenship and ban all Arab summer camps in the country.[29] That same summer, the naming of groups for destroyed Palestinian villages at the Communist Youth summer camp in Nazareth was attacked in a local Hebrew newspaper that dedicated its front page to the issue.[30]

Since the late 1990s all the major Palestinian political movements in Israel, including the NDA and the Islamic movements, have developed their own summer camps. In these camps educators and children openly display the symbols and themes forbidden at school—especially the Right of Return of the Palestinian refugees. Sometimes the camp curriculum includes a visit to the ruins of a Palestinian village destroyed in 1948.

The NDA has organized an annual children's camp since 2001 called "The Identity Camp." The NDA secretary general, 'Awd 'Abd al-Fattah, ascribes much importance to the summer camp because he considers it

> a school of a special nature. It has a unique role in bringing up a generation who acquires skills and capacities that would enable it to cope with policies aimed at distorting and marginalizing it [. . .] from the Identity Camp have graduated

a great list of promising youth who can be trusted in the political, cultural, and social positions, within a national vision we are proud of.[31]

In other words, the political impact of these camps is expected to extend beyond its actual participants. Rather, the summer camp is an opportunity to train a cadre of future leadership that would influence their social environment beyond the immediate context of the camp. Indeed, many of the party leaders in student organizations were politically socialized through the party's summer camps and other party activities.

With the authorities' continuous attempts to reorganize surveillance of Palestinian memory and identity since 2000 (see Chapter 7), summer camps, and particularly camps of the nationalist and Islamist streams, have become a highly contested battlefield between camp organizers and the Israeli state authorities. To understand these dynamics, in July 2009 and July 2011 I visited the summer camps of the NDA.

The NDA Summer Camps

My first visit to the NDA Identity Camp was coordinated with the director, the Dr. Rawda 'Atallah (1953–2013), whom I met in advance of my visit and who was very helpful in introducing me to the different aspects of camp life. Dr. 'Atallah had been active previously in the Movement of Democratic Women, which had a major role in organizing the first communist children's camps in the 1980s. Unlike the camps of the Communist Party, which are organized on a regional basis, the NDA organizes a single country-wide camp for children. This setting allows a rare interaction between children from different regions—the Galilee, the Triangle, the Naqb, and the mixed Arab-Jewish cities—and thereby promotes the ideological goal of national solidarity. Dr. 'Atallah and other camp organizers were proud to emphasize this aspect in their conversations with me.

After entering the summer camp and as I was walking through it, I was immediately struck by the density of the Palestinian and Arab national symbolism. Icons such as Palestinian flags, refugee house keys, images of Handala, kufiyas, and maps of Palestine were at every corner, hanging on the walls, worn by the children and the camp counselors, hung on their bodies as medallions, or sometimes painted on their faces. The approximately five hundred children were divided into teams, each of which carried the name of a famous Palestinian cultural or intellectual icon such as Khalil Sakakini, Naji al-'Ali, Mahmoud Darwish, Edward Said, Fadwa Tuqan, and others. Every morning the camp's activities began with the singing of "Mawtani." The children wore orange (the party's color) t-shirts with a portrait of the party's leader, Azmi Bishara.[32] The counselors wore similar white t-shirts. This semiotic thickness is a reflection of the role assigned to the camp by its organizers: to counterbalance, within five condensed days, the denationalizing orientation of the formal education system in which the children spent the entire academic year.

During five days the children participated in various workshops including: music, singing, drama, debka dancing, drawing, clay sculpturing, painting on wood, painting on glass, handicrafts, storytelling, creative writing, developing Arabic linguistic skills, Arab and Palestinian literature, caricature drawing, chess, swimming, and a knowledge competition titled "Know Your Country."

The five days of camp culminated in a gathering of all the children at which leaders of the party came to congratulate them. The children themselves presented an exhibit of the artwork they had created—a large map of Palestine made of wax, paintings of iconic elements like Palestinian flags and figures such as Handala, and paintings depicting soldiers shooting Palestinians. The final ceremony was opened by singing "Mawtani." While singing, some counselors marched between the children, two of them waved Palestinian flags, and others encouraged the children with bold arm movements to take active part in the singing and follow the leading singer on the stage. The singer also encouraged the children to join her and sometimes allowed them to sing without her (since the song includes frequent repetition, it can be sung and taught at the same time).

The simultaneous teaching and singing of the national anthem was followed by a concert at which the children performed songs and recited poems of well-known Arab poets.[33] The songs and the poems were chosen by the children, but the counselors had to pre-approve them for inclusion in the program. Behind the children a large Palestinian flag and an election poster of the party were displayed, and each performer stood on the stage and recited or sang with much devotion and enthusiasm in front of hundreds of other children and staff, as well as some parents who came especially for the closing ceremony. The repertoire chosen for this concert reflected much of the political atmosphere of the camp, as well as the dilemmas of its organizers.

Except for one poem that dealt with a woman who committed suicide after being forced to marry a man she did not love ("Hamda Died" by 'Omar al-Fara), all other poems came from a core of explicitly Arab and Palestinian nationalist poetry: "A letter to Gamal Abdel Nasser," written by the Syrian poet

Nizar Qabbani following the death of the Egyptian president in 1970; "Write down: I am an Arab," by Mahmoud Darwish, a poem describing the proud stand of an Arab in Israel against the humiliation of military rule; more recent poems including "Palestinian, you are not allowed to live!" by Bilal 'Abdallah (a Palestinian poet born in 1976 in Lebanon who lives in Denmark and has become popular since the al-Aqsa Intifada), and "Rebel " by 'Omar al-Fara, a poem full of national pathos, including lines such as: "Rebel! From Haifa to the Golan and from Gaza to the Ghore valley," and "Death is easier than life in an oppressed homeland." The most intriguing choice was the poem that opened the series: "Those who pass between fleeting words," written by Mahmoud Darwish and first published in 1988 during the first weeks of the First Intifada.

Mahmoud Darwish

The importance of the poem "Those who pass between fleeting words," lies in its status in Israeli-Palestinian relations. Shortly after appearing in Arabic it was translated into Hebrew, and it elicited furious reactions from Jewish Israelis along the entire political spectrum.[34] The following lines were at the eye of the storm:

> Live where you wish but do not live among us
> It is time for you to get out
> and die where you wish but do not die among us.
>
> . . .
>
> Get out of our land
> our continent, our sea
> our wheat, our salt, our wound
> our everything, and get out
> of the memory of memories.

The poem touched a primal anxiety shared by Jewish Israelis, that the Palestinian national movement wanted the expulsion of Jews from Israel. Since its publication it has been cited countless times in Hebrew, usually to make the point that there is no room for Israeli-Palestinian compromise. Frequently, the supposed text did not even appear in the original poem: "Take your dead," "Take your graves," "Return to your countries." In 2010 and 2011 alone, some of these fabricated lines were cited by Knesset Speaker Reuven Rivlin (elected in 2014 as president of Israel) in three different sessions of the Knesset assembly; another Jewish Knesset member misquoted it once.

In response to the fierce criticism it elicited, Darwish himself argued that it was written in a moment of anger.[35] He was not especially proud of this poem and did not reprint it in any of his poetry books that were published later. In a conversation with an Israeli reporter who asked about the poem, he once answered: "Haim Guri [a famous Israeli poet] also wrote bad poems." However, Darwish's partial distancing did not change the public status of the poem among Jews, and therefore when Arab citizens of Israel read it, they do so either only in Arabic (not directed at a Jewish audience) or as an extreme form of protest. The wave of anti-Arab legislation in the Eighteenth Knesset (2009–2013), and especially the Nakba Law, once again brought this poem center stage.

For example, Zuheir Andrews, an Arab journalist, published an article in the Arabic newspaper *Kul al-'Arab* in which he protested against the Nakba Law. He ended with a stanza from "Those who pass between fleeting words": "Get out of our land / our continent, our sea / our wheat, our salt, our wound / our everything, and get out / of the memory of memories."[36] Two days earlier, a slightly shortened and softened version of the same article was published in Hebrew in *Haaretz.* Interestingly, the Hebrew version included only one line from the poem, which is less controversial: "Ours is the past here / and the present and the future / from the beginning until the end of the days." Andrews knew that to keep his Jewish audience attentive to his messages, he should avoid antagonizing them by including Darwish's demand for them to leave. Similarly, in a discussion about the Nakba Law in the Knesset assembly, Arab MK Taleb al-Sani' quoted lines from the poem, but only the "benign" lines, not any of the lines starting with "get out."[37]

The recital of Darwish's poem, like other poems recited at the final ceremony of the NDA camp, was a clear sign that the organizers considered it a safe space, where a consideration of the sensitivities of Jewish Israelis was unnecessary, and caution could be suspended. At the same time, it is evident that Darwish's poem, similar to other texts with an obvious potential for public scandal or intervention by the police, were contextualized as part of the children's creativity and not part of the official camp curriculum.

Abdel Nasser

The NDA summer camps take place around or shortly before 23 July, the anniversary of the 1952 Free Officers' revolution in Egypt, which is identified mostly with one of its leaders, Gamal Abdel Nasser. When the revolutionary date coincides with the camp dates, it is celebrated at the camp, and the image of Abdel Nasser is central to the event.

Abdel Nasser's image is another domain of contestation between Jews and Arabs. From the mid-1950s until 1967, Abdel Nasser, a pan-Arab hero, was a source of hope for the Palestinians who anticipated that the Arab countries would be able to turn back the wheel of history and liberate Palestine. The Communist Party at the time was ambivalent toward Abdel Nasser due to his oppression of communists in Egypt.[38] However this ambivalence did not prevent his popularity among Palestinians in Israel, to the extent that Sallah Baransi, one of the founders of the al-Ard movement (a forerunner of the NDA), implicitly compared him to Prophet Mohammad.[39] The sociologist Honaida Ghanim has argued that for many secular Palestinian intellectuals in those years, Abdel Nasser replaced God.[40] His death in September 1970 sent a shockwave throughout the Middle East and triggered a wave of mass memorial gatherings and symbolic funerals in many Palestinian towns and villages in Israel.[41]

In my 2008 survey, 7.4 percent of the Palestinian interviewees mentioned Abdel Nasser when asked to mention the most important persons in the history of the country over the past hundred years. This rate was higher than that of any Palestinian leader in Israel, such as Tawfiq Zayyad or Azmi Bishara— even though Abdel Nasser's political career was in Egypt and not in Palestine and, therefore, was outside the parameters of the questionnaire. Overall, among Arab historical leaders who died before the twenty-first century Abdel Nasser was ranked first, with a significant lead over the second ranked leader, 'Izz al-Din al-Qassam (1.8 percent).

Among Jews in Israel, Abdel Nasser was considered the arch-enemy, sometimes compared by various Israeli leaders to Adolf Hitler.[42] In the 1960s during the annual Lag Ba'Omer holiday (a Jewish holiday that is celebrated in Israel with picnics and by lighting bonfires), Jewish children used to burn an Abdel Nasser puppet in the bonfire. As in the case of the Darwish poem, the main aspect that remained in the Israeli Jewish collective memory of him is a fabricated quote about his desire to "throw the Jews into the sea." No valid reference for this quote exists,[43] although Abdel Nasser did call for the destruction of Israel. This means that, as in the case of Darwish, the remembered misquote primarily reflects Jewish anxieties. The extent to which the fears of Jewish Israelis about Abdel Nasser were internalized by the Arabs is evident in the following numbers, based on my 2008 survey: among interviewees who said that the family is the most important source for historical knowledge, 14.7 percent mentioned Abdel Nasser, while among the rest of the interviewees only 6.2 percent mentioned him. This gap suggests that talking about Abdel Nasser among Arabs largely was restricted to the private sphere.

For example, Ayman 'Odeh, the general secretary of the DFPE since 2007, was born five years after Abdel Nasser's death. He told me that at the age of six he knew by heart approximately twenty different poems about Abdel Nasser, who remained the most important figure in his life until the age of twenty. However, although 'Odeh's family listened regularly to 'Abd al-Halim's song about Abdel Nasser at home, he was warned not to speak about Abdel Nasser among Jews. This concern had not disappeared in 2008:

> Two months ago I gave this picture [showing me a picture of Abdel Nasser] to my parents. My mother had Jewish children as patients. [Even] after forty years [since his death], whenever the family of a Jewish child came to my parents, they removed the picture [from the wall] and put it aside, and returned it after the family left. Five days ago I told them: "Either you leave it on the wall or I will take it." My father told me: "Take it." My mother said: "No, we will keep it on the wall all the time." After an argument, I took it. My father even told me that it is insolence to show the Jews a picture of Abdel Nasser.[44]

Given the highly charged feelings about Abdel Nasser among Palestinians in Israel, the visible presence of his image in the NDA camp and his glorification in the poetry reciting is evidence of both the attempts to bring national memory from the private to the public sphere and of efforts to shape the camp as a safe place for displaying this memory.

Surveillance

Given this tendency to display "forbidden" knowledge in the camps, the Israeli authorities do attempt to monitor the curriculum of Arab camps but with limited success. Since 2010 police approval to run the camp is conditioned on the approval of the Ministry of Education, and the camp director and his deputy are required to be employees of the Ministry of Education (a requirement that makes them much more vulnerable to state pressure). In addition, in the last several years the Ministry has sent its superintendents several times during the camp on surprise inspections (a classic panopticonian form of institutional gaze).[45]

The person directly responsible for tightening the state's surveillance over the NDA camp is Jalal Safadi, himself belonging to a family of internally displaced Palestinian from Safad. In 2010 Safadi was nominated as the director of the Arab Section in the Administration of Youth and Society in the Israeli Ministry of Education, which includes responsibility for supervising various aspects of informal education, including summer camps and the informal curriculum in schools. In other words, Safadi was placed on the frontlines of the Ministry of Education's aspiration to restrict Palestinian national commemoration in the summer camps.

Safadi aspires for a future as a politician in one of the ruling parties in Israel (in his words, he does not "want to be a member of the Knesset in the opposition"). He told me that he is proud that the Ministry has better control over the summer camps, compared to the period before he entered office. When I met him in his office, I insisted on understanding how he reconciles his personal knowledge of the expulsion and the land taken from his family with his enthusiasm for limiting public discussion of this biography. He answered:

> I am a person of *today*. There *were* lands. OK, I know where the lands *were*. I told my daughters. I even took them once during Independence Day to that place. Until noon we were mourning, but then I said: "We are today in the State of Israel, let's go to Haifa, let's make a barbecue. Not to suck up to the Jews, [but] because I believe that this is how Arabs in Israel should behave.

Safadi believes that waving Palestinian flags and hanging pictures of Abdel Nasser are forms of "incitement" and instructed his team of superintendents to ban them. While Safadi presents the shift as his own initiative, it is noteworthy that in 2009 a new Minister of Education, Gid'on Sa'ar (Likud), was appointed. Even before his appointment, Sa'ar was involved in legislation attempting to restrict Palestinian commemoration in Israel, and it is not unlikely that the tightening of state surveillance on Palestinian summer camps is directly related to Sa'ar's world view.

In accordance with the new regulations, on my visit in the NDA summer camp in 2011, Abdel Nasser's smile, which a year earlier welcomed the participants at the gate was no longer there.[46] I later learned from the camp director that a superintendent from the Ministry of Education who visited the camp on the first day explicitly asked him not to talk about the Egyptian leader.[47]

On my first visit to the 2011 summer camp, I happened to arrive during the visit of the superintendent of the Ministry of Education and was allowed to attend his meeting with the camp director. The camp director is a young high school teacher (as required by the new regulations) and an activist in the NDA party although he is not an official member. His family is originally from a village destroyed in 1948. The superintendent, like his supervisor Jalal Safadi, belongs to a group of carefully chosen Arab employees in mid-level administrative positions at the Ministry of Education. Although his mere appointment to his position indicates that he is not considered a trouble maker by the ministry or by the security services, I got the impression that the hardening line toward Palestinian citizens is a burden on the superintendent. He specifically complained to me that since the appointment of Sa'ar as Minister of Education "things became tougher." As much as the superintendent and other Arab functionaries in the ministry have been seen in the past as collaborators,[48] their position became even more contested as tensions between Arab grassroots educators and the government intensified.

The meeting took place in the director's compound in the camp, separated only by a rope from the rest of the camp. The director told the superintendent that he got a phone call from an Arab man who said: "I heard that you are inciting against the state; you should stop it." The following is the conversation that then ensued:

> Superintendent: You have to draw a line between providing education and incitement.
> Director: What do you mean? What I teach here is exactly what I teach at school [his body language reflects a lack of patience].
> Superintendent: Be careful of this issue, in order to avoid your camp being shut down.

Later the superintendent added: "The most important thing is conveying to the children the message that using force does not help. Dialogue is most important." Talking to me, the superintendent commented that before his arrival at the camp, he had visited another camp organized by the DFPE, where he saw signs with slogans protesting against the Civil Service. He said that he ordered the removal of those signs, and the director argued that children hung the signs without his knowledge or permission.

At the end of the meeting, the superintendent went over the official NDA camp program, checked if all the necessary documents were available, and signed them. Throughout, his tone was not threatening; rather his message sounded more like a warning he had to provide because of his role as a representative of the state in this situation, especially when a third party (T. S.) was witnessing the interaction. Still, after he left, the director told me privately that he felt "stressed out" by the superintendent's visits. When I asked to what extent the official program represents the actual curriculum, he answered honestly: "If you want to get the approval, you cannot include all the details."

Although the Ministry of Education superintendents and the NDA camp staff reflected different choices made by Arab citizens of Israel—the former represented the state's interests and ideology while the latter challenged them—all of them, and especially the camp director who was also a state employee, were familiar with the dilemmas that preceded the choice made by the others. Therefore, it appears that there was a tacit mutual understanding in this case to avoid embarrassing each other. The superintendent did not want to see anything that he had to report, and the camp director tried to help him by not displaying any problematic content while the superintendent was there.

Not everyone in the camp knew about the superintendent's visit. While he was on his way out of the camp, a group of children passed in front of him with their counselor. The specific theme of the camp that year was the Right of Return and, therefore, every group of children was named after a Palestinian village destroyed in 1948; that particular group's name was al-Qastal. In earshot of the superintendent, the children shouted rhythmically: "We are from al-Qastal—the Zionists expelled us." The superintendent then sent a helpless look to the camp director, who, in turn, summoned the counselor and asked him to halt the slogans. I assume that the superintendent was aware that he did not witness an exceptional scene, but he could not stand by without correcting it.

SUMMER CAMPS IN THEIR BROADER CONTEXT

Over the past several decades, summer camps have become an important element in the alternative education system of the Palestinian citizens of Israel, a space for processing national memory and transmitting it to children and youth. Themes banned at school are openly discussed in a space considered relatively safe. At the same time Israeli state agencies, through trial and error tactics, check the limits of their ability to monitor and discipline the curriculum of these camps. In a sense, summer camps and the political struggle around them represent the broader challenge of Arab Palestinian national education in Israel. Since the 1990s, Palestinian activists in Israel increasingly have challenged the monopoly of the state over representation of the official historical narrative in mass education. If before the 1980s the counter-hegemonic nationalist narrative was introduced to Palestinian children and youth only in family circles or by a small number of non-conformist school teachers, afterward a wide range of challenges to the state monopoly were developed by Palestinian NGOs and political movements. The exclusion of Palestinian citizens from meaning-ful influence on the state-sanctioned curriculum has led to the creation of an alternative web of collective-memory producers who implement diverse strate-gies. These strategies include both attempts to influence the curriculum in the formal education system, as well as efforts to bypass it.

The Israeli state is currently renewing its attempts to regain control, but its ability to do so is limited for several reasons. First, school is far from being the major source of historical remembrance among Palestinian citizens, and public education does not have much credibility among them. Second, since the 1990s historical education in the informal education system usually has been seen as falling within the legal boundaries of freedom of speech in Israel. This is why the state is trying to enhance its position in the summer camps by demand-ing that directors be state employees. Clearly, however, this requirement is not enough to shape the unofficial curriculum not included in the official docu-ments submitted for approval. Third, Arab municipalities have a certain level of autonomy that is used efficiently by some of them to promote aspects of educa-tion excluded from the state system.

Still, the ability of Palestinian collective-memory agents to inculcate their own version of history among the next generation also is limited. First, the state implements a mandatory universal education system and, therefore, almost every Arab child has to attend state-supervised schools, which in the academic year 2012/13 included 422,968 Arab students from the first to twelfth grades.[49] In summer 2013, however, only fifteen thousand Arab children and youth took part in summer camps and this number includes "a-political" camps such as those organized by the Arab scouts and some municipalities.[50] In a rough estimate, at least two-thirds of the Arab participants attend these depoliticized camps. Thus, only a minority of Arab children in Israel are exposed to the Palestinian national narrative in summer camps, as well as in various other channels of in-dependent, history-teaching projects outlined in this chapter and Chapter 8. Collectively, Palestinians in Israel lack the coercive power of a central govern-ment that can impose universal "required knowledge." This lack of coercion al-lows a great deal of variation between the various Palestinian political forces,[51] but at the same time it compromises the ability of the Palestinian intellectual elite to shape a more coherent and unified national narrative. It is reasonable to assume that many of those children sent to summer camp are already di-rectly pre-equipped with national consciousness and national memory by their parents. Second, the dependency on local authorities of Palestinian producers of historical remembrance means that they cannot rely on those local authorities who are too weak or antagonistic to the Palestinian national narrative. The political survival of many local Arab politicians depends on their ability to recruit resources from different state ministries and, therefore, they invest great efforts to ensure open communication with government ministers.

.   .   .

Children's education is but one sphere of the struggle over collective memory, along with memorial monuments and the emergence of a political calendar. The most common themes that provoked a direct conflict between the Israeli state and its Palestinian citizens have been the themes of victimhood (when Palestinian victimhood, especially concerning the Nakba, is linked to Israeli responsibility) and the themes of Arab or Palestinian prowess (as in the case of the Palestinian armed struggle or Abdel Nasser), both of which trigger existential anxieties among Jewish Israelis. The next chapter provides a closer look at the dialectical relationship between these two themes.

10 THE QUEST FOR VICTORY

ON 18 MAY 2006, Azmi Bishara, then an Arab-Palestinian member of the Knesset, delivered a speech at an NDA party event commemorating the fifty-eighth year since the Nakba. In his speech, Bishara linked the Nakba with another event: "We have to convene every 15th of May to commemorate the Nakba, and on the 23rd of July to celebrate the answer to the Nakba."[1] Bishara was referring to the 1952 Free Officers' revolution in Egypt that toppled the pro-Western monarchy and established an Arab nationalist and anti-colonialist regime that set the tone in Arab politics for the next fifteen years. Although there is probably a causal relation between the Egyptian defeat in the 1948 war and the revolution, naming this event an "answer to the Nakba" requires some intellectual effort. The 1948 war resulted in the forced uprooting of at least seven hundred thousand Palestinians and the eradication of hundreds of villages. Although the revolutionary Egyptian regime was very sympathetic to the Palestinians in its rhetoric, it was unable to bring home even one refugee. However, the 23 July revolution is popularly considered a *victory* for Arab nationalism, which contributed to a discursive change in the Arab world and, in the eyes of Bishara, partly restored a symbolic balance of victories and defeats, humiliation and pride.

Bishara's linkage is a statement against the widely accepted convention that victimization is a central aspect of the Palestinian collective ethos.[2] The underlying assumption behind the juxtaposition of the Nakba and the 1952 revolt is the futility of constructing a stable and compelling national narrative in which the nation is primarily depicted as a subjugated entity. No matter how central a collective, victimizing experience might be in the national narrative, a certain level of historical agency, or even victory, must be added to the equation. In other words, the inclusion of a victory in the narrative serves the purpose of "semiotic instrumentalism," whose aim is to maintain a certain symbolic structure.[3]

The interdependency between different symbolic themes of a collective narrative is best illustrated in Yael Zerubavel's work on Zionist collective memory.[4] According to Zerubavel, selective choices from Jewish history incorporated into the Zionist commemorative narrative were shaped to a large extent by the drive to create a counter-image to that of diasporic Jews as passive and weak. Therefore, themes of active heroism were especially valuable for balancing themes of victimization prevailing in the pre-Zionist Jewish tradition. The collective memory of the Palestinians in Israel is evidence that "semiotic instrumentalism" is a useful conceptual category of analysis, beyond the particular case of Zionist commemoration.

HEROISM, VICTIMIZATION, VICTORIES, AND DEFEATS

Yael Zerubavel identified an inherent tension in national myths of martyrdom between the two poles of heroism and victimization.[5] While the first is identified with activism and self-empowerment, the second represents passivity and downplays the nation's power. Heroism is related to the sacrifice one makes to achieve national goals or ensure national survival. Emphasis on victimization in national conflicts, on the other hand, is based on beliefs about the justness of national goals, while emphasizing the evil of the opponents' goals and delegitimizing their characteristics.[6] Furthermore, since World War II, the international sphere has become a stage of competition over the status of victim,[7] since "there is a tremendous moral capital in suffering, even if you aren't suffering any more."[8] Victimhood has become an important asset.

The distinction between myths of heroism and victimization is between two ideal types. In reality, the two complement each other, and every national myth merges elements from both. This distinction, however, needs further refinement because heroic myths can be related to both victories and defeats. While heroic victories hold a central place in many national narratives and are frequently commemorated by major national holidays, some national heroic defeats are also celebrated as evidence of the nation's ability to sacrifice—even without achieving a tangible goal. This is the case of the Battle of the Alamo myth in Texan identity,[9] the Battle of Gallipoli in Australian identity,[10] and the Battle of Tel Hai in early Zionism.[11] The interesting question is whether these events could have been used successfully as national myths had they not been part of a set of myths that included victories as well. In the case of Zionist commemoration, for example, it was especially important to present certain events as victories, regardless of their actual outcome. Perhaps the best example of this is the commemoration of the Bar-Kokhba revolt against the Roman Empire (135–137 CE):

> National pride was a central Zionist theme, and the revolt was important because it symbolized the ancient Hebrews' proud and courageous stand that led them to defend their nation's freedom at all cost rather than yield to the oppressors. The Zionist commemorative narrative thus shifted the focus from the outcome of the revolt to the act of rebelling; it emphasizes the initial success that brought about the liberation of Judea rather than the defeat that led to exile.[12]

In this chapter I argue that Zerubavel's argument about the importance of victorious myths is extremely relevant for the Palestinians in Israel as their collective memory is based on a continuous attempt to balance themes of victimhood with themes of prowess. Modern Palestinian and Arab histories make themes of victimhood significantly more available, and the frequent attempts to construct various events as victories have been evident in the Palestinian national narrative since the 1930s.[13] For example, the obituaries announcing the execution of Hijazi, al-Zir, and Jamjum in 1930 have frequently referred to them as "the roots of Arab independence."[14] Compared with other Palestinians, however, the tandem of victories and victimhood in the case of the Palestinians in Israel has particular characteristics since in their case the audience of the narrative includes the Jewish citizens of Israel, who are also casted in the role of the victimizers who should be defeated.

FROM KAFR QASIM TO THE DAY OF NAKBA AND STEADFASTNESS

The introduction of heroism into the public discourse of the Palestinians in Israel coincided with the political mobilization around the commemoration of the Kafr Qasim massacre. In the first decade after the massacre, poetry was a major medium of commemoration, and it heralded what would be known as "the literature of resistance."[15] As Barbara Harlow showed, literature written in the context of a struggle for liberation inevitably includes a strong element of commitment to a utopian future.[16] Therefore, it is not surprising that the presentation of past and present predicaments is commonly sprinkled with promises for overcoming them. "The world of 'victory,'" writes the Egyptian literature critic Abdelwahab Elmessiri, "is largely a world of noble visions and beautiful dreams, for there is very little in the refugee camps or the occupied territory that would support either. But this is the nature of the revolutionary imagination—that it refuses to succumb to the status quo, to the old or new facts."[17]

The common thread in the commemorative poems written at the time by Samih al-Qasim, Tawfiq Zayyad, Mahmoud Darwish, Hanna Abu Hanna, and others, is the presentation of the massacre not only as a hideous crime but as a starting point for resistance as well, usually by describing or calling for a transformation of the pain into resisting power. Many of the titles of their poems explicitly illustrate this, such as Zayyad's "Kafr Qasim, stand your dead and rebel! (awqifu amwatakum wa-inhadu!). Similarly, Darwish wrote in his famous poem "The blood's residency": "Kafr Qasim / I came back from death, to live, to sing [...] / we will sing in strong determination / we will bring back the right / that refused to vanish / we will return it / the executioner's hit taught me to walk on my wound / and I walk / then I walk / and I rebel!" Even a poem by Fawzi 'Abdallah published three decades after the massacre conveys a similar theme in its title: "The rebelling sadness" (al-huzn al-thair).

Sometimes heroism and prowess is introduced to the narrative by a reference to another event that had already gained the public image of a national victory. In her review of Palestinian poetry and the press under the military government, Maha Nassar concluded that writers had to walk a fine line between celebrating a victory and insisting that they are not a fifth column. As a result they frequently adopted opaque language.[18] Nevertheless, in some instances the Kafr Qasim commemorative poetry does include direct and explicit references to concrete triumphal myths.

In the first years after the massacre, the closest relevant event to rely upon as a victory was the battle of Port Said, which was considered a turning point in the 1956 tripartite attack of Britain, France, and Israel on Egypt. At least until the Algerian victory in 1962, Port Said had been the major triumphal myth of Arab nationalism. Al-Ittihad's editorial on 11 December 1956 was very explicit in connecting the two events: "The policy of the Kafr Qasim massacre was crashed in the gates of Port Said." Al-Qasim referred to this myth in his widely known poem about the massacre: "To a hand that still resists" (li-yadin dhalat tuqawimu):

In the day they said: "There are dead and injured"
How I cried!
I said: The last regiment goes on
And from house to house I went to tell the news that yielded in the new year

On the radio, news of the glorious year:
"Egypt is a volcano . . . and all the people went to defend Port Said
Dear brothers . . . the victory is guaranteed!"

Similarly, the poet Mahmud al-Dasuqi ended his poem "Memory" about the massacre with the following lines:

Oh Port Said—Over the ages commemorate
the victory of Arabness and remind
our nation's glories and our people's power.
Our history is in the middle of the passing time
and let the history write you in its pages.

Several years later, the Algerian victory in 1962 was celebrated and glorified in Palestinian poetry in Israel in a similar way.[19] These years would be remembered as the golden age of pan-Arabism, which is personified by the image of Nasser (which literally means victor) as a triumphant leader. This image would remain valid regardless of future defeats. His death in September 1970 triggered a wave of nostalgia to his glorious days as the Arab leader who defied colonialism. In the symbolic funerals in Palestinian towns and villages in Israel that followed his death, people called: "Gamal Abdel Nasser, O fighter, O the triumphant over colonialism" (Gamal Abdel Nasser, *ya mighwar, ya qahir al-isti'mar*).[20]

The tendency to balance victimhood with heroism and triumph is more than a reflection of the artistic tendencies of individual poets and writers since poems are subject to editorial-ideological monitoring of their texts. In 1965, for example, when Emile Toma (then *al-Ittihad*'s editor) felt that the poetical tendency started to lean too much toward the victimhood pole, he explicitly protested this inclination and demanded that the poets observe the developments "from the point of view of the fighter."[21]

The Arab defeat in 1967 provided further incentive to cultivate victorious Arab myths. Following the downfall, Al-Qasim wrote his poem "The Thunderbird":

It surely will come,
Will come with the sun;
Its face deformed by the dust of textbooks.

It surely will come,
After the wind has died in my voice,
Something whose wonders have no bounds;

Something that is named in songs:
The Thunderbird!

It is bound to come:
For we have reached it,
We have reached the summit of death![22]

Al-Qasim promised in his poem a redemptive event, and then he went looking for it. After the Qadafi revolution in Libya in September 1969, al-Qasim published a poem titled "The Return of 'Omar al-Mukhtar" in which he glorified the recent revolution.[23] al-Mukhtar led the resistance against Italian rule from 1911 until his execution in 1931. His resurrection in al-Qasim's poem aimed to eliminate the defeat by a new victory for the Arab nation.

The October 1973 war, in which Egyptian and Syrian armies achieved impressive tactical aims by their surprise offensive of 6 October, has been intensively commemorated in Arab artistic, cinematic, musical and literary works.[24] This war looked much more like the thunderbird al-Qasim was waiting for, and it provided much stronger discursive material for the construction of a victorious myth than most of the previous events discussed. In the section "The world is not the same world anymore" of his ode "The Great Crossing," published shortly before the first anniversary of the war, Tawfiq Zayyad wrote:

The night was long, long it was
And heavy was the shame, heavy it was
And deep was the wound, deep it was
Even our bread was full of
humiliation and degradation
But now . . . now . . . now
The joy, which is hosed by blood
sprouted in each entity and entity.[25]

The celebration of the 1973 war in *al-Ittihad* was later toned down, probably because of the pro-Western turn of the Egyptian president Anwar al-Sadat, who, from 1975 onward, was casted in the role of the villain who betrayed the revolutionary legacy of Gamal Abdel Nasser.

In the light of the enthusiasm to adopt any hint of Arab triumphal myth, the silence of *al-Ittihad* regarding the al-Karameh battle (see Chapter 6) is perplexing. One possible reason is that references to non-Palestinian, Arab myths are safer. As long as Fatah and the PLO were defined as "terrorist organizations" by Israel, an explicit identification with their military battles might have been risky. Another possible reason for this silence is that the Communist Party considered Fatah as a rival in mobilizing national sentiments. The party leaders tended to express sympathy and solidarity but avoided giving the PLO too much credit. Glorifying Egyptian and Algerian victories or a revolution in Libya did not involve any competition with the glorified actors. It is not a coincidence that in a rare reference to Karameh in *al-Ittihad*, it is called a "Jordanian battle" (see Chapter 6).

Soon, however, the Communist Party would have a triumphal myth of its own: Land Day. Note the thoughtful construction of the balance between victimhood and prowess in Saliba Khamis's text published on the occasion of the first anniversary in 1977:

> On the last 30 March, we, the Arabs in Israel, experienced a new episode of crime and defense. The crime is the dispossession and land confiscation by the government of Israel. The defense is the adherence of the Arab masses to their land.[26]

With the emergence of the Land Day myth, Samih al-Qasim, whose attraction to pan-Arab martyrology is evident, was able to contextualize it within this martyrology. Soon after Land Day, al-Qasim published a poem titled "With the martyrs" that locates Land Day among other known massacres and battles. For al-Qasim, Land Day belongs both to the category of massacres of innocent civilians, such as the killing of forty Egyptian children by the Israeli air force, and to the category of epic Islamic and Arab victories such as the battle in 'Ayn Jalut:[27]

Announce among the peoples, announce in our name
Your blood is our voice!
Where is Sakhnin, 'Arabeh, Kafr Kana?
Where is Bahr el-Baqr?[28]
Where is, my brothers, Deir Yasin or Kafr Qasim?
Where is, my brothers, Nur al-Shams?[29]
Where is, my brothers, 'Ayn-Jalut or Maysalun?
Where?
We will not ask!
[...]
Your blood unifies the map
Not the Naqb or the Galilee
Your blood is a sign in a long way![30]

The triumphal aspect of Land Day enabled a public processing of one specific aspect of the Kafr Qasim saga: the humiliating forced "reconciliation party" (*sulha*) that the military government imposed on the residents of Kafr Qasim. This ceremony "remains an indelible stain on the historical record, an assault on the dignity of the victims and the Arab community as a whole."[31] Although it had been well known, this episode is relatively neglected in the first two decades of commemorative rhetoric. While the theme of resistance served the need of political mobilization, and the theme of victimization enabled the accumulation of moral capital, the theme of humiliation, embodied by the *sulha* did not serve any purpose. Land Day, however, enabled the presentation of the humiliation as something that belongs to the past. In an article published on the twenty-ninth anniversary of the massacre in 1985, when Hakim Rabi from Kafr Qasim wrote about the *sulha*, he commented that "Land Day was the pure rain that wiped out the black stain, which stuck to the martyrs' families."[32]

The tendency to balance victimhood with heroism became especially apparent with the formalization of commemoration of the Nakba. In its March 1998 meeting (see Chapter 5), the FUC decided to name the day of remembrance for the collective tragedy in 1948 as *Yawm al- Nakba wal-Sumud* (day of catastrophe and steadfastness), not simply Nakba Day, as it is called by Palestinians elsewhere. To a certain extent, this decision echoes the official commemoration of the Holocaust in Israel. In 1951 Israel inaugurated a day of remembrance for the Holocaust, but named it "Yom ha-shoah ve-ha-gvura" (day of holocaust and heroism). The date that was chosen as a remembrance day is the supposed date of the beginning of the Warsaw Ghetto uprising in 1943 (according to the Hebrew calendar). Beyond being a particular example of the aspiration to balance victimhood and heroism, this similarity might be another illustration for the way Palestinian commemoration in Israel is shaped by its proximity and exposure to Jewish Israeli discourse.

THE JULY 2006 WAR

Thus far I have examined "the quest for victory" through texts written by a small number of individuals. Now I widen the scope of examination. The findings from my 2008 survey provide an opportunity to examine the topic from the angle of popular historical remembrance. As described earlier, interviewees were asked to mention a maximum of three events that they considered to be the most important in the history of the country. In addition, they were asked to describe their identity in an open-ended way. Figure 8 presents the most frequently mentioned events by gender and by self-identification.[33]

Event	Entire sample	Gender		Self-Identification		
		Women (N=268)	Men (N=270)	Palestinian (N=227)	Israeli (N=214)	Palestinian and Israeli (N=61)
July War (2006)	34%	40%***	27%	32%	36%	44%*
1948	28%	25%	31%	33%***	30%	34%
1948 with mention of Nakba[b] terms[c] vocabulary	13%	10%	15%*	18%****	13%	19%
Al-Aqsa Intifada (2000–)	12%	16%****	7%	15%*	8%*	10%
1967 war	7%	4%	10%**	8%	8%	6%
POW exchange 2008[b]	7%	7%	6%	5%	4%**	3%
Iraq war(2003–)	6%	4%	8%*	7%	7%	8%
October 2000 events	5%	6%	4%	5%	6%	5%
Israel-Egypt peace treaty (1979)	4%					
Israel-Jordan peace treaty (1994)	4%					
Rabin's assassination (1995)	4%					
Saddam's execution (2006)	3%					
World War II (1939–1945)	3%					
September 11th (2001)	3%					
Collapse of the US dollar (2007–2008	3%					
First Intifada (1987–1993)	2%					
Palestinian uprisings[d]	17%	23%****	11%	20%*	14%	15%

[a] Asterisks in the table refer to a 4 cell χ^2 test: *p<0.1; **p<0.05; ***p<0.01: ****p<0.001

[b] This is a subcategory of "1948"; it includes only responses that explicitly used the terms Nakba, expulsion, or occupation.

[c] The POW exchange between Israel and Hizballah occurred while the survey was being conducted and after some of the interviews already had taken place.

[d] This is an aggregation of three uprisings: First Intifada, Al-Aqsa Intifada, and October 2000.

Figure 8. The most frequently mentioned events by gender and self-identification (Arab sample only)

The most surprising and thought-provoking finding is the high frequency of the mention of the Israel-Hizballah confrontation in the summer of 2006, known in the Arab world as the July War and in the West and in Israel as the Second Lebanon War (although the latter term is also common in the Arabic press in Israel, which is another expression of the "Israeliness" of some Arabic newspapers). It was mentioned even more frequently than the 1948 war (or the Nakba) as among the three most important events in the history of the country (although not as the single most important event). We should be careful, however, when interpreting the ranking of these two events because it is likely that the mention of the 1948 war was affected by the political sensitivity of the Nakba. It is not unlikely that face-to-face interviews would have led to a higher frequency of reference to the events of 1948. At the same time, the frequency of the mention of the 2006 war is still impressive, regardless of whether or not it surpasses the Nakba.

There might be several reasons for this finding, some of them circumstantial and others more substantive. To begin with, it is known that relatively recent events tend to be more accessible in human memory than earlier events. In a parallel Jewish sample, however, only 4.8 percent of the respondents mentioned this war, seven times less than in the Arab sample. What can explain, then, the gap between the Jewish and Arab respondents regarding this war?

I would like to suggest two mutually complementing explanations for this gap: First, the vulnerability felt by many Palestinians in Israel during the war; and second, its popular interpretation as an Israeli defeat. To a large extent these two themes overlap with the distinction between victimhood and heroism discussed earlier.

In the 2006 confrontation, Palestinians in Israel were vulnerable and suffered casualties. In fact, nineteen out of the forty-four civilians killed on the Israeli side of the border were Arabs. Although the Arabic press usually did not refer to them as martyrs, it did dedicate much attention to them, not only during the war, but even on the first and second anniversaries of the war. One year after the war, for example, *al-Sinnara* returned to the bereaved families and described their suffering under the title "A Year since the Second Lebanon 'War' and the Victims' Families Are Still under the Brunt of the Shock."[34] On the second anniversary, *al-Sinnara* published a table of casualties on both the Lebanese and Israeli side, in which the Palestinian citizens who were killed in the war were included on the Israeli side.[35]

The vulnerability explanation seems to have validity because the mention of this war was highly associated with geographic location. All of the Israeli civilian victims in the war were killed less than 40 km. from the Israeli-Lebanese border. Indeed, among the northern respondents who live in this area, 38 percent mentioned the war whereas among other respondents, only 24 percent mentioned it (significance of χ^2 test < 0.01). Women who lived in the north of Israel most frequently mentioned the July war (44 percent) whereas men who did not live in the north referred infrequently to the war (19 percent).

Furthermore, women were much more likely to refer not only to the July war but also to relatively recent events that resulted in the death of young Palestinian victims (the intifadas and October 2000). Men were more likely to refer to events in ways that had the potential to be interpreted as a national humiliation (the Nakba, the 1967 war, and the war in Iraq),[36] but that were distant enough in time and space that they did not experience them directly (only 10% of the interviewees were born in 1948 or earlier and in this subgroup, men and women mentioned the Nakba with equal frequency—48 percent). What I suggest here is that the unmediated-vulnerability aspect of the 2006 war is remembered much more vividly by women than by men.

The other likely reason for the prevalence of mentioning the 2006 war is the almost unequivocal presentation of the war in the Arab media as an unprecedented defeat for Israel. Especially important were the discursive strategies of Hizballah's leader, Hasan Nasrallah (which literally means God's victory), who projected the self-confidence of a self-reliant winner. Photos of Nasrallah, as wall posters or on key chains, became popular among many Palestinian nationalists in Israel. In a survey of a representative sample of the Palestinian adult population in Israel from January 2007 (N=508), 60.5 percent said that there was no winner in the war. However, 28 percent said that Hizballah was the winner and only 2.4 percent argued that Israel won.[37]

The casualties among the Palestinians in Israel did not prevent the majority of them from seeing Nasrallah as an ally. In a survey conducted by the Truman Institute in September 2006, 70 percent of the interviewees said that they believe Nasrallah is concerned about their fate.[38] Azmi Bishara, whose attraction to triumphal mythology was illustrated earlier, wrote about it during the first days of the war: "The [Hizballah] resistance is not playing the role of the victim and does not ask for international sympathy with the victim—but a combative solidarity from those who are free. These are new rules of the game that the Arabs forgot."[39]

The real importance of the war, however, lies in its perception as an Israeli defeat rather than as identification with Nasrallah. Although religious affiliation was not associated with mentioning the war, Muslims were more than four times more likely to mention Nasrallah as one of the most important figures in their history than Palestinians of other religions (9.2 percent vs. 2.1 percent, respectively). Among Muslims, Nasrallah appeared to be especially popular with highly religious people (11.3 percent)[40] and less popular with secular Muslims:[41] only one out of forty-four secular Muslims in the sample mentioned his name (2.1 percent). At the same time, the level of religiosity among Muslims was not associated with mentioning the war. It means that while religious Muslims were much more likely to identify with Nasrallah as the winner, the Israeli defeat by itself was an attractive theme for much wider social circles.

Arabic media in Israel celebrated an Israeli defeat. Leading this tendency is Arab48, the website of Bishara's party, which has frequently glorified the "unforgettable lesson" that Hizballah taught the "invincible army."[42] The website has kept referring to the war around 14 August (the day fighting ended in 2006) every year since then, sometimes accompanying the text by photos depicting Israeli soldiers weeping and their body language reflecting anguish or fatigue (see Figure 9).

6 سنوات على »14 آب«: حربٌ قوّضت أسطورةً

عـ48ـرب/ حسن عبد الحليم

تاريخ النشر: 17/08/2012 - آخر تحديث: 00:31

قبل ست سنوات، وتحديدا في 14 آب، وبعد 33 يوما من التلعثم والتلكأ والتخبط والترنّح، انسحبت إسرائيل من لبنان تجر ذيول الفشل مهيضة الجناح، رغم النيران الهائلة التي أسقطتها على لبنان برا وبحرا وجوا، والدمار الذي زرعته، خرجت وفاض اليدين تلملم فشلها وتلفي به أمام لجان التحقيق، فتقوضت أساطير، وبانت ما قبل حرب لبنان لا يشبه ما بعدها.

Figure 9. The website Arab48 celebrates the sixth anniversary of the 2006 war with a photo of Israeli soldiers weeping. Source: http://www.arabs48.com/?mod=articles&ID=93846.

The title of Hasan ʿAbd al-Halim's article celebrating the first anniversary of the war was: "The July War was an Israeli defeat and not only a failure."[43] In the text itself he compared the 2006 war with the 1973 war.

Following the sixth anniversary of the war, the same author continued to celebrate the defeat of Israel:

> Six years ago, on 14 August, and after thirty-three days of hesitation, delays, confusion, and grogginess, Israel withdrew from Lebanon dragging the tails of failure with broken wings. Despite the enormous bombardment of Lebanon from the land, sea, and air, and the destruction it caused, Israel came out empty-handed, gathered its failure, and faced the commissions of inquiry. Legends collapsed, and what was happening before the Lebanon war is not similar to what followed it."[44]

Defeating Israel in Order to Be Israeli

Previously I presented examples of the triumphant rhetoric in the poems of the "poets of resistance." This group is admired in the Arab world for its intellectual leadership of the resistance against Israel.[45] It is important, though, to evaluate this image in the light of their self-understanding of it, as well as later biographical details. First, some of them did not unambiguously adopt this title, because they were keenly interested in a dialogue with Jewish Israelis. Mahmoud Darwish, in an interview with Joseph Algazy in 1969 referred to the term "resistance poetry" by quoting an Egyptian literary critic who argued that the point of departure of these poets (Darwish named Al-Qasim, Zayyad, Salem Jubran, and himself) is the recognition of the rights of Jews and Arabs in Palestine. "They recognize Israel's right of existence, and therefore, they should be named: poets of protest and opposition."[46] In 1970 Darwish could not stand the constant harassment and persecution and left the country. Except for Darwish, however, all the other poets who frequently have been associated with the resistance genre proved once and again that their politics is practiced from within the boundaries of Israeli citizenship. Tawfiq Zayyad was a member of the Knesset for sixteen years (1974–1988; 1992–1994); Samih al-Qasim and Hanna Abu Hanna were candidates in elections for the Knesset; Salem Jubran received an award for his poetry from the Israeli Ministry of Culture in 2006; Rashid Husayn thought of himself as both Palestinian and Israeli.[47] Although people might change their view in the course of a lifetime, this common biographical thread, as well as the very early insight of Darwish about the politics of his colleagues, imply that the nurturing of triumphant myths was not necessarily the reflection of a revolutionary future vision but was compatible with an aspiration to reform the existing State of Israel.

This insight brings us to discuss the significant association between mentioning the 2006 war and self-definition (in an open-ended question) as both Israeli and Palestinian. Among men, this association was especially strong: 43 percent of the men who described themselves using both terms mentioned the war, compared with only 24 percent in the rest of the sample. Furthermore, a multivariate analysis revealed that self-definition as both Israeli and Palestinian was the strongest predictor of mentioning the 2006 war, even when gender, education, generation, religion, religiosity, and self-labeling as either Israeli or Palestinians were controlled for (see the first table in the Appendix, p. 243). One possible reason is that for those Arab citizens who are both proud Palestinians and seek ways to integrate into Israeli society as equal citizens, an Israeli defeat at the hands of Arabs paves the way for imagining a more egalitarian interaction with Jews.

In this context, it is noteworthy that celebrating an Israeli defeat was evident not only in the rhetoric of politicians who preach for separate national institutions for the Arabs in Israel (like Bishara), but also of citizens who hold explicit stands in favor of Arab-Jewish integration and cooperation. Raja Za'tra, a member of the editorial board of the communist *al-Ittihad* newspaper told the Hebrew newspaper *Haaretz* in September 2006: "People appreciate Nasrallah because he hurt Israel, he broke the nose of Israel's aggressive policy [...] people do not forget the blood spilled in Gaza. Nasrallah proved that the Arabs are not an inferior species, they are not powerless people."[48]

When the war ended, the author Sayed Kashua, who was educated in a Jewish boarding school and publishes only in Hebrew, published the following confession in his weekly column in *Haaretz*:

> Well, it's like this: I was against the war, but after it started I wanted the army to lose, or at least not to feel victorious. My hands tremble as I write, but in this war I was against Israel—make no mistake—my country. This has nothing to do with the other side; it has nothing to do with what I think about the side that fought in this round against the IDF. It's true that I would prefer that the IDF, that the State of Israel lose without the consequence being that soldiers die. I would like to see it lose in arm-wrestling—[imagine] rows of tables in which soldiers from both sides sit and arm-wrestle. I would prefer a loss by penalty kicks.

The past few weeks were so confusing, and included phone calls to friends I grew up with, whom I lived with and who I knew were fighting; looking for the names of victims with my heart pounding and my head exploding; and ending with a feeling of relief when I did not identify friends in the lists of names. You can say it's treason, you can say what you want, but I am still unable to understand how I can be happy when I hear that another IDF tank has been hit and at the same time afraid that I have friends inside it and then cringe when I see the photographs and under them the ages of the fallen.[49]

Maybe the most telling monologue that illustrates the link between the quest for victory and integrative aspirations is the interview I conducted with J., a physician who grew up in a communist family with a clear universalistic orientation. In his clinic in a mixed Jewish-Arab city, he treats both Jewish and Arab patients. Since the mid-2000s, he has been part of a Jewish-Arab group who meet during Israel's Independence Day to discuss the most difficult and dividing collective memories face to face. To understand the significance of the way J. experienced and remembers the July 2006 war, we should first understand his wider perspective on Arab-Jewish relations:

With all the pain involved in the struggle and the encounter between the two nations, I consider it a blessing—a blessing in the cultural sense, in the diversity that it brings to my personal life. [Had I have been given the choice] I would have liked to live in such a society. This is a choice. It does not eliminate my love of my identity, of the components of my identity—who I am, where I come from. But I would have liked to live in such a society that enriches me: Jewish-Arab.

It is very, very challenging, interesting, and educational. I do not want this separation. I would fight that we stay together.[50]

Later, J. mentioned the different moments of Arab failures he remembers from his lifetime:

The failure of 1967 and the occupation of the West Bank, the failure of the Arab peoples in the war—personally, I tried to escape from it, I tried . . . what does it tell me? That I belong to a people who failed in the war. All the time. All the political events, the intifadas. Take even the last event of the Gaza war [the Israeli assault on the Gaza Strip in December 2008]. Beyond the issue of justice or lack of justice. Look at the equation of military and technological power between the two peoples. Personally I felt insulted about the inferiority of my side, the Arab. This is something at a level that I did not know how to deal with. It was there, I felt it [. . .]. This is the insulting thing—the shame of seeing on the first day when they attacked the police in Gaza—and I saw the policemen spread around in half bodies and people injured. There is something personally humiliating and I felt part of this humiliation [. . .]

[During the 2006 war] I had mixed feelings. On the one hand was the feeling that there is someone who can resist this entire military doctrine and sophisticated technology even with primitive tools. I felt schadenfreude—"don't think that you can control the world" [. . .] something in me identified with the resistant power of Hizballah. I am not connected at all to their values, but something in me was happy [saying]: "I will show you"; "you cannot do everything." There is something that can break this domineering conception. It was very strong in me—not to break and fail as every time. On the other hand, I was afraid of the ability of such a [religious] force to gain power.

WHICH VICTORIES ARE REMEMBERED?

Earlier in this chapter I referred to many other events that were publicly celebrated as Arab victories over Israel. Almost none of them left its footprint on the findings of the 2008 survey. In Egypt and Syria, the state has imposed the remembrance of the 1973 war extensively in school textbooks, in the naming of various sites, in promoting 6 October as a national holiday, in dedicating museums to the war, and issuing stamps.[51] Due to the lack of similar supportive mechanisms among the Palestinians in Israel, the war has lost its status in popular memory. In the 2008 survey, the 1973 war was mentioned by only seven respondents (1.3 percent), only one of them under the age of fifty. Without the support of a state apparatus, triumphs (real or imagined) that occurred only one generation ago but were not directly experienced by most of the population seem to fade away from the collective memory. The 1973 war might have promoted collective pride among Palestinian citizens of Israel in the months and even several years after its occurrence, but its memory was not maintained, nor was it transferred to the next generation (unlike the 1948 war that had lasting consequences for almost every Palestinian household and, therefore, was transferred in the private sphere). At the same time, the quest for victory might be strong enough to overcome the state's antagonism by nurturing the victorious aspects of recent events and using them to balance the victimization ethos.

One might ask what would have been the result had this study been conducted prior to the 2006 war. If the argument about the need for a semiotic balance is correct, I would have expected other triumphal myths to take its place. Indeed, Israel's continuous involvement in Lebanon since the 1970s provided more than one opportunity for celebration. In March 1978 Israel launched an attack on the PLO forces in South Lebanon, named in Israel "The Litani Operation" and the March 1978 War by Palestinians and Lebanese. The PLO presented the event as an Israeli defeat, and an annual memorial for the event took place for several years. Although there is no evidence for similar ceremonies inside Israel, *al-Ittihad* did report on ceremonies in Lebanon. On the third anniversary of the war, *al-Ittihad* celebrated the event as an Arab victory, with rhetoric very similar to that used in reference to the 2006 war:

> The Litani Operation, as is well known, in which the ugliest kinds of destructive weapons have been used, failed quickly, facing the brave resistance of Palestinians and patriotic Lebanese. This resistance forced the invading Israeli force to retreat after suffering heavy casualties in lives and equipment.[52]

Similarly, the withdrawal of Israel from South Lebanon in May 2000 was celebrated in the Arabic-language media as a great Arab victory. At that time, the NDA convened to celebrate the victory, and Bishara himself stated: "Hizballah triumphed and for the first time since 1967, we tasted the taste of victory." Following the drama of the summer of 2006, the 2000 withdrawal drastically lost its centrality, but the rhetoric remained the same. This last quote could have appeared in summer 2006 as well. The July 2006 war was simply the most available victory in popular memory in 2008, only two years after its occurrence. Self-agency and prowess are too important for national identification to be neglected and, therefore, victorious myths are constructed and reconstructed in different times and under changing circumstances.

•   •   •

The quest for victory was born out of the experience of collective humiliation. Since the humiliating actors are Jewish Israelis, they are also cast in the role of the defeated party in the triumphal mythology. This is only one way in which Arab-Jewish interactions shape the representation of the past by Arab citizens of Israel. Another pattern is the suspension of memories of humiliation and dispossession as an attempt to begin a new chapter. Such an attempt was evident in the way many Palestinians in Israel reacted to the assassination of Israeli

Prime Minister Yitzhak Rabin in 1995. By adopting Rabin as a symbol of peace and hope, they omitted his responsibility for the Nakba and other key events in Palestinian history. The adoption of Rabin as a symbol of hope, the disillusion that followed, and what was left of the optimistic representation of the Israeli leader, are the topics of the next chapter.

11 LATENT NOSTALGIA FOR YITZHAK RABIN

AS ONE OF THE MAJOR FIGURES responsible for the Nakba, the way the late Prime Minister Yitzhak Rabin is remembered by Palestinian citizens of Israel is an excellent example of a strategic suspension of the memory of the Nakba. On the evening of 4 November 1995, following the end of a mass demonstration in support of the Israeli-Palestinian peace process, Rabin was assassinated by an Orthodox Jewish Israeli student. Rabin's assassination resulted from, and expressed, fundamental differences among Jewish Israelis, not only about the future status of the territories Israel occupied in 1967 but about the very definition of Israeli identity.[1] These controversies have been reflected in a 'fragmented commemoration' in terms of time, space, and content.[2] The Palestinian citizens of Israel were far from being neutral or indifferent to this Jewish controversy since it had far-reaching implications on their status and their identity as well. The collective political consciousness and behavior of the Palestinians in Israel are highly informed by their need to navigate between different expectations of non-Israeli Palestinians and Jewish Israelis. The way they have commemorated, remembered, and later ignored Rabin has been shaped by the same dynamics.

In this chapter I suggest the existence of a latent nostalgia for Rabin's time. This nostalgia is latent because it cannot be identified in the public sphere. This insight is derived from juxtaposing an analysis of references to Rabin's assassination in the Arabic press in Israel from November 1995 until July 2008 with an analysis of three surveys of representative samples of Arab and Jewish citizens of Israel from the same period of time. An examination of memories of Rabin by relying exclusively on materials available in the public sphere would reveal a transition from intensive and mostly sympathetic references immediately after the assassination to an almost complete ignoring of him after 2000. Furthermore, at the first stage, the representation of Rabin and his assassination became a contested terrain, in which integrative aspirations among the Arab citizens were translated into attempts to join Jewish Israeli expressions of mourning and commemoration, while concerns about "Israelification" were reflected in reserved attitudes or even contempt. Therefore, if we rely exclusively on public representations, the post-2000 muteness might be interpreted as a disappearance of this internal Arab controversy.

Silence, however, is not identical to forgetting.[3] While studying collective memory, we should take into consideration the existence of a latent layer of memory that does not have a public expression and can be revealed only by active investigation that focuses on the perspectives of ordinary people who do not necessarily have access to formalized and public commemorative tools. An examination of individual-centered surveys reveals continuity from the pre-2000 to post-2000 period, not only in the evident remembering of Rabin, but also in the association between the remembrance of Rabin and certain political orientations. In other words, the association between remembering Rabin and integrative aspirations that was publicly visible from 1995 to 1999 did not disappear but became latent and can be detected only by active investigation based on interviews of individuals. Individual remembrances in 2008 correlate with certain sociopolitical orientations that were evident in the public sphere in the late 1990s; this is a finding that illustrates both the interdependence and the relative independence of these two levels of investigation.

RABIN AND THE PALESTINIAN CITIZENS OF ISRAEL

Rabin's pre-1992 biography made him one of the least probable candidates for being remembered positively by Palestinians. In 1948 Rabin, as a young but senior officer, commanded the expulsion of tens of thousands of Palestinians from the Ramleh region to the West Bank.[4] In the 1967 war, Rabin was the IDF Chief of Staff. Rabin was the prime minister of the government that decided in 1975 to confiscate lands, a confiscation that led to Land Day in 1976, during which Rabin was still the prime minister. In 1984, while the IDF was occupying a region of Lebanon that reached to the Awali River, he was appointed Minister of Defense. He led a heavy-handed policy in Lebanon that cost the lives of hundreds of Palestinians and Lebanese. In a 1985 Land Day rally, Tawfiq Zayyad named him "the cutthroat from Tel Aviv." From 1987 to 1990, still as Minister of Defense, Rabin implemented harsh measures for oppressing the Palestinian uprising in the West Bank and the Gaza Strip. Rabin was quoted frequently as having ordered the Israeli military in the early stages of the uprising to "break the legs and bones" of the Palestinian rebels. Although the context of this comment was his demand to avoid fatal casualties,[5] this statement was inscribed in the collective consciousness of Palestinians in Israel as epitomizing his harsh policy. Consequently, in the 1988 election, the campaigners for the Labor Party among Arab citizens made an effort to hide Rabin and belittle his importance.

After his election as Prime Minister in 1992, however, Rabin led three historic interrelated political processes that were highly applauded by Arab citizens. Rabin's government began the Oslo process, which included a formal recognition of the PLO, breaking a long-standing taboo in Israeli politics. Rabin's coalition also relied on the passive support of the Arab parties (to form a "blocking majority") as legitimate actors in Israeli politics, including a formal agreement between the Labor party and the Arab parties,[6] breaking a second historical taboo.

Finally, Rabin's government led the most serious attempt to date to diminish state discrimination against Arab citizens in various spheres. Although the new policy was not as revolutionary as some pro-integration Arab leaders presented it later,[7] the change was tangible enough to influence the political atmosphere. Public opinion polls conducted by Smooha showed that the percentage of Arab citizens who considered the term "Israeli" as relevant to their identity, those who had some reservations about whether Zionism is racism, and those who accepted the "right of Israel to exist as a Jewish-Zionist state" peaked at an unprecedented high level in 1995. Similarly, anti-Arab attitudes among Jewish citizens in the same year were the lowest since a similar survey was first conducted in 1980.[8]

Under the above-mentioned sociopolitical circumstances, Arab citizens were considered a legitimate part of the mass pro-Oslo demonstration on 4 November 1995. The Public Committee for the Peace Demonstration that organized the event published ads in Arabic newspapers with the identical content and slogans that appeared in Hebrew newspapers, inviting the public to join the demonstration. It also organized and funded buses to bring in demonstrators from various Arab towns and cities.

This background might explain why the dominant voice among the Arab-Palestinian public in the days after the assassination was one of shock mixed with sympathy for the assassinated leader. This sympathy was intimately related to a real hope that Rabin's policies signaled a turning point toward more inclusion and more equality for Arab Palestinians inside Israel. It was also related to the widespread belief that Rabin's policy was a step toward redefining the boundaries of Israeli identity, and his assassination was seen as a proof of the seriousness of his intentions.[9] Therefore, all the Arab political parties and Arab municipalities published mourning notices in the newspapers and sent condolences to the government and the family. School sessions began with a discussion of the assassination and the need for tolerance and pluralism. The National Committee of Arab Mayors convened a special meeting and dispatched a large delegation to the funeral.[10]

These sentiments were expressed as well on the popular level. Merchants in the Arab city of Nazareth set up a memorial for Rabin in the local outdoor market; some Arab schools held art exhibits in which children presented their works on the assassination; and in various Arab localities, residents stood during the mourning siren that was sounded across the country to coincide with Rabin's funeral.[11]

As Lev Greenberg has argued, the historic process Rabin led was one of democratization, not only of peace. To legitimize his policy, Rabin created a new collective identity. "The new 'us' was based on Israelis and Palestinians who aspired to peace, and 'they' are extremist religious Jews and Muslims who act to perpetuate the war."[12] His assassination was seen by many Arab citizens as a validation of this new set of identities. Perhaps one of the most poignant expressions of this expectation was the following text, written in Hebrew by Riad 'Ali, an Arab journalist of a Druze background who has worked in the Hebrew media for years but apparently still did not feel that he was accepted as a full Israeli:

> I cried! And I wrote about it in my diary—"I was absentminded for moments. I would never be able to explain it, but my cry was mixed with a strange joy. Not a malicious joy but its opposite. It was the joy of a nomad who found his destination. The joy of a child who lost his mother for a short while, and a second after he started bitterly weeping, he noticed her appearing from beyond the corner and his face lifted up!" Two weeks later I added another comment: "Now I understand . . . ! My latent and honest longing to be a full-fledged citizen was rising inside me . . . ! For the first time in my life I felt Israeli . . . ! In his death, Rabin gave me what he tried extensively in his life to keep from me . . . the feeling of home!"[13]

Many Arab citizens expected the Hebrew media to pay attention to Arab expressions of sorrow and mourning and were disappointed and frustrated that their painful reaction was mostly ignored.[14] As I illustrate in the next sections, this disappointment did not deter some dominant public figures from the continuous attempt, during the first five years after the assassination, to use the memory of Rabin's assassination as a tool to promote their integrative worldview. "Rabin's legacy" kept the dream of equality and integration alive even while Rabin's successors reversed his policy of integration.

To what extent did the association between remembering Rabin and an integrative orientation remain valid in the years following the assassination, years in which the relations between Jewish and Arab citizens of Israel drastically deteriorated?[15] The investigation of this question would be bifocal: one lens focuses on public expressions in the Arabic media in Israel, and the other focuses on memories of individuals as they expressed themselves in responses to a research questionnaire.

BEFORE OCTOBER 2000

Analyzing the reference in the Arabic press to Rabin during the first five years after the assassination reveals a significant gap between an extremely sympathetic tone and extensive coverage in *al-Ittihad* (the newspaper of the Communist Party) and the reserved tone of *Sawt al-Haq wal-Hurriyya* (published by the northern faction of the Islamic Movement) and *Fasl al-Maqal* (published by the NDA); both of them began to ignore Rabin even before 2000. The commercial newspapers were closer to the supportive tone of *al-Ittihad* and to a limited extent covered Rabin's memorial days until 2000. Some of them even complained about the exclusion of Arabs from these ceremonies.[16]

It is noteworthy that until the 1980s, *al-Ittihad* dominated non-governmental Arabic newspapers in Israel. By the late 1990s, however, it already faced competition from both the commercial press, for example, *al-Sinnara* and *Kul al-'Arab*,[17] which became the most widely read newspapers and from newspapers owned by other political parties. On the ideological front since the late 1990s, especially challenging was *Fasl al-Maqal*, which targeted the same secular and politically-aware audience of *al-Ittihad* but with a clearer Arab nationalist tone, and it articulated objections to Israelification tendencies among the Palestinian citizens of Israel.

Since the appearance of its political competitors, *al-Ittihad* has provided the most consistent support for Arab-Jewish political partnerships, and the way it treated Rabin's memory was closely related to this orientation. While in the mainstream Hebrew press Rabin was characterized by a mix of six characters (in the following order): the Sabra, the peacemaker, the Zionist, the Americanophile, the anti-politician, and an empathic figure,[18] *al-Ittihad* presented Rabin almost exclusively as a peacemaker, with some sporadic reference to his transformation from a hawk into a dove. Any concrete reference to the role he played in 1948 was completely absent.

In addition, even though Arab representatives were not invited to speak at the central annual memorial rally in Tel Aviv each year, these events were highlighted by *al-Ittihad* and celebrated as evidence of the vitality of Rabin's legacy.

Two years after the assassination, the domestic political conditions were already significantly different from those that prevailed during the period of Rabin's government. The May 1996 elections resulted in the rise to power of Binyamin Netanyahu and his Likud party, who promptly emptied the Oslo process of its reconciliatory potential. Furthermore, Netanyahu's government abolished most of the budgetary anti-discriminatory improvements introduced by the former government.[19]

The mass rally on Rabin's memorial day was an opportunity for the opposition to demonstrate its power. For *al-Ittihad*, the second anniversary of the assassination was still an opportunity to promote an integrative agenda. It was especially important for the editors to convey the message that Netanyahu's policy had strong opposition among the Jewish public, implicitly advocating Arab-Jewish cooperation. The front page of the issue on 9 November 1997, the day after the annual commemorative rally in Tel Aviv, trumpeted "Half a million people applauded peace at Rabin square," referring to the event as "the largest rally in the history of Israel." The editorial column, entitled "A Brave Demonstration," stated:

> The brave demonstration seen yesterday, Saturday night, commemorating the second anniversary of the assassination of the former Prime Minister Yitzhak Rabin, requires all political forces in the country, and especially the peace forces, to take a stand. There is a consensus among observers that this is the largest demonstration in the history of Israel. The number of attendees exceeded even the 400,000 participants in the demonstration against the Lebanon War and its massacres in 1982. Some estimate that half a million people attended and some estimate that even more. [...]
>
> Why did they come in such a magnitude? [...] As it is well known, by killing Rabin the assassin Amir wanted to kill the peace process. The election of Netanyahu and the actions we have witnessed during his term testify that

Amir's goals have begun to be realized and the peace process is careening toward the abyss. Has the public of peace seekers in Israel regained its own senses
and come in the hundreds of thousands to rescue the peace process?

Anyway, this demonstration is considered a big positive sign. If it continues
on the correct path, great results can be achieved, as the 1982 demonstration did
which shook off Likud rule and led to the withdrawal from Lebanon.

There is certainly much exaggeration in the number of participants mentioned
by *al-Ittihad*. The demonstration was exceptionally large, but the official police
estimate was only 200,000 and even the organizers, who usually tend to inflate
numbers, estimated that 400,000 people attended.[20] *Al-Ittihad*'s emphasis on
the record attendance and the repeated comparison to the mythic 1982 demonstration, which is considered one of the zenith points of what is commonly
named the "Zionist Left," clearly was aimed at convincing the Arab reader of
the possibility of sharing a political struggle with Jewish citizens.

Al-Ittihad maintained a similar approach the following year. On 2 November
1998,[21] the newspaper provided extended coverage of the commemorative rally
in Tel Aviv, also showing a large photo of Rabin singing the "Song of Peace" on
the stage moments before his assassination. The editorial reminded its readers:

> Rabin was engraved in Israeli history as the person who broke the traditional
> hostile attitude toward the Palestinian people and its legitimate leadership [...]
> This was due to his realistic and correct view of global and regional developments
> and his conviction, as an experienced military commander, that there is no se-
> curity and no peace without legitimate rights. In this, he was a courageous and
> wise leader.

On the following day the newspapers covered a commemorative rally by Peace
Now, including a photo from the demonstration in which Israeli flags were very
visible. The Friday supplement also gave significant attention to Rabin's assassination. An op-ed column by Anton Shalahat argued that Rabin's assassination
and anti-Arab attitudes in Israeli society have similar origins. It was an explicit
attempt to demarcate the political boundaries in Israel based on moral criteria
rather than the usual Arab-Jewish divide.

The commemorative events in 1999 were the last to receive significant attention by *al-Ittihad*. On 3 November the newspaper extensively covered the
commemorative ceremony in Oslo, attended by Israeli Prime Minister Ehud
Barak, Palestinian President Yasser Arafat, and U.S. President Bill Clinton. The

accompanying photo depicted Yasser Arafat delivering his speech with a picture of Rabin behind him.

Not everyone shared the enthusiastic desire to join in the commemoration of Rabin. More specifically, mourning Rabin and, later, the commemoration of his assassination, was limited to those circles that aspired to be part of an inclusive definition of Israeli citizenship and considered it a realistic option. Expressions of sorrow and mourning immediately after the assassination were evident in the three commercial newspapers and in *al-Ittihad*, while the Islamist *Sawt al-Haq wal-Hurriyya* kept a restrained tone of coverage (the secular nationalist *Fasl al-Maqal* began to appear only in 1996).

The immediate reactions to the assassination in *Sawt al-Haq wal-Hurriyya* included celebration of the failure of the Israeli Security Services,[22] alongside its protest that political assassination is only condemned selectively. A week before Rabin's assassination, Fathi Shiqaqi, the leader of the Islamic Jihad was assassinated in Malta (Israel has never denied reports in foreign publications that this was a Mossad operation). The first editorial published after Rabin's assassination stated: "We must ask those who condemn the assassination of Rabin the following question: Where were these voices when Dr. Fathi Shiqaqi was assassinated a week ago? Is it permissible [to pour out] the blood of a Muslim and the blood of others is forbidden?"

The next year, following the first anniversary of the assassination, *Sawt al-Haq wal-Hurriyya* reported an incident in a high school in the Arab town Kafr Kana, where the school administration censored the speech prepared by the head of the student council for the commemorative ceremony. According to the newspaper, the student, Kamal 'Awawde, intended to talk not only about the assassination but also about "what Rabin did to the Arabs and the Palestinians," but was forced to deliver a truncated speech. *Sawt al-Haq wal-Hurriyya* criticized the school administration for commemorating Rabin's assassination while at the same time rejecting the students' initiative to commemorate the 1956 massacre at Kafr Qasim (the anniversary of which occurs a few days earlier).

Fasl al Maqal adopted a similar line. In a central article following the first anniversary, the newspaper accused Rabin of partial responsibility for his own assassination, since he tolerated violence against Arabs.[23] In both "oppositional" newspapers, the religious *Sawt al-Haq* and the secular *Fasl al-Maqal*, even this reserved reference to Rabin soon disappeared and replaced by an almost complete silence after 1996. A rare exception was a sarcastic comment in *Fasl al-Maqal* following the commemoration ceremony in Oslo in 1999. While mocking this ceremony, Azmi Bishara mentioned that some American newspapers were trying to make Rabin "The Man of the 20th Century," in another attempt to "turn Israeli legends into world legends."[24]

Findings from Surveys before 2000

This association between sympathy for Rabin and an integrative orientation is well reflected in a survey conducted in May 1996.[25] In this survey the interviewees were presented a list of groups and persons with a scale one to ten for each of them, representing level of sympathy (1 representing strong rejection, 10 representing strong support). The four persons mentioned in the questionnaire were Rabin, Arafat, Shimon Peres (then Prime Minister of Israel), and Netanyahu, the leader of the opposition in the Knesset. The survey was conducted shortly before the 1996 elections, in which Peres and Netanyahu were the two candidates for prime minister.

The findings show that a majority of the Arab citizens of Israel were much closer to the sympathetic line of *al-Ittihad* than to the cynicism of the other two political newspapers. The average sympathy index for Rabin was 7.15 compared with 7.31 for Peres, 5.81 for Arafat, and 2.83 for Netanyahu. The high level of sympathy for Peres is probably related to his being the successor of Rabin and the candidate in the upcoming election against the right-wing candidate Netanyahu.

To measure integrative tendencies, I used two variables. One of them was a dummy variable that indicated whether the interviewee clearly intended to vote for one of the candidates for prime minister in the elections scheduled for 29 May or alternatively did not intend to vote, intended to use a blank ballot, did not know yet, or refused to answer. Since voting for either candidate (Peres or Netanyahu) represented an active attempt to influence the Israeli political sphere, I considered the intention as an indicator of the interviewee's orientation toward political integration. Indeed, those who intended to vote had significantly higher sympathy for Rabin than the other interviewees (7.53 vs. 5.33, respectively, $p<0.001$ in t-test).

A second indicator was a connection with Jews, a reflection of social integration. This aspect was measured by the question: "Do you have any connections with Jews?" The optional answers were: "Not at all," "Only work relations," "Yes, a friend, or two," "A lot of relationships, including friendships." The results are presented in Figure 10.

The numbers show that sympathy for Rabin was significantly associated with personal connections with Jews—the deeper the connection, the higher

	Arafat	Netanyahu	Peres	Rabin
No connections	5.77	2.83	7.13	6.63
Business connections	6.01	2.64	7.0	6.89
1-2 friends	5.3	3.27	7.62	7.21
Many connections, including friends	5.82	2.84	7.48	7.51
F-value in ANOVA test	1.219	1.186	1.698	3.442*

* $p < 0.05$

Figure 10. Sympathy for various politicians and depth of personal connection with Jews in May 1996

the sympathy for Rabin. The value of Analysis of Variance (ANOVA) test is an indication to the strength of the association. Furthermore, a similar association was not found in relation to any other leader, including Prime Minister Peres. In this regard there is a complete congruence between the public references to Rabin after his assassination and the personal answers in the survey. The gap between the tendency of the Communist Party to connect Rabin's memory to themes of Arab-Jewish partnership as opposed to the separatist tendencies of the NDA and the Islamic Movement is well reflected in this survey. At that point in history, public memory and individual memories displayed similar patterns.

FOLLOWING OCTOBER 2000

The events of October 2000 reshuffled the political cards of Arab-Jewish relations in Israel. The frustration that spread among the Palestinian citizens of Israel led to an almost complete withdrawal from participating, even passively, in further commemorations of Yitzhak Rabin. As part of the fifth anniversary of Rabin's assassination, the Rabin Center organized a conference for Arab school principals aimed at increasing their awareness of the importance of Rabin's memorial day.[26] Initially, 550 principals and 70 superintendents confirmed their participation.[27] The event took place on 5 November, only a few weeks after the eruption of the al-Aqsa Intifada and the October 2000 events inside the Green Line. Arab school principals are known to be one of the most conservative groups among the Arabs in Israel, due to a strict selection process guided by the Shabak (see Chapter 8). Nevertheless, only fifteen principals and a similar number of superintendents attended the events.

From the year 2000 onward, *al-Ittihad* stopped covering the annual commemorative rally in Tel Aviv, and pictures of Rabin did not appear in the newspaper on or around 4 November, as they had in the years 1995–1999. This sudden silence is evident in other Arabic newspapers, as well, and in Arab schools.[28] As a general tendency, since 2000 Rabin's name has almost disappeared from the Arabic press. The sporadic mentioning of his name since then was usually related to his pre-1992 history and was done by actors who reject Israelification. For example, the website Arab48 (belonging to the secular nationalist NDA) referred to a report in the Hebrew daily *Haaretz* about a new book that discovered that Rabin had suggested in 1956 to expel the Palestinians from the West Bank.[29] Arab speakers were invited to and did appear at the central annual memorial rally in Tel Aviv in the years 2000–2002, probably as a conciliatory gesture by Zionist left-wing parties following October 2000, but they stopped participating soon after.

This silence stems partly from the active exclusion of the Arabs from the commemoration by the Jewish side.[30] The Rabin Center itself, for example, invested much energy in projects aimed at mutual rapprochement between Jews only.[31] However, this exclusion started immediately after the assassination and, therefore, the abstention of *al-Ittihad* from referring to Rabin can be easily linked to the frustration and anger that followed the October 2000 events.

A rare crack in this wall of silence was the participation of Samih al-Qasim in a poetry evening dedicated to the memory of Rabin on 29 October 2009. He was harshly criticized by a rising star of Palestinian poetry, Najwan Darwish from Jerusalem, who blamed him for contributing to normalization and Israelification.[32]

UNDER-CURRENT MEMORY

Unlike before 2000, in the post-October 2000 period the compatibility of public memory and personal reference to Rabin disappeared. Rabin's absence from public discourse in Arabic does not mean that Arab citizens of Israel forgot him. Public polls showed not only that sympathy for Rabin among Arab citizens did not vanish; it even increased—at the same time that it decreased among the Jewish population. The July 2005 survey replicated the sympathy index from 1996 and the comparison is presented in Figure 11.[33] It is noteworthy as well that in the 2005 survey the sympathy for Rabin among Arab citizens exceeded by far that of any other former prime minister. The second highest index was ascribed to Peres and it was only 5.95, compared with 7.57 for Rabin. This gap implies that the sympathy for Rabin has not spilled over to other Zionist leaders. Rather, in 2005

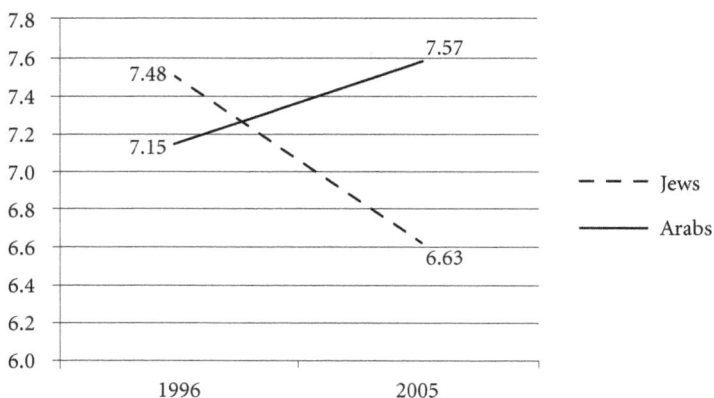

Figure 11. Sympathy for Rabin among Jews and Arabs in 1996 and 2005

Rabin is remembered as a positive exception among Israeli leaders. Among the Jewish interviewees, Rabin ranked third, after Ben Gurion and Begin.[34] Rabin was ranked first by Jews who stated that the definition "Israeli" suites them more than the definition "Jew,"[35] so the nostalgia for Rabin is shared by Arabs and Jews who aspire to emphasize Israeli citizenship, and it distinguishes both of them from Jews who prefer to emphasize Jewish identity.

In the same survey, Arab interviewees were much more likely than Jewish interviewees to think that Rabin's assassin, Yigal Amir should have been sentenced to death (67.1 percent vs. 28.1 percent); and they tended more to argue that his assassination was the most important event in the history of the state since its founding (47 percent vs. 37 percent).[36] Similar results were found in a survey conducted three months later by the Tami Steinmetz Center for Peace Studies at Tel Aviv University. The survey was conducted among a representative sample of 585 Israeli citizens and showed again that Rabin is remembered more positively by Arab citizens than by Jewish citizens. The interviewees were asked to choose an adjective to describe Rabin as a leader from the following: outstanding, fairly good, mediocre, fairly bad, failing. Among Arabs 39 percent described Rabin as an outstanding leader while among Jews, only 20 percent described him as such.[37]

Accordingly, among the Arab respondents, there was more longing for Rabin's era. Among the Jewish sample, 30 percent said that Israeli society has changed for the worse due to Rabin's assassination while in the Arab sample, 61 percent expressed the same opinion. Although due to the small size of the Arab sub-sample in this particular survey (N=80), one should be careful with the interpretation of these results, the gap is still statistically significant and impressive in its magnitude.

Returning to the July 2005 survey with the larger sample, there are many indications that the association between Israelification tendencies and remembering Rabin among the Arab citizens remained valid in 2005. One such an indication is the answer given to the question: Who is primarily responsible for the assassination? Arab interviewees tended much more to accuse "the Israeli right" than did Jewish interviewees (36.6 percent vs. 14.7 percent).[38] This gap echoes Lev Greenberg's insight that Rabin tried to redesign political identities in Israel based on pro-peace and anti-peace camps,[39] rather than as Arabs versus Jews. The fact that more than one-third of the Arab interviewees pointed their fingers at the right suggests that a significant portion of them adopted this distinction.

Another indication of the integrative orientation of Rabin's remembrance is the differential sympathy for Rabin among people with different levels of pride in their Israeli identity, as seen in Figure 12.

The survey I conducted in July–August 2008 showed a similar tendency and it is particularly important for validating my argument as Rabin was not even mentioned in the questionnaire. Therefore, mention of his name by the interviewees reflects the status of Rabin in an interviewee's memory much more than in the other surveys. In one significant question in the survey, respondents were asked to mention as many as four persons whom they considered to be

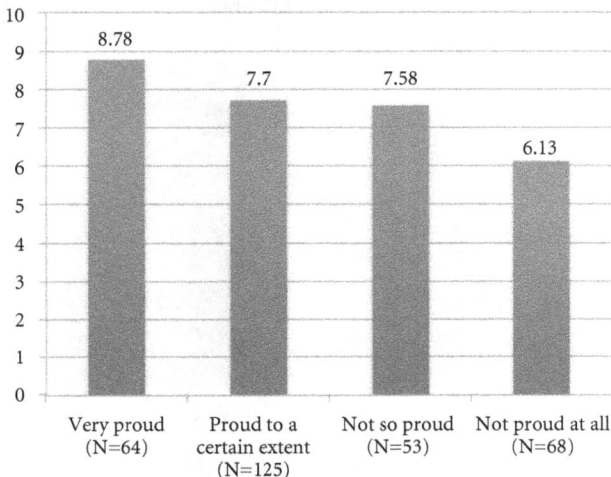

Figure 12. Sympathy for Rabin by level of pride in Israeli identity, 2005

the most important in the history of the country.[40] Unexpectedly, Rabin was the name most frequently mentioned by the Arab sample (38.6 percent), exceeding even that of the mythic Palestinian leader Arafat (31.1 percent). Among the Jewish respondents, Rabin was mentioned by only 27.4 percent, ranked fourth after Israel's first prime minister, Ben Gurion (74.0 percent); former prime minister, Begin (39.4 percent); and Herzl (29.4 percent).

Beyond the evidence for the strong presence of Rabin in the collective memory of the Arab citizens in Israel in 2008, this survey indicates, as well, that the integrative orientation of Rabin's remembrance was maintained. The political implications of mentioning various historical figures can be traced by cross-tabulating the answers to the above-mentioned question with another open-ended question that appeared in the questionnaire: How do you define your identity? The question sounds as vague in Arabic as it sounds in English, and the aim was to avoid steering the respondent toward any particular self-definition. Based on the answers given, I distinguished in the Arab sample between those who included the term "Israeli" in their self-definition (including "Israeli citizens") and those who did not.

It turns out that among those Arab respondents who included the term "Israeli" in their self-definition, 45 percent mentioned Rabin, while among the other respondents only 34 percent mentioned him ($p<0.01$ in χ^2 test). Similarly, when I asked the respondents to respond to the question "To what extent does the definition "Israeli" fit you?" on a scale of one to four, a clear correlation between the level of Israeliness and the likelihood of mentioning Rabin was revealed (see Figure 13).

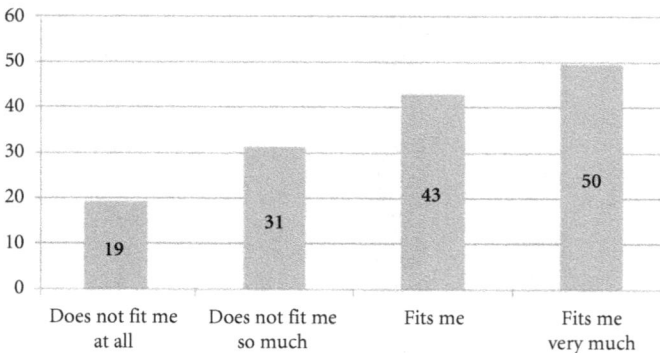

Figure 13. Percentage of respondents who mentioned Rabin in answer to the question: "To what extent does the definition 'Israeli' fit you?" (2008 survey)

NOSTALGIA FOR THE INTEGRATIVE OPTION

The first decade of the twenty-first century was characterized by a deterioration in the relations between Arab and Jewish citizens of Israel. The events of October 2000, the al-Aqsa Intifada, the 2006 war in Lebanon, and the several cycles of violence in Gaza Strip had detrimental effects on these relations.[41] Several cases of localized violent clashes did not deteriorate into the gravity of those of October 2000 mainly because of a "fear balance" between the state and its Arab citizens.[42]

Looking back from this sociopolitical reality, the years of Rabin's government have a special meaning. In those three years (1992–1995), the "Zionist Left," and the Palestinian citizens of Israel were as close as they have ever been to political cooperation, and optimistic predictions about the future of the Israeli-Palestinian conflict were widespread.

Under these circumstances, it is not surprising that among Arabs in Israel the belief that it is possible to reconcile their Palestinian identity with their Israeli citizenship reached its zenith at the same time. Rabin became a symbol of this hope and in the days after his assassination, many Arabs in Israel even believed that the political earthquake would leave them and the Israeli "Peace Camp" on one side of the political map while a defeated Israeli right wing would remain on the other side. The assassination of Rabin immediately became a symbol for the feasibility of the integrative option, and it is this meaning that shaped the remembrance of Rabin among Palestinian citizens of Israel in the ensuing period. For this purpose, Rabin's pre-1992 past, including his central role in expelling Palestinians in 1948, was ignored. The omission of this episode and the sympathy for Rabin do not reflect in any way the acceptance of the Zionist narrative but rather the opposite. They are tightly connected to the general antagonism that Palestinian citizens have with Israeli official memory and the legacy of all leaders. Following Rabin's assassination, the pro-integration actors strove to *separate* Rabin from the antagonizing Zionist narrative by emphasizing the inclusive policy he led in the last years of his life.

Paradoxically, Rabin's image among Arab citizens of Israel moved in opposing directions in each of the two spheres of memory examined. At the public level, the extensive attention given by some political actors before 2000 was transformed into silence in the post-2000 period. At the individual level, Rabin's image remained salient and the sympathy for him even increased.

How can we explain this paradox? First, the Arabic-language media in Israel is a major component in the counter-hegemonic public sphere of Arabs in Israel.[43] It is likely, therefore, that this silence is a form of protest by Arab journalists against the state authorities and the Jewish public following October 2000. If this is indeed a protest, then the importance of Rabin in the history of the country is not ignored but, rather, there is a suspension of its acknowledgment. Accordingly, this protest is not activated in a personal interview because outside of the public sphere, people are not always constrained by a sense of collective responsibility and concern for the political effect of their answers. Following this line of thought, it appears that both the journalists who are silent about Rabin in the public sphere, as well as ordinary people who mention him in a survey, do so because of Rabin's association with integrative tendencies. Rabin symbolizes similar themes in his appearance and in his absence. The silence could have become a form of protest only because it has a certain meaning in the public sphere.

A possible complementary explanation is that silence is needed, especially for those agents of memory who led the initial public commemoration and now prefer to downplay their role out of shame, due to the failure of the integrative approach whereas ordinary people have fewer reasons to be ashamed and do not feel they have to compensate for past mistakes by ignoring Rabin. For those among them who still aspire to be recognized as Israelis, the impasse of the Israeli-Palestinian conflict makes the reconciliation of Israeli and Palestinian identities particularly challenging and demanding. The latent nostalgia for Rabin's time is a longing for the ephemeral period when being Israeli looked like a realistic and plausible option for Palestinian citizens of Israel.

CONCLUSION

EARLY IN MY FIRST CONVERSATION with Wakim Wakim, before talking with him about the March of Return, I raised the intersecting points of our biographies. Wakim was born in 1958 to a family of internal refugees from the village of al-Bassa in the western Galilee and grew up in the Christian village of Maʿiliya. I was born eleven years later and grew up in Hanita, a kibbutz located on the mountain one kilometer in air distance from al-Bassa. Established in 1938, Hanita was an iconic symbol of the Zionist project of settling and defending the land. In the 1948 war, Hanita's residents took part in the occupation of al-Bassa and later gained some of the village's agricultural lands. As a teenager I used to work in these fields, unaware of their history. Wakim expressed interest in visiting Hanita and, especially, its small historical museum.

In June 2012 I met Wakim, accompanied by his father Elias and some younger members of the Committee of al-Bassa's Uprooted, in the Hanita Museum. I was accompanied by my father, my late uncle, and ʿEzer Argaman, a member of Kibbutz Hanita and a member of the museum staff—all three were born either in the late 1940s or early 1950s and spent decades of their lives on the kibbutz. During the visit, Argaman and E. Wakim had a long discussion about what exactly was agreed upon in the May 1948 meeting that had taken place between representatives of al-Bassa and Hanita shortly before the IDF's occupation of al-Bassa (a meeting that E. Wakim attended personally and that Argaman learned about second hand).

The specific details of the event need not concern us here, but what is significant is that their differing versions is an example of the ways history is remembered differently by both sides. Being aware of that, Argaman made a suggestion to the visitors from al-Bassa: "What do you think about taking one of the museum walls and presenting your own story on this wall?" Argaman did not have the authority to make such a proposal, and it was unlikely that it would have been approved by the museum director or by the residents of Hanita. Nevertheless, it was an original idea. The co-habitation of Palestinian and Zionist narratives is not common in Israeli museums, certainly not in a museum that originally aimed to glorify a specific settlement as the jewel in the crown of the Zionist project.

At the same time, I thought to myself that the people of al-Bassa would have good reasons to reject the proposal. First, why should they frame their story within the context of a Zionist institution dedicated to glorifying the colonial project? Second, as long as they are still actively demanding the return of their lands, why would they agree to freeze their narrative in a museum as if their dispossession is a closed chapter in history? This "framing" of their story might be interpreted as giving up their concrete political claim.

To my surprise, W. Wakim was quite enthusiastic and expressed great interest in the proposal. This went far beyond mere politeness since he continued to raise the issue in phone conversations with me after the visit was over. In his view, this was an unprecedented opportunity to tell his story to mainstream Jewish Israelis. He decided to bring up the proposal for discussion with the rest of al-Bassa's Committee of the Uprooted. Two weeks after the visit in Hanita, W. Wakim called me and informed me that the committee rejected the proposal. However, my assumptions of the reasons for the rejection appeared to be wrong. "For us," he said, "cooperating with you [Jewish Israelis] is self-evident. But people in the committee said: 'How can we explain this to our relatives in Lebanon?'"

CAUTIOUS COMMEMORATION

Palestinians in Israel have to adapt themselves to the expectations of both other Palestinians outside of Israel as well as Jewish Israelis. As much as W. Wakim wanted his story to be told and to be recognized by Jewish Israelis, a common aspiration among Palestinians in Israel that I illustrated throughout this book, he and other members of the committee remained restricted by the expectations of their family members in Lebanon and the broader Palestinian diaspora.

These cross-pressures are part of the broader tension between being Palestinians and being Israeli citizens, which is a major force that shapes Palestinian commemoration in Israel. While some other axes of conflict (integration-separation;

local-national; elite-masses; intra-Palestinian communal relations) are not simple derivatives of this tension, they are commonly related to it in one way or another. Together, these tensions create frequent discrepancies between various forms and spheres of historical remembrance and commemoration, as well as internal inconsistencies in the commemorative rhetoric. While consistency is certainly not a natural condition that should be expected by default and whereas these discrepancies and inconsistencies might be found in many other cases of national historical remembrance, it seems that the peculiar status of Palestinians in Israel makes them even sharper and more common. As Amal Jamal has phrased it, "the Israeli 'Palestinianness' is a combination of historical and cultural memories that do not always cohere and in many cases collide."[1] This is a multidimensional collision.

First, the Nakba dominates the collective memory of Palestinians in Israel, and at the same time, it is suspended in some contexts to enable their inclusion in the Israeli political community. For example, while nationalist Palestinian intellectuals frequently describe the massacre in Kafr Qasim as another chapter of the Nakba, the readiness of the mayor of Kafr Qasim to sit on the advisory board of Israel's sixtieth anniversary celebration in 2008, contradicts their efforts to draw a connecting line between these two events and creates discordance in their narrative. In another example, the Knesset deputy chair, a Druze member of a party that has been very active in the attempts to outlaw the Nakba commemoration, delivered a speech at the unveiling of a memorial dedicated to Druze soldiers who fought in 1948 *against* Zionist forces, while Israeli flags flapped in the wind behind him. Similarly, one of the major actors involved in the expulsion of Palestinians in 1948, Yitzhak Rabin, gained much sympathy in popular memory among Palestinians in Israel because he was considered to be the first Israeli leader to open the doors of Israeliness to Arab citizens. For intellectuals who aspire to a harmonious nationalist narrative, this discordance is disturbing and might explain another inconsistency: the gap between the popular Palestinian sympathy for Rabin expressed in public opinion polls and the exclusion of his remembrance from the public discourse of Palestinian intellectuals and the Arabic media since 2000.

In a certain sense, then, memory of the Nakba is located at the juncture of Palestinian identity and Israeli citizenship. Its remembrance plays a central role in defining Palestinian identity today, but it also produced a deep-seated fear of expulsion among Palestinians, a fear that historically has been a major reason for the attractiveness of Israeli citizenship. Tellingly, when the Palestinian writer

Emile Habibi agreed to accept the Israel Prize (Israel's most prestigious award) in 1992 and was harshly and widely criticized in the Arab world, he justified his decision by claiming, "I was convinced that into my hands had fallen an additional tool with which to fight the threat of expulsion."[2] These two aspects of the memory of the Nakba have created internal tensions in Palestinians' commemorative rhetoric. The major events on the Palestinian political calendar are commonly presented as links in a long chain of Palestinian victimization, and at the same time, their commemoration aims to ensure that these events remain *isolated and exceptional cases*. In addition, while the commemoration of the Kafr Qasim massacre, Land Day, and al-Aqsa Day commonly celebrate Palestinian steadfastness and overcoming the Israeli intention to expel them, each commemoration is also a reminder to the state that the victims were Israeli citizens and *therefore* should have been protected.

Because of the Palestinian aspiration to make Israeli citizenship a protective shield, it is exactly those events that revealed its limited protective value that are especially alarming and are deeply inscribed in the collective consciousness of Palestinians in Israel. Therefore, paradoxically, the rhetorical commitment to Palestinian national unity is effectively challenged by the selective exclusion of Palestinian non-citizens from the collective martyrology. The selection of major events for the Palestinian political calendar also effectively redrew the line between citizens and non-citizens, a line that those same events threatened to blur.

In addition, we have seen that Palestinian national and local narratives and agendas frequently differed. For example, among residents of 'Aylabun, many preferred to disconnect their expulsion and massacre from the general context of the Nakba and instead framed their tragedy as a local event in order to secure their shaky status as Israeli citizens. A similar tendency had characterized the struggle to return to their land of the people of Kafr Bir'im. It has been only since the late 1990s that some of the second and third generation of internal refugees from the village began to contextualize their case in the broader Palestinian national narrative.

CAUTION AND ITS DECLINE

The above-mentioned tensions, as well as the surveillance and disciplinary methods imposed on Palestinian commemoration, have made this commemoration hesitant and cautious. Both the content and the form of Palestinian commemoration in Israel have been sensitive to changes in the potential to extend the meaning of Israeli citizenship from merely permission not to be expelled into a broader tangible legal and political set of rights. However, this potential has fluctuated since 1948.

Until 1966, the meaning of Israeli citizenship for Palestinians under military rule was extremely limited. Although egalitarian citizenship remained remote even after the end of military rule, nonetheless the civil and political rights of Arab citizens in Israel gradually and incrementally developed until the mid-1990s under the second government of Yitzhak Rabin. As a result, over the years Palestinian commemoration practices have gradually become more explicit, embodied, and spatialized. Initially, poetry reading played a central role in producing historical remembrance among Palestinians, cyclic memorial marches were added in the 1960s, and memorial monuments appeared in the 1970s. The sanitized language that characterized some monuments in the 1970s and 1980s was replaced in the 1990s by a clear reference to the perpetrators of atrocities. Around that same time Palestinian national symbols that had been actively excluded from commemorative rallies in the 1980s were displayed openly.

Since Rabin's assassination in 1995 and, especially, since the beginning of the Second Intifada in 2000, the gradual extension of Palestinian citizenship rights in Israel has ended and even reversed, expressed by a wave of discriminatory legislation against Palestinian citizens,[3] including legislation against commemoration itself. This wave, along with frustration over the failed emancipatory process of the 1990s, has pushed many Palestinians in Israel to reconsider their integrative aspirations. In addition, the widespread feeling among Palestinians that the two-state solution to the Israeli-Palestinian conflict has reached an impasse, has also contributed to imagining alternative political solutions in which Israeli citizenship would be replaced with the citizenship of a future binational, non-national, or Islamic state.

There are many indicators of this growing frustration and reassessment of the value of Israeli citizenship in the early twenty-first century. In terms of political behavior, there has been a gradual decline in the voter turnout of Palestinian citizens for Knesset elections. This tendency corresponds with various striking attitudes expressed in public opinion polls. For example, the Index of Arab-Jewish relations conducted by Smooha shows that between 2003 and 2012 there has been a sharp decline in the number of Palestinian citizens who: are happy with their lives as Israeli citizens; feel pride when Israel gains a major international achievement; trust the Israeli judiciary; trust the Knesset; think that Israel has the right to exist as an independent state; think that the country between the Jordan River and the Mediterranean Sea is a shared homeland for Arabs and Jews (this declined from two-thirds to one third in less than a decade!); see their Israeli citizenship as more important than their national identity as Palestinians or their religious affiliation (declined from 30 percent to 12 percent); and believe that their way of life and behavior is more similar to that of Jewish Israelis than to that of Palestinians in the West Bank and the Gaza Strip (from 72 percent to 54 percent). At the same time, there has been a sharp increase in the number of Palestinian citizens who reported that they were personally harmed by threats, humiliation, or assault by Jews; personally affected by discrimination; and were afraid of being expelled.[4]

A related process is the emergence of the northern faction of the Islamic Movement over the last fifteen years as a major political power among Palestinian citizens. As evidenced by the integrative orientation of the southern faction, political Islam in and of itself is not necessarily an obstacle for cross-confessional cooperation. The northern faction, however, has become the stronger and more influential of the two, with triple the number of supporters as the southern faction.[5] The movement's tendency to withdraw from the Israeli public sphere and its aspiration to minimize cooperation with Jewish Israelis have influenced the parameters of Palestinian commemoration, as evidenced by the creation of a separate central event for commemorating the Nakba in which Jewish speakers are absent.

The erosion of Palestinian civil rights in Israel has had clear implications for Palestinian commemoration in the first decades of the twenty-first century. Commemoration in general and the commemoration of the Nakba, in particular, have become even less cautious than they were in the 1990s. The monumentalization of Palestinian memory indicates the readiness of Palestinians to carve their national identity on public space. The sea of Palestinian flags, waving at commemorative events, is also evidence that displays of Palestinian identity are seen less as a risk or, alternatively, that people are much more willing to take that risk.

This change, however, has its own limits. A central museum that would tell the story of the Palestinians in Israel has not been established yet. Even though several initial steps were taken in this direction, none of the initiatives came to fruition. This absence is partly explained by lack of financial resources, but there is also a deeper reason: such a museum would have to confront directly many sacred cows of the official narrative of the Israeli state through direct reference to the relationship between the Nakba and the establishment of Israel.

This is a risk that many are still reluctant to take. According to Ayman 'Odeh, the general secretary of the DFPE who proposed the establishment of a large commemorative site for Palestinian history, none of the Arab local authorities was willing to include the site in its jurisdiction.[6] Still, the growing assertiveness of Palestinian commemoration in Israel in the early twenty-first century suggests that the emergence of such a site or museum might only be a matter of time.

In addition, there has been a gradual change in the relative importance of Jewish Israelis versus Palestinians outside Israel as audiences for Palestinian citizens' commemorative rhetoric. Jewish citizens of Israel are still considered as a potential audience of Palestinian commemoration, but there has been a noticeable decline in the tendency to approach Jewish audiences. The direct appeal to Jewish Israeli audiences in Hebrew that was so evident at the 1986 Kafr Qasim commemoration has not been repeated at any of the central events of the four major commemorations on the political calendar in the early twenty-first century. At the same time, the availability of satellite television and the Internet has enabled direct and immediate communication with Arab audiences in the region. In the last decade, the four major events of the Palestinian political calendar have been covered by Arabic satellite channels from outside Israel. The fiftieth anniversary of the Kafr Qasim massacre was even broadcast live by al-Jazeera. Clips from commemorative rallies are uploaded to YouTube and can be watched worldwide.

The shift in audience is clearly related to the decreasing universalistic orientation of the commemoration. The use of universalistic discourse in the hope of gaining rights, and its decline when it fails to guarantee these rights, are known from other contexts. The sociologist Brian Conway described how in the first years following 1972, Bloody Sunday was predominantly framed in a global struggle for human rights, but later the nationalist discourse of Irish republicans gained dominance,[7] a change that reflected their failure to achieve a political settlement. Similarly, the changing relative weight of the national versus universalistic aspects of the political calendar of Palestinians in Israel has been indicative of changes in the level of hope that Israeli citizenship can guarantee Palestinians' rights.

Finally, as a result of both the decline in caution and the increased exposure to Palestinians elsewhere, the content of Palestinian commemoration inside and outside Israel is more similar than ever. The simultaneous development of the temporal commemoration of the Nakba by Palestinian citizens and non-citizens alike is evidence of this process, as well as the growing weight of forces that promote complete withdrawal from Israeliness in the commemorative ceremonies. At the same time, however, the calendar of mass processions inside Israel remains distinct (the March of Return, al-Aqsa Day, and the commemoration of Kafr Qasim). The content of commemoration as a whole certainly keeps its peculiar characteristics (such as the constant demand for civic equality in commemorative rhetoric, the insistence on legality and respect for Israeli law, and the symbolic inclusion of Jewish Israelis in commemoration events).

At the moment of writing these lines in summer 2014, Palestinian citizens of Israel stand at a critical juncture. Earlier this year the Knesset decided to increase the threshold of votes for achieving parliamentary representation to 3.25 percent, which is, not coincidentally, almost identical to the percentage of votes won by the three Arab parties represented in the Knesset. In other words, this is part of a broader wave of anti-Arab legislation, this time manifesting as an attempt to exclude Palestinian citizens from the parliament. In a parallel path, the Israeli government is promoting a Basic Law that would define Israel as a Jewish State and would practically provide legal justification to many forms of anti-Arab discrimination that so far have been illegal.[8] This legislation might add to the growing frustration among Palestinian citizens over the ineffectiveness of the parliamentary and legal paths as forms of struggle.

Furthermore, another round of violent escalation in the Israeli-Palestinian conflict is accompanied this time by sporadic physical attacks of Arabs in Israel by Jewish mobs. While this sort of attack has occurred in the past, their frequency and intensity is unprecedented,[9] and they further undermine the sense of personal security among Palestinian citizens. Attacks on Jewish cars on the main roads near Arab localities by Arab mobs led to Jewish customers distancing themselves from Arab businesses in some Arab towns, leading to an ever-growing social distance between Arabs and Jews.

In the long term, the above mentioned processes might join into a centrifugal power that would reduce Palestinian involvement in the Israeli public sphere. Once the legal forms of struggle are blocked and once Palestinian citizens give up the possibility of influencing Jewish Israeli public opinion, the forms of struggle of Palestinian Israeli citizens might become more similar to the forms of struggle of other Palestinians. Under these circumstances, the forces that have maintained the separate character of Palestinian commemoration in Israel might disappear as well.

REFERENCE MATTER

APPENDIX

ODDS RATIOS FROM LOGISTIC REGRESSIONS, PREDICTING THE MENTION OF VARIOUS EVENTS BY PALESTINIAN INTERVIEWEES (2008 SURVEY)

	July 2006 War	1948	1948 as Nakba	Al-Aqsa Uprising
Women	1.85***	.86	.72	2.64***
Attended college	.69	1.95***	1.974**	1.32
Age 60+	1.07	2.85***	2.375**	.577
Age 18–29	2.22****	1.06	.671	1.218
Galilee resident	2.23****	.71	.882	.762
Muslim	.87	.85	1.533	1.235
Secular	1.69*	1.264	1.391	.128**
Palestinian (self-labeling)	.83	1.98**	2.681***	1.717
Israeli (self-labeling)	1.06	1.62*	1.549	.842
Palestinian and Israeli (self-labeling)	3.01***	.62	.557	.753

* p< 0.1; ** p< 0.05; *** p< 0.01; **** p<0.001

MEMORIAL MONUMENTS FOR MARTYRS BUILT BY PALESTINIAN CITIZENS OF ISRAEL

	Year of completion	Commemoration of	Town/ Village	Location	Initiated by
1	1976	Kafr Qasim massacre (1956)	Kafr Qasim	Cemetery	Municipal Council
2	1978	Land Day Martyrs (1976)	Sakhnin	Cemetery	Land Committee
3	1978	The martyr Rafaet Al-Zuhayi (Land Day, 1976)	Taybeh	Secondary square in town	Municipal Council
4	1983	Sabra and Shatila massacre (1982)	Kafr Kana	Cemetery	Sons of the Village movement
5	1983	Sabra and Shatila massacre (1982)	Laqiyya	Central square	Local Committee
6	1983	'Aylabun massacre (1948)	'Aylabun	Cemetery	Private
7	Mid-1980s	The Mawasi massacre (1948)	'Aylabun	Cemetery	Private
8	1994	Kafr Qasim massacre (1948)	Kafr Qasim	Central square	Municipal Council
9*	1998	'Aylabun and Mawasi massacres (1948)	'Aylabun	Secondary square in town	Municipal Council
10*	1998	Martyrs of Shefa'amr and the region (1948)	Shefa'amr	Central square	Municipal Council
11	1998	The martyr Muhammad Abu Jami' (1994)	Rahat	Central square	Local Committee
12	2000	Martyrs of Kafr Kana (1936–2000)	Kafr Kana	Central square	Municipal Council
13	2001	The martyr Muhammad Khamaysi (October 2000)	Kafa Kana	Entrance to town	Family
14	2002	13 al-Aqsa martyrs (October 2000)	Kafr Manda	Entrance to town	Family
15	2002	The martyr Muhammad Jabarin (October 2000)	Um al-Fahm	Central square	Municipal Council

16	2002	The martyr Ahmad Jabarin (October 2000)	Um al-Fahm	Central square	Municipal Council
17	2002	The martyr Muslih Abu Jarad (October 2000)	Um al-Fahm	Central square	Municipal Council
18	2002	13 al-Aqsa martyrs (October 2000)	Nazareth	Entrance to city	Municipal Council
19	2002	13 al-Aqsa martyrs (October 2000)	Jat	Entrance to town	Municipal Council
20	2003	13 al-Aqsa martyrs (October 2000)	Sakhnin	Central square	Municipal Council
21	2003	Martyrs of Kafr Manda (1936–2000)	Kafr Manda	Central square	Municipal Council
22*	2005	The martyr Muhammad Khatib (2004)	Near Kafr Kana	Main road outside of town	Family
23	2006	Kafr Qasim massacre (1956)	Kafr Qasim	Central square	Municipal Council
24	2009	Assault in Shefa'amr (2005)	Shefa'amr	Central square	Municipal Council
25	2009	'Aylut Massacre (1948)	'Aylut	Central square	Municipal Council
26	2004	Martyrs of 'Arabeh (1936–2000)	'Arabeh	Entrance to town	Local Committee
27	2013	Soldiers of the Druze battalion (1948)	Shefa'amr	Site of mass burial	Druze communal leadership
28	2014	The martyr Khayr al-Din Hamdan (November 2014)	Kafr Kana	Site of death—major juncture	Local Committee

* Destroyed or distorted

NOTES

INTRODUCTION

1. Interview with Iyad Barghuthi, 3 March 2012.
2. Robinson, *Citizen Strangers*, 74–84.
3. Ibid., 111.
4. Kimmerling, "Boundaries and Frontiers," 265–84.
5. Yiftachel, "Ethnocracy."
6. On the predicament of Palestinians in Israel facing the ethnic character of the state, see Ghanem and Rouhana, "Citizenship and the Parliamentary Politics of Minorities in Ethnic States." For details about current days discrimination, see Haider et al., *The Equality Index.*
7. Jamal, "Palestinian Dynamics of Self Representation."
8. Jamal, "Nationalizing States," 447.
9. Jamal, *Arab Public Sphere in Israel,* 97.
10. Ibid.
11. Ibid., 99.
12. Bishara, "He-'Arvi ha-Yisraeli," 176.
13. Landau, *Arab Minority in Israel;* Stendel, *Arabs in Israel;* Kaufman, *Arab National Communism;* Ghanem, *Palestinian-Arab Minority in Israel;* Bashir, *Land Day;* Bauml, *Tsel Kahol-Lavan;* R. Cohen, *Strangers in Their Homeland;* Reiter, *National Minority, Regional Majority;* Frisch, *Israel's Security and Its Arab Citizens;* Haklai, *Palestinian Ethnonationalism;* Jamal, *Arab Minority Nationalism;* Pappé, *Forgotten Palestinians;* Peleg and Waxman, *Israel's Palestinians;* Schueftan, *Falastinin be-yisrael;* Robinson, *Citizen Strangers.*
14. Lewin-Epstein and Semyonov, *Arab Minority in Israel's Economy.*
15. Al Haj, *Education, Empowerment, and Control.*
16. Jamal, *Arab Public Sphere in Israel.*
17. Rabinowitz, *Overlooking Nazareth.*
18. Rabinowitz and Abu-Baker, *Coffins on Our Shoulders.*
19. Ghanim, *Livnot et ha-uma me-hadash.*
20. H. Cohen, *Good Arabs.*
21. Gvion, *Beyond Hummus and Falafel.*

22. Ben Porat, *Biladi Biladi*; Sorek, *Arab Soccer in a Jewish State*.

23. Zerubavel, *Recovered Roots*, 9.

24. Cressy, *Bonfires and Bells*; E. Zerubavel, "Easter and Passover"; E. Zerubavel, "Calendars and History"; Y. Zerubavel, *Recovered Roots*.

25. E. Zerubavel, "Easter and Passover," 316–317.

26. For this typology, see Ghanem, *Palestinian-Arab Minority in Israel*.

27. Coser, "Introduction: Maurice Halbwachs 1877–1945."

28. Mannheim, *Essays on the Sociology of Knowledge*.

29. Assmann and Czaplicka, "Collective Memory and Cultural Identity."

30. Popular Memory Group, "Popular Memory."

31. Ibid., 255.

32. Popular Memory Group, "Popular Memory."

33. Olick, "Collective Memory: The Two Cultures."

34. Popular Memory Group, "Popular Memory."

35. Jamal, *Arab Public Sphere in Israel*.

36. Inevitably, my focus on actors who hold a certain level of public power is reflected in an imbalance of the gender distribution of the interviewees, given the extreme overrepresentation of men in positions of power.

37. In August 2005 an Israeli Defense Forces (IDF) deserter killed four Shefa'amr residents in a calculated attempt to prevent the withdrawal of Israel from the Gaza Strip. For more information, see Chapter 5.

38. On a similar problem, see Rabinowitz, *Overlooking Nazareth*. It is noteworthy that this suspicion is based on a concrete social reality—at an early stage of my academic career, after my first articles had been already published, Shabak representatives contacted me and suggested that I utilize my academic credentials to collect information for them. I firmly rejected the offer and have never received a similar offer since then, but the incident taught me the extent to which I must work hard to gain trust in my fieldwork.

39. The reliability of telephone interviews for the Arab minority in Israel has been frequently criticized. It has been argued that Arab respondents are suspicious and tend to feel threatened when being asked questions with a potentially political connotation (especially by phone), and that their answers might reflect a tendency to satisfy the authorities (Smooha, "Suvreys among the Arab Population in Israel"). As Smooha notes, however, in surveys he has taken since the mid-seventies, the high rate of support for the Palestinian Liberation Organization (PLO: considered a terrorist organization by Israeli law until 1993) and a long list of anti-establishment attitudes indicate that, collectively, the Arabs in Israel are not a frightened public.

40. The survey was conducted by the B. I. Lucille Cohen Institute for Public Opinion Research at Tel Aviv University. The samples were based on a proportional sampling of statistical areas, within layers defined by religion, geographical region, and socio-

economic status. In the second stage, numbers of households were sampled from each statistical area. In each household selected for the sample, one adult aged eighteen or older was interviewed. The response rate was 35 percent, which is compatible with the known response rate of phone interviews in Israel. Arabs were interviewed by native Arabic speakers and Jews were interviewed by native Hebrew or Russian speakers. The phone conversation typically lasted no more than ten minutes. The questionnaire was part of a larger research project about memory and identity among Jews and Arabs in Israel, and this book uses only answers to specific questions from the survey.

41. Rabinowitz, " Palestinian Citizens of Israel."

42. Brubaker, *Nationalism Reframed*, 4–6. The homeland is "external" since it is beyond the political boundaries of the state even though "the trapped minorities" do not see themselves as living outside of their homeland.

43. Csergo and Goldgeier, "Kin-State Activism."

44. Yiftachel, "Between Nation and State," 289.

45. Bray and Keating, "European Integration and the Basque Country," 139.

46. Brubaker and Feischmidt, "1848 in 1998."

47. Conway, *Commemoration and Bloody Sunday*.

48. Cheskin, "History, Conflicting Collective Memories, and National Identities."

49. For an evaluation of the applicability of the term in various contexts, see Goldberg and Bram, "Sephardic/Mizrahi/Arab-Jews."

50. Historically in the mandate period, this was not an issue as it reflected Palestinian citizenship.

51. Brubaker et al., *Nationalist Politics and Everyday Ethnicity*, 299.

52. Gündüz-Hoşgör and Smits, "Intermarriage between Turks and Kurds."

53. Monden and Smits, "Ethnic Intermarriage in Times of Social Change."

54. Wigfall-Williams and Robinson, *A World Apart*.

55. On the gap between national and vernacular perspectives and on ethnically mixed families in Transylvania, see Brubaker et al., *Nationalist Politics and Everyday Ethnicity*.

56. Rabinowitz, "The Palestinian Citizens of Israel."

57. For example, some of the Soviet war monuments built in republics that gained independence in the post-Soviet era became contested sites between the Russian ethnic minority and the new nationalizing states: Smith, "Woe from Stones."

58. Csergo and Goldgeier, "Kin-State Activism."

59. For this distinction see Brubaker, "Nationalizing States Revisited."

60. For studies that analyze the relations between the State of Israel and its Palestinian citizens from the colonial paradigm, see Zureik, *The Palestinians in Israel*; Shafir and Peled, *Being Israeli*; and Robinson, *Citizen Strangers*.

61. Yiftachel, "Ethnocracy."

62. For examples of analyzing the territory between the sea and the river as one unit, see Yiftachel, "Ethnocracy"; Meron Benvenisti, "The binational option," *Haaretz*,

7 November 2003; and Yehuda Shenhav, *Beyond the Two-State Solution*. For an example of considering Israel in its pre-1967 borders as the relevant unit of analysis, see Smooha, "The Model of Ethnic Democracy."

63. Kimmerling, "Exchanging Territories for Peace."

64. Lyn Spillman, "When Do Collective Memories Last?"

CHAPTER 1

1. On Ottoman identity in Palestine after the end of the Empire, see A. Halabi, "Liminal Loyalties."

2. In this context it is worth emphasizing that my aim here is not to illustrate the relative salience of Palestinian particularism but to show the important role of calendars and martyrs in the attempts to cultivate this collective identity. I also do not intend to analyze the socio-political developments that led to the emergence of Palestinian nationalism as these processes have been discussed in detail elsewhere. See, e.g., Porath, *Emergence of the Palestinian-Arab National Movement*; Muslih, *Origins of Palestinian Nationalism*; Kimmerling and Migdal, *Palestinians*; R. Khalidi, *Palestinian Identity*; Litvak, *Palestinian Collective Memory and National Identity*, Gerber, *Remembering and Imagining Palestine*.

3. On pre-modern elements of Palestinian collective memory, see R. Khalidi, *Palestinian Identity*; Gerber, *Remembering and Imagining Palestine*.

4. On these organizations in Palestine, see Porath, *Emergence of the Palestinian-Arab National Movement*; Al-Hut, *Al-Qiyadat Al-Mu'assasat Al-Siyasiyya fi Filastin*; Tamari, "Confessionalism and Public Space in Ottoman and Colonial Jerusalem"; Tamari, "With God's Camel in Siberia."

5. Sakakini, *Yawmiyat, Al-Kitab Al-Thalith*, 142 (3 May 1919).

6. Sakakini, *Yawmiyat, Al-Kitab Al-Thalith*, 145–146 (9 May 1919).

7. Although the shrine was most likely constructed by the Mamluk Sultan Rukn al-Din Baybars (1223–1277), the poplar Palestinian narrative ascribes the initiation of the Nabi Musa holiday to Saladin (1138–1193). Some scholars believe that Saladin had been part of the collective memory of the Palestinians since the twelfth century (Gerber, *Remembering and Imagining Palestine*, 63–68), while others argue that his glorification is part of a wider modern mythology that was created as a response to the mounting challenges Middle Eastern and Islamic societies confronted in the nineteenth century (Halabi, "The Transformation of the Prophet Moses Festival," 91). In any case, there is a consensus that in modern times the Nabi Musa holiday was popularly associated with Saladin and the struggle against the crusaders.

8. Halabi, "The Transformation of the Prophet Moses Festival," 91.

9. Sakakini, *Yawmiyat, Al-Kitab Al-Thalith*, 219 (10 April 1920).

10. Al-Hut, *Al-Qiyadat Wal-Mu'assasat Al-Siyasiyah Fi Filastin*.

11. Halabi, "The Transformation of the Prophet Moses Festival," 149. See also Betty S.

Anderson, *Nationalist Voices*, 89, on the meaning of the event as an Arab nationalist celebration.

12. Halabi, "The Transformation of the Prophet Moses Festival," 168.

13. Ibid., 212–215.

14. Ibid., 100.

15. Ibid., 266.

16. The flag was the green-red-black-white Arab national flag that was used during the 1916–1918 Arab Revolt and later became known as the Palestinian flag. See Sorek, "The Orange."

17. Friedland and Hecht, "The Nebi Musa Pilgrimage," 100.

18. Ibid., 101.

19 "The Birth of the Honorable Arab Prophet," *al-Karmil*, 21 October 1921, 1.

20. "Mihrajanat al-mawasim wa-istighlaluha," *Filastin*, 2 April 1936, 1.

21. Yuval, "Mifleget al-Istiqlal."

22. The mufti is a Sunni Islamic scholar who is an interpreter or expounder of Islamic law. The title Grand Mufti of Jerusalem, however, was a British innovation.

23. The *waqf* is a collection of donated assets, given to the Islamic community under Islamic religious law and held by a charitable trust.

24. Halabi, "Transformation of the Prophet Moses Festival," 217–239.

25. Friedland and Hecht, " Nebi Musa Pilgrimage," 107–108.

26. Sakakini, *Yawmiyat, Al-Kitab Al-Thalith*, 128.

27. Renan, "What Is a Nation?"

28. Sakakini, *Yawmiyat, Al-Kitab Al-Thalith*, 142 (3 May 1919).

29. Podeh, "Shonut betokh mifgan shel ahdut." In the first few years after the declaration the celebrations included public rallies as well.

30. "Al-ijtima' al-kabir fi Yafa," *Filastin*, 2 November 1923, 1.

31. Quandt et al. "The Politics of Palestinian Nationalism," 26.

32. Ricks, "Khalil Totah," 61; Betty S. Anderson, *Nationalist Voices*, 100–101.

33. *Al-Jami'a al-'Arabiyya*, 2 November 1931, 1.

34. *Filastin*, 3 November 1932, 1.

35. The Department of Public Works (DPW) was an engineering unit of the British government in Palestine, responsible for paving roads and building bridges and ports. Its priorities were biased toward Zionist needs and *Filastin* sporadically complained about the preference given to Jews as employees and contractors of the DPW.

36. Sakakini, Yawmiyat, *Al-Kitab Al-Rabi'*, 358 (5 November 1932).

37. The Palestinian Arab Party was established by the Husayni family in 1935 and was dismantled during the revolt.

38. *Al-Difa'*, November 3, 1946, 1.

39. Budeiri, "The Palestinians."

40. For a discussion of the prevalence of the Islamic notion of martyrdom in the

discourse of the Palestinian national movement in the 1960s and 1970s, see Johnson, *Islam and the Politics of Meaning*, 68–79.

41. The theme of crucifixion would continue to be evident in Palestinian national poetry, including in the text of poets with Muslim origins and a secular world view, such as Mahmoud Darwish, Mu'in Bseiso, and Tawfiq Zayyad. See Davies, *The Crucified Nation*, 89–107. For more on Christian symbolism in Palestinian poetry, see Elmessiri, *Palestinian Wedding*.

42. Campos, *Ottoman Brothers*, 66.

43. Ibid., 77–80.

44. Campos, "Shared Homeland," 56–57.

45. Kayyali, *Palestine*. For details on the Palestinians who were executed in 1915 and 1916, see Al-Hut, *Al-Qiyadat Wal-Mu'assasat*, 46–52.

46. According to Bayan al-Hut (*Al-Qiyadat Wal-Mu'assasat*, 48), they were not commemorated in Palestine. In Syria their commemoration was especially noticeable under the short-lived (October 1918–July 1920) Arab government in Damascus. On this commemoration, see Gelvin, *Divided Loyalties*, 175–181.

47. Segev, *One Palestine*, 106.

48. According to popular mythology, Ya'rub (a name that appears in Islamic genealogies) is the forefather of the Arabs. Mentioning him in this context probably was aimed at emphasizing the Arab identity of Palestine.

49. Kayyali, *Palestine*, 50.

50. Porath, *Emergence of the Palestinian-Arab National Movement*.

51. Presumably Palestinians who died during the Nabi Musa riots in 1920 also could have qualified as Palestinian martyrs. Nevertheless, I have not found any attempt to commemorate them as martyrs during the British Mandate period. It is noteworthy that I could not access two Arab-Palestinian newspapers published at the time of the riots, *Surya al-Janubiyya* and *al-Sabah;* further investigation of the topic through these newspapers might reveal new findings.

52. *Filastin*, 14 May, 1921, 1.

53. See *Filastin*, 11 June, 1921.

54. The practice of mourning for forty days after the death is shared by Islam and Eastern Christianity.

55. Buraq is the mythological horse of the prophet Muhammad, who, according to Islamic tradition, was tethered to the wall in Jerusalem before the prophet's nocturnal journey from Jerusalem to Mecca. Therefore, one of the Palestinian names for this site is al-Buraq. The wall itself is the remaining part of the external wall of the ancient Jewish temple destroyed in 70 CE and in Jewish tradition, it is known as the Western Wall. Because the 1929 eruption of violence was triggered by a local conflict around this site, this historical episode is named in Palestinian historiography and collective memory as the Buraq Revolt.

56. *Al-Yarmuk*, 18 June 1930.

57. Porath, *Emergence of the Palestine Arab National Movement*, 6.

58. Ibid.

59. A telegram sent by the Officer Administering the Government of Palestine to the Secretary of State for the Colonies, 30 July, 1930. British National Archive, CO733/181/5.

60. Porath, *Emergence of the Palestinian-Arab National Movement*, 5–6.

61. Abu-Ghazaleh, "Arab Cultural Nationalism."

62. One prominent exception was an article by As'ad Shuqayri, the mufti of Acre, published in *Mirat al-Sharq* on 24 June 1930. Shuqayri argued against considering the three as martyrs because they did not actively sacrifice their lives. It is noteworthy that both al-Shuqayri and the newspaper *Mirat al-Sharq* had received money from the Zionist movement for publishing pro-Zionist articles (see Cohen, *Army of Shadows*, 29, 117), and therefore it is possible that this article was one of them. At the same time, unlike most of the commissioned articles, this one was signed by its author and not under a pseudonym.

63. Ben-Zaqen, *Qomonizm ke-imperialism tarbuti*, 236.

64. See "The crucifixion conspiracy," *Al-Yarmuk*, 23 June, 1930, 1; "On the cross," *al-Jami'a al-'Arabiyya*, 26 June 1930, 1; "The situation in Palestine and the Arab countries before the crucifixion of the three martyrs of Palestine," *Filastin*, 26 June 1930, 2.

65. Appeared in a black frame on the first page of *al-Jami'a al-'Arabiyya* 26 June, and 27 June 1930.

66. *al-Jami'a al-'Arabiyya*, 25 June 1930.

67. *al-Jami'a al-'Arabiyya*, 28 July 1930, 3.

68. *Filastin*, 17 June 1931, 1.

69. *Al-Difa'*, 17 June 1934.

70. Husri, *Day of Maysalun*.

71. See, e.g., *Al-Jami'a al-'Arabiyya*, 30 July 1930, 1; 24 July 1932, 1; *Filastin*, 24 July, 2.

72. *Al-Jami'a al-'Arabiyya*, 30 July 1930, 1.

73. On the representation of 'Omar al-Mukhtar in Arab poetry, see al-Karaki, *Hamasat Al-Shuhada*, 193–202.

74. "Shahid Tab'un," *Al-Difa'*, 27 December 1935.

75. On the Tel Hai myth, see Y. Zerubavel, "Politics of Interpretation."

76. Kabaha, " Role of the Press," 131–132.

77. Kanafani, *1936–39 Revolt in Palestine*; Johnson, *Islam and the Politics of Meaning*; Hamuda, *Al-wa'i wal-Thawra*.

78. *Filastin*, 22 November 1935.

79. "Evel ha-Qdoshim," *Davar*, 27 December 1935.

80. Kanafani, *1936–39 revolt in Palestine*, 33.

81. Johnson, *Islam and the Politics of Meaning*.

82. Haiduc-Dale, "Nationalism and Religious Identification," 206.

83. Ibid., 35.

84. Ibid.; Porath, *Palestine Arab National Movement*, 142.

85. Haiduc-Dale, "Nationalism and Religious Identification," 205.

86. *Filastin*, 2 November, 1935.

87. Haiduc-Dale, "Nationalism and Religious Identification," 205.

88. *Al-Difaʻ*, 7 February 1936.

89. Swedenburg, *Memories of Revolt*.

90. Johnson, *Islam and the Politics of Meaning*.

91. For detailed statistics, see W. Khalidi, *From Haven to Conquest*, 846–52.

92. Al-Sifri, *Filastin Al-ʻArabiyyah*.

93. Al-Ansari was a member of a secret armed organization in Jerusalem, established in 1934. Initially the organization focused on burning Jewish stores and storages. From the beginning of the revolt, the group was involved in shooting British police and Jewish residents. The attempt to kill Allan Seacrest, the Jerusalem police chief, on 12 June 1936 was part of the escalation of the revolt. See Abu Gharbiya, *Fi khidam al-nidal*, 48–56; 72–77.

94. Sakakini, *Yawmiyat, Al-Kitab Al-Sadis*, 263 (13 June 1936).

95. "Al-shahid al-majhul," *Filastin*, 20 November 1936, 2.

96. The local National Committees were established at the beginning of the Arab Revolt in 1936 and were subjected to the AHC but kept a large degree of autonomy.

97. This is a reference to the locations of three mythological battles. The battle in Yaʻbad was the battle in which al-Qassam was killed on 19 November 1935. The battles in Balʻa and Bait Imrin took place in September 1936.

98. "Al-Shahid al-majhul," *Al-Difaʻ*, 3 December 1936, 4.

99. Al-Sifri, *Filastin Al-ʻArabiyyah*, 192.

100. Swedenburg, *Memories of Revolt*.

101. Haiduc-Dale, "Nationalism and Religious Identification," 227–268.

102. Al-Hout, " Palestinian Political Elite."

103. Haiduc-Dale, "Nationalism and Religious Identification," 227–268.

104. Ayalon, *Reading Palestine*, 143.

105. Najjar, " Arabic Press," 82.

106. Ibid., 82–99.

107. Ibid., 100–103.

108. Ibid., 153–157.

109. Sorek, *Arab Soccer in a Jewish State*.

110. Still, newspapers found indirect and subtle ways to highlight the importance of 17 June. In 1936, *Filastin* republished the cartoon that appeared on Balfour Day in 1932, and except for the accurate date, the entire first page looked like it appeared on Balfour Day.

111. Slyomovics, *Object of Memory*, 184–187.

112. Shabeeb, "Poetry of Rebellion."

113. Nimr Murqus wrote in his memoirs that as a child in Kafr Yasif he was taught the poems of Nuh Ibrahim and other poets. Also, when Murqus was in third grade, Nuh Ibrahim himself came to their classroom. Murqus, *Aqwa Min Al-Nisyan*, 37–38.

114. Haiduc-Dale, "Nationalism and Religious Identification," 231–233.

115. Shabeeb, "Poetry of Rebellion."

116. 'Awd, *Nuh Ibrahim*; Hajab, *Al-Sha'ir Al-Sha'abi*.

CHAPTER 2

1. Jiryis, *Arabs in Israel*; Lustick, *Arabs in the Jewish State*; Bauml, *Blue and White Shadow*; Robinson, *Citizen Strangers*.

2. Kaufman, *Arab National Communism*; Ghanem, *Palestinian-Arab Minority in Israel*, 66–67; Jamal, "Nationalizing States"; Beinin, *Was the Red Flag Flying There?* See also Nahas, *Israeli Communist Party*.

3. Following the split in 1965, there were two parties that called themselves the Israeli Communist Party, one of them with Jewish members only and the other with an Arab majority and a Jewish minority. Officially, only the "Jewish" party kept the name (and was known by the Hebrew acronym *Maqi*); the other party was officially registered as the New Communist List (known by the Hebrew acronym *Raqah*). *Maqi*, however, gradually disappeared, and in 1989 *Raqah* reclaimed its original name. For convenience, I refer to *Raqah* (1965–1989), which was the more active branch, as the Communist Party.

4. See Jamal, "Nationalizing States."

5. Ghanem, *Palestinian-Arab Minority in Israel*, 201.

6. Ibid., 69; see also an earlier argument about the consensus around these themes in Rouhana, "Intifada and the Palestinians of Israel."

7. Ghanem, *Palestinian-Arab Minority in Israel*, 69–70.

8. For a detailed outline of the Kafr Qasim massacre, see Rosenthal, "Who Killed Fatma Sarsur."

9. B. Morris, *Israel's Border War*, 145–147.

10. Ibid., 257–276. The unit was instructed by the Central Region Headquarters to commit "maximal killing and damage to property."

11. Amira Hass, "Thin Black Line," *Haaretz*, 11 February 2010. See also Rashid, *Qisat Madinat Ghaza*.

12. http://www.maannews.net/arb/ViewDetails.aspx?ID=236254.

13. Hass, "Thin Black Line."

14. David Ben Gurion during a discussion in the Knesset. See Hass, "Thin Black Line."

15. On these efforts, see Rosenthal, "Who Killed Fatma Sarsur."

16. "Text of Arab U.N. Protest," *The New York Times*, 15 December, 1956, 9.

17. "Ma'sat Rafah yanda li-hajibin al-insaniyya fi al-'alam," *al-Difa'*, 30 November 1956, 4.

18. "Bin Ghurion wa-ma'sat 'Arab Kafr Qasim," *al-Difa'* 13 December 1956, 2.

19 Robinson, *Citizen Strangers.*

20. Arendt, *Eichmann in Jerusalem.*

21. For an outline of these plans, see Arik Ariel, "Ha-historiya ha-sodit shel ha-transfer," *Haaretz*, 27 November 2013.

22. On "Operation Mole," see Rosenthal, "Who Killed Fatma Sarsur"; for an outline of various plans, see a speech of Meir Vilner, "Fi iktirah li-naz' al-thiqa 'an al-hukuma," *al-Ittihad*, 6 August 1987.

23. Nassar, *Palestinian Citizens of Israel.*

24. Tawfiq Tubi, "Ba'ad al-majzara," *al-Ittihad*, 31 December 1956.

25. Robinson, "Local Struggle, National Struggle."

26. Rosenthal, "Who Killed Fatma Sarsur." According to Rosenthal, the IDF plan (Operation Mole) was to send the residents to "relocation camps" for the duration of the war (similar to the internment of Japanese Americans in World War II) but in the Border Patrol units, it was interpreted as expulsion eastward. Troops in the region were prepared for it, and officers learned only a day before the massacre that the war front would be in the south, against Egypt, and not in the east. Operation Mole was officially suspended a day before the massacre but remained in the mind of officers and regular troops.

27. Robinson, *Citizen Strangers,*167–69.

28. Ibid.

29. Kabaha, " Conspiracy and the Victim," 89.

30. "Madhbahat al-Qibya—14 October 1953," *Falastinuna*, December 1960.

31. "Black September" refers to the armed conflict that began in September 1970 between the PLO and the Jordanian armed forces. Thousands of Palestinians were killed and the PLO forces were expelled and relocated to Lebanon.

32. Robinson, *Citizen Strangers,*176.

33. Bishara, " Arabs in Israel," 175–177.

34. Ibid.

35. See the analysis of Asaf Oron on the *Ha-'Okets* website "Ha-sod he-afel shel Dr. Karnit Plog," 1 September 2013, http://www.haokets.org/2013/09/01/קרנית-פלוג-של-ד"ר-ה-סוד-האפל/

36. Between the years 1961 and 1975 the median number of years of schooling grew from 1.2 to 6.5, while the percentage of adults with academic education tripled from 1.5 percent to 4.5 percent. Lewin-Epstein and Semyonov, *Arab Minority in Israel's Economy*, 23.

37. After 1948 Israel took over not only land belonging to Palestinian refugees but also two-thirds of the land owned by Palestinians who had become Israeli citizens. See Yiftachel, *Ethnocracy.*

38. Bashir, *Land Day.*

39. Y. Zerubavel, *Recovered Roots*, 9.

40. Rouhana, *Palestinian Citizens in an Ethnic Jewish State*, 100.

41. Yiftachel, "Minority Protest."

42. Yousef Farah quotes memoirs of 'Ali Muhammad Shla'ata from Sakhnin, "Dhi-kriyat min yawm al-ard," *al-Ittihad* supplement, 26 March 1993, 5.

43. Interview with Mas'ud Ghenayem, 29 July 2001. Ghenayem, born in 1965, was the chairman of the Islamic Movement in Sakhnin from 2000 to 2007 and was elected to the Knesset in 2009. Ghenayem was very active in cultivating the memory of Land Day in Sakhnin.

44. Interview with 'Omar Sa'id, 14 July 2001. Sa'id is a political activist from Kafr Kana who was a high school student and a member of the Communist Youth in 1976. Following Land Day Sa'id shifted his political orientation from the communist to the national stream.

45. Sarsur, "Between the Sulha and the Monument," 199.

46. "Yawm al-ard, 'id al-wihda al-wataniyya," *al-Jadid* editorial, March 1986, 1–3.

47. Benedict Anderson, *Imagined Communities*.

48. Salem Jubran, "Afkar hawla wad'ina bimunasabat yawm al-ard," *al-Ittihad*, 29 March 1991, 3.

49. Interview with 'Omar Sa'id, 14 July, 2001.

50. Ghanem and Ozacky-Lazar, *Arab Vote to the 15th Knesset*.

51. *Al-Ittihad*, 29 March 1977.

52. *Al-Ittihad*, 29 March, 1987.

53. See, e.g., "Sha'ab al'khalil yatadaman ma'a sha'ab al-jalil," *al-Ittihad*, 31 March 1980, p.1.

54. 'Atallah Mansur, "Mi-shnei 'evrei ha-kav ha-yaroq," *Haaretz*, 1 August 1980.

55. Bashir, *Land Day*.

56. Ibid., 100–101.

57. Ilan Dar, "Ha-roman bein Raqah ve-Ashaf," *Davar*, 23 June 1978, 17.

58. Saliba Khamis, *al-Ittihad*, 25 March 1977, 4.

59. Bashir, *Land Day*, 100–102.

60. Saliba Khamis, "Event in the Tragic History of Our Land," *al-Ittihad*, 28 March 1980, 3.

61. Rekhess, *Arab Minority in Israel*.

62. Ehud Ya'ari, "Hey'arkhut la-bhirot ba-migzar he-'Arvi," *Davar*, 24 December 1976, 3.

63. A reference to Menachem Begin, Israel's Prime Minister and leader of the right-wing Likud party at the time of writing.

64. Tawfiq Tubi, "Yawm al-ard al-khalid, al-dhikra wal-mustaqbal," *al-Ittihad*, 28 April 1978, 2.

65. Robinson, *Citizen Strangers*.

66. See *al-Ittihad*, 16 March 1984, 1.

67. Fawzi 'Abdallah, "Yawm al-ard, bayna al-falastana wal-asrala" (Land Day—between Palestinization and Israelization), *al-Watan*, 18 April 1986.

68. See, e.g., *al-Watan*, "Al-'alam al-Falastini yumaziquhu al-shuyu'iyun," 4 April 1986; *Davar*, 1 April 1990, 5.

69. Yoel Dar, *Davar*, 31 March 1979, 3.

70. See "Sha'ab al'khalil yatadaman ma'a sha'ab al-jalil," *al-Ittihad*, 31 March 1980, 1.

71. Rouhana, " Intifada and the Palestinians of Israel," 71.

72. Kaufman, *Arab National Communism*, 53.

73. Saliba Khamis, "Kayfa nuhayi al-dhikra al-'ashira li-majzarat Kafr Qasim," *al-Ittihad*, 28 October 1966.

74. *Al-Ittihad*, 9 April 1976.

75. Conversation with Joseph Algazy, 22 February 2014.

76. *Davar*, 1 April 1979.

77. Islamist awakening in Israel began in the 1970s and drew from the ideology of the Muslim Brotherhood, which demanded that religion be afforded a place in every part of social existence (Aburaiya, *Developmental Leadership*, 118). The Islamic Movement started as a loose network of organizations that emerged throughout the country, whose leadership was based mainly among lower-middle-class graduates of Islamic seminaries in the West Bank (Rubin-Peled, *Debating Islam*, 131–132). 'Abdallah Nimr Darwish was a prominent figure among them. After failing to set up a quasi-military clandestine organization, Islamist leaders chose to focus on educational, cultural, and welfare projects. In the 1980s the movement gained control over several local councils.

78. The unofficial titles "northern" and "southern" refer to the initial split between the two major centers of power in Kafr Qasim and Umm al-Fahem. The latter is located 35 miles north of the former. Practically, however, supporters of both factions could be found throughout the country.

79. Slyomovics and Khleif, "Palestinian Remembrance Days and Plans."

80. In the 1950s the state confiscated approximately 38 percent of Kafr Qasim's lands. In the late 1990s the Kafr Qasim local council was involved in a legal process that aimed to transfer a small portion of these lands to within Kafr Qasim's municipal boundaries.

81. Kafr Qasim Local Council, *Diwan Al-Shahid*, 4.

82. Ibid., 11–12.

83. Ibid., 7–8.

84. Joseph Algazy, *Haaretz*, 3 November 1997.

85. Joseph Algazy, *Haaretz*, 29 October 1997.

86. *Davar*, 2 April 1990.

87. *Al-Ittihad*, 31 March 1994, 5.

88. "Min Ihtilal Sakhnin Ila Ihtilal al-wa'i" (from the occupation of Sakhnin to the occupation of consciousness), *Sawt al-Haq wal-Huriyya*, 29 March 1995.

89. Nasim Abu Khayt, *Al-Ittihad*, 26 March 1984.

90. See, e.g., Kamal Khatib, "Yawm al-ard wal-manakh al-Falastini," *Sawt al-haq wal-Hurriyya*, 2 April 1993, 2; 'Abd al-Hakim Mufid, *Sawt al-Haq wal-Hurriyya*, 31 March, 1995.

91. The communists' rivals tend to emphasize the Israeli identity of the party.

92. *Al-Ittihad*, 31 March 1993, 1.

93. 'Omar Sa'di, "Safhat min al-taarikh lam taktab 'an yawm al-ard: dor al-mara fi al-ma'araka," *al-Ittihad*, 23 March, 1994, 8.

94. *Al-Ittihad*, 11 November 1977.

95. *Al-Ittihad*, 15 November 1977.

96. Morris, *Birth of the Palestinian Refugee Problem*, 478.

97. For a report on the fortieth-day ceremony, see *al-Ittihad*, 20 December 1977.

98. Until the 1980s, references by Palestinians in Israel to the 1948 massacres were rare, but there was one exception: the massacre at Deir Yasin. The exceptionality of Deir Yasin stems from the early acknowledgement of the massacre by Israeli leaders, who presented it as a horrible diversion committed by a subversive extreme faction.

CHAPTER 3

1. British rule over Palestine officially ended on 15 May 1948, but since it was a Saturday, the Zionist leadership decided to declare the establishment of the state a day earlier, on 14 May. Israeli celebrations of independence refer to the Hebrew date of 14 May 1948 (5 Iyar).

2. "Idrab wa-mudhaharat wa-a'alam soda," *al-Difa'*, 16 May 1949, 1 and 4.

3. Beinin, *Was the Red Flag Flying There?*; Nassar, "Palestinian Citizens of Israel"; Robinson, *Citizen Strangers*.

4. Beinin, *Was the Red Flag Flying There?* 47.

5. For an example of the way the party wished to attract Jewish supporters and avoid antagonizing them, see Kaufman, *Arab National Communism*, 37.

6. "Fi al-dhikra al-'Ishrin li-qiyam dawlat Israil," *al-Ittihad*, 30 April 1968.

7. Rekhess, *Ha-mi'ut he-'arvi*, 115.

8. *Al-Ittihad*, 15 May 1986, 1.

9. For a detailed report on the related discussions, see *al-Ittihad*, 20 March 1998.

10. 'Awd Abd el-Fatah, "Al-mufaraqat al-'ajabiya," *Fasl al-Maqal*, 1–3 April 1998, 7.

11. *Dardashat*, a television program of the Israel Broadcast Authority, 22 March 1998.

12. In the 1996 Knesset election, about one-third of the Arab voters voted for Zionist parties. This ratio shrank to 18 percent in 2009.

13. To hear the arguments of both sides, listen to the program "La samt ba'ad al-yawm," on Radio al-Shams, broadcasted on 19 May 2013 and available at: http://www.youtube.com/watch?v=_NEB-UG_vsE.

14. Ben-Ze'ev and Aburaiya, "Middle-Ground."

15. Jamal, *Arab Minority Nationalism in Israel*, 148.

16. H. Cohen, "Land, Memory, and Identity."

17. Rekhess, " *Ha-mi'ut he-'Arvi.*"

18. Jamal, *Arab Minority Nationalism in Israel*,124.

19. Sammy Smooha, unpublished data from the 2010 sequence of the Jewish-Arab relation index.

20. Ben-Ze'ev and Aburaiya, "Middle-Ground."

21. Based on the 2012 sequence of the Jewish-Arab relations index, in answer to the question "To which political party or movement you feel the closest?" 25 percent of the internally displaced Palestinians mentioned the Islamic Movement, more than any other party or movement. The level of support for the movement in the rest of the Arab sample was only 10 percent.

22. Ben-Ze'ev and Aburaiya, " Palestinian Struggle."

23. Mahmoud abu Shanb, "Al-musharadun wa-abna'uhum wa-ahfaduhum: 'an Bir'im ma binhid'!" *al-Ittihad*, 18 November 1984.

24. On the case of Kafr Bir'im and its neighboring village Iqrit, see Kimmerling, "Sovereignty, Ownwership and Presence."

25. Jamal, *Arab Minority Nationalism in Israel*, 127.

26. Numbers of participants is always difficult to assess due to the interests involved. Some of the organizers argued that 30,000 participated in the 2014 March of Return. I am convinced that this is an exaggeration, but there is no doubt that many thousands participate annually and that this number is generally on the rise.

27. Muhammad 'Ali taha, "Taghridat al-sabah–al-'awda ila lubya," Al-Haya al-Jadida, 7 April 2014, http://www.alhayat-j.com/newsite/details.php?opt=1&id=232601&cid =3264.

28. Sammy Smooha, unpublished data from the 2010 sequence of the Jewish-Arab relation index.

29. The most common of them, "Khaybar Khaybar ya yahud, Jaysh Muhammad sawfa ya'ud" [Khaybar, Khaybar, O Jews, Mohammad's army will return] is taken from the Hamas repertoire and refers to a town that was populated by Jewish tribes before the rise of Islam and was defeated by Muslim forces in 629 CE.

30. 'Aida Toma-Suleiman, "Muqata'at masirat al-'awda . . . bidayat sira' um I'lan hazima?" al-Jabha, 20 April 2013, http://www.aljabha.org/index.asp?i=76160.

31. Conversation with 'Aida Toma-Suleiman, 17 March 2014.

32. "La samt ba'd al-yawm." For details, see note 13.

33. "Biladi, Biladi," *al-Ittihad*, 25 July 1989.

34. These gaps between Palestinian citizens and non-citizens were reflected in a comparative survey among Arab education students in the West Bank and inside Israel conducted by Hillel Cohen in 2013. It turned out that Palestinian students in Israel were significantly more likely to support joint Arab-Jewish struggle for their rights (H. Cohen, "Palestinians in Israel and the Territories").

35. Jamal, " Political Ethos."

36. Editorial in *Fasl al-maqal,* 26 September 2003, 3.

37. Ahmad Sa'ad, *al-Ittihad* supplement, 5 October 2001, 2.

38. *Sawt al-Haq wal-Hurriyya*, 28 September 2011.

39. Ayman Odeh, "The Kafr Qasim massacre," al-Jabha, 25 October, 2008, http://www.aljabha.org/?i=37334.

40. Based on the 2012 Index of Arab-Jewish Relations conducted by Sammy Smooha. Data received from the Guttman Center at the Israel Democracy Institute.

41. See a statement of Jamal Zahalqa on this issue, Yoav Stern, *Haaretz*, 30 September 2007.

42. It is noteworthy that President Rivlin took part in a separate ceremony that took place three days before the traditional ceremony. Officially, the mayor of Kafr Qasim explained a need to hold two separate ceremonies for security reasons, but it is likely that creating a distance between the president, who was speaking with the Israeli flag in the background, and the more blatant messages of protest, was convenient for everyone involved.

43. In a 2012 survey of the Arab adult population 12.6 percent of the interviewees mentioned the northern faction of the Islamic Movement as the movement they feel the closest to, and only 3.6 percent mentioned the Sons of the Village. Parties and movements who are represented in the parliament or who support this representation were mentioned by 65.8 percent of the respondents (Smooha, *Still Playing by the Rules*, 186).

CHAPTER 4

1. On this concept, see Koselleck and Presner, *Practice of Conceptual History*, 292.

2. On the commemoration of martyrs by the Faysal government in Damascus, see Gelvin, *Divided Loyalties*, 175–181.

3. Mayo, *War Memorials as Political Landscape*; Mosse, *Fallen Soldiers*; Handelman and Handelman, " Presence of Absence"; Hoffenberg, "Landscape, Memory."

4. Handelman and Handelman, " Presence of Absence."

5. On Kenya, Congo, Sudan, and India, see Larsen, "Re-Placing Imperial Landscapes." On Algeria, see Benslama, " Cause Identitaire."

6. "Al-Idrab yubalwar al-'azm 'ala taharur min al-istiqlal," *al-Ittihad*, 7 June 1967, 1.

7. Benvenisti, *Mul Ha-Homah Ha-Segurah*, 283–287; Benvenisti, *'Ir ha-mnuhut*. See also "Azmat al-nusub al-tidhkariyya li-dahaya alharb fi al-Quds al-'Arabiyya," *al-Ittihad*, 27 December 1968.

8. H. Cohen, *Good Arabs*.

9. "Ihtifal tidhkari fi Kafr Qasim li-munasabat al-dhikra al-'ashira lil-majzara," *al-Ittihad*, 1 November 1966, 4.

10. Interview with Ibrahim Sarsur from Kafr Qasim, August 2003.

11. "Limadha yajib an nansa," *al-Ittihad*, 29 August 1969.

12. The exact date of transformation cannot be determined, and it depends on the perspective of the observers and their differential sympathy to various previous mayors.

Ibrahim Sarsur ("Bein ha-sulha la-andarta" [Between the Sulha and the monument], 200) mentions the year 1974, while an earlier *al-Ittihad* report mentions both 1979 and 1981 as the year of change (*al-Ittihad*, 29 October 1985, 4).

13. Sarsur, "Bein ha-sulha la-andarta," 200.

14. Kafr Qasim Local Council, Protocol of session no. 30, October 27, 1976, *Israel State Archive*, Protocol of Municipal Meetings, GL 8/3535.

15. Galtung, "Cultural Violence."

16. The Land Day monument stood at the center of the exhibition: "The Story of a Monument: Land Day Sakhneen 1976–2006" (curator: Tal Ben-Zvi). The exhibition was presented at the Musawa Center in Haifa in March 2008. See http://www.hagar-gallery .com/landay/home.html.

17. Ibrahim Malik, "Qadiat al-nasb al-tidhkari li-yawm al-ard," *al-Ittihad*, 7 July 1978.

18. *Al-Ittihad*, 16 December 1977.

19. Interview with 'Abed 'Abdi, 27 July 2001.

20. Interview with Jamal Tarabiyeh, 5 July 2001.

21. *Al-Ittihad*, 2 April 1976.

22. E.g., see "The 40th day," *al-Ittihad*, 14 May 1976, 5.

23. Conway, *Commemoration and Bloody Sunday*, 47–55.

24. Interview with 'Abed 'Abdi, 27 July 2001.

25. Schiff and Yaari. *Israel's Lebanon War*.

26. Interview with 'Omar Said from Kafr Kana, 14 July 2001.

27. Interview with Nabhan al-Sani', 11 March 2014.

28. Al-'Arif, *al-Nakba*, 1053.

29. Young, *At Memory's Edge*, 94.

30. Morris, "Revisiting the Palestinian Exodus of 1948," 57.

31. Morris, *The Birth of the Palestinian Refugee Problem*.

32. Srur, *Nakba*.

33. Interview with Elias Srur, 20 July 2003.

34. Interview with Naif Sam'an, 15 July 2003.

35. Sa'ar, "Carefully on the Margins."

36. Ghanem, "Shulaym be-hevra shulit."

37. Sorek, "Between Football and Martyrdom."

38. Sorek, *Arab Soccer in a Jewish State*.

39. Tamari, "Local and the National in Palestinian Identity," 3–4.

40. Lustick, *Arabs in the Jewish State*.

41. Rosenfeld and al-Haj, *Arab Local Government in Israel*.

42. See, e.g., the protest against naming a street and building a memorial for a Jewish Irgun combatant who was killed during the attack on Jaffa in 1948, in a predominantly Arab residential neighborhood (Monterescu, "Estranged Natives," 271), or the

demand by Arab residents to restore the pre-1948 name of a major street in Haifa (*Al-Ittihad*, 1 April 2001, 9).

43. Bishara, *al-'Arab fi Israi'l*, 7–10.

44. Confino, *Nation as a Local Metaphor*.

45. Robinson, "Local Struggle, National Struggle"; Sorek, "Between Football and Martyrdom."

46. Swedenburg (*Memories of Revolt*, 19) argued that Israel's harassment of those institutions that sustained support for the PLO limited the PLO's capacity to harness subaltern opinion to disseminate hegemonic and highly elaborated interpretations of Palestinian history. The result was that Palestinians adopted the mere outline of the canonic national narrative, but many local versions of history remained untouched.

47. The title "The Martyrs' Village" appeared in the past on a sign at the entrance to Kafr Qasim. For several years in late 1990s and early 2000s, the town's official website http://www.kufur-kassem.com named it "The Martyrs' Village" but later this name was removed. Sakhnin is also referred to sometimes as the "The Martyrs' Village" in the press (see, e.g., *al-Ittihad*, 3 April 1982, 2). In a memorial book published by the local branch of the Islamic Movement in Sakhnin following October 2000, Sakhnin gained the same title.

48. Amara and Schnell, "Identity Repertoires"; Sorek, "Between Football and Martyrdom."

49. Lustick, *Arabs in the Jewish State*.

50. Litvak, " Islamization of Palestinian Identity."

51. Tsimhoni, " Ha-notsrim be-yisrael."

52. Ben-Ze'ev and Aburaiya, "Middle-Ground."

53. Amara and Schnell, "Identity Repertoires."

54. Smooha, *Still Playing by the Rules*, 116.

55. Sa'ar, "Carefully on the Margins."

56. Among the forty Palestinian Christians in the sample who did not use Christian identity to define themselves in an open-ended question, 32 (80 percent), included the Nakba among the three most important events, compared with only 37 percent (4 out of 15) among interviewees who did describe their identity with reference to Christianity ($p < 0.05$).

57. Abu-Saad et al. "Identity and Political Stability."

58. Smooha, *Orientation and Politicization*.

59. Sorek, "The Quest for Victory."

60. Abu-Saad et al. "Identity and Political Stability."

61. Ghanem, " Shulaym be-hevra shulit."

62. Smooha, unpublished data from the 2010 sequence of the Arab-Jewish Relations Index.

CHAPTER 5

1. *Al-Ittihad*, 20 March, 1998, 1.

2. From an interview with MK Muhammad Barakah: "The memory merges the ugliness of the Nakba with the beauty of the steadfast journey," *Al-Ittihad*, 20 March 1998, 2.

3. *Al-Ittihad*, 15 April 1998.

4. *Dardashat*, a television program of the Israel Broadcast Authority, 22 March 1998.

5. Interview with Muhammad 'Ali Taha, 22 July 2003.

6. Ibid.

7. *Al-Ittihad*, 1 November 1998, 9.

8. Interview with Elias Srur, 20 July, 2003.

9. Interview with Hanna Swayd, mayor of 'Aylabun from 1993 to 2003, 20 November, 2008.

10. Protocol of the Shefa'amr Municipal Council, session no. 3/98, 1 April 1998, 3.

11. Al Haj, *Social Change and Family Process*, 76.

12. See Joseph Algazy, *Haaretz*, 7 February, 1998.

13. Interview with Ahmad Hamdi, member of the Shefa'amr local council and Abu Hatem's confidante, July 2001.

14. *Al-Ittihad*, 4 April 1998. In addition, the local magazine, '*al-Hadir wal-mustaqbal*, published a call to the inhabitants to provide martyrs' names.

15. Gal Sharon, *Haaretz*, 15 November 1998.

16. Ibid. In this report Yasin is quoted, saying: "I feel closer to the Israeli flag than to the Palestinian flag."

17. A letter from Ahmad Khatib to 'Orsan Yasin, 15 July 1999 (provided by the Shefa'amr city hall).

18. A letter from Ahmad Hamdi to 'Orsan Yasin, 13 July 1999 (provided by the Shefa'amr city hall).

19. "Go to the monument and find the reasons for the flare-up," David Retner, *Haaretz*, 9 May 2000.

20. Interview with 'Abed 'Anbtawi, FUC Secretary, 29 July 2003.

21. Ibrahim, "Israel's Ethnic Project."

22. Firro, *The Druzes in the Jewish State*, 4.

23. The Arab Salvation Army was an army of volunteers from Arab countries set up by the Arab League in 1948. On the Druze battalion, see Firro, *The Druzes in the Jewish State*, 43–50.

24. Ibid., 50–51.

25. Ibid., 55.

26. Ibid., 248.

27. Amara and Schnell, "Identity Repertoires"; R. Halabi, "Invention of a Nation."

28. Conversation with Shaykh 'Awni Khnayfas, chairman of the DNC, 12 May 2014.

29. Ibid.

30. Zaid Khunayfas, "Izahat al-sitar fi Shefa'amr 'an al-nasb al-tidhkari lil-shuhada al-duruz fi ma'rakat hawsha wal-kasair," 21 April 2013, shefa-amr.com, http://www.shefa -amr.com/nv/?todo=news&id=15&subid=57&tid=16140.

31. Mu'in Abu 'Ubayd, "Shefa'amr, Izahat al-sitar 'an al-nasb al-tidhkari lishuhada ma'rakat hawsha wal-kasair," al-Bayan, 25 April 2014, www.albayan.co.il/page.php?id= 3187.

32. Ibid.

33. Rafik Halabi, *Haaretz*, 7 August 2005.

34. Interview with Municipal Council Member, Nasim Jarus, 11 December 2006.

35. Interview with Wasel Taha, mayor of Kafr Kana at the time of the establishment of the memorial, 14 July 2001.

36. Elmessiri, *Palestinian Wedding*.

37. On the other hand, the name of Muhammad Khatib, killed by the Israeli police in April 2004, was not added to the monument. According to the police, Khatib was killed after opening fire on a police patrol, and he was earlier involved in killing an Israeli soldier. In April 2005 his family built a monument to commemorate him at the location of his death, but a week later it was destroyed by an order of the Minister of Interior. The municipal council rejected demands to add his name to the central memorial monument. Maintaining a safe distance from the armed struggle is another major characteristic of Palestinian commemoration inside Israel (see Chapter 6).

38. Shamir, *Hantsaha ve-zikaron*, 147–148.

39. Interview with Wasel Taha, 14 July 2001.

40. During the occupation of 'Aylut in July 1948 and after its surrender, the IDF killed thirty-four local men. See 'Araf and 'Abud, *'Aylut Al-Sumud Wal-Istimrar*.

41. Conversation with Mahmoud Yazbak, 13 June 2011.

42. In Sakhnin, for example, since the municipality decided to name the main street after the Al-Aqsa martyrs, the families of Land Day martyrs demanded that they also have streets named after them. The municipality complied.

43. Conversation with Maqbula Nassar, a member of the local committee in 'Arabeh, 29 June 2011.

44. Conversation with Mahmoud Yazbak, 13 June 2011.

45. Husam Ibrahim, "Majhulun yaqumun bi-a'mal takhribiyya 'ala miftah al-'awda bil-nasira," *Mawqa' al-Shams*, 8 May 2014.

46. Shamir, *Zikaron ve-Hantsaha*.

47. Segev, "Ma 'osot ha-'andartaot baleylot," *Haaretz*, 27 April 1990.

48. Interview with 'Abed 'Anbetawi, 29 July 2003.

49. D. Handelman and L. Handelman, " Presence of Absence."

50. Ibrahim Abu-'Ata, "Zawaj Saddam Husayn fi Umm al-Fahm," al-Arab, 14 May 2009, http://www.alarab.net/Article/137415.

CHAPTER 6

1. Abdel Nasser's blatant secularist ideology and his oppression of the Muslim Brotherhood explain the exclusion of these events from Islamist commemoration.

2. Kanafani, *The 1936–39 Revolt in Palestine.*

3. Budeiri, "The Palestinians."

4. Zayyad, *Suwar Min Al-Adab Al-Sha'bi Al-Filistini.*

5. Zayyad, *'An Al-Adab Wal-Adab Al-Sha'bi Fi Filastin.*

6. See ibid. On the renewed interest in the revolutionary poetry of the 1930s, see Nassar, "Affirmation and Resistance," 260–261.

7. McDonald, "Geographies of the Body."

8. "Thalathun 'am 'ala rahil al-shahid Abd al-rahim Mahmud," *al-Ittihad,* 14 July 1978.

9. *Haaretz,* 7 September 1981.

10. "Fi half takrim al-sha'ir 'Abd al-Rahim Mahmud," *al-Watan,* 18 April 1986, 5.

11. 'Awd, *Nuh Ibrahim,* 115; *al-Ittihad,* 18 November 1986.

12. Interview with Adib abu-Rahmun, who lived in Acre from 1948 to 1965, 5 January 2009.

13. Saliba Khamis mentioned their execution briefly in an article about the 1929 uprising; "Thawrat al-buraq," *al-Ittihad,* 7 March 1980. This reference is a rare exception.

14. Swedenburg, *Memories of Revolt.*

15. The military branch of Hamas, as well as missiles fired from the Gaza Strip at Israelis, is named for 'Izz al-Din al-Qassam.

16. *Sawt al-Haq wal-Huriyya,* 12 April 2012, 6.

17. Swedenburg, *Memories of Revolt,* 6.

18. Brubaker, *Nationalism Reframed,* 4–6.

19. Birnbaum, "Historical Discourse."

20. *Al-Watan,* 25 April 1986.

21. Kaufman, *Arab National Communism,* 37; Ghanem, *Palestinian-Arab Minority in Israel,* 88–89; for more on the careful approach to the armed struggle by the communists, see Rekhess, *Ha-mi'ut he-'arvi,* 42–43.

22. Terrill, "Political Mythology."

23. "Al-Karama badal Aylul al-Aswad" (Karameh instead of Black September), *al-Ittihad,* 27 May 1975, 1.

24. The numbers are based on reports in the Israeli press at the time.

25. "Al-thawra al-falastiniyya mustamirra," *al-Ittihad,* 4 January 1984, 4.

26. See, e.g., the reference to Sana Muhaidli who killed twelve Israeli soldiers in South Lebanon in April 1985. Even *al-Ittihad* referred to her as the "Bride of the South," as she was called in Lebanon.

27. True, the rare cases commemorating 'Ayash might force Palestinians in Israel to confront state authorities, as we see in Chapter 9. However, the demand to implement the Right of Return and the insistence on the linkage between the Nakba and Israel's

Independence Day are not less sensitive, but Palestinians in Israel do not avoid raising these issues publicly, despite intimidations.

28. Smooha, *Still Playing by the Rules*, 12.

29. H. Cohen, "Palestinians in Israel and the Territories," unpublished paper.

30. The three organizations are the Ibn Khaldoun Institute inside Israel, Badil (a non-profit organization mandated to defend and promote the rights of Palestinian refugees located in Bethlehem, West Bank), and the 'Aidoun Group (a group of Palestinian intellectuals and academics active in refugee camps in Lebanon and Syria). The publication is available at http://www.bettna.com/personal/haweya-intma/hawya-intma.htm.

31. Conversation with Mohanad Mustafa, one of the booklet's authors, 22 September 2008.

32. See *al-Ittihad*, 11 July 1984, 4; 13 July 1984, 2.

33. Cobban, *Making of Modern Lebanon*; Sayigh, *Armed Struggle*.

34. Khalili, *Heroes and Martyrs of Palestine*, 179.

35. 'Ali 'Ashur, "Tal al-Za'tar—ramz al-tadhiya wal-sumud," *al-Ittihad*, 17 August 1976.

36. "Bluzat 'sabra wa-shatila' wa-alwan al-'alam al-falastini," *al-Ittihad*, 5 October 1984, 1.

37. Rouhana, "Intifada and the Palestinians of Israel," 62.

38. Rekhess, "'Arvim be-yisrael," 129–139.

39. "Al-tajamu' fi al-nasira yunadhim nadwa li-dhikra al-shahid 'Adnan Khalaf," 13 October 2009, http://www.alarab.net/Article/194229.

40. "Ihyaa dhikrat shahid Rahat," *al-Ittihad*, 28 February 1995, 4.

41. "Ighlaq al-khalil wa-hamlat mudahamat wa-i'itiqalat fi al-dafa," *al-Ittihad*, 26 February 1995, 3.

42. Jamal, " Political Ethos."

43. *Dardashat*, a television program of the Israel Broadcast Authority, 22 March 1998.

CHAPTER 7

1. Buksbaum, "Nakba—Ein Davar Kaze."

2. Kadman, *Betsidei ha-derekh*.

3. Shapira,"Hirbet Hizah."

4. Raz-Krakotzkin, "Diaspora in Sovereignty."

5. Akçam, *From Empire to Republic*, 150.

6. Onur Bakiner, "Is Turkey Coming to Terms with Its Past?"

7. Ibid.

8. http://www.armenian-genocide.org.

9. See, e.g., Sebnem Arsu, "Turkey Offers Condolences to Armenians over Killings," *New York Times*, 23 April 2014.

10. Meron Benvenisti, *Sacred Landscape*, 38–75.

11. H. Cohen, "Land, Memory, and Identity."

12. Ibid., 9.

13. Al-Haj, *Education, Empowerment, and Control*; Bauml, *Tsel kahol lavan*; H. Cohen, *Good Arabs*; Robinson, *Citizen Strangers*.

14. Bauml, *Tsel kahol lavan*.

15. Robinson, *Citizen Strangers*.

16. See, e.g., "Kafr Qasim Ahayat dhikrat shuhadai'ha bimasira dakhma," *al-Ittihad*, 1 November 1968, 6.

17. Sarsur, "Bein ha-sulha la-andarta," 200. See also Robinson, "Local Struggle, National Struggle."

18. *Al-Ittihad*, 1 April 1977.

19. In 1982 a 16-year-old boy from 'Arabeh was sentenced to four months in jail for waving the Palestinian flag on Land Day. A resident of Deir Hanna was sentenced to thirty-two days in prison for singing "In blood and in spirit we will redeem you, Galilee" (*al-'Anbaa*, 30 May 1982). Following Land Day 1983, a resident of Sakhnin was sentenced to five months in jail for waving the Palestinian flag in the annual march (*Davar*, 12 May 1983).

20. *Al-Ittihad*, 24 December 1982.

21. Letter from Arab Affairs Advisor, 27 March 1984, "Advisor to Prime Minister for Arab Affairs, October 1983–August 1984," Israel State Archive, a-4632/13.

22. See the telegram from 'Ezra Kopelewitz, Department of Arab Education, directed to a high school director in Sakhnin on 29 March 1981: "It was brought to our attention that there is a proposal to stop classes tomorrow Tuesday, 30 March on the occasion of Land Day. You are required to maintain teaching as usual in all teaching hours in your institution." From "Arab School Institutions: High School in Sakhnin," Israel State Archive, GL 17664/5.

23. For example, "Jamahir al-tulab li-lmusharaka fi yawm al-ard," *al-Ittihad*, 28 March 1985, 5.

24. A letter from Yehezqel Shemesh from the Office of the Minister Responsible for Minority Affairs to the Ministry of Education, 11 December 1986, in "Arab Education," Israel State Archive, GL-8/18643. 1 January is the date commemorated by the Fatah movement as the beginning of the armed struggle.

25. Shira Robinson, unpublished seminar paper.

26. Ben-Bassat and Dahan, *Political Economics of the Municipalities*, 31–32.

27. Matspen (Hebrew: compass) was a Marxist anti-Zionist organization active in the 1960s and 1970s. Most of its members were urban Jewish Israelis.

28. Protocol of a special 'Arabeh Local Council meeting, no. 8/84, 18 March 1984, Israel State Archive, GL-11932/2.

29. Shafir and Peled, *Being Israeli*.

30. al-Ard (lit., the land), a political group with an Arab nationalist agenda, emerged in 1959 and was banned by the Israeli authorities in 1964.

31. A discussion of the Central Committee for Security at the Arab Affairs Advisor office, 18 September 1984, "Policy of the Education System," Israel State Archive, GL-18642–8.

32. The "New Historians" are a loosely-defined category of Israeli historians who since the mid-1980s have published studies challenging the traditional Zionist narrative, especially regarding the 1948 war.

33. Ram, "Postnationalist Pasts."

34. Rosenfeld and Al-Haj, *Arab Local Government in Israel.*

35. Ben-Bassat and Dahan, *Political Economics of the Municipalities*, 31–32.

36. Stendel, *Arabs in Israel;* Caspi and Kabaha, "From Holy Jerusalem to the Spring."

37. Popular Memory Group, "Popular Memory."

38. The 35th assembly session of the 13th Knesset, 9 December 1992, "Arab students association at the University of Haifa," http://82.166.33.81/divrey/Qform.asp.

39. Gonen Segev himself later became a symbol of corruption. In September 1995 his vote in the Knesset assembly was crucial for the approval of the second stage of the Oslo Accords. In exchange for his support of Rabin's government, he became the Minister of Energy. In 2005 Segev was jailed for attempting to smuggle Ecstasy pills to Israel using his expired diplomatic passport.

40. Benvenisti, *Sacred Landscape*, 268.

41. Tom Segev, *Elvis in Jerusalem*, 151.

42. Smooha, *Still Playing by the Rules.*

43. Haklai, *Palestinian Ethnonationalism in Israel;* Payes, *Palestinian NGOs in Israel;* Jamal, *Arab Minority Nationalism in Israel*,188–225.

44. Calhoun, *Nations Matter.*

45. For a detailed study of one of the organizations that focuses on historical remembrance, Baladna, see Gutman, "Past before Future."

46. Rabinowitz and Abu-Baker, *Coffins on Our Shoulders.*

47. Jamal, *Arab Public Sphere in Israel.*

48. The internet seems to have special importance for shaping historical remembrance as compared to obtaining news: in another survey of a representative sample, when Arab interviewees were asked about the medium they relied on most to obtain *news* (compared to historical knowledge in my survey), 75 percent mentioned television and only 4 percent mentioned the Internet. See Jamal, *Arab Public Sphere in Israel*, 76.

49. Ibid.,115.

50. Smooha, unpublished data.

51. Sharon Rofe-Ofir, "Kafr Kana Residents: Why Are We Forbidden from Commemorating the Nakba," Y-net, 26 April 2008, http://www.ynet.co.il/articles/0,7340,L-353 6017,00.html.

52. Foucault, *Discipline and Punish.*

53. Sabbagh-Khoury, "Palestinian Predicaments."

54. See, e.g., a report about confrontation at the University of Haifa on Land Day 1996 in: "Migbelot ba-qampus," Joseph Algazy, *Haaretz*, 14 March 1997.

55. See report and photos at the Tawfiq Zayyad Institution's website, http://www .Zayyad.com/index0.asp?f=oldnews.asp&m=menu0.asp&t=frontmenu0.asp.

56. See, e.g., later public comments: Ahia Rabed, "Acre: March in Memory of the 'Martyrs' Who Murdered Jews in 1929," Y-net, 17 June 2005, http://www.ynet.co.il/Ext/ App/TalkBack/CdaViewOpenTalkBack/0,11382,L-3100396,00.html.

57. See, e.g., Meron Rapoport, "In Acre, Simhat Torah and Ramadan Don't Go Well Together," *Haaretz*, 22 October 2006; Gideon Levy and Alex Levac, "Lod's Arab Residents Fear Influx of Jewish 'Settlers' Will Drive Them Out," Haaretz, 7 January 2013.

58. "Lod mesarevet lehikana'," Aviv 7, 7 May 2006, http://aviv7.co.il/redac_i/redact10i .htm.

59. Sabbagh-Khoury, "Palestinian Predicaments."

60. Connerton, *How Societies Remember*, 72.

61. Three days before the demonstration, a participant in the forum of the right-wing website HAYAMIN.ORG called other participants to do at the march "what [we] do to the leftists in Tel Aviv" (http://hayamin.org/forum/index.php?topic=4278.0). It is unclear if this call is related to the confrontation that actually took place at the march, but the photos from the event published by PLS48 (a website operated by the northern faction of the Islamic Movement) did show that the counter-demonstrators were dressed as religious Jews.

62. Shim'on Cohen, "A Demand from Dichter to Ban the March of Return, Aruts 7, 7 May 2008, http://www.inn.co.il/News/News.aspx/174762.

63. The Conquest of Labor (*kibbush ha-'avoda*) was one of the explicit goals of Ha-Shomer.

64. "Whose Land Day?" *Maariv*, 30 March 2008.

65. Interview with Yoel Zilberman, 23 June 2009.

66. Interview with Wakim Wakim, 5 January 2012.

67. Zochrot is a Jewish Israeli NGO founded in 2002 to promote awareness of the Nakba among Jewish Israelis.

68. Interview with 'Abed Nimarnah, 1 July 2012.

69. 'Abed Mawad, "An Answer to the Nakba Law," Bokra, 23 March 2011, http://www .bokra.net.

70. A conversation with Maqbula Nassar on 29 June 2011, a member of the committee whose mother was born in Hittin.

71. "Al-tahdirat li-masirat al-'awda li-lrweis wal-damun" (the preparations for the March of Return to Rweis and Damun), http://www.youtube.com/watch?feature=player _embedded&v=7TxsS9–z6bo#!

72. Ben Kaspit and Yonatan Hilleli, "Increase in the Identification of the Arabs of Israel with Iran," NRG, 3 January 2007, www.nrg.co.il/online/1/ART1/555/618.html.

73. Ori Nir, *Haaretz*, 12 May 2001.

74. Tamar Trabelsi, "Livnat to Arab Schools: Give Loyalty—Get Money," Y-net, 19 August 2001, http://www.ynet.co.il/articles/0,7340,L-1029929,00.html.

75. Ibid.

76. The Association for Civil Rights in Israel sent a letter to both Lieberman and Livnat to protest and explain the problematic aspects of their proposals from a legal point of view. See http://www.acri.org.il/he/5567.

77. Dichter, "Malkodet Shel Dmei Shtika."

78. Itamar Inbari and Uri Yablonka, "The Arab Boycott," NRG, 6 December 2007, http://www.nrg.co.il/online/1/ART1/668/029.html.

79. David Retner, "Go to the monument and find the reasons for the flare-up," *Haaretz*, 9 May 2000.

80. Avinadav Vitkon, "The Likud Mayor of Shefa'amr," *Makor Rishon*, 3 November 2008.

81. Inbari and Yablonka, "The Arab Boycott."

82. Ahia Rabed, "Dichter: whoever cries about the Nakba—will have a Nakba," Y-net, 17 December 2007, http://www.ynet.co.il/articles/0,7340,L-3483382,00.html.

83. Meron Benvenisti, "Time to stop mourning," *Haaretz*, 23 December 2007.

84. Bakiner, "Is Turkey Coming to Terms with Its Past?"

85. Brubaker at al., *Nationalist Politics and Everyday Ethnicity*, 137.

86. Interview with MK Alex Miller, 11 August 2008. The interview was conducted in Hebrew, which is not Miller's mother tongue. It might explain some of the awkward sentences.

87. In 2012, 12.1 percent of the Arab citizens who reported participating in Land Day events and 14.7 percent of those who reported participation in Nakba commemoration also reported that they were harassed by the authorities. Smooha, *Index of Arab-Jewish Relations in Israel 2003–2011*, 51.

88. Muhammad Muhsin Watad, "Most of the mayors were absent from the March of Return, including the host, the mayor of Tira," *Kul al-'Arab*, 23 April 2011, 2.

89. Mana Abu Shehada, "tahrid 'unsusri did a'da baladiyyat natsirit 'ilit," al-'Arab, 20 May 2011, http://www.alarab.net/Article/373474.

CHAPTER 8

1. A letter from Tawfiq Abu Ahmad to the general director of the Ministry of Education, 22 May 1986, Israel State Archive, "Ha-hinuch he-'Arvi", GL-6/18643.

2. Mar'i, *Arab Education in Israel*, Copty, "Knowledge and Power in Education," Al Haj, *Education, Empowerment, and Control*.

3. Gellner, *Nations and Nationalism*, 28.

4. Monica, "Reading and Power," Johnston, "Organizational Structure."

5. Williams, *Culture and Materialism*.

6. On the attempts of Romanian authorities since the end of World War I to erode education in Hungarian, see Brubaker at al. *Nationalist Politics and Everyday Ethnicity*, 83–85.

7. Copty, "Knowledge and Power in Education," 276.

8. Ibid., 249–251.

9. Ibid., 272.

10. Ibid., 206.

11. Al-Haj, *Education, Empowerment, and Control*.

12. Yonah et al. "Neo-Liberal Reforms."

13. Rali Sa'ar, "A Shabak man nominates Arab directors in the Arab sector," *Haaretz*, 6 December 2000; Aryeh Dayan, "Ministers of Education Are Changed—the Shabak Representative Always Stays," *Haaretz*, 29 September 2004.

14. Theoretically, just mentioning the name of a historical figure is not an indication for sympathetic remembrance of this figure or for the interviewee's sentiments of belonging. We have, however, evidence that recalling Zionist or Arab historical figures was significantly associated with certain patterns of self-definition. Among those who mentioned Zionist figures, 48.0 percent used the term "Israeli" in their open ended self-definition (alone or in a combination with other terms), while in the rest of the population only 32.9 percent did so ($p<0.001$ in χ^2 test). Among those who mentioned Arab figures, 57.5 percent used the term "Palestinian," while in the rest of the Arab sample only 35.0 percent did so.

15. 'Awawdah, *Dhakirah la tamut*.

16. Unsurprisingly, when I conveyed these findings to activists in the field of Arab education, they encouraged me to make them public and to make sure they would be reported in the Arabic media in Israel (see a report on these findings on the Arabic website Panet, 9 December 2008, http://www.panet.co.il/online/articles/71/73/S-165067,71,73.html). From the activists' point of view, these numbers prove that Arab public education has negative implications on the familiarity of Arab students with their national history and justify their efforts to gain more autonomy for Arab education.

17. Handala is a character created by the Palestinian cartoonist Naji al-'Ali and an icon widely recognized as a symbol of Palestinian struggle. Handala, a refugee child whose back faces the reader, is present in every one of al-'Ali's cartoons.

18. These numbers do not include private schools in East Jerusalem, which are considered part of Israel in the official statistics.

19. Ichilov and Mazawi, *Between State and Church*, 58.

20. Abu-Asbah, *Arab Education in Israel*.

21. Al Haj, *Education, Empowerment, and Control*, 97.

22. Yair Ettinger, "Instead of Hijab, the Muslim Sisters Will Wear a Green Surgeon's Cap," *Haaretz*, 3 April 2012.

23. Al-Haj, *Education, Empowerment, and Control*, 95.

24. Ibid.

25. Copty, "Knowledge and Power in Education," 281; Mar'i, *Arab Education in Israel*, 61.

26. Wiemer, "Zionism and the Arabs," 35.

27. Mar'i, *Arab Education in Israel*, 61.

28. Order of Education: http://cms.education.gov.il/EducationCMS/Units/Zchuyot /ChukimVeamanot/Chukim/PkudatChinuchChadash1978.htm.

29. Ibid.

30. Rabinowitz and Abu-Baker, *Coffins on Our Shoulders*, 1–2.

31. Conversation with Dr. Yousef Jabareen, then chair of the Students' Council, 9 February 2012.

32. See a report about an event organized by the student council at the Yani high school in Kafr Yasif before the 1984 Land Day, *al-Ittihad*, 28 March 1984.

33. To a large extent this Arab national orientation echoes the historical connection between the Arab Orthodox community and the emergence of Arab nationalism in the Levant.

34. http://www.youtube.com/watch?v=2TUh7YZ6gso.

35. Supreme Court Ruling from 5 January 2012, http://www.psakdin.co.il/fileprint .asp?filename=/minhali/private/ver_srjw.htm

36. This is based on the assessment of Dr.Yousef Jabareen, an activist in the field of Arab education and himself a graduate of the St. Joseph school.

37. "Kinus be-Natseret mita'am ha-va'ad le-haganat admot he-'Arvim nin'al lelo hahlatot," *Davar*, 18 February 1979, 3.

38. The general director of the Ministry of Education, Eli'ezer Shmueli, instructed all superintendents and school directors not to attend the inaugural conference of the FUCAE. See a discussion of the Central Committee for Security at the Arab Affairs Advisor office, 18 September 1984, "Policy of the Education System," Israel State Archive, GL-18642–8.

39. Rosenfeld and Al-Haj, *Arab Local Government in Israel*; As'ad Ghanem, "Ha-manhigut ha-munitsipalit."

40. Ghanem and Sarah Ozacky-Lazar, *Ha-hatsba'ah he-'Arvit*.

41. See Copty, "Knowledge and Power," 129.

42. The Ta'awun Fund, founded by a group of Palestinian businessmen abroad, supports Palestinian cultural institutions.

43. Tomer Zarhin, "The Palestinian Identity Program Will Not Be Implemented Next Year," Y-net, 30 July 2000, http://www.ynet.co.il/articles/0,7340,L-41350,00.html.

44. E.g., a letter sent by Raji Mansur, head of the FUCAE, to directors of departments of education in the Arab municipal councils, 24 September 2002.

45. The Or Commission was appointed by the Israeli government to investigate the

events of October 2000. The commission criticized the functioning of Prime Minister Ehud Barak and the Minster of Internal Security Shlomo Ben Ami. It also criticized the Israeli police for using excessive force. Despite these conclusions, none of the policemen involved in the killing was ever brought to trial.

46. A letter from the director general of the Ministry of Education, Culture, and Sports, to the directors of Arab schools, 21 October 2004 (Reference 591841).

47. A letter from the director general of the Ministry of Education, Culture, and Sports, to the directors of Arab schools, 18 November 2004 (Reference 594989).

48. Jabareen and Agbaria, *Education on Hold.*

49. Interview with Hala Espanioly, 25 November 2008.

50. https://sites.google.com/a/motran.tzafonet.org.il/mainpage/home/ywmyat -altrbyte-alajtmayte-2012–2013/ahyadhkryalaqsy.

51. Saba-Sa'di, "The Disputed Role."

52. Interview with Orna Simhon, 1 July 2012.

53. Samar 'Odeh, "Arab Schools in Haifa Will Report on Teachers Who Were Absent Protesting the October 2000 Events," 107.5 Online, 7 October 2009. http://radiohaifa .mediacast.co.il/article.aspx?id=4777.

54. Jack Khoury, "Education Ministry Hunting for Arab Teachers Absent on Land Day," *Haaretz*, 11 April 2011.

55. Interview with Orna Simhon, 1 July 2012.

56. Jabareen and Agbaria, *Education on Hold.*

57. FUCAE website, http://arab-education.org/?p=1043.

58. Ayman Dahamshe, "Lajnat mutaba'at qadaya al-ta'lim al-'Arabi tusdiru kitab al-hawiyya," 29 March 2011, http://www.panet.co.il/online/articles/1/2/S-389865,1,2.html.

59. Peled, "The 100 Terms Program."

60. Ibn Khaldun, The Arab Society for Research and Development, is a public, non-profit center for applied research established in 2002.

61. Ghanem, "Identity and Belonging," 1.

62. Interview with Mohanad Mustafa, one of the booklet's editors, 20 September 2008.

63. The local Community Center, known in Israel as *matnas* (the Hebrew acronym for Center for Culture, Youth, and Sport) is a potential educational tool of the municipal government. Although the center is part of a country-wide network of the Israel Association of Community Centers (which is a governmental entity operated by the Ministry of Education), the municipality provides most of its budget and appoints 40 percent of the board members. Another 40 percent of the board members are representatives of the local residents. The meaning of this structural arrangement is that each *matnas* has a significant degree of local autonomy from the central government. Therefore, in some Arab localities, commemoration of events such as Land Day or October 2000, which cannot be commemorated at schools, find a home at the *matnas.*

CHAPTER 9

1. Uri As and Yair Ettinger, "The Police Closed the Camp of Return in Kabul," *Haaretz*, 31 July 2003.

2. According the Hebrew newspaper *Haaretz*, the police found a booklet that was distributed to the children that included praises for Yahia 'Ayash, known for planning several suicide attacks before being killed by Israel in 1996. Inside pre-1967 Israel it is uncommon to find public praises of 'Ayash, and this inclusion in the curriculum of the Sons of the Village is an indication of the location of the movement at the margins of the political spectrum among Palestinians in Israel.

3. Cupers, "Governing through Nature."

4. Goffman, *Asylums*.

5. Kahane and Rapoport, *The Origins of Postmodern Youth*, 106.

6. Kahane and Rapoport, *The Origins of Postmodern Youth*.

7. Paris, *Children's Nature*, 11.

8. Ibid.

9. Hoffmann, *Stalinist Values*.

10. E. Greenberg, "Majallat Rawdat al-Ma'Arif"; Degani, Arnon, "They Were Prepared."

11. *Davar*, 26 July 1949.

12. Rekhess, *Ha-Mi'ut he-'Arvi*, 57.

13. Ibid., 70–71.

14. Kaufman, *Arab National Communism*, 54.

15. Muhammad Abu Asba', "Liqa taarikhi lil-shabab fi al-Taybeh bayn shuyu'i al-jalil wal-muthalath," *al-Ittihad*, 6 August 1976.

16. Samih al-Ghanadri, "Al-mukhayam al-tatawu'i yatahawal ila mihirajan ra'i," *al-Ittihad*, 17 August 1976, 2, 6.

17. Kahane and Rapoport, *Origins of Postmodern Youth*, 108.

18. Samih al-Ghanadri, "Jabarat al-'amal—yughayiruna wujh al-Nasira," *al-Ittihad*, 20 August 1976; the Palestinian national movement has more than one anthem, reflecting the variety of geo-political conditions of Palestinian existence. Among them, *Mawtani* has the strongest connection to the pre-1948 Palestinian struggle since it was authored by Ibrahim Tuqan in 1934 and was used during the 1936–1939 revolt.

19. Ibid.

20. "Talkhis al-'amal al-tatawu'i al-awal fi al-Nasira," *al-Ittihad*, 24 August 1976.

21. "Iftitiah 'urs al-'amal wal-karameh al-thani fi il-Nasira," *al-Ittihad*, 12 August 1977.

22. 'Atallah Mansur, "Mahane 'im dgalim Falastiniin," *Haaretz*, 28 August 1981.

23. Rekhess, *Ha-mi'ut he-'Arvi*, 177.

24. Conversation on 11 November 2014 with Issam Aburaya from Sakhnin, who as an adolescent, attended the Nazareth working camp in the mid-1980s.

25. See "Ahaly Kafr Bir'im 'ala al-'ahd," *al-Ittihad*, 18 September 1985.

26. Maget, *Bir'am*, 48.

27. See, e.g.,, Nasim abu Khayt, "al-mukhayam al-sayfi al-awal," *al-Ittihad*, 27 July 1986.

28. Ibtihaj Majali, "Madrasa minhajuha . . . durus al-haya wal-kifah," *al-Ittihad*, 1 September 1987.

29. "Al-shurta taqatahim mukhayam al-atfal," *al-Ittihad*, 25 July 1989, 8.

30. "Ikhtitam mukhayam al-salam wal-tufula fi al-Nasira," *al-Ittihad*, 6 August 1989, reported how the news was handled in the Hebrew newspaper.

31. Tawfiq 'Abd al-Fattah, "Intiba'at shababiya 'an mukhayam al-hawiya," Arab48, 25 July 2012, http://www.arabs48.com/?mod=articles&ID=93265.

32. Fifteen months earlier, following a police investigation against him as a suspect of "assisting the enemy in wartime" (referring to his communication with people in Lebanon during the 2006 war), Bishara resigned from the Knesset via the Israeli Embassy in Cairo. Bishara has denied the allegations and declared that he is staying abroad because he does not believe he would receive a fair trial in Israel. His portrait on the camp T-shirts, therefore, was a statement of solidarity. Rawda 'Atallah, the camp director, was Bishara's sister.

33. Although poetry recitation is a major Arab and Palestinian cultural tradition, ending camp with a poetry citation by children is a tradition that goes back to the communist summer camps in the 1980s.

34. Darwich, *Palestine, mon pays*; Alcalay, *Memories of Our Future.*

35. Yosi Sarid, "Darwish ke-mashal," *Haaretz*, 18 June 2010.

36. Zuheir Andrews, *Kul al-'Arab*, 1 April 2011.

37. Session no. 230 of the 18th Knesset, 22 March 2011.

38. Nassar, "Affirmation and Resistance."

39. Ibid., 198–199.

40. Ghanim, *Livnot et ha-uma.*

41. "Masirat fi al-muthalath", *al-Ittihad*, 9 October 1970, 4.

42. Podeh, "Demonizing the Other."

43. This quote was originally ascribed to the founder of the Palestine Liberation Organization Ahmad Shuqayri, whose statement in the same spirit was quoted in a Lebanese newspaper two days before the 1967 war. (Shemesh, "Did Shuqayri Call for Throwing the Jews into the Sea.") The attribution of the quote to Abdel Nasser probably relates to the fact that he was the strongest Arab leader that Israel faced at the time.

44. Interview with Ayman 'Odeh, 30 October 2008.

45. On the panopticon metaphor, see Foucault, *Discipline and Punish.*

46. See https://www.youtube.com/watch?v=TpSWVpcMukk.

47. Nevertheless, in 2012 an image of Abdel Nasser again appeared at the entrance.

48. On the collaborators among the Palestinian citizens of Israel, see H. Cohen, *Good Arabs.*

49. Data is based on the official database of the Ministry of Education, available at http://ic.education.gov.il/mabatrachav/startprod.htm.

50. Estimate provided by the Administration of Youth and Society in the Israeli Ministry of Education.

51. In the summer camps of the Islamic Movement, for example, there is a strict separation of boys and girls from an early age, a dress code calling for modesty in the swimming pool, and much less time for cultural activities such as music and dancing.

CHAPTER 10

1. "During the 58th Memorial Day of Nakba in Lydda," *Kul al-'Arab*, 19 May 2006.

2. Oren at al., "Conflict, Identity, and Ethos."

3. On "semiotic instrumentalism," see Schwartz et al.,"Recovery of Masada."

4. Y. Zerubavel, *Recovered Roots.*

5. Y. Zerubavel, " Politics of Interpretation."

6. Frank, *Sanity and Survival.*

7. Chaumont, *La Concurrence Des Victimes.*

8. Benjamin, "Victimology."

9. Flores, *Remembering the Alamo.*

10. Haltof, "Gallipoli."

11. Y. Zerubavel, " Politics of Interpretation."

12. Y. Zerubavel, *Recovered Roots,* 96.

13. R. Khalidi, *Palestinian Identity,* 194–201.

14. *Mirat al-Sharq,* 17 June 1930, 1.

15. Nassar, "Affirmation and Resistance"; Slyomovics and Khleif, "Palestinian Remembrance Days and Plans."

16. Harlow, *Resistance Literature.*

17. Elmessiri, *Pale*stinian Wedding: Major Themes," 99.

18. Nassar, "Affirmation and Resistance," 9.

19. Ibid., 269–271.

20. *Al-Ittihad,* 9 October 1970, 5.

21. Emile Tuma, "Al-Shi'r al-'Arabi al-Thawri fi isra'il," *al-Jadid* 12, no.1, 1965, 5–8, cited by Nassar, "Affirmation and Resistance," 258.

22. Translated by Elmessiri, *Palestinian Wedding,* 217.

23. Samih al-Qasim, "'Awdat 'Omar al-Mukhtar," *al-Ittihad,* 15 May 1970, 4.

24. Meital, "Who Is Egypt's 'Hero of War and Peace.'"

25. Tawfiq Zayyad, "Al-'Ubur al-Kabir," *al-Ittihad,* 4 October 1974, 2.

26. *Al-Ittihad,* 25 March 1977, 4.

27. In 1260 Mamluks forces defeated the Mongols in southeastern Galilee and stopped their expansion westward. The battle has been remembered as a great Islamic victory and later as an Arab national victory.

28. On 8 April 1970, the Israeli air force bombarded an elementary school in the Egyptian village of Bahr el-Baqr, killing 40 children.

29. Rafat al-Zuhayri, one of the six Land Day martyrs, was a resident of Nur al-Shams in the West Bank. He was killed in Taybeh, inside pre-1967 Israel, and was the only Land Day victim who was not an Israeli citizen.

30. *Al-Jadid*, March 1977, 11.

31. Robinson, *Citizen Strangers*, 175.

32. Hakim Rabi, "Kafr Qasim, al-majzara—al-ʿibra," *al-ittihad*, 29 October 1985, 4.

33. For creating the variable "Palestinian," answers that included the term Palestinian alone or in any possible combination (Palestinian-Israeli, Palestinian-Muslim, Arab-Israeli-Palestinian, etc.) were coded as 1, while all other cases were coded as 0. For the variable "Israeli," answers including the term Israeli or Israeli citizen were coded as 1 while all other cases were coded as 0.

34. Husayn Swayti, *al-Sinnara*, 13 July 2007, 66–68.

35. *Al-Sinnara*, 11 July 2008, 2.

36. If we include in the "War in Iraq" category those interviewees who mentioned the execution of Saddam Hussein, the frequency would rise to 10 percent (12 percent among men, 8 percent among women).

37. Rekhess and Rudnitzky, *Seqer ʿamadot ha-ukhlusiya he-ʿarvit be-yisrael.*

38. Itamar Inbari "A Survey: The Palestinians Want to Adopt Hizballah's Model," NRG, September 26 2006, http://www.nrg.co.il/online/1/ART1/484/016.html.

39. Azmi Bishara, "Al-azraq wal-ahmar wa-sabghat ukhra," Arab48, 16 July 2006.

40. "Religious" was defined as those who described themselves as observing religion at a "high" or "very high" level.

41. "Secular" was defined as those who described themselves as observing religion at a "low level" or not at all.

42. See for example, Zuheir Andrews, "Fi qadaya tasdir al-azmat," Arab48, 19 August, 2006, http://www.arabs48.com.

43. Hasan ʿAbd al-Halim, "Harb tamuz kanat hazima israiliyya wa-laisat mujarad fashl," Arab48, 5 August 2007.

44. Hasan ʿAbd al-Halim, "6 sanawat ʿala 14 Ab": Harb qawadat ustura," Arab48, 17 August 2012, http://www.arabs48.com/?mod=articles&ID=93846.

45. Elmessiri, *Palestinian Wedding: A Bilingual Anthology*; Harlow, *Resistance Literature*.

46. Joseph Algazy, "In Memory of Mahmoud Darwish 1941–2008," http://www.defeatist-diary.com/index.asp?p=articles_Darwish. The interview appeared originally in Hebrew in *Zo Haderekh* on 19 November 1969 and in Arabic in the November 1969 issue of *al-Jadid*. Darwish's choice to rely on the Egyptian scholar is interesting by itself, and it might have been a shield against accusations of lack of patriotism by Arab nationalists.

47. Hoffman, *My Happiness*, 266.

48. Meron Rapaport, "Even to Talk with You Is No Longer Possible," *Haaretz*, 18 September 2006.

49. Sayed Kashua, "Through the Looking Glass," *Haaretz*, 17 August 2006.

50. Interview with J. in his clinic, 29 June 2009.

51. Wedeen, *Ambiguities of Domination*; Meital, "Who Is Egypt's 'Hero of War and Peace'?"

52. *Al-Ittihad*, 20 March 1981, 1.

CHAPTER 11

1. Peri, "The Assassination."

2. Vinitzky-Seroussi, "Commemorating a Difficult Past."

3. Ben-Ze'ev et al., *Shadows of War*; Vinitzky-Seroussi and Teeger, "Unpacking the Unspoken."

4. Morris, *Birth of the Palestinian RefugeeProblem Revisited*, 424–476.

5. Mordekhai Haymovitz, "Yeuhda Meir lo hit'orer mileil he-alot ha-shvurot," NRG, 5 January 2008, http://www.nrg.co.il/online/1/ART1/678/702.html.

6. Reiter, *National Minority, Regional Majority*, 155–158.

7. Ibid.

8. Smooha, "Advances and Limits of the Israelization."

9. Al-Haj, "Illusion of Belonging."

10. Ibid., 167.

11. Ibid.

12. L. Greenberg, "Lama lo himshakhnu be-darko?"

13. 'Ali, "Ha-ah ha-13", 75.

14. Al-Haj, "Illusion of Belonging," 172–173.

15. Smooha, *Index of Arab-Jewish Relations in Israel 2003–2009*.

16. Vinitzky-Seroussi, *Yitzhak Rabin's Assassination*.

17. Jamal, *Arab Public Sphere in Israel*, 83.

18. Peri, *Yad ish be-ahiv*, 162.

19. Reiter, *National Minority, Regional Majority*, 179–181.

20. "Rabin's Commemorative Rally—the Largest in the History of the State," *al-Ittihad*, 9 November 1998.

21. Ironically, this is the date of the Balfour Declaration of 1917, which is considered a tragedy in the Palestinian national narrative, and was ignored by *al-Ittihad* on that same day.

22. The headline in the first issue after the assassination (10 November 1995) was: "Earthquake under the Feet of the Israeli Shabak."

23. Muhammad Hamze Ghenayem, "The Monster That Acted in the Name of Its Creator," *Fasl al-Maqal*, 8 November 1996.

24. 'Azmi Bishara, "Oslo 3," *Fasl al-Maqal*, 5–11 November 1999.

25. The survey was directed by Asher Arian and Michal Shamir and carried out by Modi'in Ezrahi Research. It included a stratified sample of the adult (18+) popula-

tion in Israel (N=1,168 Jews, 503 Arabs; the Arab-Jewish ratio is non-proportional). Jews and Arabs were interviewed by means of face-to-face interviews in Hebrew and Arabic, respectively.

26. The Rabin Center is an institute established in 1997 by a parliamentary law and is "dedicated to improving the shape of Israeli society by ensuring that the legacy of Yitzhak Rabin continues to impact the youth and the people of Israel" (from the center's website, http://www.rabincenter.org.il).

27. Tamar Rotem, "They Teach Them Democracy—but Forbid Them from Demonstrating," *Haaretz*, 16 October 2000.

28. Vinitzky-Seroussi, *Yitzhak Rabin's Assassination*.

29. "New Book: Rabin Suggested to Expel the Palestinian from the West Bank in 1956," Arab48, 18 December 2005, http://www.arabs48.com/?mod=articles&ID=29326.

30. Vinitzky-Seroussi, *Yitzhak Rabin's Assassination*.

31. Uriya Shavit, "Goodbye, Friend," *Haaretz* 13 April, 2001.

32. Najwan Darwish, "Samih al-Qasim wa-huma al-asrala," Arab48, 17 November 2009, http://www.arabs48.com/?mod=articles&ID=66944.

33. The survey was conducted in July 2005 by the Guttman Institute at the Israel Democracy Institute among a representative sample of Israel's adult population (ages 18 and over), both Jews and Arabs. The sample included 1684 Jewish and 320 Arab respondents, who were interviewed over the telephone in Hebrew, Arabic, and Russian.

34. Arian et al., *Auditing Israeli Democracy*.

35. Peri, *Yad ish be-ahiv*, 241.

36. Arian et al., *Auditing Israeli Democracy*.

37. Ya'ar and Herman, "Rabin? He Was Not a Bad Leader."

38. Arian et al., *Auditing Israeli Democracy*.

39. L. Greenberg, "Lama lo himshakhnu bedarko?"

40. I used the Arabic term *balad*. This can refer to a country or a certain geographical region—not necessarily a political unit. This terminological choice was made to enable respondents to bring up names from both Israeli and Palestinian histories, based on their own choice.

41. The major confrontations in the Gaza Strip (2008–2009 and 2014) occurred after the last survey in this research was conducted, but they are mentioned here since they are related to the same path of escalation.

42. Smooha, *Index of Arab-Jewish Relations in Israel 2003–2009*.

43. Jamal, *Arab Public Sphere in Israel*.

CONCLUSION

1. Jamal, " Ambiguities of Minority Patriotism."

2. Hoffman, *My Happiness*, 371–372.

3. Adala, *New Discriminatory Laws*.

4. Smooha, *Still Playing by the Rules.*

5. Ibid.

6. Conversation with Ayman ʿOdeh, 6 May 2014.

7. Conway, *Commemoration and Bloody Sunday.*

8. Eyal Gross, "Hoq ha-Leom," *Haaretz,* 8 June 2014.

9. See a letter from the Association for Civil Rights in Israel to the attorney general, 10 July 2014, http://www.acri.org.il/he/31954.

BIBLIOGRAPHY

BOOKS AND JOURNAL ARTICLES

Abu-Asbah, Khaled. *The Arab Education in Israel: Dilemmas of a National Minority.* Jerusalem: The Floersheimer Institute for Policy Studies, 2007.

Abu Gharbiya, Bahjat. *Fi khidam al-nidal al-'Arabi al-Filastini: Mudhakkirat al-munadil Bahjat Abu Gharbiya, 1916–1949* [In the service of the Arab-Palestinian struggle: Memories of the fighter Bahjat Abu Gharbiya, 1916–1949]. Beirut: Mu'assasat al-Dirasat al-Filastiniyyah, 1993.

Abu-Ghazaleh, Adnan. "Arab Cultural Nationalism in Palestine during the British Mandate." *Journal of Palestine Studies* 1, no. 3 (1972): 37–63.

Aburaiya, Issam. "Developmental Leadership: The Case of the Islamic Movement in Umm Al-Fahim, Israel." MA thesis, Clark University, 1991.

Abu-Saad, Ismael, Yossi Yonah, and Avi Kaplan. "Identity and Political Stability in an Ethnically Diverse State: A Study of Bedouin Arab Youth in Israel." *Social Identities* 6, no. 1 (2000): 49–61.

Adalah. *New Discriminatory Laws and Bills in Israel.* Adalah, 2012. http://adalah.org/Public/files/English/Legal_Advocacy/Discriminatory_Laws/Discriminatory-Laws-in-Israel-October-2012-Update.pdf.

Akçam, Taner. *From Empire to Republic: Turkish Nationalism and the Armenian Genocide.* London and New York: Zed Books, 2004.

al-'Arif, 'Arif. *Al-Nakba: Nakbat bait al-maqdas wa-l-firdaws al-mafqud, 1948–1955* [The Nakba: The Nakba of Jerusalem and the lost paradise, 1948–1955]. Sidon and Beirut: Manshurat al-Maktaba al-'Asriyya li-l-Tiba'a wa-l-Nashr, 1956.

Alcalay, Ammiel. *Memories of Our Future: Selected Essays 1982–1999.* San Francisco: City Lights, 1999.

'Ali, Riad. "Ha-ah ha-13" [The thirteenth brother]. *Panim* no. 1 (1997): 73–76.

Amara, Muhammad, and Izhak Schnell. "Identity Repertoires among Arabs in Israel." *Journal of Ethnic and Migration Studies* 30, no. 1 (2004):175–193.

Anderson, Benedict. *Imagined Communities: Reflections on the Origin and Spread of Nationalism.* New York: Verso, 1983.

Anderson, Betty S. *Nationalist Voices in Jordan: The Street and the State*. Austin: University of Texas Press, 2005.

'Araf, Shukri, and Yusef Gharib 'Abud. *'Aylut: al-Sumud wal-istimrar* [Aylut—steadfastness and continuity]. 'Aylut: 'Aylut Local Council, 2008.

Arendt, Hannah. *Eichmann in Jerusalem: A Report on the Banality of Evil*. New York: Penguin Group US, 2006.

Arian, Asher, Shlomit Barnea, Pazit Ben-Nun, Raphael Ventura, and Michal Shamir. *Auditing Israeli Democracy, 2005: A Decade after the Assassination of Prime Minister Yitzhak Rabin*. Jerusalem: The Israel Democracy Institute, 2005.

Assmann, Jan, and John Czaplicka. "Collective Memory and Cultural Identity." *New German Critique* no. 65 (1995): 125–133.

'Awawdah, Wadi'. *Dhakirah la tamut: Shuhud a'ayan fatahu qulubahum wa-hajarat dhakiratihim li-yarwu ma Jara lahum fi al-'am 1948, 'am al-Nakbah*. [A memory not dying: Eye witnesses opened their hearts and the chambers of their memories to tell what heppenned in 1948]. Haifa: The National Committee for the Defense of the Rights of the Uprooted, 2000.

'Awd, Khalid. *Nuh Ibrahim: Sha'ir Thawrat 1936–1939* [Nuh Ibrahim: The poet of the 1936–1939 revolt]. Nazareth: 'Ayn Aabl Assocation, 1995.

Ayalon, Ami. *Reading Palestine: Printing and Literacy, 1900–1948*. Austin: University of Texas Press, 2004.

Bakiner, Onur. "Is Turkey Coming to Terms with Its Past? Politics of Memory and Majoritarian Conservatism." *Nationalities Papers* 41, no. 5 (2013): 691–708.

Barkan, Elazar. *The Guilt of Nations: Restitution and Negotiating Historical Injustices*. New York: Norton, 2000.

Bashir, Nabih. *Yawm al-Ard: Bayna al-qawmi wal-yawmi* [Land Day: Betwixt and between—national and civic]. Haifa: Mada al-Carmel, 2006.

Bauml, Yair. *Tsel kahol lavan: Mediniyut ha-mimshal ha-yisraeli ve-pe'ulatav be-kerev ha-ezrahim he-'arvim: Ha-shanim ha-me'atsvot, 1958–1968* [A blue and white shadow: The Israeli establishment's policy and action among the Arab citizens: The formative years: 1958–1968]. Haifa: Pardes, 2007.

Beinin, Joel. *Was the Red Flag Flying There? Marxist Politics and the Arab-Israeli Conflict in Egypt and Israel, 1948–1965*. Berkley: University of California Press, 1990.

Ben-Bassat, Avi, and Momi Dahan. *Ha-kalkala ha-politit shel ha-rashuyot ha-mekomiot* [The political economics of the municipalities]. Jerusalem: The Israel Democracy Institute, 2009.

Ben-Zaken, Avner. *Qomonism ke-imperyalism tarbuti: Ha-zika bein ha-qomonism ha-artsi-yisraeli la-qomonism he-'arvi 1919–1948* [Communism as cultural imperialism: The affinities between Eretz-Israeli communism and Arab communism 1919–1948]. Tel Aviv: Resling, 2006.

Ben-Ze'ev, Efrat, and Issam Aburaiya. "'Middle-Ground' Politics and the Re-

Palestinization of Places in Israel." *International Journal of Middle East Studies* 36, no. 4 (2004): 639–655.

———. "*Ha-maavak ha-falastini 'al 'itsuv ha-merhav be-yisrael: me-'aliya le-regel ishit le-hantsaha qvutsatit*" [The palestinian struggle on shaping the space in Israel: From personal pilgrimage to organized collective commemoration]. *Politika* no. 19 (2009): 105–119.

Ben-Ze'ev, Efrat, Ruth Gino, and Jay Winter. *Shadows of War: A Social History of Silence in the Twentieth Century.* Cambridge: Cambridge University Press, 2010.

Ben Porat, Amir. *Biladi Biladi.* Tel-Aviv: Babel, 2001.

Benjamin, Jessica. "Victimology." *Tikkun* 4, no. 2 (1988): 75–77.

Benslama, Fethi. "La Cause Identitaire." *Cahiers Intersignes* no. 10 (1995): 47–66.

Benvenisti, Meron. *'Ir ha-mnuhut: Batei he-'almin shel Yerushalaim* [Jerusalem's city of the dead]. Jerusalem: Keter, 1990.

———. *Mul ha-homah ha-segurah: Yerushalayim ha-hatsuyah ve-hame'uhedet* [In front of the closed wall: Divided and united Jerusalem]. Jerusalem: Vaydenfeld, 1973.

———. *Sacred Landscape: The Buried History of the Holy Land since 1948.* Berkeley: University of California Press, 2002.

Berlin, Isaiah. *The Power of Ideas.* Princeton, N.J: Princeton University Press, 2000.

Birnbaum, Sariel. "Historical Discourse in the Media of the PNA." In *Palestinian Collective Memory and National Identity,* edited by Meir Litvak, 135–168. New York: Palgrave-Macmillan, 2009.

Bishara, Azmi. "He-'Arvi ha-Yisraeli: 'Iyunim be-siah politi shasu'a" [The Israeli Arab: Reading in a fragmented political discourse]. In *Bein ha-ani la-anahnu* [Between the "me" and the "us"], edited by Azmi Bishara, 169–191. Jerusalem: Van Leer Institute and Hakibbutz Hameuchad, 1999.

———. *al-'Arab fi Israi'l: Ru'ya min al-dakhil* [The Arabs in Israel: A view from within]. Ramallah: Muwatin, 1998.

Bray, Zoe, and Michael Keating. "European Integration and the Basque Country in France and Spain." In *Divided Nations and European Integration,* edited by Tristan James Mabry, John McGarry, Margaret Moore, and Brendan O'Leary, 127–156. Philadelphia: University of Pennsylvania Press, 2013.

Brubaker, Rogers. *Nationalism Reframed: Nationhood and the National Question in the New Europe.* Cambridge, UK: Cambridge University Press, 1996.

———. "Nationalizing States Revisited: Projects and Processes of Nationalization in Post-Soviet States." *Ethnic and Racial Studies* 34, no. 11 (2011): 1785–1814.

Brubaker, Rogers, and Margit Feischmidt. "1848 in 1998: The Politics of Commemoration in Hungary, Romania, and Slovakia." *Comparative Studies in Society and History* 44, no. 4. (2002): 700–744.

Brubaker, Rogers, Margit Feischmidt, Jon Fox, and Liana Grancea. *Nationalist Politics* and *Everyday Ethnicity in a Transylvanian Town*. Princeton, NJ: Princeton University Press, 2006.

Budeiri, Musa. "The Palestinians: Tensions between Nationalist and Religious Identities." In *Rethinking Nationalism in the Arab Middle East*, edited by Israel Gershoni and James Jankowski, 191–206. New York: Columbia University Press, 1997.

Buksbaum, Tova. "Nakba: Ein davar kaze" [Nakba: There is no such thing]. Presentation at the Conference Discourse on Trauma, Rememberence, and Forgetting, Tel Aviv, 21 February 2010.

Buruma, Ian. *The Wages of Guilt : Memories of War in Germany and Japan*. New York: Farrar, Straus, and Girou, 1994.

Calhoun, Craig J. *Nations Matter: Culture, History, and the Cosmopolitan Dream*. London: Routledge, 2007.

Campos, Michelle. *Ottoman Brothers: Muslims, Christians, and Jews in Early Twentieth-Century Palestine*. Stanford: Stanford University Press, 2010.

———. "'Shared Homeland' and Its Boundaries: Empire, Citizenship and the Origins of Sectarianism in Late Ottoman Palestine, 1908–1913." PhD diss., Stanford University, 2003.

Caspi, Dan, and Mustafa Kabaha. "*Miyerushalaym ha-qdosha ve'ad ha-ma'ayan*" [From holy Jerusalem to the spring]. *Panim* no. 16, 2001.

Chaumont, Jean-Michel. *La concurrence des victimes: Genocide, identite, reconnaissance* [The competition of victims: Genocide, identity, recognition]. Paris: Éditions la Découverte, 2002.

Cheskin, Ammon. "History, Conflicting Collective Memories, and National Identities: How Latvia's Russian-Speakers Are Learning to Remember." *Nationalities Papers* 40, no. 4 (2012): 561–584.

Cobban, Helena. *The Making of Modern Lebanon*. Boulder, Colorado: Westview Press, 1985.

Cohen, Hillel. *Army of Shadows: Palestinian Collaboration with Zionism, 1917–1948*. Berkley: University of California Press, 2008.

———. *Good Arabs: The Israeli Security Agencies and the Israeli Arabs, 1948–1967*. Berkeley: University of California Press, 2010.

———. "Land, Memory, and Identity: The Palestinian Internal Refugees in Israel." *Refuge: Canada's Periodical on Refugees* 21, no. 2 (2003): 6–13.

———. "Palestinians in Israel and the Territories on Peace, Violence and Jewish Rights: Comparative Study and Some Initial Observations." Unpublished paper, 2014.

Cohen, Raanan. *Strangers in Their Homeland: A Critical Study of Israel's Arab Citizens*. Brighton: Sussex Academic Press, 2009.

Confino, Alon. *The Nation as a Local Metaphor: Württemberg, Imperial Germany, and National Memory, 1871–1918*. Chapel Hill: University of North Carolina Press, 1997.

Connerton, Paul. *How Societies Remember*. Cambridge: Cambridge University Press, 1989.

Conway, Brian. *Commemoration and Bloody Sunday: Pathways of Memory*. Basingstoke, Hampshire, UK: Palgrave Macmillan, 2010.

Copty, Makram I. "Knowledge and Power in Education: The Making of the Israeli Arab Educational System. PhD diss., University of Texas, 1990.

Coser, Lewis A. "Introduction: Maurice Halbwachs 1877–1945." In *On Collective Memory*, edited by Lewis A. Coser, 1–36. Chicago: Chicago University Press, 1992.

Cressy, David. *Bonfires and Bells: National Memory and the Protestant Calendar in Elizabethan and Stuart England*. Berkeley: University of California Press, 1989.

Csergo, Zsuzsa, and James M. Goldgeier. "Kin-State Activism in Hungary, Romania, and Russia: The Politics of Ethnic Demography." In *Divided Nations and European Integration*, edited by Tristan James Mabry, John McGarry, Margaret Moore, and Brendan O'Leary, 89–126. Philadelphia: University of Pennsylvania Press, 2013.

Cupers, Kenny. "Governing through Nature: Camps and Youth Movements in Interwar Germany and the United States." *Cultural Geographies* 15, no. 2 (2008): 173–205.

Darwich, Mahmoud. *Palestine, mon pays: L'affaire du poème* [Palestine, my country: The poem affair]. Paris: Éditions de Minuit, 1988.

Davies, Alan. *The Crucified Nation: A Motif in Modern Nationalism*. Brighton, UK: Sussex Academic Press, 2010.

Degani, Arnon. "They Were Prepared: The Palestinian Arab Scout Movement 1920–1948." *British Journal of Middle Eastern Studies* 41, no. 2 (2014): 200–218.

Dichter, Shalom. "Malkodet shel dmei shtika" [A trap of hush money]. *Kan* no. 5 (2001): 29.

Einaudi, Jean-Luc. *La Bataille de Paris: 17 Octobre 1961*. Paris: Éditions du Seuil, 1991.

———. *Octobre 1961: Un massacre à Paris*. Paris: Fayard, 2001.

Elmessiri, Abdelwahab M. *The Palestinian Wedding: A Bilingual Anthology of Contemporary Palestinian Resistance Poetry*. Washington, DC: Three Continents, 1982.

———. "The Palestinian Wedding: Major Themes of Contemporary Palestinian Resistance Poetry." *Journal of Palestine Studies* 10, no. 3 (1981): 77–99.

Firro, Kais. *The Druzes in the Jewish State: A Brief History*. Leiden: Brill, 1999.

Flores, Richard R. *Remembering the Alamo: Memory, Modernity, and the Master Symbol*. Austin: University of Texas Press, 2002.

Foucault, Michel. *Discipline and Punish: The Birth of the Prison*. New York: Vintage, 1995.

Frank, Jerome David. *Sanity and Survival: Psychological Aspects of War and Peace*. New York: Vintage, 1967.

Friedland, Roger, and Richard Hecht. "The Nebi Musa Pilgrimage and the Origins of Palestinian Nationalism." In *Pilgrims and Travelers to the Holy Land,* edited by Bryan Le Beau and Menachem Mor, 89–118. Omaha: Creighton University Press, 1996.

Frisch, Hillel. "Ethnicity or Nationalism? Comparing the Nakba Narrative amongst Israeli Arabs and Palestinians in the West Bank and Gaza." *Israel Affairs* 9, nos. 1–2 (2002): 165–184.

————. *Israel's Security and Its Arab Citizens*. New York: Cambridge University Press, 2011.

Galtung, Johan. "Cultural Violence." *Journal of Peace Research* 27, no. 3 (1990): 291–305.

Gellner, Ernest. *Nations and Nationalism*. Oxford: Blackwell, 1983.

Gelvin, James L. *Divided Loyalties: Nationalism and Mass Politics in Syria at the Close of Empire*. Berkeley: University of California Press, 1998.

Gerber, Haim. *Remembering and Imagining Palestine: Identity and Nationalism from the Crusades to the Present*. Basingstoke, UK: Palgrave Macmillan, 2008.

Ghanem, As'ad. "Ha-manhigut ha-munitsipalit etsel he-'arvim be-yisrael: Hemshekhiyut ve-shinuy" [The municipal leadership of Arabs in Israel: Continuity and change]. *Ha-mizrah he-hadash* no. 37 (1995): 151–165.

————. "Identity and Belonging": A Pioneering Project, Which Must Be the Starting Point for an Alternative, Comprehensive Educational Plan." *Adalah's Newsletter* no. 27 (2006).

————. *Palestinian-Arab Minority in Israel, 1948–2000: A Political Study*. Albany: State University of New York Press, 2001.

————. "Shulayim be-hevra shulit: Ha-yihudiut ha-beduit" [Margins in a marginal society: The Bedouin uniqueness]. In *He-'arvim ba-politiqa ha-yisraelit: Dilemot shel zehut* [The Arabs in Israeli politics: Dilemmas of identity], edited by Elie Rekhess, 85–90. Tel Aviv: Tel Aviv University, Moshe Dayan Center, 1998.

Ghanem, As'ad, and Sarah Ozacky-Lazar. *Ha-hatsba'ah he-'Arvit babhirot la-kneset ha-15* [The Arab vote in the elections for the 15th Knesset]. Giv'at Haviva: Institute for Peace Research, 1999.

Ghanem, As'ad, and Nadim N. Rouhana. "Citizenship and the Parliamentary Politics of Minorities in Ethnic States: The Palestinian Citizens of Israel." *Nationalism and Ethnic Politics* 7, no. 4 (2001): 66–86.

Ghanim, Honaida. *Livnot et ha-uma me-hadash: Intelectualim falastinim be-yisrael* [Rebuilding the nation: Palestinian intellectuals in Israel]. Jerusalem: Magnes Press, 2009.

Goffman, Erving. *Asylums: Essays on the Social Situation of Mental Patients and Other Inmates*. Garden City, NY: Anchor Books, 1961.

Goldberg, Harvey E., and Chen Bram. "Sephardic/Mizrahi/Arab-Jews: Reflections on Critical Sociology and the Study of Middle Eastern Jewries within the Context of Israeli Society." *Studies in Contemporary Jewry* 22 (2007): 227–256.

Greenberg, Ela. "Majallat Rawdat al-Ma'arif: Constructing Identities within a Boys' School Journal in Mandatory Palestine." *British Journal of Middle Eastern Studies* 35, no. 1 (2008): 79–95.

Greenberg, Lev. "Lama lo himshakhnu bedarko?" [Why did we not continue in his way?]. In *Zikaron be-mahloqet* [Controversial memory], edited by Lev Greenberg, 123–151. Beersheba: Ben Gurion University, 2000.

Gündüz-Hoşgör, Ayşe, and Jeroen Smits. "Intermarriage between Turks and Kurds in

Contemporary Turkey: Inter-Ethnic Relations in an Urbanizing Environment." *European Sociological Review* 18, no. 4 (2002): 417–432.

Gutman, Yifat. "Past before Future: Memory Activism in Israel-Palestine." PhD diss., The New School, 2011.

Gvion, Liora. *Beyond Hummus and Falafel: Social and Political Aspects of Palestinian Food in Israel.* Berkley: University of California Press, 2012.

Haider, Ali, Yaser Awad, and Manar Mahmoud. *The Equality Index of Jewish and Arab Citizens in Israel (2009).* Jerusalem: Sikkuy, 2010.

Haiduc-Dale, Noah. "Nationalism and Religious Identification: Palestinian Christians in Mandate Palestine, 1918–1948." PhD diss., New York University, 2010.

al-Haj, Majid. *Education, Empowerment, and Control: The Case of the Arabs in Israel.* Albany: State University of New York Press, 1995.

———. "An Illusion of Belonging: Reaction of the Arab Population to Rabin's Assassination." In *The Assassination of Yitzhak Rabin*, edited by Yoram Peri, 163–174. Stanford: Stanford University Press, 2000.

———. *Social Change and Family Process: Arab Communities in Shefar-am.* London: Westview Press, 1987.

Hajab, Nimr Hasan. *Al-Shaʿer al-shaʿabi al-shahid Nuh Ibrahim* [The popular poet the martyr Nuh Ibrahim]. Amman: Al-Yazuri, 2006.

Haklai, Oded. *Palestinian Ethnonationalism in Israel.* Philadelphia: University of Pennsylvania Press, 2011.

Halabi, Awad. "Liminal Loyalties: Ottomanism and Palestinian Responses to the Turkish War of Independence, 1919–22." *Journal of Palestine Studies* 41, no. 3 (2012): 19–37.

Halabi, Edie. "The Transformation of the Prophet Moses Festival in Jerusalem, 1917–1937: From Local and Islamic to Modern and Nationalist Celebration." PhD diss., University of Toronto, 2007.

Halabi, Rabah. "Invention of a Nation: The Druze in Israel." *Journal of Asian and African Studies* 49, no. 3 (2014): 267–281.

Haltof, Mark. "Gallipoli, Mateship, and the Construction of Australian National Identity." *Journal of Popular Film and Television* 21, no. 1 (1993): 27–36.

Hamuda, Samih. *Al-waʿi wal-thawra. Dirasa fi hayat wa-jihad al-shaykh ʿIzz alq al-Qassam* [The consciousness and the revolt: Study on the life and jihad of Shaykh ʿIzz al-Din al-Qassam]. Jerusalem: Dar al-Shuruq, 1986.

Handelman, Don, and Lea Shamgar Handelman. "The Presence of Absence: The Memorialism of National Death in Israel." In *Grasping Land: Space and Place in Contemporary Israeli Discourse and Experience*, edited by Eyal Ben Ari and Yoram Bilu, 85–128. Albany: State University of New York Press, 1997.

Harlow, Barbara. *Resistance Literature.* New York: Methuen, 1987.

Hoffenberg, Peter H. "Landscape, Memory and the Australian War Experience, 1915–18." *Journal of Contemporary History* 36, no. 1 (2001): 111–131.

Hoffman, Adina. *My Happiness Bears No Relation to Happiness: A Poet's Life in the Palestinian Century.* New Haven, CT: Yale University Press, 2009.

Hoffmann, David. L. *Stalinist Values: The Cultural Norms of Soviet Modernity, 1917–1941.* Ithaca, NY: Cornell University Press, 2003.

House, Jim. "Antiracist Memories: The Case of 17 October 1961 in Historical Perspective." *Modern & Contemporary France* 9, no. 3 (2001): 355–368.

al-Hout, Bayan N. "The Palestinian Political Elite during the Mandate Period." *Journal of Palestine Studies* 9, no. 1 (1979): 85–111.

———. *Al-qiyadat wal-mu'assasat al-siyasiyyah fi filastin, 1917–1948* [The leaders and political institutions in Palestine, 1917–1948]. Beirut: Institute of Palestine Studies, 1981.

Husri, Sati'. *The Day of Maysalun: A Page from the Modern History of the Arabs: Memoirs.* Washington: Middle East Institute, 1966.

Ibrahim, Ibtisam. "Israel's 'Ethnic Project' in the City of Shafa-Amr: Particularization of Identity along Religious Lines." PhD diss., University of Wisconsin—Madison, 2000.

Ichilov, Orit, and André Elias Mazawi. *Between State and Church: Life-History of a French-Catholic School in Jaffa.* New York: P. Lang, 1996.

Ighbariyah, 'Umar. *Remembering the Nakba in 'Eilabun.* Tel Aviv: Zochrot, 2010.

Jabareen, Yousef T., and Ayman Agbaria. *Education on Hold: Israeli Government Policy and Civil Society Initiatives to Improve Arab Education in Israel.* Nazareth: DIRASAT, 2010.

Jamal, Amal. "The Ambiguities of Minority Patriotism: Love for Homeland Versus State among Palestinian Citizens of Israel." *Nationalism and Ethnic Politics* 10, no. 3 (2004): 433–471.

———. *Arab Minority Nationalism in Israel: The Politics of Indigeneity.* London: Routledge, 2011.

———. *The Arab Public Sphere in Israel: Media Space and Cultural Resistance.* Indiana University Press, 2009.

———. "Nationalizing States and the Constitution of 'Hollow Citizenship': Israel and Its Palestinian Citizens." *Ethnopolitics* 6, no. 4 (2007): 471–493.

———. "Palestinian Dynamics of Self Representation: Identity and Difference in Palestinian Nationalism." In *Israelis in Conflict: Hegemonies, Identities and Challenges,* edited by Adriana Kemp, David Newman, Uri Ram, and Oren Yiftachel, 123–143. Brighton; Portland: Sussex Academic Press, 2004.

———. "The Political Ethos of Palestinian Citizens of Israel: Critical Reading in the Future Vision Documents." *Israel Studies Forum* 23, no. 2 (2008): 3–28.

Jelen, Brigitte. "17 octobre 1961—17 octobre 2001: Une commemoration ambigue." *French Politics, Culture and Society* 20, no. 1 (2002): 30–41.

Jiryis, Sabri. *The Arabs in Israel.* Beirut: The Institute for Palestine Studies, 1969.

Johnson, Nels. *Islam and the Politics of Meaning in Palestinian Nationalism.* London: Kegan Paul International, 1982.

Johnston, Bill. "Organizational Structure and Ideology in Schooling." *Educational Theory* 35, no. 4 (1985): 333–343.

Kabaha, Mustafa. "Hamezima ve-ha-qorban: Tevah kfar qasem ba-historiografia he-'arvit ve-ha-falastinit" [The conspiracy and the victim: The Kafr Qasim massacre in Arab and Palestinian historiography]. In *Kafr Kassem: Myth and History,* edited by Ruvik Rosenthal, 87–116. Tel Aviv: Hakibbutz Hameuchad, 2000.

———. "The Role of the Press and Its Discourse in the Arab-Palestinian National Struggle." PhD diss., Tel-Aviv University, 1996.

Kadman, Noga. *Betsidei ha-derekh u-veshulei ha-toda'ah* [On the sides of the roads and on the margins of consciousness]. Tel Aviv: November Books, 2008.

Kafr Qasim Local Council. *Diwan Al-Shahid: Al-Shi'r 'an majzarat Kafr Qasim* [*Diwan Al-Shahid:* Poems on the Kafr Qasim massacre]. Kafr Qasim: Kafr Qasim Local Council, 1999.

Kahane, Reuven, and Tamar Rapoport. *The Origins of Postmodern Youth: Informal Youth Movements in a Comparative Perspective.* New York: Walter de Gruyter, 1997.

Kanafani, Ghassan. *The 1936–39 Revolt in Palestine.* Washington, DC: Committee for Democratic Palestine, 1972.

Al-Karaki, Khalid. *Hamasat al-shahada* [The enthusasism of martyrdom]. Beirut: Al-mu'assasa al-'arabiyya li-ldirasat wal-nashr, 1998.

Kaufman, Ilana. *Arab National Communism in the Jewish State.* Gainesville: University Press of Florida, 1997.

Kayyali, Abd al-Wahab. *Palestine: A Modern History.* London: Croom Helm, 1978.

Khalidi, Rashid. *Palestinian Identity: The Construction of Modern National Consciousness.* New York: Columbia University Press, 1997.

Khalidi, Walid. *From Haven to Conquest: Readings in Zionism and the Palestine Problem until 1948.* Washington, DC: Institute for Palestine Studies, 1971.

Khalili, Laleh. *Heroes and Martyrs of Palestine: The Politics of National Commemoration.* Cambridge: Cambridge University Press, 2007.

Khuri, Elias. *Bab Al-Shams* [Gate of the sun]. Beirut: Dar Al-Aadab, 1998.

Kimmerling, Baruch. "Boundaries and Frontiers of the Israeli Control System: Analytical Conclusions." In *The Israeli State and Society : Boundaries and Frontiers,* edited by Baruch Kimmerling, 265–84. Albany: State University of New York Press, 1989.

———. "Exchanging Territories for Peace: A Macrosociological Approach." *Journal of Applied Behavioral Science* 23, no. 1 (1987): 13–33.

———. *The Israeli State and Society: Boundaries and Frontiers.* Albany: State University of New York Press, 1989.

———. "Sovereignty, Ownwership and 'Presence' in the Jewish-Arab Territorial Conflict: The Case of Bir'im and Ikrit." *Comparative Political Studies* 10, no. 2 (1977): 155–176.

Kimmerling, Baruch, and Joel Migdal. *Palestinians: The Making of a People.* New York: Free Press, 1993.

Koselleck, Reinhart, and Todd S. Presner. *The Practice of Conceptual History: Timing History, Spacing Conepts.* Stanford: Stanford University Press, 2002.

Landau, Jacob M. *The Arab Minority in Israel, 1967–1991: Political Aspects.* Oxford: Clarendon Press, 1993.

Larsen, Laragh. "Re-Placing Imperial Landscapes: Colonial Monuments and the Transition to Independence in Kenya." *Journal of Historical Geography* 38, no. 1 (2012): 45–56.

Lewin-Epstein, N., and M. Semyonov. *The Arab Minority in Israel's Economy: Patterns of Ethnic Inequality.* Boulder, CO: Westview Press, 1993.

Litvak, Meir. "The Islamization of Palestinian Identity: The Case of Hamas." *Middle Eastern Studies* 34, no. 1 (1998): 148–163.

———. *Palestinian Collective Memory and National Identity.* New York: Palgrave-Macmillan, 2009.

Lustick, Ian. *Arabs in the Jewish State.* Austin: University of Texas Press, 1980.

Maget, Ilan. *Bir'am: Qehilat Zikaron Meguyeset.* Giv'at Haviva: Institute for Peace Research, 2000.

Mannheim, Karl. *Essays on the Sociology of Knowledge.* Memphis, TN: General Books, 2010.

Mar'i, Sami Khalil. *Arab Education in Israel.* Syracuse, NY: Syracuse University Press, 1978.

Mayo, James M. *War Memorials as Political Landscape. The American Experience and Beyond.* New York: Praeger, 1988.

McDonald, David A. "Geographies of the Body: Music, Violence and Manhood in Palestine." *Ethnomusicology Forum* 19, no. 2 (2010): 191–214.

Meital, Yoram. "Who Is Egypt's 'Hero of War and Peace'?" The Contest over Representation." *History and Memory* 15, no. 1 (2003): 150–183.

Monden, Christiaan W. S., and Jeroen Smits. "Ethnic Intermarriage in Times of Social Change: The Case of Latvia." *Demography* 42, no. 2 (2005): 323–345.

Monica, Maria Filomena. "Reading and Power: A Debate on Popular Education in the Beginning of the Twentieth Century." *Analise Social* 16, no. 3 (1980): 499–518.

Monterescu, Daniel. "Estranged Natives and Indigenized Immigrants: A Relational Anthropology of Ethnically Mixed Towns in Israel." *World Development* 39, no. 2 (2011): 270–281.

Morris, Benny. *The Birth of the Palestinian Refugee Problem: 1947–1949.* Cambridge: Cambridge University Press, 1987.

———. *The Birth of the Palestinian Refugee Problem Revisited.* Cambridge: Cambridge University Press, 2004.

———. *Israel's Border Wars, 1949–1956: Arab Infiltration, Israeli Retaliation, and the Countdown to the Suez War.* Oxford: Clarendon Press, 1993.

———. "Revisiting the Palestinian Exodus of 1948." In *The War for Palestine: Rewriting the History of 1948*, edited by Eugene Rogan and Avi Shlaim, 37–59. New York: Cambridge University Press, 2007.

Mosse, Goerge L. *Fallen Soldiers: Reshaping the Memory of the World Wars*. Oxford: Oxford University Press, 1990.

Murqus, Nimr. *Aqwa min al-nisyan: Risala ila ibnati* [Stronger than oblivion: A letter to my daughter]. Kafr Yasif, 1999.

Muslih, Muhammad Y. *The Origins of Palestinian Nationalism*. New York: Columbia University Press, 1988.

Nahas, Dunia. *The Israeli Communist Party*. London: Croom Helm, 1976.

Najjar, Aida Ali. "The Arabic Press and Nationalism in Palestine, 1920–1948." PhD diss., Syracuse University, 1975.

Nassar, Maha. "Affirmation and Resistance: Press, Poetry and the Formation of National Identity among Palestinian Citizens of Israel, 1948–1967." PhD diss., University of Chicago, 2006.

———. "Palestinian Citizens of Israel and the Discourse on the Right of Return, 1948–59." *Journal of Palestine Studies* 40, no. 4 (2011): 45–60.

Nora, Pierre. "Between Memory and History: Les lieux de memoire." *Representations* no. 26 (1989): 7–24.

Nordmann, Charlotte, and Jerome Vidal. "La politique de la memoire." In *Le 17 octobre 1961: Un crime d'etat à Paris*, edited by Nils Andersson and Olivier Le Cour Grandmaison, 171–181. Paris: La Dispute, 2001.

Olick, Jeffrey. K. "Collective Memory: The Two Cultures." *Sociological Theory* 17, no. 2 (1999): 333–348.

Olick, Jeffrey K., and Daniel Levy. "Collective Memory and Cultural Constraint: Holocaust Myth and Rationality in German Politics." *American Sociological Review* 62, no. 6 (1997): 921–936.

Oren, Neta, Daniel Bar-Tal, and Ohad David. "Conflict, Identity, and Ethos: The Israeli-Palestinian Case." In *The Psychology of Ethnic and Cultural Conflict (Psychological Dimensions to War and Peace)*, edited by Yueh-Ting Lee, Clark McCauley, Fathali M. Moghaddam, and Stephen Worchel, 133–154. Westport, CT: Praeger, 2004.

Pappé, Ilan. *The Forgotten Palestinians: A History of the Palestinians in Israel*. New Haven, CT: Yale University Press, 2011.

Paris, Leslie. *Children's Nature: The Rise of the American Summer Camp*. New York: New York University Press, 2008.

Payes, Shany. *Palestinian NGOs in Israel: The Politics of Civil Society*. London: Tauris Academic Studies, 2005.

Peled, Yoav. "The 100 Terms Program: A Rawlsian Critique." Adalah's Newsletter 27 (2006). http://adalah.org/newsletter/eng/jul-aug06/ar1.pdf.

Peleg, Ilan, and Dov Waxman. *Israel's Palestinians: The Conflict Within*. Cambridge: Cambridge University Press, 2011.

Peri, Yoram. "The Assassination: Causes, Meaning, Outcomes." In *The Assassination of Yitzhak Rabin*, edited by Yoram Peri, 25–62. Stanford: Stanford University Press, 2000.

———. *Yad ish be-ahiv: Retsah Rabin umilhemet hatarbut be-yisrael* [Brothers at war: Rabin's assasination and the cultural war in Israel]. Tel Aviv: Babel, 2005.

Podeh, Elie. "Demonizing the Other: Israeli Perceptions of Nasser and Nasserism." In *Rethinking Nasserism: Revolution and Historical Memory in Modern Egypt*, edited by Elie Podeh and Onn Winckler, 72–99. Gainesville: University Press of Florida, 2004.

———. "Shonut betokh mifgan shel ahdut: Hagigot yovel ha-zahav le-hatsharat Balfour (1967) be-Yisrael." [Variance within a display of uniformity: The celebrations of the Balfor Declaration's golden jubilee (1967) in Israel]. *Yisrael* no. 17 (2010): 59–90.

Popular Memory Group. "Popular Memory: Theory, Politics, Method." In *The Oral History Reader*, edited by Robert Perks and Alistair Thomson, 75–86. New York: Routledge, 1998.

Porath, Yehoshua. *The Emergence of the Palestinian-Arab National Movement, 1918–1929*. London: Frank Cass, 1974.

———. *The Palestine Arab National Movement: From Riots to Rebellion*. London: Frank Cass, 1977.

Quandt, William B., Paul Jabber, and Ann Mosely Lesch. *The Politics of Palestinian Nationalism*. Berkeley: University of California Press, 1973.

Rabinowitz, Dan. *Overlooking Nazareth: The Ethnography of Exclusion in Galilee*. Cambridge: Cambridge University Press, 1997.

———. "The Palestinian Citizens of Israel, the Concept of Trapped Minority and the Discourse of Transnationalism in Anthropology." *Ethnic and Racial Studies* 24, no. 1 (2001): 64–85.

Rabinowitz, Dan, and Khawla Abu-Baker. *Coffins on Our Shoulders: The Experience of the Palestinian Citizens of Israel*. Berkeley: University of California Press, 2005.

Ram, Uri. "Postnationalist Pasts." *Social Science History* 22, no. 4 (1998): 513–545.

Rashid, Harun Hashem. *Qisat Madinat Ghaza* [The story of the city of Gaza]. Al-Munathama al-'Arabiyya li-ltarbia wal-thaqafa wal-'ulum, 1987.

Raz-Krakotzkin, Amnon. "Diaspora in Sovereignty: Towards a Criticism of 'the Negation of Diaspora' in Israeli Culture." *Teoria Uvicoret*, no. 4 (1994): 23–55.

Reiter, Yitzhak. *National Minority, Regional Majority: Palestinian Arabs Versus Jews in Israel*. Syracuse, NY: Syracuse University Press, 2009.

Rekhess, Elie. *Ha-mi'ut he-'arvi be-yisrael: Bein qomunism le-le'umiyut 'arvit 1965–1991* [The Arab minority in Israel: Between communism and Arab nationalism 1965–1991]. Tel-Aviv: Hakibbutz Hameuchad, 1993.

———. "He-'arvim be-yisrael le-ahar tahalikh Oslo: Loqalizatsia shel ha-maavaq ha-le'umi" [The Arabs in Israel after the Oslo process: Localization of the national struggle]. *Ha-mizrah He-hadash* no. 43 (2002): 275–304.

Rekhess, Elie, and Arik Rudnitzky. *Seker 'amadot ha-ukhlusiya he-'arvit be-yisrael, yanuar 2007* [Public opinion poll among the Arab population in Israel, January 2007]. Tel Aviv: Tel Aviv University, Moshe Dayan Center, 2007.

Renan, Ernest. "What Is a Nation?" In *Becoming National: A Reader*, edited by Geoff Eley and Ronald Grigor Suny, 41–55. New York and Oxford: Oxford University Press, 1996.

Ricks, Thomas M. "Khalil Totah: The Unknown Years." *Jerusalem Quarterly* 34 (2009): 51–77.

Robinson, Shira. *Citizen Strangers: Palestinians and the Birth of Israel's Liberal Settler State*. Stanford: Stanford Univesrsity Press, 2013.

———. "Local Struggle, National Struggle: Palestinian Responses to the Kafr Qasim Massacre and Its Aftermath, 1956–1966." *International Journal of Middle East Studies* 35, no. 3 (2003): 393–416.

Rosenfeld, Henry, and Majid Al-Haj. *Arab Local Government in Israel*. London: Westview, 1990.

Rosenthal, Ruvik. "Mi harag et Fatma Sarsur" [Who killed Fatma Sarsur]. In *Kafr Kassem: Myth and History*, edited by Ruvik Rosenthal, 11–51. Tel Aviv: Hakibbutz Hameuchad, 2000.

Rosland, Sissel. "Victimhood, Identity, and Agency in the Early Phase of the Troubles in Northern Ireland." *Identities: Global Studies in Culture and Power* 16, no. 3 (2009): 294–320.

Rouhana, Nadim. "The Intifada and the Palestinians of Israel: Resurrecting the Green Line." *Journal of Palestine Studies* 19, no. 3 (1990): 58–75.

———. *Palestinian Citizens in an Ethnic Jewish State : Identities in Conflict*. New Haven, CT: Yale University Press, 1997.

Rubin-Peled, Alisa. *Debating Islam in the Jewish State: The Development of Policy toward Islamic Institutions in Israel*. Albany: State University of New York Press, 2001.

Sa'ar, Amalia. "Carefully on the Margins: Christian Palestinians in Haifa between Nation and State." *American Ethnologist* 25, no 2 (1998): 215–239.

Saba-Sa'di, Sylvia. "The Disputed Role of a Traditional Intellectual Group: The Case of Arab Women Teachers in Israel." *EUI Working Papers* no. 23 (2008).

Sabbagh-Khoury, Areej. "Palestinian Predicaments: Jewish Immigration and Refugees Repatriation." In: *Displaced at Home: Ethnicity and Gender among Palestinians in Israel*, edited by Rhoda Ann Kanaaneh and Isis Nusair. Albany: State University of New York Press, 2010.

al-Sakakini, Khalil. *Yawmiyyat Khalil al-Sakakini: Yawmiyyat, rasa'il wa-taammulat: Al-kitab al-rabi', bayna al-ab wal-ibn, rasai'l Khalil ila Sari fi Amrika 1931–1932*. Edited by Akram Musallam. Ramallah: Markaz Khalil al-Sakakini al-Thaqafi, Mu'assasat al-Dirasat al-Muqaddasiyah, 2005.

———. *Yawmiyyat Khalil al-Sakakini: Yawmiyyat, rasa'il wa-taammulat: Al-kitab al-sadis, rasai'l Khalil al-Sakakini ila Sari fi Amrika, 1935–1937*. Edited by Akram Musallam. Ramallah: Markaz Khalil al-Sakakini al-Thaqafi, Mu'assasat al-Dirasat al-Muqaddasiyah, 2006.

———. *Yawmiyat Khalil al-Sakakini: Yawmiyyat, rasa'il wa-taammulatt: Al-kitab al-thalith, ikhtibar al-intidab wa-as'ilat al-hawiyya, 1919–1922*. Edited by Akram Musallam. Ramallah: Markaz Khalil al-Sakakini al-Thaqafi: Mu'assasat al-Dirasat al-Muqaddasiyah, 2004.

Sarsur, Ibrahim. "Bein ha-sulha la-andarta" [Between the Sulha and the monument]. In *Kafr Kassem: Myth and History*, edited by Ruvik Rosenthal, 196–203. Tel Aviv: Hakibbutz Hameuchad, 2000.

Sayigh, Yezid. *Armed Struggle and the Search for State: The Palestinian National Movement, 1949–1993*. Oxford: Clarendon Press, 1997.

Schiff, Zeev, and Ehud Yaari. *Israel's Lebanon War*. New York: Simon and Schuster, 1984.

Schueftan, Dan. *Falastinim be-yisrael: Maavaqo shel ha-mi'ut he-'arvi ba-medina ha-yehudit* [Palestinians in Israel: The Arab minority's struggle against the Jewish state]. Or Yehuda: Kinneret, Zmora-Bitan, Dvir Publishing, 2011.

Schwartz, Barry, Yael Zerubavel, Bernice M. Barnett, and George Steiner. "The Recovery of Masada: A Study in Collective Memory." *Sociological Quarterly* 27, no. 2 (1986): 147–164.

Segev, Tom. *Elvis in Jerusalem: Post-Zionism and the Americanization of Israel*. New York: Metropolitan, 2002.

———. *One Palestine, Complete: Jews and Arabs under the Mandate*. New York: Metropolitan, 2000.

Shabeeb, Samih. "Poetry of Rebellion: The Life, Verse and Death of Nuh Ibrahim during the 1936–39 Revolt." *Jerusalem Quarterly* no. 25 (2006): 65–78.

Shafir, Gershon, and Yoav Peled. *Being Israeli: The Dynamics of Multiple Citizenship*. Cambridge: Cambridge University Press, 2002.

Shamir, Ilanah. *Zikaron ve-hantsaha* [Memory and commemoration]. Tel Aviv: Am Oved, 1996.

Shapira, Anita. "Hirbet Hizah: Between Remembrance and Forgetting." *Jewish Social Studies* 7, no. 1 (2000): 1–62.

Shemesh, Moshe. "Did Shuqayri Call for 'Throwing the Jews into the Sea'?" *Israel Studies* 8, no. 2 (2003): 70–81.

Shenhav, Yehuda. *Beyond the Two-State Solution: A Jewish Political Essay*. Cambridge: Polity Press, 2012.

al-Sifri, 'Isa. *Filastin al-'Arabiyyah bayna al-intidab wal-Sahyuniyyah* [Arab Palestine between the mandate and Zionism]. Jaffa: Matba'at maktabat falastin al-jadida, 1937.

Slyomovics, Susan. *The Object of Memory: Arab and Jew Narrate the Palestinian Village*. Philadelphia: University of Pennsylvania Press, 1998.

Slyomovics, Susan, and Waleed Khleif. "Palestinian Remembrance Days and Plans: Kafr Qasim, Fact and Echo." In *Modernism and the Middle East: Architecture and Politics in the Twentieth Century*, edited by Sandy Isenstadt and Kishwar Rizvi, 186–217. Seattle: University of Washington Press, 2008.

Smith, David J. "'Woe from Stones': Commemoration, Identity Politics and Estonia's 'War of Monuments.'" *Journal of Baltic Studies* 39, no. 4 (2008): 419–430.

Smooha, Sammy. "The Advances and Limits of the Israelization of Israel's Palestinian Citizens." In *Israeli and Palestinian Identities in History and Literature*, edited by Kamal Abdel-Malek and David C. Jacobson, 9–33. New York: St. Martin's Press, 1999.

———. *Index of Arab-Jewish Relations in Israel 2003–2009*. Haifa: The Jewish-Arab Center, University of Haifa, 2010.

———. *Index of Arab-Jewish Relations in Israel 2003–2011*. Haifa: The Jewish-Arab Center, University of Haifa, 2012.

———. "The Model of Ethnic Democracy: Israel as a Jewish and Democratic State." *Nations and Nationalism* 8 no. 4 (2002): 475–503.

———. *The Orientation and Politicization of the Arab Minority in Israel*. Haifa: University of Haifa, The Institute of Middle Eastern Studies, 1984.

———. "Sqarim be-qerev ha-ukhlusiya he-ʿarvit be-yisrael" [Surveys among the Arab population in Israel]. In *Emet Veseqer*, edited by Kamil Fux and Shaul Bar Lev, 173–198. Haifa: Hakibbutz Hameuchad, 1998.

———. *Still Playing by the Rules: Index of Arab-Jewish Relations in Israel 2012*. Jerusalem: Israel Democracy Institute and University of Haifa, 2013.

Sorek, Tamir. *Arab Soccer in a Jewish State: The Integrative Enclave*. New York: Cambridge University Press, 2007.

———. "Between Football and Martyrdom: The Bi-Focal Localism of an Arab-Palestinian Town in Israel." *British Journal of Sociology* 56, no. 4 (2005): 635–661.

———. "The Orange and the Cross in the Crescent: Imagining Palestine in 1929." *Nations and Nationalism* 10, no. 3 (2004).

———. "The Quest for Victory: Collective Memory and National Identification among the Arab-Palestinian Citizens of Israel." *Sociology* 45, no. 3 (2011): 464–479.

Spillman, Lyn. "When Do Collective Memories Last? Founding Moments in the United States and Australia." *Social Science History* 22, no. 4 (1998): 445–477.

Srur, Elias. *Nakba fi ʿAylabun*. ʿAylabun: ʿAylabun local authority, 1998.

Stendel, Ori. *The Arabs in Israel*. Brighton, UK: Sussex Academic, 1996.

———. *The Arabs in Israel: Between Hammer and Anvil*. Jerusalem: Academon, 1992.

Swedenburg, Ted. *Memories of Revolt: The 1936–1939 Rebellion and the Palestinian National Past*. Minneapolis: University of Minnesota Press, 1995.

Takei, Milton. "Collective Memory as the Key to National and Ethnic Identity: The Case of Cambodia." *Nationalism and Ethnic Politics* 4, no. 3 (1998): 59–78.

Tamari, Salim. "Confessionalism and Public Space in Ottoman and Colonial Jerusalem." In *Cities and Sovereignty: Identity Politics in Urban Spaces*, edited by Diane Davis and Nora Libertun de Duren, 59–83. Bloomington: Indiana University Press, 2011.

———. "The Local and the National in Palestinian Identity." In *Israeli and Palestinian Identities in History and Literature*, edited by Kamal Abdel-Malek and David C. Jacobson, 3–8. New York: St. Martin's Press, 1999.

———. "With God's Camel in Siberia: The Russian Exile of an Ottoman Officer from Jerusalem." *Jerusalem Quarterly* 35 (2008): 31–50.

Terrill, W. Andrew. "The Political Mythology of the Battle of Karameh." *The Middle East Journal* 55, no. 1 (2001): 91–111.

Trouillot, Michel-Rolph. "Abortive Rituals: Historical Apologies in the Global Era." *Interventions* 2, no. 2 (2000): 171–186.

Tsimhoni, Daphne. "Ha-notsrim be-yisrael: Bein dat u-politiqa" [The Christians in Israel: Between religion and politics]. In *He-'arvim ba-politiqa ha-yisraelit: Dilemot shel zehut* [The Arabs in Israeli politics: Dilemmas of identity], edited by Elie Rekhess, 63–72. Tel-Aviv: Tel-Aviv University, Moshe Dayan Center, 1998.

Vinitzky-Seroussi, Vered. "Commemorating a Difficult Past: Yitzhak Rabin's Memorials." *American Sociological Review* 67, no. 1 (2002): 30–51.

———. *Yitzhak Rabin's Assassination and the Dilemmas of Commemoration*. Albany: State University of New York Press Press, 2009.

Vinitzky-Seroussi, Vered, and Chana Teeger. "Unpacking the Unspoken: Silence in Collective Memory and Forgetting." *Social Forces* 88, no. 3 (2010): 1103–1122.

Wedeen, Lisa. *Ambiguities of Domination: Politics, Rhetoric, and Symbols in Contemporary Syria*. Chicago: University of Chicago Press, 1999.

Wiemer, Reinhard. "Zionism and the Arabs after the Establishment of the State." In *Palestinians over the Green Line: Studies on the Relations between Palestinians on Both Sides of the 1949 Armistice Line since 1967*, edited by Alexander Scholch, 26–63. London: Ithaca Press, 1983.

Wigfall-Williams, Wanda, and Gillian Robinson. *A World Apart: Mixed Marriage in Northern Ireland*. Belfast: Queen's University Belfast and the University of Ulster, 2001.

Williams, Raymond. *Culture and Materialism: Selected Essays*. London: Verso, 2005.

Winter, Jay. *Sites of Memory, Sites of Mourning: The Great War in European Cultural History*. New York: Cambridge University Press, 1995.

Yiftachel, Oren. "Between Nation and State: 'Fractured' Regionalism among Palestinian-Arabs in Israel." *Political Geography* 18, no. 3 (1999): 285–307.

———. "Ethnocracy: The Politics of Judaizing Israel/Palestine." *Constellations* 6, no. 3 (1999): 364–390.

———. "Minority Protest and the Emergence of Ethnic Regionalism: Palestinian-Arabs in the Israeli 'Ethnocracy.'" In *Ethnic Challenges to the Modern Nation State*, edited by Shlomo Ben-Ami, Yoav Peled, and Alberto Spectorowski, 145–180. London and New York: Macmillan and St. Martin's Press, 2000.

Yonah, Yossi, Yossi Dahan, and Dalya Markovich. "Neo-Liberal Reforms in Israel's Education System: The Dialectics of the State." *International Studies in Sociology of Education* 18, nos. 3–4 (2008): 199–217.

Young, James E. *At Memory's Edge: After-Images of the Holocaust in Contemporary Art and Architecture*. New Haven, CT: Yale University Press, 2002.

Yuval, Ohana-Arnon. "Mifleget al-Istiqlal: Reshito shel radiqalism falastini: 1930–1937." [The Istiqlal party: The beginning of a Palestinian radicalism, 1930–1937]. *Qatedra* no. 12 (1979): 91–109.

Zayyad, Tawfiq. *'An al-adab wal-adab al-sha'bi fi filastin* [On literarture and popular literature in Palestine]. Beirut: Dar al-'Awdah, 1970.

———. *Suwar min al-adab al-sh'abi al-filastini* [Images from the Palestinian popular literature]. Beirut: Al-muassasa al-'arabiyya lil-dirasat wal-nashr, 1974.

Zertal, Idith. *Israel's Holocaust and the Politics of Nationhood*. Cambridge and New York: Cambridge University Press, 2005.

Zerubavel, Eviatar. "Calendars and History: A Comparative Study of the Social Organization of National Memory." In *States of Memory: Continuities, Conflicts, and Transformations in National Retrospection*, edited by Jeffrey K. Olick, 315–337. Durham, NC: Duke University Press, 2003.

———. "Easter and Passover: On Calendars and Group Identity." *American Sociological Review* 47, no. 2 (1982): 284–289.

Zerubavel, Yael. "The Politics of Interpretation: Tel-Hai in Israel's Collective Memory." *Journal of the Association for Jewish Studies* 16, nos. 1–2 (1991): 133–160.

———. *Recovered Roots: Collective Memory and the Making of Israeli National Tradition*. Chicago: University of Chicago Press, 1995.

Zureik, Elia. *The Palestinians in Israel: A Study in Internal Colonialism*. London and Boston: Routledge and Kegan Paul, 1979.

ARABIC NEWSPAPERS AND WEBSITES

al-Arab (http://www.alarab.net)

Arab48 (http://www.arabs48.com/)

al-Bayan (http://www.albayan.co.il)

Bokra (http://www.bokra.net/)

al-Difa'

Falastin al-Thawra

Falastinuna

Fasl-al-maqal

Filastin

al-Ittihad

al-Jabha (http://www.aljabha.org)

al-Jadid

al-Jami'a al-'Arabiyya

al-Karmil
Kul al-'Arab
al-Mithaq
Panet (http://www.panet.co.il)
al-Raya
Sawt al-Haq wal-Huriyya
www.shefa-amr.com
al-Sinnara
al-Sirat
al-Watan
al-Yarmuk

HEBREW NEWSPAPERS AND WEBSITES
Davar
Haaretz
Ma'ariv
NRG (http://www.nrg.co.il)
Y-net (http://www.ynet.co.il)

INDEX

Stanford Studies in Middle Eastern and Islamic Societies and Cultures

Joel Beinin, *Stanford University*

Adi Kuntsman and Rebecca L. Stein, *Digital Militarism: Israel's Occupation in the Social Media Age*
2015

Laurie A. Brand, *Official Stories: Politics and National Narratives in Egypt and Algeria*
2014

Kabir Tambar, *The Reckoning of Pluralism: Political Belonging and the Demands of History in Turkey*
2014

Diana Allan, *Refugees of the Revolution: Experiences of Palestinian Exile*
2013

Shira Robinson, *Citizen Strangers: Palestinians and the Birth of Israel's Liberal Settler State*
2013

Joel Beinin and Frédéric Vairel, editors, *Social Movements, Mobilization, and Contestation in the Middle East and North Africa*
2013 (Second Edition), 2011

Ariella Azoulay and Adi Ophir, *The One-State Condition: Occupation and Democracy in Israel/Palestine*
2012

Steven Heydemann and Reinoud Leenders, editors, *Middle East Authoritarianisms: Governance, Contestation, and Regime Resilience in Syria and Iran*
2012

Jonathan Marshall, *The Lebanese Connection: Corruption, Civil War, and the International Drug Traffic*
2012

Joshua Stacher, *Adaptable Autocrats: Regime Power in Egypt and Syria*
2012

Bassam Haddad, *Business Networks in Syria: The Political Economy of Authoritarian Resilience*
2011

Noah Coburn, *Bazaar Politics: Power and Pottery in an Afghan Market Town*
2011

Laura Bier, *Revolutionary Womanhood: Feminisms, Modernity, and the State in Nasser's Egypt*
2011

Samer Soliman, *The Autumn of Dictatorship: Fiscal Crisis and Political Change in Egypt under Mubarak*
2011

Rochelle A. Davis, *Palestinian Village Histories: Geographies of the Displaced*
2010

Haggai Ram, *Iranophobia: The Logic of an Israeli Obsession*
2009

John Chalcraft, *The Invisible Cage: Syrian Migrant Workers in Lebanon*
2008

Rhoda Kanaaneh, *Surrounded: Palestinian Soldiers in the Israeli Military*
2008

Asef Bayat, *Making Islam Democratic: Social Movements and the Post-Islamist Turn*
2007

Robert Vitalis, *America's Kingdom: Mythmaking on the Saudi Oil Frontier*
2006

Jessica Winegar, *Creative Reckonings: The Politics of Art and Culture in Contemporary Egypt*
2006

Joel Beinin and Rebecca L. Stein, editors, *The Struggle for Sovereignty: Palestine and Israel, 1993–2005*
2006

The authorized representative in the EU for product safety and compliance is:
Mare Nostrum Group
B.V Doelen 72
4831 GR Breda
The Netherlands

www.ingramcontent.com/pod-product-compliance
Lightning Source LLC
Chambersburg PA
CBHW020457270326
41926CB00008B/645